FORECLOSING THE FUTURE

FORECLOSING THE FUTURE

The World Bank and the Politics of Environmental Destruction

BRUCE RICH

● ISLANDPRESS   Washington | Covelo | London

ISLAND PRESS is a trademark of Island Press/The Center for Resource Economics.

Library of Congress Cataloging-in-Publication Data
Rich, Bruce.
   Foreclosing the future : the World Bank and the politics of environmental destruction / Bruce Rich.
      pages cm
   Includes bibliographical references and index.
   ISBN-13: 978-1-61091-184-9 (hardback)
   ISBN-10: 1-61091-184-9 (cloth)
   ISBN-13: 978-1-61091-185-6 (paper)
1. World Bank. 2. Development banks—Political aspects. 3. Environmental policy—Economic aspects. 4. Economic assistance—Environmental aspects. 5. Economic development projects—Environmental aspects. I. Title.
   HG3881.5.W57R527 2013
   333.7′137–dc23

                                        2013014782

Printed on recycled, acid-free paper ✪
Text design by Joyce C. Weston
Manufactured in the United States of America
10 9 8 7 6 5 4 3 2 1

Keywords: Island Press, economics, sustainability, business, corporate responsibility, corporate externalities, environmental commons, sustainable economy

Contents

A Future in Foreclosure

IN 2000 A DEDICATED PHYSICIAN working to promote public health for the poor in developing countries condemned the World Bank for promoting "corporate-led economic globalization" that "not only failed to improve living standards and health outcomes among the poor, but also . . . inflicted additional suffering on disenfranchised and vulnerable populations." He recounted his own experience in a Latin American country where the World Bank subsidized huge multinational mining and oil investments while encouraging the weakening of environmental laws that "led to significant ecological degradation from deforestation, oil spills, and poisoned waterways."

These words were written by Dr. Jim Yong Kim, who assumed the presidency of the World Bank on July 1, 2012.

Kim's words in 2000 (in a book he co-edited, *Dying for Growth*, a macabre pun on what the World Bank model of growth was doing to the poor) were all the more disquieting in that they came the better part of a decade after the 1992 Rio de Janeiro Earth Summit, the landmark United Nations Conference on Environment and Development. In Rio, in one of the largest diplomatic gatherings in history, 118 heads of state and numerous international development institutions such as the World Bank made wide-ranging pledges and commitments to address global environmental issues while helping the poor.

More than 20 years after Rio '92 and 13 years after Dr. Kim's warnings about the effects of distorted economic globalization, scientific evidence is growing that the global economy has put the entire global climate system at risk, as well as the planetary web of biodiversity and life forms. Species are dying at an alarming and accelerating rate. Economically caused global warming is already undermining the benign, stable climate conditions that have enabled the rise of human civilizations over the past 7,000 years. The inability of our institutions to address these trends is rooted in a continuing worldwide failure of governments and of markets to deal with the impacts of human activity on the natural world.

The World Bank Group is a microcosm of this breakdown. The Bank's failures to confront the environmental challenges of economic development illuminate the political failures and hypocrisies of most of the governments of its members. The Bank is to blame, but its member governments are even more so.

This book builds on an earlier analysis I published nearly two decades ago, *Mortgaging the Earth*, which identified many of the persistent institutional and political pathologies that undermine the Bank's effectiveness. Since then, unfortunately, the environmentally unsustainable development that the Bank has continued to finance is contributing to a global ecological debt that now is foreclosing on the future of human societies.

The world urgently needs global governance at the very moment when it is failing. The World Bank Group has a unique wealth of experience that could help build governance at the local, national, and international levels, if only the Bank would learn from its experience rather than flee from it. Quite a few years ago, an internal review of the Bank's operations described the problem as unfounded institutional optimism based on pervasive institutional amnesia. In a world desperately in need of global environmental leadership, the Bank could and should play a more positive role.

The Role of the World Bank Group

In the second decade of the twenty-first century, the World Bank is no longer as financially influential as it once was. The growth of international private-sector finance, and of global public lending institutions in newly industrializing nations such as China and Brazil, mean that the Bank has now become just one financial player among others.

But the Bank remains critically important. It continues to put itself forth as an intellectual and policy leader for economic development in the United Nations system and in the global economy at large. The Rio Earth Summit chose the Bank to administer a new fund to finance environmental projects—the Global Environment Facility. After Rio the Bank and other development institutions did try to incorporate environmental concerns more fully into their decision making. More recently, the richer countries chose the World Bank to administer most of the new funds they have contributed to address climate change in developing nations. Still more important for the global environment than these new funds is the ecological impact of the activities financed by the Bank Group's core lending and finance, which has averaged around $57 billion annually in recent years.

Since the early 1990s the World Bank has also played no small role in promoting a one-sided economic globalization that has liberalized markets and unleashed capital flows. It has done so without effective regulation at either the national or international level to counteract environmental and social abuses unleashed by these flows. Of course, the Bank has been just one player, albeit an influential one, in promoting this agenda, together with the finance ministries of many industrialized countries, led by the United States, as well as private international banks and multinational corporations.

One particularly corrosive effect of this globalization agenda has been a disproportionate growth of corruption in developing nations, resulting in massive outflows of stolen funds from even the poorest countries, laundered through proliferating international tax havens. This corruption is undermining not just the Bank's environmental performance, but international development efforts across the board.

When one examines the failures to conserve ecosystems, or to mitigate the environmental impacts of development, one finds that failed governance at all levels is almost invariably at the root. The Bank itself is a prime example. Many of its problems are associated with a dysfunctional institutional culture in which the relentless pressure to move money out the door, even in violation of the Bank's own polices and rules, often overrides all other considerations. What is remarkable about this "loan approval culture" is how well documented it has been for decades through reams of internal Bank reports, and how little the Bank's management, and member-country governments, whether donors like the United States and other industrialized nations, or developing country borrowers, have done to effectively change it.

A Brief Note on Methodology and a Short Outline

Much of the analysis in *Foreclosing the Future* relies on internal Bank studies, particularly those of the Bank's operations evaluation staff. Some former high-ranking Bank professionals have criticized these analyses as lacking independence and watering down, or even misrepresenting, how bad things really are. Bank management, on the other hand, has often responded that these internal evaluations are too one-sidedly critical of the Bank's actual performance. In the final analysis, the studies provide an unparalleled insight into deep-seated, continuing institutional problems that undermine, and at times cripple, the Bank's effectiveness. I have also relied on numerous external studies and reviews, the analyses of nongovernmental organizations, reports and hearings of the U.S. Congress and federal government, and of other governments, as well as press accounts of various Bank controversies. The book's approach is roughly chronological, though some chapters bring together in one place issues that have been important over the past two decades; for example, chapters 8 and 9 address climate and energy.

The first two chapters introduce the World Bank, describe why it is important for anyone concerned with the fate of the global environment and the future of economic development, and identify a number of major themes of the book. Following the 1992 Earth Summit, the Bank strove to improve its environmental performance and to increase lending for environmental projects. But at the same time internal Bank evaluations revealed a record of poor results and continual failure to mainstream environmental concerns into its operations.

Chapters 3 through 6 examine the momentous debates over environment and development, and well-publicized efforts to reform the Bank, under the presidency of James Wolfensohn from 1995 through 2005. In the face of growing controversies over World Bank financing of large dam, mining, and oil projects, Wolfensohn convened unprecedented reviews involving the Bank, industry, civil society, and borrowing governments in an attempt to reach consensus on both the Bank's future role in supporting such activities and on good practice for any future investment. Unfortunately, Bank management and borrowing governments rejected many of the recommendations presented in these reviews. The Bank continued its financing of ecologically destructive and socially disruptive large infrastructure and extractive industries and had little to show for its attempts to improve their environmental and social performance. The Bank's efforts to promote conservation and better management of forests also failed in the face of weak governance and much stronger global market forces that reward short-term deforestation.

Wolfensohn was the first World Bank president to publicly raise the issue of massive corruption of Bank lending, but his efforts to control this corruption on the part of borrowing governments and corporations proved ineffective. During Wolfensohn's tenure, the Bank also increasingly subsidized private-sector investment through its private-sector lending arm, the International Finance Corporation (IFC). As his second term drew to an end, the pushback from Bank management and borrowing governments against the Bank's environmental standards and policies grew. There was even resistance to stronger fiduciary safeguards to prevent funds from being stolen.

Chapter 7 describes the brief and tumultuous tenure of Paul Wolfowitz from 2005 through 2007. Wolfowitz's efforts to crack down on corruption were met with strong opposition by the Bank's member countries. Controversy over Bank finance of large dams continued, and evidence of how corruption totally undermined Bank development goals became more public in a series of hearings before the U.S. Senate Foreign Relations Committee. Wolfowitz was forced to resign in disgrace because of alleged favoritism shown to a female Bank staffer who was his romantic partner.

Chapters 8 and 9 examine the Bank's role in climate and energy finance, arguably the most critical and intractable development issue facing the Bank and the world at large as global warming accelerates. The Bank's contradictions and failures in this area mirror those of its member countries as well as the failure of the international system to address the climate impacts of economic growth.

Chapter 10 examines the tenure of Robert Zoellick from 2007 through June 2012, which was characterized by an accelerated move away from lending for specific investment projects to large loans to governments, government agencies, and private financial institutions for budget support or for general investment programs. Bank environmental and social safeguards did not apply as strongly to such loans, which reinforced the "loan approval culture" that had undermined the quality of Bank operations for decades. Zoellick gave still greater priority to the operations of the International Finance Corporation, despite both its appalling record in continuing to finance environmentally and socially destructive extractive industries, and internal evaluations that found that the vast majority of IFC finance had no focus on poverty alleviation—supposedly the World Bank Group's core mission.

Chapters 11 and 12 describe the advent of the Bank's current president, Dr. Jim Yong Kim, and the disconnect between, on the one hand, his enthusiastic commitments to "end poverty" and to increase the Bank's focus on fighting global warming, and, on the other hand, the Bank's deep-seated institutional problems. These problems continue to undermine the Bank's purported goals through the pressure to lend and the growing marginalization of the Bank's hard-won environmental and social safeguards and standards. Kim, who little more than a decade before vehemently criticized the Bank and the IFC, reaffirmed the IFC as a model for the rest of the Bank despite its track record of even greater environmental and social failure than the affiliates of the Bank that lend to governments. If the Bank is to play a more positive role it must focus on improved governance in its borrowers and itself—starting with finally changing the incentives in its own internal culture to focus less on moving money out the door and more on developmental and environmental quality.

The issues, the project examples, and the policy conflicts we find in the World Bank reflect a wider battle going on throughout the world, a battle for the kind of global society that future generations will inhabit. The basic question is whether worldwide economic activity can be embedded in rules and standards that can be agreed on and enforced. A global economy calls for a global project of justice. What we call environmental sustainability is an integral part of this project of justice, ensuring a world not just for future human generations, but for the other living things with which we share this small planet. If they are in danger, then so are we.

ACKNOWLEDGMENTS

THIS BOOK WOULD NOT have come about without the involvement and superlative professionalism of the staff of Island Press. Special thanks go to the founder and president of Island Press, Chuck Savitt, for his initial interest and enthusiasm for the project, and to David Miller, senior vice president and publisher. I owe a special debt of gratitude to Island's superb editor Emily Turner Davis, whose numerous helpful suggestions improved the manuscript tremendously. Editing can sometimes be difficult for an author, and Emily's constant good cheer and thoughtfulness made working with her a true pleasure. I am also very thankful for Island's engaging a fine copy editor, Mike Fleming, who further improved the quality of the final text.

Special thanks go to the following individuals who very generously offered to read the manuscript in parts or in whole. Their comments have also been extraordinarily helpful: Elissa Parker, vice president for research and policy at the Environmental Law Institute, Washington D.C.; Tamar Gutner, associate professor of international relations and associate dean, School of International Service, American University, Washington D.C.; and Don Babai, research associate and lecturer, Harvard University. I alone am responsible, of course, for the content of the book.

Last, but not least, a very special thanks goes to Brent Blackwelder, president-emeritus of Friends of the Earth, U.S., a longtime campaigner for environmental justice in international finance. Brent put me in touch with Chuck Savitt to get this project rolling.

ACRONYMS

BNDES	National Bank for Economic and Social Development (Brazil)	ESSD	Environmentally and Socially Sustainable Development
BP	British Petroleum	FCPF	Forest Carbon Partnership Facility
CAO	Compliance Advisor/Ombudsman (World Bank Group)	FIAHS	Fund for Innovative Approaches in Human and Social Development
CDM	Clean Development Mechanism	FIP	Forest Investment Program
CEO	Chief Executive Officer	FPIC	Free Prior Informed Consent
CERs	Certified Emission Rights (carbon credits)	G8	Group of 8 (nations with eight largest economies)
CFCs	chlorofluorocarbons	G20	Group of 20 (nations with 20 largest economies)
CIFs	Climate Investment Funds	G77	Group of 77 (developing nations)
CIFOR	Center for International Forestry Research	GAO	U.S. Government Accountability Office
CITES	United Nations Convention on International Trade in Endangered Species	GAP	Government Accountability Project
CODE	Committee on Development Effectiveness (of World Bank executive board)	GDP	gross domestic product
		GHG	greenhouse gas
		GNP	gross national product
CPS	Concentrated Solar Power	GEF	Global Environment Facility
CSOs	civil-society organizations	GNI	gross national income
CSR	Corporate Social Responsibility	HFCF-22	chlorodiflouromethane, a gas used as a refrigerent and plastic feedstock
CTF	Clean Technology Fund (largest of CIFs)	HFC-23	super GHG produced as a byproduct of HFCF-22 manufacture
DNA	dioxyribonucleic acid		
DNV	Det Norske Veritas	IBRD	International Bank for Reconstruction and Development (affiliate of World Bank Group)
DRC	Democratic Republic of the Congo		
EAs	Environmental Assessments		
EBY	Entidad Binacional Yacyretá		
ECAs	Export Credit Agencies	ICDPs	Integrated Conservation and Development Projects
EIR	Extractive Industries Review		
ENDESA	Empresa Nacional de Electricidad S.A. (Spain and Chile)	ICOLD	International Commission on Large Dams

IDA	International Development Association (affiliate of World Bank Group)	OGP	International Association of Oil and Gas Producers
IDB	Inter-American Development Bank	OP	operational procedure (World Bank)
IEA	International Energy Agency	OPEC	Organization of Petroleum Exporting Countries
IEG	Independent Evaluation Group (World Bank)	PCF	Prototype Carbon Fund
IFC	International Finance Corporation (affiliate of World Bank Group)	PDLG	Participatory Development Learning Group
		P4R	Program for Results
ILO	United Nations International Labor Organization	REDs	Regional Environment Departments
IMF	International Monetary Fund	REDD	"Reduced Emissions from Deforestation and Forest Degradation"
INT	Department of Institutional Integrity (World Bank Group)		
IP	Internet Provider	T&V	Training and Visit agricultural extension system
IPIECA	International Petroleum Industry Environmental Conservation Association	TSERO	Transitional Support for Economic Recovery Operation Grant
IRGR	Investor Relations Global Rankings	UNCED	United Nations Conference on Environment and Development ("Rio '92")
IT	information technology		
IUCN	World Conservation Union (formerly International Union for Conservation of Nature)	UNDP	United Nations Development Programme
		UNEP	United Nations Environment Programme
JI	Joint Implementation mechanism	UNESCO	United Nations Educational, Scientific, and Cultural Organization
MDB	multilateral development bank	UNFCCC	United Nations Framework Convention on Climate Change
M&E	monitoring and evaluation		
MIGA	Multilateral Investment Insurance Agency (affiliate of World Bank Group)	USAID	U.S. Agency for International Development
NEAPs	National Environmental Action Plans	US EXIM	U.S. Export-Import Bank
NGO	nongovernmental organizations	WBG	World Bank Group (comprised of IBRD, IDA, IFC, and MIGA)
NTPC	India National Thermal Power Corporation	WCD	World Commission on Dams
OECD	Organization for Economic Cooperation and Development	WWF	World Wildlife Fund (U.S.); (World Wide Fund for Nature—Europe)
OED	Operations Evaluation Department (World Bank)		

CHAPTER ONE

Tiger Talk

Ιɴ Sᴀɪɴᴛ Pᴇᴛᴇʀsʙᴜʀɢ it was the most glamorous event in memory, set in an imposing nineteenth-century Tsarist palace. Supermodel Naomi Campbell attended with her billionaire companion, real estate oligarch Vladislav Doronin (known as "the Donald Trump of Russia"). Hollywood megastar Leonardo DiCaprio's first two attempted airplane flights to Russia encountered emergency delays; he scrambled to find other connections before arriving many hours late. Harrison Ford called in via videoconference. What lured them? They and hundreds of wildlife specialists and government officials were gathering in the former Russian imperial capital in November 2010 at a summit to save the world's tigers. Indeed, only 3,200 tigers remain alive in the wild, down from over 100,000 a century ago. In the first decade of the twenty-first century alone, the world tiger population declined by 40 percent.[1] If the tigers were ever going to be saved, it was now or never.

In addition to movie stars and supermodels, the summit convened officials from the 13 Asian nations where at least traces of viable tiger habitat remain, including the prime ministers of Nepal, Bangladesh, and Laos, as well as another global celebrity of sorts, Chinese premier Wen Jiabao. The stars and politicians mingled with the heads of prominent environmental organizations, such as World Wildlife Fund.

Vladimir Putin, Russia's prime minister, presided over the lavish gathering. Indeed, he had done much to bring the summit to the town where he began his career as a secret police official in Soviet times. Putin used tigers to promote his tough guy image. Once, in front of television cameras, he shot an escaped Siberian tiger with a tranquilizer gun and personally placed a tracking collar on its neck.[2] He had also been given a tiger cub as a present for his 56th birthday.[3] Putin's macho persona gave the event a certain edgy buzz. Putin hailed DiCaprio as "a real man" for his determination to attend.[4] Before the assembled hundreds he quoted Gandhi, of all people, to the effect that a nation's "moral progress could be judged by the way its animals are treated."[5] Putin's apparent conversion to Gandhian principles startled some participants as the former KGB agent continued, "Nature is the habitat of humans, so caring for tigers and their habitat is caring for all people."[6]

Yes, it was Putin's show, but the man who really made the summit happen was Robert Zoellick, president of the World Bank. Like Putin, Zoellick was a genuine aficionado of tigers. His office was reportedly decorated with a large map showing the destruction of tiger habitat over the past 160 years.[7] Unlike Putin, he headed an institution that appeared to many to have made major progress in environmental protection, and in reconciling economic development with ecology (i.e., "sustainable development," as it is called in the international development world).

Many thought Zoellick's involvement would ensure that the tiger summit did not become one more conference producing grandiose but empty promises. In 2009 he prompted the Bank to launch a Global Tiger Recovery Program that aims to increase the tiger population by more than double by 2022. The 2010 summit secured the high-level political commitment of countries where tigers still live in the wild, as well as pledges from the richer countries to raise $350 million to achieve the goal. The Bank itself proposed $100 million in new loans for tiger conservation to Nepal, Bhutan, and Bangladesh.[8] It would play a key role in coordinating the whole effort, demonstrating the Bank's heightened commitment to environmental protection.

If there were any international institution that had the potential to reconcile economic priorities and ecological challenges, it was arguably the World Bank. The Bank and its sister institution, the International Monetary Fund (IMF), were founded in 1944 by the United States, the United Kingdom, and 42 other countries to serve as linchpins of the entire post–World War II global economic system—a role they grew into over the decades and maintain to this day. The IMF was to address financial stability in the international monetary system, and the World Bank would lend to governments for economically productive projects, first in postwar Europe and then in the poorer regions of the world in need of investment.

The original World Bank, known as the International Bank for Reconstruction and Development (IBRD), was complemented in subsequent decades by the creation of new, affiliated institutions. In 1956 the International Finance Corporation (IFC) was founded at U.S. prompting to fund private sector development. The IBRD lent only to governments and government agencies. In 1960 the International Development Association

(IDA) was established to provide loans (which the IDA called "credits") at very low interest rates for longer periods of time to the poorest countries (today mainly in Sub-Saharan Africa and Southeast Asia). In 1988 the Multilateral Investment Insurance Agency (MIGA) was established to complement the IFC's support for private-sector investment through providing investment-risk insurance. Together, the IBRD, IDA, IFC, and MIGA are known as the World Bank Group (WBG); they share the same president, governance structure, and goals and can be viewed as divisions or affiliates of the same institution.[9] One hundred and eighty-seven countries are members of the World Bank Group, and governance is exercised through a board of 24 executive directors who oversee the president and a staff of over 10,000; at least technically, they approve every loan and every major policy of the institution. Over the years, voting power on the board has been approximately proportional to each country's contribution to the four main WBG affiliates, such that the richer industrialized countries, led by the United States, have always had, and continue to have, the majority of voting shares.[10]

The Bank was present at the creation of the modern project of international development and foreign aid, and from the beginning it has been conscious of a leadership role in this area, continually trying to incorporate new concerns in its policies and practices. Under the presidency of Robert McNamara (1968–81), the Bank expanded its mission from the simple financing of productive investment projects (which its charter stated was its main function) to include a focus on helping the poor in its borrowing countries. Criticism of the Bank's neglect of the environment in the 1980s led it to attempt to make ecological sustainability an important component of its lending decisions, articulated in a number of environmental policies and the addition of environmentally trained staff.

Later in the 1980s and 1990s, reflecting changing political winds in its most important donor countries, the World Bank Group put a strong emphasis on economic liberalization, free trade, and privatization as loan conditions for many of its borrowers, a set of policies known as the "Washington Consensus." From the 1980s to the present the Bank became a focal point of controversy, with some claiming it actually harmed people in developing countries, and others defended it as an institution with the money, intellectual leadership, and political clout to accelerate positive change in the world. After all, the Bank is probably the single largest employer of PhD development economists and specialists from the leading universities of the world.

The WBG's influence comes not just from the amounts of money it commits annually—some $57.3 billion in 2011—but also from its ability to attract cofinancing from local governments, other international aid agencies, and private banks and businesses. The cost of a typical Bank-financed project can often be three or four times the amount of the Bank's own financial contribution. Further, the Bank's stamp of approval on a project or even on a development approach can have widespread influence on the practices of other institutions around the globe. Finally, as a global finance institution in which nearly all of the world's governments participate, the Bank has unique convening power, coordinating development assistance for many different countries and sectors. So it is that the Bank proclaims that "Our mission is to fight poverty with passion and professionalism for lasting results and to help people help themselves and their environment by providing resources, sharing knowledge, building capacity, and forging partnerships in the public and private sectors."[11]

The Bank backs its rhetoric with billions of dollars in loans for what it characterizes as environmental purposes. Even a casual perusal of the Bank's 2011 Annual Report shows that 14 percent of its new lending commitments—some $6.1 billion of a total of more than $43 billion (for the IBRD and IDA)—was dedicated to promoting "Environment and Natural Resources Management," more than to any other theme except "Financial and Private Sector Development."[12]

It was this history, and the promise of the Bank's influence, that brought the hundreds of participants to St. Petersburg in November 2010 to witness the strange political bedfellows Robert Zoellick and Vladimir Putin trying to save the planet's tigers.

Doubts

Outside the tiger summit palace there were doubts. Putin had a dismal environmental record, to say nothing of his suppression of dissidents, growing accusations of his sanctioning human rights violations in Chechnya, and the unpunished murders of hostile journalists.[13] Right after his inauguration as president in 2000 he eliminated Russia's Environmental Protection Committee and Forestry Service. Russian environmentalists declared just months before the Tiger Summit that the country's nine UNESCO World Heritage Nature sites were "threatened with extinction."[14]

In the small world of professional wildlife conservationists, there were party poopers who chose to decline the once-in-a-lifetime opportunity to make tiger talk with Naomi Campbell. For example, Alan Rabinowitz.

Rabinowitz may be the world's best-known tiger conservationist; he has been characterized by Time magazine as the "Indiana Jones of wildlife conservation" and by the New York Times as "the Dag Hammarskjöld of biology."[15] Executive director of science and exploration at New York's Wildlife Conservation Society (formerly known as the Bronx Zoo) for nearly three decades, more recently Rabinowitz became the CEO of Panthera, a nonprofit organization dedicated to saving the world's endangered large cats. When asked by the London *Guardian* what hopes he had about the tiger summit, he replied, "None, and that's why I'm not going."[16] The summit, he explained, would be "a fiasco of more of the same" with a "preordained agenda." He noted that under the aegis of the World Bank all kinds of other things were to be discussed and funded, such as allocation of tradable carbon credits for tiger habitats, and "politically correct" programs in environmental education and helping local communities near tiger habitats. In frustration Rabinowitz exclaimed, "Money has not been focused on the one thing that will save the tigers immediately, and that's adequate protection of protected areas [from poachers]."[17]

He had a point. Growing prosperity in East Asia over the past two decades has fueled a black market in tiger body parts, which are key components of Chinese traditional remedies for ailments ranging from arthritis to erectile dysfunction. Although the trade in tiger parts has long been banned by the United Nations Convention on International Trade in Endangered Species (CITES), and outlawed in China for 18 years, the price of a dead tiger had grown to over $50,000.[18] Given that remaining tiger habitats are in poorer Asian countries (India alone has more than half of the world's remaining tigers), one can understand how these huge illegal market incentives easily overwhelm well-meaning attempts to improve rural livelihoods or provide local environmental education—certainly worthy causes, but, as Rabinowitz notes, they will not save the tigers, pushed to the edge of extinction by increasingly lucrative poaching.

Indeed, poaching drives massive corruption in the administration of protected areas, especially in India. A Kathmandu-based World Wildlife Fund expert, Bivash Pandav, appeared to the *Guardian*'s Patrick Barkham "to sound close to despair" after visiting tiger habitats in 11 countries over four years. Although the highest-level officials in India, including the prime minister, may be sincere, Pandav asserted, still the protected-area administrators are often corrupt, and there is no accountability; in fact, they are often promoted.[19] In some cases they provide false figures about the tiger populations in the parks they administer. In one of India's most famous tiger reserves, Sariska, in Rajasthan, local park administrators continued to report a tiger population even after the animals were totally exterminated by poachers, with the officials' complicity.[20] The park is also threatened by illegal mining operations.[21] Unfortunately, this is not simply a case of a few crooked miscreants, or even of special problems with wildlife officials in India or elsewhere. Over the past 20 years there has been an explosion of corruption in developing countries (and also in richer countries), which has undermined international development aid in many sectors, and particularly in risk-prone, environmentally important areas—forestry, mining, oil and gas development, large infrastructure projects such as big dams, and international carbon trading, to name just a few.

Putin's Russia provides another example. From World War II to 1990, the Soviet government rigorously enforced anti-poaching laws and maintained a closed border with China, allowing the Siberian tiger population to recover from near extinction—perhaps only 30 or 40 individuals—to over 400. The post-Soviet collapse of governance into Mafia capitalism, coupled with the growing demand from China for tiger parts and an impoverished Siberian rural population, have now combined to threaten the tigers; 20 to 30 are being poached a year.[22]

What role could the World Bank play in addressing the forces of corruption and poor governance—was it part of the solution, or complicit in making things worse, or both—or were these problems simply too overwhelming for any one institution to make a difference?

The World Bank's sponsorship of the tiger summit led some prominent conservationists in India, where the battle for tiger survival will arguably be won or lost, to denounce the Bank as a continued threat to the environment in South Asia and elsewhere. Bittu Sahgal, editor of one of India's most prestigious wildlife publications, *Sanctuary*, claimed that the Bank had "left a trail of ecosystem destruction behind virtually every large project it has financed. . . . Tigers survive [in India] largely in the precise areas where World Bank money has been kept at arm's length. . . . While they say they want to help tigers, they are simultaneously cajoling the India government to accept loans in excess of $1 billion for highways and mines that will destroy tiger and wildlife habitats."[23]

At the tiger summit Zoellick pledged that the Bank would not finance projects that would harm tiger habitats.

Zero for Twenty?

In fact, in 2011 the Saint Petersburg meeting led President Zoellick to ask the World Bank's own internal quality-control unit—known as the

Independent Evaluation Group (IEG)—to conduct a review of 20 major World Bank–supported development projects in or near tiger habitats. Approved between 1994 and 2004, these projects included road building and highway improvement, as well as agricultural and forest development schemes. The IEG reports directly to the Bank's board of executive directors and conducts audits of completed projects, in addition to evaluating performance in whole sectors, such as energy or environment. The IEG's findings are supposed to ensure that the Bank learns from experience and that errors are not repeated. It was established in the early 1970s under a different name, the Operations Evaluation Department (OED), under threats from the U.S. Congress not to approve appropriations for the World Bank unless it instituted an internal quality-control and institutional learning function.[24]

The IEG tiger study found that three-quarters of the projects it examined directly threatened tiger habitats; and two-thirds also created, or were exposed to, indirect threats. For example, a project could induce poor farmers and loggers to move into the habitat areas, or actually catalyze poaching. In the planning phase, only 11 of the 20 projects adequately applied the World Bank's environmental policies, and less than half prepared any proposals to deal with the indirect impacts.

The end result was still worse: only three projects could show that effective measures had actually been carried out to prevent direct harm to protected habitats and species, and none could demonstrate any success in dealing with the more serious indirect threats and pressures that threatened tigers.[25] Even for three projects in India, Vietnam, and Indonesia that were expressly designed to promote conservation of tiger habitat as well as local community development, the bottom line was failure: "This balancing act proved very difficult to achieve in practice, demonstrating the inseparable link between good governance and biodiversity conservation."[26] And indeed, during the study period the tiger population decline actually accelerated in the countries where the 20 projects were located, particularly in India.

The study appeared to confirm the complaints of the critics. Bank-funded projects were harming tiger habitat despite existing environmental policies, which appeared in many cases to be ignored. Even more significantly, the Bank's policies—even when followed—could not protect against the major causes of environmental destruction, such as illegal trafficking: "Addressing these issues requires policies and programs at national and international levels."[27]

The past two decades have seen weakening governance and growing corruption in many developing countries—which some claim has only been exacerbated by World Bank policies. During the 1990s and much of the 2000s it was none other than the Bank and its sister institution, the International Monetary Fund (IMF), that promoted privatization, deregulation, and global integration of markets, policies that had fostered prosperity for some, including many in Asia, but also greater inequality. Much of the economic growth that ensued was commodity intensive, unleashing other darker, more-brutal international market incentives to pillage environmental assets, incentives that increasingly seemed to overpower all efforts to constrain them.

The 2011 IEG tiger report identified troubling perversities that critics maintained had characterized much Bank lending over the past 20 years: the Bank's negligence in carrying out its own environmental policies, the inability or unwillingness of borrowing governments to adhere to these policies, and a systematic weakness of governance in many countries (which is a polite way of referring to pervasive corruption). In fact, some critics alleged that the Bank itself was rife with bad internal governance and truly perverse, powerful, unwritten incentives to move money out the door at the cost of project quality. Prioritizing loan quantity above all else meant not just a lack of attention to ecological concerns, but also negligence of basic fiduciary duties—such as ensuring that the money lent is not stolen.[28]

There were others in India, the World Bank's biggest borrower ($88 billion since 1945, about 11 percent of its total cumulative lending),[29] who had an even more damning critique: the Bank's entire lending program for the country did more harm than good, hurting both the environment and the poor.

Nothing Good from the World Bank?

In September 2007, more than 700 people from all over the subcontinent—villagers, farmers, students, and local advocates—came to Delhi for a mammoth week-long investigative tribunal to examine the World Bank's social and environmental record. One hundred and fifty representatives of communities claiming to be adversely affected by Bank projects and policies presented testimony before a "jury" that could hardly be dismissed as marginalized radicals: it included the first woman to be appointed chief justice of an Indian state (Kerala), a former justice of India's Supreme Court, and a former justice of the High Court of Mumbai. Others judging the World Bank's record included the most internationally renowned historian of ancient India (Romila Thapar), a distinguished economics professor, and Booker Prize–winning author Arundhati Roy.[30]

The 28-point indictment of the tribunal and the "jury" asserted that the Bank had actively helped to weaken Indian environmental law to benefit large corporate investments. It attacked the Bank for financing the privatization of power, water, education, and health, and for its promotion of user fees for these services, making them unaffordable for India's poor and leading to their "deepening deprivation." It lambasted the Bank's support for carbon trading as subsidizing a private market for selling greenhouse-gas emissions that "in practice is doing nothing to reduce them." "Our conclusion based on these testimonies," the tribunal wrote, "is that the majority of World Bank–sponsored projects do not serve their stated purpose, nor do they benefit the poor of India. Instead in many cases, they have caused grievous and irreversible damage to those they intend to serve."[31]

Several prominent economists who had worked at the Bank for years have been no less withering in their analysis. Take Herman Daly, who worked at the Bank from 1988 through 1994. Daly is famous worldwide as a proponent of ecological economics; for Daly our world economic system, based as it is on an assumption of limitless growth, is on an ultimate collision course with the ability of the Earth's ecological systems to sustain human populations. In his view, national economies, as well as the world economy itself, will have to adopt totally different goals and values, namely those of a steady state in terms of traditional material growth and the use of resources. A steady-state economy would not preclude development in the sense of technical progress and social welfare. It was a credit to the World Bank at the time that they employed him. But in a September 2011 interview Daly was brutally blunt. He observed that at first he thought that he and the Bank's environmental staff "at times were being persuasive. But eventually I came to believe that it was really a lost cause and mainly window dressing." In his view the fatal flaw was the ideology of free-market growth, espoused by many economists and most Bank staff like the defining creed of a religious cult. "I don't expect," he stated, "anything good from the World Bank."[32]

One of the Bank's top research economists for 17 years, William Easterly (now a professor of economics at New York University), wrote a book in 2001 concluding that every approach to economic development the Bank had undertaken since the 1950s had failed.[33] He was forced to resign after making the mistake of further publishing his findings as an op-ed piece in the *Financial Times*.[34] One of his main conclusions was that top-down, centralized institutions like the World Bank, with pretensions to global knowledge, global plans, and global solutions, inexorably fail. In 2007 he described the World Bank as the "High Church of Development." Dead serious, but also with black humor, he wrote: "A dark ideological specter is haunting the world. It is almost as deadly as the tired ideologies of the last century—communism, fascism, and socialism—that failed so miserably. It feeds some of the most dangerous trends of our time, including religious fundamentalism. It is the half-century-old ideology of Developmentalism. And it is thriving."[35]

Harvard professor Lant Pritchett worked for nearly 20 years at the World Bank, from 1988 to 2007, co-authoring a number of key policy documents in the early 2000s. In September 2010, at a seminar sponsored by the Bank, he let loose. "Economic analysis played zero role in financing decisions [at the Bank]," he declared. "To stop projects was a career killer."[36] He was reported to "liken the World Bank to a coalition of single-interest groups," observing "that entrenched single-issue advocacy groups [within the Bank] defend their political entitlement to finance their sectors, too often without adequate economic rationale."[37]

Easterly and Pritchett contend that the Bank only pretends to use rigorous economic analysis in designing its loans—in reality, the focus is on getting the money out the door, and the various Bank policies and procedures are window dressing. For Herman Daly the argument is not about reforming the Bank to be made more effective in promoting economic growth—rather, the whole ideology of growth is a dead end.

As we shall see in the course of this book, both analyses are correct, and on a deeper level not contradictory: the Bank's perverse internal incentives are a fundamental problem, and the global environment cannot be sustained without challenging the ideology of limitless economic expansion.

Environmental Failures

Despite the billions the World Bank reported it was lending for environmental and natural-resources management, allegations proliferated in the 2000s that it was more of a menace to the global environment than a solution. These accusations percolated upwards from nongovernmental groups to governments and parliaments.

In June 2011 the United Kingdom House of Commons Environmental Audit Committee lambasted the Bank, calling into question the environmental impacts of the Bank's lending for agriculture and forestry, as well as extractive industries such as mining, oil, and gas.[38] The Committee recounted that "witnesses highlighted several examples including support for asparagus cultivation in Peru which has resulted in fast depletion of ground water, investments which encourage extensive exploration in the Amazon region for oil and gas for export, and support for offshore oil exploration off the coast of Ghana which would dump the drilling waste at sea."[39] The committee chair, Joan Walley, declared that "the World Bank should not assume continued support [from the UK] unless it changes its ways."[40]

The Commons Environmental Audit Committee's biggest concern was what it characterized as the Bank's climate-destroying energy portfolio, particularly shocking given that major donor countries to the Bank had contributed many billions of additional funds to mitigate global warming by reducing carbon-intensive energy use in developing nations.

In recent years the Bank claimed to have made fighting climate change, which many scientists believe is the world's gravest ecological challenge, a top environmental priority. Under Zoellick the World Bank positioned itself to be the world's leading public climate banker; in 2008 industrialized countries chose it to administer some $6.7 billion in new "Climate Investment Funds" to finance clean, low-carbon energy in developing countries as well as to assist poorer countries in adapting to global warming that is already occurring. Later, at the Cancun, Mexico, international climate treaty negotiations in 2010, the richer industrialized countries also chose the World Bank to manage as interim trustee the first $30 billion of a Green Climate Fund, which is supposed to disburse $100 billion a year by 2020. Additionally, the Bank was a pioneer in jumpstarting the global carbon market: in the decade starting in 2000, with support from rich countries, it established 13 global funds with over $3 billion of assets to promote global trading of carbon-emission-rights offsets.[41]

All of this new climate money was managed by the Bank outside its much larger main lending portfolio. The environmentally minded British Members of Parliament seemed to think that giving more money to the Bank for climate mitigation was throwing good money after bad. "The current state of the World Bank's lending to support fossil-fuel-powered energy generation is unacceptable and counterproductive," the committee asserted.[42] In 2010 alone the Bank's total energy lending totaled about $10 billion, of which roughly $6.5 billion was for fossil fuels, and only $3.5 billion was for energy efficiency and renewable power such as wind, solar, geothermal, and small hydropower. The Bank inflated these 2010 green power figures by counting disbursements from these separate donor climate funds—by one estimate between $520 and $870 million.[43]

In fact, from 2007 to 2010 the Bank lent as much for coal-fired power development—coal being the most carbon-intensive of all fuels—as the total amount donors put into the Climate Investment Funds.[44] It financed two giant coal plants in India and South Africa that will be among the 50 biggest sources of greenhouse-gas emissions on Earth. The South African plant, Medupi, will be the fourth-largest coal plant on Earth, and its annual GHG emissions will exceed those of 135 of the world's 212 nations.[45] Thus it was no surprise that the UK House of Commons committee concluded that "the World Bank is not the most appropriate channel for future UK climate finance. It undermines our low-carbon objectives."[46]

A Decade of "Mainstreaming the Environment"

Was there indeed a pervasive culture of perverse incentives at the Bank—all the more pervasive, in fact, because it was unwritten?

The Bank's own internal studies over the years revealed that the institution's environmental failures were often rooted in deep-seated patterns of behavior. A year before the Tiger Summit, in 2009, the Independent Evaluation Group made a damning assessment of the Bank's record of sustainable development. Its institution-wide Environmental Strategy, launched in 2001, was supposed to go beyond a "do no harm" agenda, which in theory was already achieved by the Bank's environmental procedures and safeguards. (The reality was quite different, as the study of projects affecting tiger habitat shows). The strategy proclaimed that the next step would be "mainstreaming" environmental concerns into all of the Bank's lending: for example, into its infrastructure, agriculture, and forestry projects. The IEG concluded that since 2001 "preliminary indicators suggest that mainstreaming has *decreased* in some sectors, such as agriculture, energy and transport. . . ."[47]

Environmental components of projects were, on average, less successful than other aspects of Bank lending. "The Bank's record on environmental stewardship has been uneven," IEG concluded with typical understatement. In fact, it found that the Bank only attempted to systematically track the results of about one-quarter of all the environmental projects it was involved in.[48]

To understand what really drove the Bank's environmental failures, whether it was inadequate monitoring of its projects, or lending for big projects without proper consideration of environmental safeguards, the IEG singled out a finding that internal Bank reports and external studies of the institution had emphasized for many years. Like a Greek chorus, these studies had bemoaned for over two decades the Bank's pervasive "culture of [loan] approval"—the drive to get projects launched. This has resulted in tragedies for the environment and for some of the poorest people on Earth. "Staff and management performance evaluations depend greatly on project approvals," the IEG observed. *"If it were known that approvals depended on having solid information on the results of similar projects, behavior might change significantly"*[49] (emphasis added). The IEG report went on: "Internal incentives favor projects with large commitments [of money], which can disadvantage environmental initiatives." Managers and staff preferred large infrastructure, for example, for electric-power generation, rather than energy-efficiency investments.[50]

Bank finance for environmental purposes had increased in recent years, mainly because, as noted above, rich industrialized countries chose the Bank to administer special new funds dedicated to the environment, funds that were technically not part of the institution's main lending portfolio but that were used in practice to top it off.[51]

Such findings were old news, and they raised troubling questions about the credibility of the Bank as an international development institution and as a trustee of public money. Yet, as we shall see in later chapters, the Bank's donor countries, and especially the borrowers, were not particularly interested in changing this state of affairs.

A Global Suicide Pact?

It would be unfair to blame only the World Bank, which, after all, is a microcosm of global society's geopolitical and environmental contradictions. And for that very reason, the Bank offers a disturbing picture of where our world is going. Before criticizing the Bank on its record in fighting global warming, one might first scrutinize its largest donor, the United States, whose inability to take action domestically was as important an obstacle as any to an effective international agreement on climate change.

The Bank, responding to demands from both developing and some donor countries, had gradually given its borrowing countries more decision-making power on its Board; in particular, China, India, Brazil, and South Africa had grown in influence, corresponding to their increasing economic clout.[52] But India and China, backed in solidarity by all the other developing nations, objected to any limits on their borrowing for fossil-fuel projects, including new coal-fired power plants. It was the Indian and South African governments that asked for the huge loans for giant coal plants, arguing that they were poor countries and coal was the cheapest fuel for generating electricity. Why should they bear the cost of fighting global climate change, when the richer industrialized countries had achieved their wealth through the burning of cheap fossil fuels? Who was the United States to lecture them on the board of the World Bank about reducing greenhouse-gas emissions?

Developing, borrowing countries resented conditions on development aid as a matter of principle—something they had reiterated countless times in various fora of the United Nations since the 1960s. Environmental policies had been part of the Bank's conditions for lending since the 1980s—in theory, and partly in practice. But for decades a significant number of Bank staff viewed the procedures as impediments to efficiently preparing projects and getting loans approved by the board of the executive directors—that is, such procedures, to cite Lant Pritchett, were "career killers." Indeed, some characterized the procedures as cumbersome obstacles preventing the Bank from moving forward more effectively in its grand mission of helping the poor.[53] Many government officials in the Bank's borrowing countries tended to agree.[54] The environment, local and global climate, the Earth's ecosystem services, and the poor who depend most directly on these services had no powerful constituency within the World Bank, nor among most of the politicians and economic power brokers of the world. True, the Bank had its environmental staff, just as many nations had their environment ministries or departments, and environmental nongovernmental organizations have proliferated around the world over the past 30 years. But the history of the past decades had also shown the limits of their influence.

Corruption has undermined not just environmental projects and programs, but the whole development effort. Yet major borrowers from the Bank have resisted more-stringent controls on Bank lending as an infringement on their sovereignty. Some donor countries have been less than enthusiastic about pursuing corruption allegations, since their companies are often beneficiaries of it. And this is just one of many examples of how disagreements within and among the Bank's member countries have played out in debates over lending priorities.

Such contradictions were legion, and thus it is perhaps not a surprise that they would sometimes be concentrated in the world's leading public international financial institution, with 188 member nations.

The Bank asserted that its policies were promoting economic growth to achieve poverty alleviation, but many claimed the actual result was accelerating environmental deterioration and increasing inequality. To address environmental degradation caused by growth, the Bank claimed the answer was still more growth—albeit "sustainable growth."[55] The Bank's key interlocutors in many borrowing countries shared the same vision, and indeed in many cases had themselves worked at the Bank. The findings of the 2007 independent tribunal on the World Bank in India eloquently articulated the crux of the problem: "It became apparent in the course of these deliberations that in India there is little difference between the thinking of its policy makers and the World Bank. We hold the Indian government equally responsible and call for a reversal of its policies."[56] In fact,

> Detailed evidence was presented to show how former World Bank staff have occupied the key positions within the Indian Finance Ministry, the Reserve Bank, and Planning Commission for the past few decades, particularly since the early 1990s. The World Bank routinely gives lucrative consultancies and other honoraria to government policy makers to influence policies. This system creates serious conflicts of interest. . . .The World Bank has very carefully nurtured India's policy elite, who owe more to this international institution than to the Indian people.[57]

The lack of coherence in the Bank's policies and projects, often working at cross purposes (for example, financing new coal plants even while administering new funds to mitigate climate change), only reflected still crasser contradictions in the policies of its member states. The same countries that pledged to support the Bank's Tiger Initiative in Saint Petersburg played a hypocritical game in other international fora. In 2010, just months before the summit, at a meeting of the Convention on International Trade in Endangered Species, China and India opposed a proposed resolution for improved reporting on cases of tiger poaching. China is reported to have asserted that the suggested compliance measures of CITES were "a dangerous precedent."[58] At the tiger summit Chinese premier Wen Jiabao vaguely declared that "all countries should crack down on poaching and illegal trade of tigers," and then skipped the final press conference of the other heads of state present at the summit.[59]

The biggest disconnect of all was that between the growing scientific evidence of increasing destabilization of the Earth's ecosystems linked to the world economy, and the inability of the world's political leaders and key economic institutions to think beyond their own immediate interests. The self-serving culture of loan approval at the World Bank and the short-term economic and political interests of businesses, traders, and nations all meld into an irrational global system that is careening toward its own destruction.

★★★

One would not think of UN secretary-general Ban Ki-moon as an excitable man, prone to hyperbolic public outbursts. In fact, secretaries general are chosen for their discretion and ability to avoid moral condemnations of the ubiquitous hypocrisies of the UN's member governments. But in 2011 at the World Economic Forum in Davos, Switzerland (the annual global policy potlatch of many of the world's leading financiers, business moguls, and statesmen, with a sprinkling of respectable—that is, non-confrontational—nongovernmental groups), he finally could no longer contain himself:

> For most of the past century, economic growth was fueled by what seemed to be a certain truth: the abundance of natural resources. We mined our way to growth. We burned our way to prosperity. We believed in consumption without consequences. These days are gone. . . . Over time, that model is a recipe for national disaster. *It is a global suicide pact.*[60] (emphasis added)

The secretary-general asked governments for "visionary recommendations" that would feed into the June 2012 "Rio Plus 20 United Nations Conference on Sustainable Development."[61] Twenty years earlier, in 1992, representatives of 172 nations, including 118 heads of state, had gathered in Rio de Janeiro at the "Earth Summit" to attempt to reconcile economic development with sustaining the global ecosystems on which all societies depend. Scientists had already been sounding the alarm over accelerating global warming and the worldwide destruction of species and forests for over a decade. In June 2012 another UN-sponsored global gathering would take place to evaluate progress and chart a way forward.

Let us look back on those days in Rio at the "Earth Summit." After all, it was an attempt to forestall the ecological "global suicide pact" that the secretary-general would warn the nations of the world about. It was also a time when the Bank put into effect some of the most important institutional reforms since its founding. These reforms were intended to address widespread international criticism of its neglect of environmental and social concerns in its lending—and remedy the lack of accountability to the very people, the poor in developing countries, that it claimed it existed to help. And let us examine the subsequent role of the World Bank, arguably the international institution most capable of addressing what were, in 1992, new environmental priorities.

CHAPTER TWO

Present at the Creation

T HE YEARS LEADING UP TO THE 1992 Rio de Janeiro Earth Summit were increasingly uncomfortable ones for the World Bank, besieged by growing international criticism of the environmental and social impacts of its lending. Large infrastructure projects supported by the Bank, including dams, plantations, mines, and oil wells, became issues of local and global controversy. In poor countries, local communities began to protest development that threatened the forests, fisheries, and agricultural lands on which they depended. Throughout the world, growing evidence of global warming heightened concerns about greenhouse-gas emissions and the destruction of tropical forests.[1] Scientists spoke up and civil-society movements grew, with varying degrees of response from national governments.

In the late 1980s such criticism, particularly from the U.S. Congress, translated into political pressure for the Bank to change or see its funding imperiled. Reforms were launched in 1987, with admission of the Bank's then president, Barber Conable, that "the World Bank had been part of the problem in the past."[2] And indeed, Conable's Bank delivered, for the first time, major institutional resources to address ecological concerns. The reforms continued under his successor, Lewis Preston, who was president from late 1991 through May 1995.

The environmental staff increased from five in 1985 to 270 in 1990— around 6 percent of total staff resources. In 1991 a new, more rigorous environmental assessment policy for proposed Bank projects was promulgated, strengthening a weaker policy that had theoretically been in force since 1984. That same year the Bank issued a new policy that it would not, under any circumstances, finance commercial logging in primary tropical moist forests.[3] Environmental organizations viewed the ban on lending for logging as a great victory.

Lending for environmental purposes increased from merely $15 million in 1985 to $180 million in 1990 and $990 million in 1995. Similarly, the Bank's prodigious research-paper mill went into overdrive, the number of reports on environmental themes increasing from 57 (out of a total of 1,238) in 1985 to 408 (out of 1,760) in 1995. Even today it would be hard to find a university or think tank that produces over 400 environmental reports a year; in fact the Bank became "arguably the largest center for such research in the world."[4]

The public commitment to "mainstreaming" the environment into all Bank activities began in the early 1990s, and by 1995 the Bank was already declaring victory in a report entitled "The World Bank and the Environment Since the Rio Earth Summit: Mainstreaming the Environment."[5] The Bank initiated the preparation of National Environmental Action Plans (NEAPs) by almost all of its borrowing nations and moved to make environmental concerns a key part of its master loan-strategy documents for its borrowers, the Country Assistance Strategies.[6]

Throughout the early 1990s, the World Bank tried to reinvent itself as an institution where the environment was a major priority. In the words of the Bank's own half-century history, "at least in principle, environmental sustainability joined economic growth and poverty alleviation to form the core objectives for Bank work."[7] But a number of deeply rooted institutional contradictions were present at the creation, or re-creation, of the Bank as an institution of "sustainable development," contradictions that proved to be extraordinarily persistent over the next two decades.

"A Very Small Tail Wagging a Very Nasty Dog"

In the autumn of 1989, France, Germany, and several other nations asked Bank management to establish a new fund for environmental projects in developing countries.[8] The French and Germans in particular indicated they would be willing to put substantial new financial contributions into such a program. The Bank's senior management showed little enthusiasm for the idea initially, in part because they feared that donors would substitute contributions to a global environmental fund for their contributions to the International Development Association (IDA).[9] IDA, which lent to the poorest countries, had to be replenished with tens of billions of dollars every three years by the richer countries, since unlike the IBRD, its loans (technically called credits) charged no interest and had very long repayment periods of decades—in effect, IDA credits were mostly grants once inflation was figured in. But once the Ninth IDA Replenishment was agreed on in December 1989, Bank management leaped to formulate a proposal. In 1991 the Global Environment Facility (GEF) was established as a three-year pilot program housed in the World Bank. It was financed by the richer donor countries, with $860 million in a Global Environmental Trust Fund.[10]

From the beginning, the GEF had the mandate of providing grants to cover the so-called incremental, additional costs for projects in developing countries that would bring global environmental benefits. For example, building a solar array or wind farm would be more expensive than a coal plant that would produce the same amount of electric power, but would bring global environmental benefits through reduced carbon emissions; the GEF would finance the difference in the cost. The Bank emphasized "global" benefits in the hopes that rich donor countries would feel they, too, were getting something out of the extra expense. The program's four initial priorities were global warming, biodiversity, international waters, and ozone depletion. The GEF trust fund was administered by the World Bank as trustee, but there were three "implementing agencies"—the Bank, the United Nations Development Program (UNDP), and the United Nations Environment Programme (UNEP). The Bank would house the GEF Secretariat and manage the lion's share of the funds for so-called investment projects, UNDP would develop smaller technical-assistance projects, and UNEP was to provide scientific guidance.[11]

The pilot GEF embodied a number of problems that would become much more important in subsequent years as other international funds were established to address global environmental issues, most notably climate change. For one thing, defining with any precision or consistency what the "incremental" or "additional" costs would be in a given project could prove complicated. Would, for example, GEF grants for a wind farm or solar power unit in China be additional or incremental if the government was planning to build and finance it anyway?—certainly the case in terms of China's central planning targets. The baseline of what governments and project proponents claimed they were already going to do or not do without GEF finance was wide open to manipulation.[12]

Moreover, if, for example, a particular forest were to be protected under the GEF, say in Brazil, and a non-protected adjacent forest area was then logged, was the GEF really bringing any additional global benefits? This was the so-called leakage problem, i.e., that piecemeal environmental measures in the area of climate mitigation or forest protection would only push destructive activities into other areas. The Chinese would gladly take the subsidy for the wind farm that they otherwise would have paid for themselves and use the freed-up money to help finance another coal power plant; loggers would simply move from the newly protected forest area to deforest an unprotected area in the same country. Leakage could occur not just within a country but among countries—the loggers would move from Brazil to Peru, etc.

Years later, in 1998 and 1999, GEF-commissioned reports concluded that the entire GEF project-approval process was still widely unpredictable and inconsistent. Coherent criteria for calculating incremental costs were largely lacking, and in biodiversity projects it was practically impossible to distinguish between so-called global environmental benefits and local ones.[13]

The pilot GEF was a donor-driven and -controlled initiative, lodged in the World Bank, also controlled by rich industrialized-country donors. For this very reason it was initially unpopular with the developing countries (organized in the United Nations as the Group of 77, or G77), who were hoping that at the upcoming 1992 Rio Earth Summit new environmental funds would be established outside the World Bank, with a UN-like governance structure (for example, one country one vote, not one dollar one vote) in which they would have a larger say.[14] The donors had launched the GEF precisely with this eventuality in mind, so that in Rio the proposed new green fund would already be a *fait accompli*.

There was also a larger concern, raised by nongovernmental organizations (NGOs), that the new GEF would throw good money after bad, that it would be used by the World Bank to cover the external costs of the environmental harm of its own projects—costs that the Bank's environmental policies required to be covered by the project itself. There was some evidence that this was indeed happening, such as in the case of a Bank logging expansion project in the Congo that was bundled behind the scenes with a World Bank–implemented GEF "wildlands protection and management project."[15]

Some observers hoped the GEF might serve as an environmental Trojan Horse to help green the institution, the theory being that the lure of bundling green grant money with Bank loans would also improve the projects financed by the loans. But in the words of political economy author Susan George, the GEF was "a very small tail wagging a very nasty dog."[16]

Sheer Fantasy

In June 1992, the largest diplomatic gathering in history took place in Rio de Janeiro—the United Nations Conference on Environment and Development (UNCED), with 30,000 participants, including 118 heads of state. The summit was held on the twentieth anniversary of the first global conference to examine environmental issues, the 1972 Stockholm United Nations Conference on the Human Environment. Many developing nations at Stockholm saw the environmental issue as something that threatened to divert aid funds away from projects to promote economic growth; they insisted that existing development assistance not be reallocated but that completely new, additional funds be contributed by the richer countries for any environmental projects they might undertake.[17] In the words of India's then prime minister, Indira Gandhi, "poverty is the worst form of pollution." The differences were in part papered over, and Bank president Robert McNamara made a stirring keynote speech proclaiming the inextricable connection between the environment and economic development. After the speech, though, it was all downhill. The Bank created an exiguous internal environmental unit that had virtually no impact on the institution's operations from the 1970s through much of the 1980s.[18]

Nonetheless, the 1972 conference can probably be seen as a marker for the beginning of the modern international environmental movement, as reflected both in civil-society organizations and in attempts at intergovernmental cooperation.[19] Stockholm did lead to the creation of the United Nations Environment Programme (UNEP), but in its first two decades it was a weak agency with a small budget and very limited influence.

Twenty years later at UNCED, the same North–South divisions on the environment persisted. The G77 wanted foreign aid to increase, and they maintained that any new commitments to environmental purposes on their part should be financed with still more additional funds from the richer nations—funds preferably not managed by the World Bank, in which they felt they had little decision-making power. Moreover, developing countries had objected for decades to the strings attached to Bank loans—e.g., that they undertake domestic changes in policy, that they reduce budget expenditures or increase taxes, that they target development aid to the poor, etc. And they especially disliked the Bank's newest environmental conditions, which, they argued, infringed on their sovereignty over their own natural resources.[20] These official positions largely ignored their own responsibility for ecological destruction that had spurred growing protest movements in major developing countries.

The most important outcome at UNCED was the negotiation and signing of two new international conventions—the United Nations Framework Convention on Climate Change (UNFCCC) and the Convention on Biodiversity (CBD). A restructured GEF would finance activities under the two treaties. Under the UNFCCC the richer industrial nations (so-called Annex

I nations) committed to reducing their climate change emissions by 2000 to 1990 levels; they also agreed to provide financial and technical assistance to developing (Annex II) countries to help address climate change.

There was one bow to the concerns of the Annex II countries: the GEF was reorganized with a new governance structure, which required dual 60 percent majorities of votes by both industrialized and developing nations for decision making.[21] A new operating charter was drawn up, the Instrument of the Restructured Global Environment Facility, which was approved by 73 countries in March 1994 and adopted by the three implementing agencies (World Bank, UNDP, UNEP).[22] The restructured GEF was in practice still largely a World Bank operation, with the Bank acting as trustee for all GEF funds and administering most of the GEF money as the investment project manager. The core GEF funds have never been large in comparison to the annual lending commitments of the World Bank Group. For the period 1994 through 1998 the GEF Trust Fund received around $400 million a year in comparison with Bank lending averaging over $20 billion annually during the same period.

Other initiatives coming out of UNCED proclaimed ambitious goals, with little practical impact on economic development patterns or environmental deterioration. Like most UN conferences it produced a legally nonbinding declaration—the Rio Declaration—in which, among other things, the rich countries pledged to increase their foreign aid to a level of 0.7 percent of Gross National Product (GNP), the same promise they had made in Stockholm 20 years earlier and subsequently ignored. Attempts to negotiate a treaty on the management and conservation of forests floundered on the objections of leading developing countries such as India and Malaysia, resulting instead in a document with no legal status whatsoever, a "non–legally binding statement" of forest principles.[23]

More exceptionally, the participating nations all solemnly approved a nonbinding 800-page document called Agenda 21, a global environmental and development agenda for the twenty-first century. The document included a multitude of grandiose political and moral exhortations, many of which the signatory governments had no serious intention, nor in most cases even the capacity, to carry out. For example, the Secretariat of UNCED estimated that implementing Agenda 21 in developing nations for the period 1993–2000 would cost over $600 billion a year, including about $125 billion from the rich industrialized nations. This was on top of existing and promised future increases of aid to 0.7 percent of GNP in the Rio Declaration.[24] Not only were these amounts sheer fantasy, but the total of all development aid from the rich countries actually *declined* on average in the years following the Earth Summit.[25] The UNCED elephant gave birth in the end to a financial mouse, the reconstituted GEF, and even the GEF was not new, since it had already been up and running as a pilot scheme in 1991.

Agenda 21 was a predecessor of the Millennium Development Goals—a set of ambitious development, public health, and environmental goals to be reached by 2015 that was agreed on by 189 nations at a huge "United Nations Development Summit" in 2000.[26] In its financial ambitions it also anticipated calls from the United Nations in the 2000s for over a hundred billion dollars a year in new and additional funds (i.e., beyond the never-realized 0.7 percent of GNP for core development assistance) from the rich countries for climate mitigation and adaptation in developing countries.

It was not an encouraging precedent.

The Culture of Loan Approval and New Reforms

June 1992 was a watershed month in the history of the World Bank. It emerged from the Rio Earth Summit with a financial prize—practical control over most of the restructured GEF. But just days after the conclusion of the summit, two major controversies came to a head, scandals that raised profound questions about the Bank's ability to manage the many billions entrusted to it.

Since the late 1980s, international headlines had detailed the plight of more than 200,000 poor Indian farmers and tribal people who were threatened with forcible resettlement to make way for a Bank-financed dam on India's longest westward-flowing river, the Narmada. The Indian government and the World Bank had failed to carry out critical environmental plans and basic resettlement measures for the Narmada Sardar Sarovar project. The headmen and leaders of desperately poor villages in the dam's wake vowed to die on site rather than move, and hundreds of members of the U.S. Congress, the Japanese Diet, the European Parliament, and several Scandinavian country parliaments wrote letters to the World Bank urging it to withdraw its support.[27] Indian author Arundhati Roy called Sardar Sarovar and similar mega-dams, often financed by the Bank, "weapons of mass destruction . . . malignant indications of civilization turning upon itself," since they embody the severing of the link, and the understanding, "between human beings and the planet they live on."[28]

The scandal became so acrimonious that Bank president Barber Conable created an independent commission to conduct a special investigation of the project. It was chaired by Bradford Morse, a former U.S. congressman,

UN undersecretary-general, and director of the United Nations Development Program. The commission's principal finding was there was "an institutional numbness at the Bank and in India to environmental matters."[29] Moreover, the Sardar Sarovar case was not an exception but in fact revealed practices that were "more the rule" in other large Bank projects in India where resettlement was involved.[30] The commission concluded that the Bank was more concerned with pleasing borrowing countries than with implementing its own policies, and urged the Bank to "step back" from the project, i.e., threaten to withdraw if the Indian authorities did not remedy social and environmental abuses.[31] On June 18, 1992, four days after Bank staff and officials returned from Rio, the Morse Commission, as it came to be called, held a press conference in Washington releasing its findings.

At that same moment, another extraordinary internal report was circulating inside the Bank, confirming that a "culture of loan approval" was corrupting Bank operations. The Wapenhans Report, nicknamed after Willi Wapenhans, the Bank vice-president who directed it, found that the whole appraisal process for preparing projects was in danger of becoming a sham. According to internal surveys, over four-fifths of Bank staff interviewed felt that "the analytical work done during project preparation" had little to do with assuring an investment's social, environmental, or even economic quality. "Many Bank staff perceive [project] appraisals as marketing devices for securing loan approval (and achieving personal recognition.)" It was all about pushing through the loan—fast—not to speak of personal career advancement.[32]

The fundamental problem identified by these two reports was the very institutional culture of the Bank, a culture that insiders and staff often referred to as the "pressure to lend." It was the bureaucratic equivalent of original sin, which imperiled not only the Bank's environmental performance, but its overall development effectiveness.

It took Bank management nearly a year to formulate an "action plan" that would address the concerns of the Wapenhans Report. The first version of the 1993 "Next Steps" plan was so unconvincing that the Executive Board sent it back for toughening. The U.S. director worried that it would be seen as a smokescreen, fueling criticism that the Bank was not taking concrete action.[33] Even so, the changes in the final version were relatively minor. Ultimately, "Next Steps" was a charade. It was easy to declare victory in less than a year since more than two-thirds of the 87 "actions" were bureaucratic posturing: forming committees, learning groups, and task forces; holding workshops and training courses; preparing reports (some of which the Bank had already been issuing for years prior to the Wapenhans Report![34]), evaluations, and studies, and reporting on the reports and studies, etc.[35] In July 1994, right after Bank management declared that 92 percent of the "Next Steps" had been successfully implemented, former Bank vice president Willi Wapenhans wrote, "It is perhaps noteworthy that the Bank's management response to the Wapenhans report does not yet address the recommendations concerning accountability. The 'cultural change' required is, however, unlikely to occur unless the performance criteria change."[36]

The Narmada Dam controversy had a different institutional impact, one which arguably did lead to lasting changes. In the autumn of 1992 several executive directors, representing the rich donor nations, directly confronted Bank management with scathing accusations ranging from a charge of "cover-up" by the U.S. director to a statement by the Dutch executive director that Bank management could not be trusted.[37] Developing country board members unanimously opposed the findings and recommendations of the Morse Commission, and the board approved a compromise: rather than canceling Bank financing of the project, as the Morse Commission recommended, the board pushed management to set a six-month deadline for the Indian government to remedy the deficiencies in the Narmada Sardar Sarovar operation. In March 1993 the Bank effectively withdrew from the project, halting all loan disbursements in response to a face-saving statement from the Indian government that it no longer desired Bank funding for the scheme. It was the first, and one of the only, times that the Bank actually halted funding for a project because of noncompliance with environmental and social loan covenants.[38]

The precedent of the Morse Commission prompted several proposals designed to hold Bank management and staff more accountable. Ultimately, in September 1993 the Bank's board of directors approved an "Independent Inspection Panel," a three-member commission charged with investigating complaints that the Bank was violating its own policies and threatening the well-being of groups in borrowing countries.[39]

The establishment of the Independent Inspection Panel was an important precedent for accountability in multilateral organizations.[40] Unfortunately, because of resistance by many of the Bank's member countries, particularly borrowing governments, it was set up in a way such that it lacks real autonomy. After receiving a complaint, it can only proceed with an investigation with the approval of the Bank's executive board and the borrowing country's government. If the inspection request is approved, the panel then has access to relevant Bank files and staff, and prepares a report with nonbinding recommendations that it submits to the Bank's management and to the board. The report is kept secret until the board decides what action, if any, is to be taken.

The Bank also instituted a new information policy in late 1993, effective in January 1994, which was an important step forward in making many official Bank documents available to the public in member countries. Staff-appraisal reports, major country economic and sectoral studies, and Bank-required environmental assessments prepared from 1994 onward were made publicly accessible. With this new policy the Bank became one of the most transparent of all international agencies, much more transparent at the time then the bilateral national aid agencies of most countries, with the exception of the United States.

Yes We Can

These reforms took place only under the greatest of outside pressures: literally a threat by the U.S. Congress to withhold $3.7 billion unless the Bank set up the inspection panel and the new information policy.[41] On May 5, 1993, the House of Representatives Banking Subcommittee on International Development, Finance, Trade, and Urban Affairs held a hearing on the 10th three-year funding replenishment of the International Development Association. It quickly turned into a discussion of Bank controversies and the poor performance detailed in the Morse Commission and Wapenhans reports. Larry Summers, who at the time was undersecretary for international affairs at the U.S. Treasury, declared that "our job in the U.S. Government is to ensure that this [World Bank] rhetoric is translated into reality. That means no more Narmadas."[42]

Following the hearing, subcommittee chairman Barney Frank gave Bank officials an ultimatum: create the inspection panel and reform the information policy, or give up the IDA funds. His interlocutors at the Bank told him, "Look, you can't order us to do anything." Frank told them (as he recounted in a later interview), "I agree, and you can't order me to pass the bill with the money."[43]

The pressure worked, and top Bank management (particularly the senior vice president for operations, Ernest Stern, who at the time was the reputed Svengali-like, actual behind-the-scenes manager of the institution) reversed their opposition. Nonetheless, Frank and the subcommittee hedged their bets: they approved money only for the first two of the three years of the replenishment (which always before had received three-year funding authorization), and they cut $200 million from the U.S. Treasury request. "You can't do that," exclaimed Barney Frank's interlocutors in the Bank. "I said," Barney Frank recalled, "Yes we can."[44]

Even after the Bank agreed to establish the panel, the pressure continued. The following year, the House Banking Committee held a special oversight hearing in which there was bipartisan agreement about the need for further Bank reforms. John Kasich (Republican-Ohio), who subsequently left Congress to become governor of Ohio, cited a litany of environmentally destructive Bank projects: "The World Bank was involved in a project that ended up destroying a significant portion of the rain forest. And of course Sardar Sarovar. . . . [And it] forced resettlement, a situation where . . . people found themselves without anyplace to live."[45] It was indeed a different era, a time when Republicans could join environmentalists in outrage over destruction of tropical forests or social damage wrought by a big World Bank–financed dam in India.

Despite a series of environmental scandals and internally commissioned reports which documented flagrant negligence in the Bank's lending practices, it seemed that only the real threat of the Bank's largest donor cutting funds could prompt the beginnings of institutional change. How would this bode for the continuity and the sustainability of the reforms?

The Tail Did Not Wag the Dog

In its first decade the GEF suffered from the same chronic institutional perversities as its big brother trustee: pressure to move money out the door as quickly as possible, and a lack of monitoring and evaluation of projects.[46] Massive confusion remained, not just in recipient countries, but also among the staff of the World Bank and other agencies such as UNDP, over how to define and calculate the additional global environmental benefits of GEF projects and the incremental costs for these benefits.[47]

The tail did not wag the dog: the GEF greening of the Bank's main lending did not occur. In fact, according to the GEF's own internal reports, environmental objectives were rarely incorporated either into Bank projects or into the Bank's more broadly based country and economic-sector strategies.[48] The Bank continued to fund fossil-fuel power development, with little regard for growing carbon emissions. Total GEF funds for all purposes for its entire existence from the pilot project in 1991 through 2010 totaled nearly $9.5 billion; a little less than a third of this total was for addressing climate change, some $3.1 billion.[49] In contrast, in just 2009 and 2010 the World Bank Group main lending portfolio contributed just over $9.6 billion for fossil fuel power and extraction, of which nearly $5.4 billion was for coal-fired power development.[50]

The Bank also failed to "green" its lending to incorporate biodiversity protection, which also accounted for nearly a third of all GEF funding in the period 1991–2009. Some GEF biodiversity projects became scandals as local populations were displaced or impoverished by an ill-conceived model of conservation.[51] Even the supposedly better-managed projects achieved disappointing results. The failures did not lie solely at the feet of the Bank. They were also attributable to weaknesses in the host governments and to complicated, often contradictory local political and social circumstances that could not be overcome by a single project, even with the best of planning. But the Bank was often oblivious from the outset to the warning signs. Similar dynamics would bedevil many Bank efforts focused on the environment, so it is worth examining a couple of cases in greater detail.

As we saw in chapter 1, a 2011 internal review of 20 Bank projects affecting tiger habitats revealed a distressing record. Three of these were "Integrated Conservation and Development Projects" (ICDPs), that tried to combine environmental goals with development efforts for local communities. Environmental groups such as the World Wildlife Fund and development agencies began to promote ICDPs in the late 1980s as a new, hopeful approach that would gain the support of the rural poor. In theory, it seemed to be a wonderful example of putting the goals of Rio and "sustainable development" into action. Of the 20 Bank projects affecting tiger habitats that were studied, the three ICDPs were the best in terms of data gathering and evaluation, and the best, at least in terms of project design, in trying to address threats to tiger habitat. Two of the three received GEF funds that were blended with Bank loans.

The first GEF supported project (approved in late 1996, closed in September 2002) was an ambitious effort to protect the Kerinci Seblat National Park in Sumatra. The park is home to the Sumatran tiger, rhinoceros, and 142 other mammal species—an astounding 1/30th of all the mammal species on Earth. Unfortunately, the project was based on mistaken premises. It emphasized economic development of local villages, assuming that poverty and a lack of alternative livelihoods were driving deforestation. In fact, the villages targeted were some of the wealthiest communities in Sumatra. They saw the ICDP development grants as supplements rather than alternatives to lucrative cash crops such as cinnamon. Moreover, much of the logging and forest clearance for cash crops was instigated by rich, influential individuals who often lived far from the park. The area suffered from a general, chronic breakdown of law and order, and the responsible government ministries, all the while receiving economic support from the project and other aid donors, had no interest in controlling illegal logging and poaching. Under these conditions, unenforceable conservation agreements with local villages proved almost useless.[52] The conclusion of the Bank's own case-study review is worth citing verbatim:

> Although the global conservation community often complains about inadequate funding for parks and protected areas, the Kerinci story illustrates that even generous budgets will not ensure success where there is little political commitment or local support for conservation.[53]

The second GEF-supported ICDP was the flagship India Ecodevelopment project (approved in May 1995, closed in June 2004). It was the only one of the 20 projects reviewed that demonstrated it had conducted tiger population surveys and mitigated indirect threats to the tigers and their habitats.[54]

The India Ecodevelopment Project was a large one for the GEF: $20 million in grants managed by the World Bank, with additional cofinancing of a $36 million IDA credit, and $13 million from the Indian government. The goal was to promote conservation in seven protected areas, five of which were (and are) critical tiger habitats, along with environment-friendly local village development—for which 60 percent of the costs of the project costs were allotted.[55]

Despite some positive impacts, the project was overwhelmed by poaching, habitat destruction, and corruption.[56] In one of the reserves, the state government pocketed an "ecotax" charged to visitors that was supposed to go for its maintenance. Local hotels kept profits from wildlife tourists without giving back a portion to manage the reserves or help local people, as they were supposed to do.[57]

Worse still, the project displaced thousands of people from traditional forestlands, while opening these areas to the private sector.[58] More than half the people affected were tribal Adivasi communities, which are among the most marginalized and impoverished population groups in India. Indian researchers charged that the Adivasi had been turned into "development and conservation project refugees of the twenty-first century."[59] The project also ignored pervasive problems with graft in Indian federal and state forest departments, and it even catalyzed corruption at the level of tribal hamlets, where such graft had not existed before.[60]

In 1998 tribal groups in Nagarhole, one of the seven protected areas, filed a complaint with the Bank's Independent Inspection Panel.[61] They contended that they had not been consulted about their impending resettlement and that the concrete houses built for them outside the park were "airless." Lacking farming tools and skills for life outside the forest, most "oustees" soon returned to the forest and/or local plantations.[62] The project proceeded with the construction of a luxury four-star hotel of the Taj chain inside the park (finally halted by court order in 2000) as protests of the affected people grew, resulting in hunger strikes and police beatings.[63] Along with their complaint, the local groups submitted an alternative plan for conservation and development in the park, managed by Adivasi communities, but it never received serious consideration.

The Panel found the complaint justified, noting "a significant potential for serious harm," and recommended a full inspection.[64] The reality on the ground blatantly contradicted the politically correct rhetoric of the project documents. Very little analysis had been undertaken of the real threats to the park, which did not include the subsistence tribal communities living in the forest. Rather, populations living outside of the park zone were increasingly encroaching onto park lands to grow cash crops such as tobacco and coffee. According to the panel, the World Bank and the GEF were aware of the lack of data on the real threats to the park, but pushed the project through anyway—another example of the pressure to lend and the "approval culture" at work.[65]

But under Indian government pressure, the Bank's executive board refused to authorize a full Independent Inspection Panel investigation, instead asking Bank management to improve the implementation of the project and address some of the issues in the Inspection Panel's initial report. The Nagarhole conflict was arguably the worst-performing part of the Ecodevelopment Project; relations between the local authorities and people in other instances actually improved, but unfortunately with little positive benefit for conserving biodiversity.

The failures of the Ecodevelopment project were certainly not exclusively the fault of the World Bank. Large-borrowing governments like India have considerable negotiating power and can chose to fulfill—and not fulfill—Bank conditions according to their own priorities, with little consequence for future borrowing. The Indian government failed on many accounts and the conflicts between rural Adivasi people and state agencies were deep rooted, dating back to British colonial days in the nineteenth century. There is a strong argument to be made that no long-term solution to managing protected areas in India can be achieved without major reforms of the way government agencies deal with local people dependent on forest resources.[66]

In fact, the whole ICDP model may be flawed, as in some cases it attempts to reconcile the irreconcilable (local development needs and habitat conservation) and has no impact on the powerful external economic forces that threaten biodiversity. Indeed, a 2001 review of 134 ICDP projects (funded by various aid agencies, including the Bank and GEF) showed that most were failures.[67] Part of the problem is that the rush by aid agencies to move projects in a relatively short time span (typically five to seven years) does not allow staff to develop an adequate understanding of local communities.[68]

Yet the hope that things will improve always remains, despite the record of failures, since that hope keeps the money flowing and the bureaucratic superstructure afloat. The standard reply of Bank management to uncomfortable evaluations has often been "that was then and this is now," i.e., the projects reviewed or criticized were designed years before and since then the problems have been, or are being, or will be, addressed.[69]

In many of these projects, the agenda—fundamentally changing how local populations behave and make their livings—might well seem hubristic to someone without a vested interest in the development business.[70] The Bank has often appeared oblivious to the possibility that the behavior of the aid agencies may be in greater need of change. Nor is there a recognition that the rural poor living next to fragile habitats are rarely the main threat.[71]

Many well-intentioned projects often reinforce, rather than remedy, the institutional and governance weaknesses of borrowers. Frequently, the Bank makes things worse by ignoring local political, social, and cultural realities—though some staff may be, in vain, all too aware of them.

"As Much Money Out the Door as Possible"

Yet, in theory, there was no reason why the Bank could not green its portfolio along the general lines of its promises of the early 1990s. Now it even had a financial incentive of sorts, with the added grant money it managed under the GEF. Why couldn't the Bank ensure that individual environmental projects were well prepared, with real sensitivity to local conditions, and with continued monitoring? Why couldn't such projects be successful not only on their own terms, but serve as examples of best practices? And why couldn't the Bank "mainstream" environmental concerns into its larger portfolio—in energy, infrastructure, agriculture, extractive industries, and transport?

In 1993, after six years of widely publicized reforms, the fundamental problem remained—a culture of loan approval without accountability. The internal signs were not good. At the highest levels there were moments of total candor, followed by . . . nothing. In a public speech before the Foreign Policy Association in March 1993, President Lewis Preston claimed that the Bank was focusing more than ever on "follow-up," "results," and "implementation." But that same month, at an internal senior management retreat, he berated the institution's managerial culture: "What we say is often what is politically correct but not what we really feel or do. . . . There is no accountability for failure."[72]

Former Bank staffer Steve Berkman, who headed many projects in Africa and Latin America in the 1980s and early 1990s, and who later served as one of President James Wolfensohn's chief anti-corruption investigators, observed:

> There was one overriding objective in our work at the Bank, and that was to get as much money out the door as possible. Of course, this was never stated openly. . . . One could easily observe the differences between those who were sincerely dedicated and committed to improving conditions in Africa and those whose primary focus was on the advancement of their careers. For the latter, this meant moving money. . . . This contradiction between those Bank staff and managers who devoted their efforts to make things work in Africa and those who devoted their efforts to advancement in the bureaucracy created a constant tension that tended to resolve itself in favor of the bureaucrats.[73]

The Bank's official 50-year history, published in 1997, identified the disastrous implications of this perverse culture. In examining the Bank's record in the 1980s through the early 1990s, it concluded that attention to "poverty was seen as an obstacle to lending performance, defined for the most part as lending volume."[74] In South Asia, the region that even today has received the greatest amount in cumulative loans, "the strategy of continued lending linked to promises rather than performance has had its inevitable consequences. The enforcement of basic covenants, whether related to financial performance [i.e., corruption], environmental standards, or institutional reform, has had to be soft pedaled. Lending has had to proceed despite clear evidence of systemic sectoral problems."[75]

Robert Wade of the London School of Economics, in his chapter on "Greening the Bank" in the same official 50-year history, concluded:

> The Bank . . . moved from Old Testament harshness ("environment versus growth") to New Testament reconciliation (environmentally sustainable development) . . . without reforming the command and control style of management and introducing ways to evaluate staff by the effectiveness of their projects more than by their reliability in moving them to the Board. Failing some change in the system of internal incentives, there is a danger that New Testament reconciliation may remain at the level of images and values and bring little improvement in what happens on the ground.[76]

CHAPTER THREE

"I Can Change the Approval Culture to an Effectiveness Culture"

IT WAS AN ASTOUNDING SCENE, unprecedented in the history of the World Bank. Just nine months into his tenure as president, James Wolfensohn was delivering a passionate tongue-lashing to the institution's top management. Internal surveys, he declared, showed that nearly 40 percent of staff had little confidence in their supervisors. He berated the managers, "They may not trust me, but they don't trust you. . . ."[1]

Wolfensohn took office in June 1995, shortly after his predecessor, Lewis Preston, died from pancreatic cancer. From his very first day, Wolfensohn promised to revolutionize the Bank, to finish the long-overdue business of internal reform. The institutional culture had to change from one of loan approval, where staff were rewarded above all else for pushing money, to a culture of "effectiveness," "accountability," and "results." In his inaugural speech, he vowed that the "smile on a child's face" would be the real test of the Bank's success.[2]

But months later his frustration was boiling over. Wolfensohn's office leaked the transcript of the March 1996 management meeting to the London *Financial Times*, which proclaimed on its front page: "World Bank chief accuses staff of resisting reforms."[3] Wolfensohn's speech was, the *Financial Times* said, a "cry from the heart." He implored the Bank's management to finally address the problems that had perpetuated years of continual crisis. "I don't know what else we can do, in terms of standard and even nonstandard approaches, to try and bring about change in the institution. I just don't know what else to do."[4]

A Renaissance Man

When people first heard of James Wolfensohn, he seemed too good to be true. An international investment banker and financier, he was also an Olympic fencer (a member of Australia's national team at the 1956

Melbourne Games), a musician, and a philanthropist. He led New York's campaign to raise $60 million to save Carnegie Hall—where he also gave a cello concert accompanied by Vladimir Ashkenazy and Itzhak Perlman. He had been chairman of the board of the Princeton Institute for Advanced Studies (where Einstein spent his last years), and just before coming to the World Bank was chairman of the board of the Kennedy Center. For years he had given 20 percent of his income to charity.

Wolfensohn's interest in international development and environment issues was long-standing. He had been involved in the original 1972 United Nations Stockholm Conference on Human Environment, and already in 1980 he was on the board of directors of the Rockefeller Foundation and the Population Council, two organizations dedicated to development issues in poorer countries. That he reminded old-timers of Robert McNamara was more than a coincidence; Wolfensohn had admired McNamara for two decades and indeed was McNamara's choice to run the Bank when McNamara retired in 1981. At that time Wolfensohn abandoned his Australian citizenship to become an American (the president of the World Bank is traditionally an American, since the United States is the largest shareholder) and thus improve his chances, but the Reagan administration chose the older, better-known A. W. Clausen of the Bank of America [5]

Now, a decade and a half later, Wolfensohn had the job he had wanted for so long. But his very virtues carried the seeds of potential failure. More than his predecessors, he personalized the office of the presidency, making his own sincerity an alibi for the Bank's ongoing failures. He was also prickly, irascible, and, some would say, thin-skinned. Though he was, himself, publically candid about the institution's shortcomings, on his first day he sent an open letter to all Bank staff declaring, "I will regard externally voiced criticism of the Bank—of ourselves—as an indication of a desire to find alternative employment."[6]

He assiduously courted the press, which responded with a cascade of positive articles—full of praise for him personally, at times approaching adulation, but also full of questions about whether the Bank could change. Wolfensohn appeared as the institution's last, best chance. Intentionally or not, he set up a public context where eventual failure would inevitably appear to be the fault of the institution. If the cello-playing, Olympic-fencing, Medici-like financier, who could also outperform the most self-righteous NGOs in his public concern for the poor, for the environment, and for children—if James D. Wolfensohn could not change the Bank, well then, no one could.

The Miraculous Banana Tree

In his memoir, Wolfensohn recounts how his predecessor, Lewis Preston, warned him:

> Once you get to know the Bank, he [Preston] said, you realize that the invisible internal structures—the hierarchies and networks and fiefdoms that had solidified over the years—are very bit as massive and immovable as the expensive new headquarters edifice. He didn't have to tell me that this meant trouble for any would-be leader.[7]

So the new president hit the Bank like a whirlwind, determined to show that he would not be "a figurehead, a presentable emissary to the many officials and heads of state I would meet, while the Bank went about its business as usual."[8] One of his first priorities was to gain a sense of what was really happening in the field. In his first six months in office he visited dozens of projects in more than 40 countries, vowing to spend 80 percent of his time in the field, and only 20 percent with governments.[9] Citing this commitment in an interview, he recounted a conversation with a poor Kenyan farmer in front of a banana tree. The tree, Wolfensohn said,

> . . . had been grown with technical advice from Danny Benor—a brilliant Israeli agronomist who works for the World Bank. . . . "I'm so proud of these bananas. They're giving me the possibility," and he [the Kenyan farmer] grabbed his son, "of sending my son to school and maybe even university. And I can't even read."[10]

But even for James Wolfensohn, things were not always what they seemed. What he thought was a spontaneous encounter with a poor farmer was in fact the outcome of bitter behind-the-scenes fighting among Bank staff as to what kinds of projects he would be exposed to and what version of reality would be scripted for him. Wolfensohn met the banana farmer while on a site visit to see the Bank's "Training and Visit" (T&V) approach to agricultural extension. The program, which emphasized farmer training and visits by village extension agents, seemed like a plausible means of scaling up agricultural technology in the developing world. But even in the late 1970s, independent studies of Bank T&V projects in India lambasted the program for ignoring the needs of local farmers and the conditions of local ecologies. T&V also was expensive for poorer countries, with high recurring costs that could only be covered by more and more Bank loans.[11] As Wolfensohn began his presidency in 1995, younger, already embittered technical staff cynically referred to T&V as "Talk and Vanish."[12]

Kenya was supposed to be one of the Bank's success stories in promoting T&V, but an internal Bank audit of the Kenya "National Extension Project," for which a follow-up project provided technical advice for the miraculous banana tree, concluded that there was no evidence that the Bank's efforts improved agricultural production, particularly for maize, the major crop. The audit found many serious problems in the project, and rated its outcome "marginally unsatisfactory."[13]

As the new president learned about the Bank, senior management and staff positioned themselves to repeat, in uniquely Machiavellian variations, the scenario of the miraculous banana tree and T&V. In fact, the incident showed just how difficult it was to understand what was really happening on the ground.

Monster of the Himalayas

There could be no better example of the challenge Wolfensohn faced than the proposed Arun III Dam in Nepal. On his first day at the Bank—June 1, 1995—Wolfensohn was confronted with a potential public relations disaster that had been brewing for over two years.

Once again, a large infrastructure project was the source of rancorous debates both outside and inside the Bank. Arun III was to be built in a pristine Himalayan valley that is the deepest on Earth: the Arun River runs between Mount Everest and Kanchenjunga (the world's third-highest mountain).[14] For Nepal, it was an enormous project: its more than $1 billion price tag was nearly twice the country's entire annual development budget at the time.[15] The project would have entailed the construction of a 75-mile-long road through the valley, an influx of some 10,000 construction workers, threats to over 100 species of rare plants and animals, and sociocultural shock to some 450,000 people belonging to over 24 different ethnic groups living in traditional farming communities.[16] Biologists viewed the valley as a wildlife haven, having more species of birds than the continental United States; its upper reaches in the 1970s were the site of efforts to gather evidence on the existence, or nonexistence, of the yeti—the abominable snowman.[17] The Bank would lend $175 million to catalyze a financing package involving five other donors.

Nepalese nongovernmental groups protested the project vehemently, accusing the Bank of violating its own policies on environmental assessment, information disclosure, involuntary resettlement, and protection of indigenous peoples. They were not opposed to hydropower projects per se, but they thought the Arun proposal was the wrong use of the country's limited development resources; indeed, in their arguments they

emphasized the Bank's lack of economic analysis of alternatives and suggested that a series of small hydro projects would be more economically
efficient, and much more appropriate for the country's needs.[18] The Arun
controversy came on the heels of the Narmada Sardar Sarovar debacle, and
indeed some of the same senior management were involved, claiming to
U.S. treasury officials and even in public that the Bank had to "take a stand"
on Arun. In the words of Vice President for South Asia Joe Wood, if the
Bank did not push ahead with Arun, "the signal we'd send out is that the
Bank can no longer support infrastructure projects like this."[19]

But some things had changed; the newly created Independent Inspection Panel, for one thing, was open for business. It had already received
its first complaint months before Wolfensohn started his tenure, on October 24, 1994, from a Nepalese NGO coalition called the "Arun Concerned
Group." Bank management, led by Wood, lobbied intensely to try to prevent an investigation. But the board finally approved an inspection in February 1995, delaying approval of the project. At the same time that the inspection panel process was proceeding, the growing international controversy
over Arun engulfed the Bank.

After 29 years in the Bank working on poverty alleviation and population issues, Martin Karcher had had enough. As division chief for health,
education, and population programs in several South Asian countries, he
saw the monster dam as a major threat to poor Nepalese citizens. Much of
the power generated would not go for domestic use, but to one potential
customer, India. The Nepalese would be burdened with a large loan relative to the size of their economy, maintenance costs for an infrastructure
project of a scale unprecedented in the country's history, and dependency
on the goodwill of their giant southern neighbor for much of the revenue
stream the project would generate. Karcher was appalled that the Bank was
planning to push the project through without Nepal even having negotiated a power-purchase agreement with the Indians.

He decided to go public with his doubts and to retire early from the
Bank in protest. On September 9, 1994, he debriefed staff members of the
Environmental Defense Fund and agreed to make a transcript of his comments public.[20] Karcher noted that poverty alleviation in a country like Nepal called for prioritizing totally different investments: "broad-based, labor-
intensive investments in basic social services"—investments that would also
have a much more benign environmental footprint.[21]

Karcher was the senior Bank official responsible for poverty alleviation in Nepal, but he claimed that Bank management blocked his access

to information on the project's economic analysis until the end of project preparation. When a draft staff-appraisal report finally leaked out, he and many both inside and outside the Bank concluded that the economic analysis was a shambles. The Bank estimated an economic rate of return for the project of 18 percent, but based on assumptions that valued Arun's electricity at 53 cents per kilowatt hour—seven and a half times greater than the price of electricity in Washington, D.C., at the time. "Obviously," Karcher observed, "if you use these kinds of values, then any project becomes feasible and justified."[22]

In early 1995 Karcher visited Germany, one of the major proposed cofinancers of the project. He appeared on prime-time German television to present his case against the project. The growing protests led the German Federal Audit Office (the German counterpart of the U.S. Government Accountability Office, or GAO) to undertake its own evaluation of Arun, which concluded that that "the economic viability of the project" was "insufficiently secured."[23] Germany withdrew its financing in the spring of 1995. Soon after, on June 21, the inspection panel sent its final report to the Bank's board, finding that the project would violate several Bank environmental and social policies.[24] Wolfensohn acted quickly and decisively. On August 3, he announced that the Bank was withdrawing support for the project.[25]

The Arun case was in some respects a victory for Bank accountability. It was also another example of the shockingly shoddy economic rationales the Bank used to justify many of its biggest, most dubious investments. Bank management often tried to justify controversial projects by maintaining there were trade-offs between poverty alleviation, economic development, and the environment. The Arun case illustrated that this was often a false dichotomy: although the environmental risks of the project were significant, the main argument against it was that it was a misuse of scarce development funds and would actually undermine long-term poverty alleviation in Nepal. The Bank's new public information policies were beginning to make independent analyses possible—analyses that could expose the dubious economic rationalizations for environmentally destructive investments.

But Arun also revealed troubling bureaucratic countercurrents. For one thing, the panel's mandate did not allow it direct access to the Bank's board once a complaint was filed, or even afterwards if an investigation was approved. Management, on the other hand, could constantly intervene with new information and suggestions in order to derail the panel. Worse, many board members from the borrowing countries had opposed the panel from the beginning as an infringement on their sovereignty.[26] Richard Bissell, who served as the panel's first chairman from 1994 to 1997, dryly concluded that "the debate over the [Arun] case revealed the extent to which a majority of the board thought they had voted for the establishment of the panel as a 'fig leaf' to placate the environmental community, rather than out of any genuine interest in ensuring compliance with the bank's policies and procedures."[27]

Despite a groundswell of international criticism, an investigation by the Independent Inspection Panel, a damning report from the German Federal Audit Office, and the public defection of the Bank's single most experienced expert on poverty alleviation in Nepal—in the face all of this, senior Bank management furiously lobbied for the project to the bitter end.

Plus Ça Change . . .

With Arun, Wolfensohn showed a willingness to shut down destructive projects, but instituting widespread change was another matter. Yet he seemed determined to try. "I can change the approval culture to an effectiveness culture," Wolfensohn proclaimed at his March 1996 meeting with management and staff.[28] He launched a number of initiatives that showed potential for transforming the Bank into an institution that might deliver on its promises. He did much to encourage greater Bank consultation with nongovernmental groups, and he initiated a debt-relief program for highly indebted poor countries (the inadequacies of which were not the Bank's fault but more a reflection of the parsimony of some of the leading industrialized countries).[29] His support for the newly created Independent Inspection Panel was critical, given the often hostile reaction of many Bank staff and management, to say nothing of borrowing governments' representatives on the Bank's executive board.

But many of these efforts aged poorly, due to a lack of continuity and follow-through. A particularly important case in point was a much-heralded initiative on "mainstreaming" participation in Bank projects, i.e., ensuring that communities affected by Bank investments would be better informed and would have some input into the planning process. This program began before Wolfensohn's tenure, but was implemented on his watch, receiving considerable publicity. A Bank-wide "Participatory Development Learning Group" (PDLG) was established in 1991, and in May 1994 the Bank established a $4.24 million "Fund for Innovative Approaches in Human and Social Development" (FIAHS).[30] Over the next three years there were action plans, training manuals, reports, the publication with fanfare of a *World Bank Participation Sourcebook*, and 20 pilot projects—all of which added up to a lot of paper, but not much change. By 1997 the projects had become defunct and the Bank terminated funding for the program. In the end, affected communities had no more input than they'd had when the "Participation Action Plan" was launched in 1994. In fact, the Bank abandoned documenting whether participation was "mainstreamed."[31]

All of these initiatives, even if there had been effective follow-up, were secondary to Wolfensohn's ambitious "change bureaucracy": a "high level" "Change Management Group" headed up by three of the five managing directors, and a new "Department of Institutional Change and Strategy" with its own director. Responsibility for public and external relations was handed over to a newly created vice-presidency, which also launched an in-house "Change Bulletin" that attempted to explain to the bewildered staff what was . . . changing.

The cultural changes Wolfensohn sought to promote at first might seem complementary, but in practice often were contradictory: improved project quality (i.e., better development results on the ground), and, simultaneously, more responsiveness to the Bank's clients.[32] The problem was that often the Bank's clients were not necessarily interested in better development results, at least not in terms of environmental and social protection. The culture of loan approval had become so overwhelming precisely because of the Bank's desire to please, or least not offend, its borrowing governments. In many development debacles, the Bank continued to disburse funds despite systematic violations of loan conditions. This was documented in countless OED reports—and ignored not just for years but for decades by management and the executive board.

Wolfensohn appeared to be responding to two external criticisms of the Bank that would be difficult, if not impossible, to reconcile. On the one hand, borrowers complained about the Bank's cumbersome loan-processing procedures and reporting requirements—especially about the relatively new environmental and social protection policies. On the other hand, nongovernmental groups and parliamentarians in many donor countries complained that the Bank was not doing enough to ensure that those policies were being followed. Wolfensohn seemed to be claiming he could square the circle.

The Bank's real priorities soon became clear. First, management streamlined business procedures to promote speedier preparation and approval of loans. Second, the Bank engaged in a process to convert existing, detailed, binding Bank policies known as Operational Directives (including key ones on environmental assessment, rehabilitation of forcibly resettled populations, etc.), into a simpler, shorter, less rigorous format. Leaked internal memos revealed that one of the main motives behind this initiative was that the inspection panel posed the threat that Bank staff might actually be held accountable for carrying out the Bank's environmental and social policy requirements.[33]

To put "change management" into high gear, Wolfensohn hired the consultant firm McKinsey and Company, which had been involved in several earlier Bank reorganizations. The catchwords of the McKinsey-led restructuring were familiar ones in the business-school-speak catechisms of the 1990s: "decentralization," "matrix management," "reengineering," "knowledge management," "internal market." The package of reforms would be known as the "Strategic Compact."

Some of the rationales that Bank documents cited for the "Strategic Compact" were not reassuring: "There are complaints from our clients . . . our processes are seen as slow and cumbersome, and our products as static and inflexible. . . . Demand for the Bank's standard loan product is flat . . . income is on a declining path."[34] What did this have to do with overcoming the infamous culture of approval or helping the poor? "Deflecting expected criticism that the new restructuring would be no different from previous ones," the London *Financial Times* reported, "the Bank said: 'This one will work because it's different.'"[35]

One major reform, decentralization, was aimed at making the Bank more responsive to the actual on-the-ground needs of borrowing counties. More staff would be assigned to the Bank's in-country resident offices, and for certain pilot countries, such as Mexico, the country directors would reside in the local Bank mission rather than in Washington.

But with decentralization, which political and social realities would prevail? Corruption, as well as capture of Bank staff by client-government priorities that had nothing to do helping the poor or sustaining the environment, were risks that might increase with decentralization.

Local Bank offices in major countries such as India and Indonesia had often proven to be even less rigorous in ensuring environmental and social protections than Washington-based staff. The local staff worked side by side in capital cities with officials from the borrowing government bureaucracies, and were eager not to offend their hosts. In fact, not a few of the local staff had been employed with the host-country government and might return some day. Without changes in internal incentives (or reforms on the part of borrowing counties), decentralization would make things worse and would reinforce the culture of approval.

A second element of the McKinsey reorganization, dubbed "the Matrix," was intended to leverage expertise within the Bank. Under the new structure, country managers (in many cases, Bank activities in borrowing nations would be overseen by both a Bank country director and a country manager) would command over $600 million of the Bank's $733 million operating and administrative budget, while the vast majority of staff would be assigned to four Bank-wide "Technical Networks" or "matrixes."[36] These networks purportedly embodied the Bank's four major self-proclaimed priorities: "Human Development"; "Poverty Reduction and Economic Management"; "Private Sector Development and Infrastructure"; and "Environment, Rural, and Social Development."[37] The new networks would compete with one another to "sell" their services in an "internal market" to the country managers, who would oversee project directors (called task managers), who would, in turn, put together teams to prepare and appraise loans.[38]

This marked a significant change from the late 1980s and early 1990s, when much of the newly hired environmental staff was anchored in separate Regional Environment Departments (REDs). REDs had their own independent budgets and the power to approve or reject environmentally sensitive projects. By the beginning of the Wolfensohn regime, the REDs' clout was diminished, and they were losing the power struggle with country departments. The McKinsey-inspired matrix management neutered the regional environmental staff, rendering them bureaucratically impotent by eliminating most of their remaining independent budgets and casting them into the newly created internal market.

Almost all ultimate power for quality control was now in the hands of the very people under the greatest pressure to promote loan approval, the country managers and task (project) managers.[39] The Bank had made a choice; it was certainly turning itself inside out to be more responsive to some of its clients: government bureaucracies and big business. This meant nothing else than embracing the "approval culture" while claiming the opposite.

The Wolfensohn reforms actually resolved what appeared to be irreconcilable pressures, but rather perversely allowing, as Robert Wade describes, the bank to be responsive to both its borrower governments and its nonborrower governments, especially the United States, by decoupling itself internally so as to allow its parts to say and do things with different parties that if spotlit all at once would seem inconsistent. The reform, in other words, was a way to institutionalize the capacity to be hypocritical and get away with it.[40]

The Knowledge Bank and Institutional Amnesia

One of the ironies of the Strategic Compact was its emphasis on the comparative advantage of the World Bank in the future as "the knowledge bank." According to the Compact, the Bank's future influence would lie not so much in its relative financial clout—diminishing in many respects because of the rapid growth of private-sector financial flows to some developing countries in the 1990s—but in its supposedly unique ability to share decades of learning about economic development with clients around the world. In April 1997, only weeks after the Bank's board approved the Compact, a new internal audit unit known as the Quality Assurance Group completed a yearlong review of the Bank's ongoing lending portfolio, examining 150 projects in detail across in fourteen major lending areas. The Group's final report concluded that *"the lessons from past experience are well known, yet they are generally ignored in the design of new operations. . . . Institutional amnesia is the corollary of institutional optimism"* (emphasis added).[41]

And what was behind this pervasive "institutional amnesia?"

Many factors are at work: pressure to lend; fear of offending the client . . . fear that a realistic, and thus more modest, project would be dismissed as too small and inadequate in its impact . . . and more generally, a conviction held by many staff members that the function of the Bank is to help create the conditions for operations to go forward, not to "sit around and wait."[42]

The higher up one went in the Bank's management, the more lending volume became "a proxy or surrogate for development contribution."[43] The portfolio review's characterization of technical assistance projects—an area where one would think that the "Knowledge Bank" would be particularly strong—concluded that "there is a sense of boredom and fatalism in this sector, which is well known for its poor performance."[44] Technical assistance loans had a lower professional status, receiving little recognition from senior management since they could not "compare in size and importance to other resource flows" such as big, quick-disbursing, structural-adjustment lending (that is, loans that went directly for budget support of governments instead of financing specific projects, with conditions to promote changes in economic policy attached).[45]

These findings would be particularly important and prescient for the prospects of the Bank's growing involvement in environmental matters, such as promoting energy efficiency and locally attuned environmental management efforts. Such projects and interventions often involved a higher degree of novel and evolving technical assistance and knowledge than conventional infrastructure lending, not to speak of adjustment loans.

The Failure of Environmental Assessments and National Environmental Action Plans

Wolfensohn's institutional changes proceeded as more information became available to Bank management regarding the Bank's failures in carrying out its self-proclaimed goal of environmentally sustainable development. In June 1996, a new OED study revealed major failures in two of its key environmental policy instruments—Environmental Assessments (EAs) and National Environmental Action Plans (NEAPs).

Although Bank environmental assessments were often very comprehensive, most of them were conducted too late in the project cycle to have any effect on project design or choice of alternatives.[46] Environmental action plans that were supposed to mitigate the impacts of projects that posed major environmental threats were often not implemented, and Bank supervision of the environmental components of projects was often lax or nonexistent.[47]

Given that the single most important factor undermining the effectiveness of the EAs was their tardy preparation in the project cycle, Wolfensohn's efforts to speed up loan approval would only worsen the problem:

> If the Bank continues to reduce the number of days available for project preparation and appraisal, finding time for meaningful consultation (and quality control of EA reports) will be increasingly problematic. . . .[48]

The National Environmental Action Plans (NEAPs) were supposed to be a flagship in shaping Bank environmental lending. The Bank prepared the first ones in the late 1980s, and accelerated their preparation following the 1992 Rio Earth Summit. The Bank's assistance in preparing NEAPs was supposed to contribute to the non–legally binding pledge countries undertook in Agenda 21 to prepare national sustainable development plans.

By 1995, 42 countries had completed a NEAP, and some 50 others were preparing them. In most cases they had little or no effect on the Bank's overall country-lending strategies, and in some instances, were even counterproductive. "In most countries," OED concluded, "few environmental professionals and staff working on Bank-financed projects had ever heard of the NEAP."[50] In many cases, the NEAPs duplicated national environmental planning initiatives already undertaken by other donors. The main beneficiaries were World Bank environmental consultants:

> NEAPs often force the use of international consultants or the creation of secretariats whose staff salaries far exceed local levels. This disparity can have a demoralizing effect on government staff and inhibit cooperation.[51]

These very issues concerning the poor performance of technical assistance, and the perverse effects of the ubiquitous use of international consultants in undermining local capacity, were again of particular relevance for environmental projects and efforts. The challenges would only increase in the 2000s, when Bank assistance for environmental projects would turn heavily toward increasingly complicated climate-change mitigation and adaptation schemes through novel financial instruments, such as carbon-trading funds.

The Culture of Corruption

The culture of loan approval had much more far-reaching effects than the Bank's supporting too many projects of dubious quality: it was a major factor contributing to the corrupt misuse of Bank funds in a number of the Bank's major borrower countries. World Bank presidents in the past had ignored corruption. Wolfensohn recounts that when he first discussed the issue with staff:

> There was a wall of silence. . . . "What's going on here," I kept asking my staff. Finally, Ibrahim Shihata [the Bank's general counsel] took me into the hall outside my office. Looking over his shoulder as if someone might hear, he warned that in the Bank, there was no room to discuss the "C-word." "It would be offensive to our shareholders and risk political repercussions," he said. Attacking corruption, he made me understand, would insult some of the executive directors who represented [borrowing] countries where corruption reached the highest levels. It would also insult some of the rich

countries that were well aware of the problem but used it to their advantage. . . . I pondered his words and concluded there was no way I could accept or condone corruption.[52]

In June 1996 he began by launching an initiative to conduct periodic spot financial audits on Bank lending programs in selected countries. The Bank hired an independent accounting firm, the Swiss Société Générale de Surveillance, to conduct the first three audits, in Poland, Kenya, and Pakistan.[53] At the 1996 annual Bank/Fund Meeting Wolfensohn called corruption a "cancer" that "diverts resources from the poor to the rich . . . a major barrier to sound and equitable development."[54]

Wolfensohn began to raise the C-word with heads of state, but with mixed results. He recounts how in early 1997 he told President Suharto of Indonesia that "we couldn't talk about development without addressing corruption. Suharto replied, 'Well, you come out here from Washington with these high ideas to tell us about corruption. But what you call 'corruption,' I call 'family values.'"[55]

The Bank under Wolfensohn also announced it would put more emphasis on "good governance," i.e., encouraging greater respect for the rule of law, including human rights and the environment. Although the Bank's charter prohibits it from taking noneconomic "political" concerns into account in making decisions, the vagueness of the charter actually gives it considerable leeway. In November 1995, Wolfensohn personally halted a $100 million IFC loan to Nigeria to support a liquefied natural gas project the day after the Nigerian military junta hanged writer and Nobel Peace Prize nominee Ken Saro-Wiwa and eight other activists. The nine had been leaders of the "Movement for the Survival of the Ogoni People" that had protested the environmental devastation caused by oil development (led by Royal Dutch Shell and Chevron) of the Niger River Delta homelands of the Ogoni tribe.[56] In 1996 the Bank halted major lending programs in Papua New Guinea and Cambodia, pending major reforms of government-sponsored unsustainable logging.[57]

Wolfensohn could point with pride to all of these initiatives; they showed that the Bank could, at least on a limited scale, promote the values of civil society, transparency, and sound governance. But how significant were these efforts compared to the other major developments under his tenure?

As the Strategic Compact, the Change Agenda, and the anti-corruption initiatives careened forward, the consequences of years of Bank complicity in the corruption of its major borrowers finally began to surface in an unprecedentedly public way, first in Russia and Indonesia. *Business Week* alleged in September that "at least $100 million" from a $500 million Russian coal sector loan was either misspent or could not even be accounted for. Noting that the Bank was preparing a new half-billion-dollar loan for the Russian coal sector, *Business Week* observed that "World Bank officials seem surprisingly unperturbed by the misspending. They contend offering loans to spur change is better than micromanaging expenditures."[58] A little over a year later the *Financial Times* estimated the amount stolen from the Bank in the coal sector loan to be much higher, as much as $250 million.[59]

An American professor of political economy at Northwestern University, Jeffrey Winters, alleged in a July 1997 Jakarta press conference that shoddy accounting practices by the World Bank had allowed corrupt Indonesian officials to steal as much as 30 percent of Bank loans over a 30-year period—a mind-boggling total approaching $10 billion.[60] At about the same time, the Bank's Jakarta Office commissioned a study of corruption in lending programs to Indonesia. The resulting report, known as the "Dice Memorandum" (Stephen Dice was the Bank staffer who wrote it), estimated that Indonesian ministries were "diverting" (i.e., stealing) between 15 and over 25 percent of the funds.[61]

In the fifteen months after the Dice Memorandum, the Bank committed and disbursed over $1.3 billion more to Indonesia without any effective measures to contain the grand larceny detailed in the memo. In October 1998, as the Bank planned to lend Indonesia another $2 billion over the next nine months, a second internal memo argued that massive corruption was not limited only to Indonesia: *"Many of our conclusions appear to be relevant to all country programs in the East Asia Region, some indeed related to Bank-wide systems/procedures"* (emphasis added).[62]

These scandals were the consequences of past practices—practices that Wolfensohn was determined to change. Moreover, theft of development aid funds, in Indonesia and elsewhere, was certainly not limited to the World Bank: almost all aid institutions were implicated in corruption. Under Wolfensohn, the Bank was at least beginning to acknowledge the problem. Building on his earlier anti-corruption initiatives, in the summer of 1998 Wolfensohn set up an Internal Audit Department Investigation Unit, initially with a half dozen staff and support from an outside investigative team from PricewaterhouseCoopers. For the first time the Bank was actively investigating fraud by its borrowers. The Investigation Unit was expanded in 2001 into a new Department of Institutional Integrity (known by the acronym INT in the Bank). As word of the department spread, there were more and more "walk-ins" by Bank staff with allegations of corruption on projects they had managed.[63]

In retrospect, it is remarkable how little public attention was paid to the corruption embedded in the very institutional DNA of the World Bank, and in much of the international development enterprise in general. For those who might think this is an exaggeration, one could refer to a World Bank Staff Association memorandum sent to Wolfensohn in early 1998:

> There are two kinds of [Bank] complicity: the passive one where Bank staff do not want to see, investigate, record, or report the evidence, and the active complicity where misappropriation of funds is done with the approval or the assistance of Bank staff. . . . *Stealing from Bank funds is the rule, not the exception* (emphasis added). Although there has been recently some indication that the Bank is wanting to fight corruption, many managers are unwilling to do so.[64]

A Monument to Corruption

The large-scale corruption revealed in the late 1990s affected all Bank projects, but it had especially strong implications for the environmental sector. Forestry was one of the most corrupt sectors not just in Indonesia, but in many developing countries. Likewise, projects involving extractive industries—mining, oil, and gas—were particularly prone to massive misuse of revenue. Large dams figured among the most controversial projects of all because they not only required enormous funds that could be easily diverted, but they also often caused significant environmental damage and displaced large numbers of people from their homes.

No project was more rife with corruption than the proposed Yacyretá Dam, a 3,100-megawatt power-generating facility on the Paraguay River between Argentina and Paraguay. Yacyretá was administered by a binational project entity, the Entidad Binacional Yacyretá (EBY): the power would go to Argentina, and Paraguay would share in some of the profits. Paraguay would bear most of the environmental and social costs, including displacement of 50,000 urban poor and the flooding of 122,000 hectares of land.[65]

Construction for the dam began in 1983, helped by a $200 million World Bank loan to support the originally estimated $2.35 billion cost. By the early 1990s delays and overruns had escalated the cost to over $8 billion. Argentine president Carlos Menem himself characterized Yacyretá as "a monument to corruption,"[66] and by 1994, according to a subsequent study by the

World Commission on Dams, $6 billion had been stolen from the project.[67] All through the years the Bank continued to pour money into it, with a $252 million loan in 1989, another $300 million in 1992, and a reallocation of $146.6 million from another Bank loan to Argentina in 1994, for a grand total of $895.5 million in IBRD support.[68]

In September 1996 the Paraguayan affiliate of Friends of the Earth, Sobrevivencia, submitted a complaint to the panel about Yacyretá. It alleged major violations of the Bank's resettlement and environmental policies, citing the lack of adequate resettlement measures, massive pollution of water supplies, destruction of fisheries and livelihoods, and health problems such as skin diseases and the spread of intestinal parasites, all caused by the filling reservoir.[69] Bank staff working on the project as well as borrowing-country members of the board (led by Argentina) challenged the allegations and the panel's recommendation for a full investigation. In a compromise, the board approved a more limited review of the project's problems.[70]

In its September 1997 report to the Board, the panel found that many of the allegations in the complaint were justified; among other things the number of people being forcibly resettled was actually over 70,000, of whom fewer than 19,000 had been resettled by the time the reservoir started filling. Despite the hundreds of millions of dollars received from the Bank, there was not enough money left in the project coffers to address the environmental and social problems.[71]

Meanwhile, right on the heels of its Yacyretá report, the panel recommended full investigations for complaints leveled at two other Bank projects affecting populations impoverished through lack of attention to resettlement: the India Singrauli National Thermal Power Corporation (NTPC) Project and the Brazil Itaparica Resettlement and Irrigation Project.[72] The Singrauli project involved the construction of coal-fired power plants that displaced thousands. Itaparica was a Bank project whose goals were laudable—a stand-alone loan to provide for the compensation and resettlement of some 40,000 people displaced by a dam that the Bank itself did not finance; unfortunately, the resettlement project was largely a failure. Both Brazil and India successfully mobilized borrowing-country support to block full investigations for these projects.[73]

The growing North–South acrimony on the board led President Wolfensohn to suggest that the board set up a working group to review the role and functioning of the panel; Wolfensohn hoped such a review would convince the board of the panel's value. The board, rather than acting on the panel's recommendations on Yacyretá, then made the review of the panel the priority, what one account characterized as "shooting the messenger."[74] The board continued to be split along North–South lines with regard to Yacyretá, and it ultimately decided in late 1997 to ask Bank management to follow up with progress reports on how the Yacyretá resettlement was proceeding.[75]

In February 1998 the acting vice-president for Latin America and the Caribbean, Isabel Guerrero, wrote to the Yacyretá claimants on behalf of President Wolfensohn that "the Bank is satisfied with the recommendations of the [panel] report which affirm that its policies on resettlement, environment, community participation, and others were fully respected and applied in the case of Yacyretá. . . ." This was a total misrepresentation of the panel's conclusions. The scandal became an issue for Wolfensohn to resolve personally when the London *Financial Times* published an article comparing the Guerrero letter and the panel review.[76]

Nearly three years into his tenure, Wolfensohn was confronted with a situation where senior management was blatantly lying, and invoking his name, to people affected by a Bank project and to the public at large. Now apparently under some pressure to respond, the newly appointed vice-president for Latin America and the Caribbean, Javed Burki, sent a letter to the claimants admitting that "Ms. Guerrero's letter . . . conveyed an *incomplete* description of the Inspection Panel's Report"[77] (emphasis added). After further outraged protests from Sobrevivencia, Burki sent a second letter four days later that explained that "Ms. Guerrero's letter conveyed an *erroneous* description of the Bank Inspection Panel's Report" (emphasis added); the Bank publicized this second letter in the Paraguayan press early in June.[78] In a subsequent meeting in June 1998 with Burki, representatives of the claimants, and Alvaro Umaña, chairman of the inspection panel, Wolfensohn apologized for the way the Bank had handled the Yacyretá project and personally affirmed that he fully supported the panel. Burki led a high-profile site mission to the area affected by the dam. At a public meeting attended by more than one thousand citizens, he declared, "I come from one of the poorest countries on earth [Pakistan] and I have never seen such misery as I have seen here today."[79]

Unfortunately, it is much harder to remedy a social and environmental disaster than to prevent one. Despite the preparation of remedial environmental and resettlement measures by EBY at Bank prompting, many of the problems remained, and in May 2002 a new complaint was filed by more than 4,000 households affected by the project. The Bank's board approved a full investigation this time, and the panel's report in February 2004 found further violations of the Bank's environmental and resettlement policies, despite remedial efforts.[80] By this time the total cost of the project was approaching $11.5 billion. Bank management responded with still more remedial action plans. Yacyretá was finally inaugurated on February 1, 2011—31 years after the first IBRD loan for the project.

The Yacyretá controversy, along with the concurrent disputes over the Singrauli and Itaparica investigation complaints, illustrates just how difficult the environmental debate remained at the Bank, splitting the Bank's executive board along North–South lines, and pitting Bank management against the inspection panel. Yacyretá also was a prime example of the nexus of massive corruption and negligence of environmental and social safeguards. Wolfensohn was trying to do the right thing, but a divided board, recalcitrant management, and corrupt borrowers demonstrated the immensity of the challenge.

Moreover, as in every other such case, no one in the Bank's management was held accountable. In any normal private-sector company, knowingly lying in the name of the CEO without his or her knowledge would be grounds for dismissal; in the case of Yacyretá, such a lie harmed tens of thousands of people displaced by the dam, people who had already been waiting for years for some sort of redress. So what happened to Isabel Guerrero? On July 1, 2008, she was appointed to be the Bank's vice-president for the South Asia Region, overseeing, among other countries, the Bank's lending for its biggest borrower, India.

The Safeguards

Despite these board struggles and the movement toward speeding up lending and weakening policies in the "Change Agenda," in the early years of Wolfensohn's tenure there was also a move to give greater prominence to the Bank's core environmental and social policies. In 1997 the Bank identified 10 "Safeguard Policies" for the lending of the IBRD and IDA, key requirements to ensure that the Bank would "do no harm" in its lending. There were six environmental policies (on environmental assessment, protection of natural habitats, forests, pest management, protection of cultural heritage and resources, and dam safety), for which the environmental assessment policy was key, since it provided a framework for screening and analyzing proposed projects and identifying potential impacts that could trigger the application of the other more-specialized policies, such as protection of natural habitats or pest management. There were two social policies, one dealing with involuntary resettlement, and the other with protection of indigenous peoples. Finally, there were two legal safeguard policies: one concerning projects that would impact international waterways; and the other for projects that would involve politically disputed areas, such as contested border regions between countries.[81]

Implementing these policies had been, and remained, problematic. On the other hand, the very existence of the policies, and the undeniably higher visibility they received under Wolfensohn, had an important impact in the entire world of international development. The other multilateral development banks—for example, the Inter-American Development Bank, the Asian Development Bank, and the African Development Bank—all drew up their own environmental and social safeguard policies based on those of the World Bank. The Bank's policy on involuntary resettlement was adopted as a model best-practice guideline for bilateral development assistance by the 30 industrialized-country members of the Organization for Economic Cooperation and Development (OECD).[82]

The safeguard policies were a prime example of the powerful, normative value of what the World Bank declares to be its priorities. Local communities and civil-society groups in major Bank-borrowing countries cited the policies as standards to help catalyze action by their own governments in projects financed by the Bank, even (or perhaps especially) when the Bank itself was failing to ensure the policies were carried out. In India, for example, national laws on resettlement compensation had existed for decades, but Bank involvement in a project gave local communities international leverage to at least increase the chances that the laws would be carried out. Moreover, the Independent Inspection Panel was not just important in establishing accountability within the Bank for the implementation of the safeguards, but it also served as the model for the creation of similar inspection and accountability mechanisms in the other multilateral development banks, as well as several bilateral export credit agencies.

But at first the safeguards and the inspection panel concerned only lending to governments and public agencies, and not support by the Bank for the private sector. Environmental groups pointed out that both the environmental policies and technical capacity of the IFC and MIGA were much weaker than those of the main World Bank lending operations, and in some important sectors (e.g., resettlement), there was no formalized policy whatsoever.

Sustainable Development or Corporate Welfare?

With the Yacyretá scandal, Wolfensohn had to navigate between the welfare of local people in borrowing countries and the political motivations of their government representatives. When the borrowing entities were private companies, questions about who was really benefitting grew even stickier. Wolfensohn strengthened the institution's support of private corporations through loan guarantees, risk insurance, and direct financing. In the name of poverty alleviation and "environmentally sustainable development," he supported increasing the scale of the International Finance Corporation (IFC) and the Multilateral Investment Guarantee Agency (MIGA).

Many NGOs saw this growing focus on the private sector as little more than corporate welfare. For one thing, the lion's share of IFC and MIGA finance went to subsidize investments of larger corporations, many of them with headquarters in rich industrialized countries, including some of the largest multinationals on Earth. MIGA and the IFC approved guarantees and loans for Coca Cola bottling plants in Kyrgyzstan in 1996 and in Azerbaijan in 1997; and in 1997 the Bank was preparing a huge IDA/IFC project to assist Elf-Aquitaine, Royal Dutch Shell, and Exxon in oil-field development and pipeline construction in Chad and Cameroon. MIGA guarantees had helped to support huge gold-mining operations in Irian Jaya (the Indonesian western half of New Guinea, now known officially as Papua) and independent Papua New Guinea (the eastern half of the island) run by giant multinational mining operations with execrable environmental records: Freeport McMoran and Rio Tinto Zinc. How were projects like these helping the poor or protecting the environment? The Bank's standard response was that they promoted growth and created employment—a rationale that could justify almost any project.

In 1996, public pressure mounted on Wolfensohn to bring IFC/MIGA environmental and developmental policies up to the same standard as the Bank's. Just as he was beginning to institute reforms of Bank private-sector lending, yet another international dam controversy shed light on the environmental and social problems plaguing World Bank Group operations. This time, the scandal centered around an IFC loan to a Spanish private electric utility, ENDESA, for the proposed Pangue Dam on the Bío-Bío River in southern Chile.

The upper Bío-Bío River basin was home to some 9,000 Pehuenche Indians and was one of the last refuges in Chile for the formerly numerous Mapuche people (of which the Pehuenche were a part). These indigenous communities opposed the project. The proposed IFC environmental and social measures were so unconvincing that the U.S. executive director of the Bank refused to approve the loan, stating that the IFC's role in the Pangue project demonstrated again "what we see as a general failure of recent World Bank hydroelectric projects to assess adequately, and in a timely manner, the likely impacts of proposed projects to fisheries and aquatic biodiversity."[83]

A network of groups representing the Pehuenche filed a complaint with the inspection panel alleging that the Bank was violating its own environmental and social policies. The panel had to reject the complaint, since it was set up only to have jurisdiction over the IBRD and IDA. Once again Wolfensohn personally intervened, establishing in 1996 an independent internal evaluation of the project conducted by Jay Hair, president-emeritus of the U.S. National Wildlife Federation and past president of the World Conservation Union (IUCN).[84]

The Hair report, as it came to be called, accused key IFC staff of "fail[ing] to disclose key documents to the IFC Board of Directors (and perhaps senior management). . . ." "At each stage of the project approval process, *key decision-support documents often did not faithfully or accurately reflect the contents of underlying environmental studies"*(emphasis added). The IFC, Hair concluded, added little, if anything of value to the project to address environmental and social risks.[85]

After personal interventions by Wolfensohn, the IFC threatened to declare its loan to ENDESA in default because of violations of environmental and social covenants in the loan agreement. For the Pehuenche, it was already too late: the dam had been completed and the reservoir filled.

Yet the scandal did prompt reform. Thanks to Wolfensohn's leadership, in 1998 the IFC adopted new policies on public disclosure of information and environmental assessment. That same year also saw the establishment of environmental and social "safeguards" for IFC and MIGA projects. And in 1999 a compliance advisor/ombudsman (CAO) office was created to review complaints about IFC and MIGA projects. Its function was similar to that of the Independent Inspection Panel, but its approach was more conciliatory—trying first to work with affected communities and project sponsors in order to find solutions. While some questioned the independence of the CAO, as well as the on-the-ground effectiveness of the new private-sector safeguard policies, these reforms did set a normative standard for other private-sector projects around the world.

In 2003, 10 leading international private banks adopted environmental and social safeguards based on the IFC reforms.[86] These so-called Equator Principles were strengthened in 2006, and as of early 2013 some 78 financial institutions in 35 countries including Brazil, Mexico, Nigeria, South Africa, and China are signatories, accounting for over 70 percent of global private-sector-project finance.[87] An international nongovernmental campaign helped pressure industrialized-country governments to agree on voluntary environmental and social standards for their publicly supported export-import banks and export-finance agencies (technically known as Export Credit Agencies, ECAs). These standards (known as the "Common Approaches on Environment" of the Organization for Economic Cooperation and Development, or OECD), approved in 2003 and strengthened in 2007, were also based on IFC safeguards and policies.[88]

Thus, Wolfensohn catalyzed a process through which the IFC environmental and social policies became a proxy for international good practice in private-sector finance in areas such as environmental assessment, resettlement of displaced people, and protection of cultural heritage and indigenous minorities. That is the good news. The bad news is that the IFC itself, like the rest of the World Bank Group, continued to have a very mixed record in carrying out its own policies. Even more than the rest of the World Bank, the IFC is driven by a deal-making culture rooted in the private sector, where developmental and environmental impacts are secondary priorities. The pressure to lend and push projects forward quickly—the loan-approval culture—was even more prevalent in the IFC than in the other parts of the Bank.

A Contradictory Record

Wolfensohn seemed to be in a race against the legacy of not just years but decades of Bank neglect. He was so vocal in promoting environmental and social policy reforms, and in engaging with civil society, that he was accused by some of surrendering to the NGOs.[89] Yet the more he pushed for reform, the more outside pressure grew to do still more, for reasons entirely beyond his control. He happened to be on the hot seat in a period when the environmental and social debts of careless development finance were finally coming due, at the same time that globalization of communication empowered activists in both borrowing and donor countries.

Wolfensohn promoted what appeared to be contradictory goals—better implementation of policies, but also speeding up the lending process to please client borrowing countries; helping the poorest of the poor, but promoting privatization and Bank subsidization of multinational corporations that were more interested in the revenue from Bank contracts and loans for massive infrastructure projects than in the people affected. Despite the sound and fury of Wolfensohn's reforms, the Bank's bureaucratic culture seemed impervious to real change from above.

Would it ever change?

CHAPTER FOUR

High Risk, High Reward

THE DALAI LAMA WAS WORRIED. Right after meeting with President Bill Clinton on June 27, 2000, he took the extraordinary action of publicly criticizing a World Bank project. The project, he said, should not proceed and "would be the source of more problems" for Tibetans.[1] Indeed, the "China Western Poverty Alleviation Project" entailed using $40 million of a $160 million loan to move some 58,000 poor, mainly ethnic Chinese Han and Chinese Muslim farmers into an area traditionally inhabited by some 4,000 Tibetan and Mongol nomads in China's Qinghai Province. The rest of the loans would provide assistance to two other Chinese provinces.[2] The Qinghai component would also involve the construction of a 40-meter-high irrigation dam and two irrigation canals, 29 and 56 kilometers long, to promote agriculture on lands that hitherto had been used for grazing, as well as schools and clinics for the migrants.[3]

The target resettlement area was not far from the Dalai Lama's birthplace. Qinghai was a traditionally Tibetan area, and since the 1950s the communist regime had aggressively promoted the resettlement of ethnic Han Chinese in western provinces with large minority populations. The Chinese government had also chosen Qinghai and the neighboring eastern Tibet Autonomous Region as a site for forced-labor prison camps; after release, former prisoners often stayed as a part of the new influx of non-Tibetans.[4] Local Tibetans argued that the project was "evidence of the Chinese policy of ethnic cleansing of the Tibetan people. . . . In the event the resettlement project is carried out with World Bank financing, then the World Bank will have participated in passing a death sentence to us here."[5]

The Dalai Lama was not the only one who was upset about the project; over the year preceding his comment, the World Bank had somehow managed to unite against itself a mind-boggling coalition: Jesse Helms, Nancy Pelosi, and 58 other members of the U.S. Congress; the European Union Parliament; U.S. treasury secretary Larry Summers; former U.S. treasury secretary Robert Rubin; the hip-hop group the Beastie Boys; and movie stars Harrison Ford and of course Richard Gere; to name just a few.[6] The *Economist* magazine, normally sympathetic toward the Bank, noted that "it is hard to imagine a more explosive cocktail of political issues than Tibet, dams, and prison labor. . . . The World Bank has probably never before faced such an enormous fax and email campaign. Executive Directors' fax machines have been breaking down from overuse."[7]

Despite a remarkably rapid mobilization of international opinion, Bank management appeared determined to push through approval of the project. Eleven of the 24 members of the Bank's Executive Board wrote to Wolfensohn, urging him to abandon the Qinghai resettlement.[8] But on June 17, 1999, the Bank's vice-president for East Asia and the Pacific asserted that the project met World Bank criteria and that it was not the role of his staff to consider "moral and political" matters.[9] The next day, the International Campaign for Tibet filed a complaint with the Bank's Independent Inspection Panel on behalf of local Tibetans, including Buddhist clergy, who requested that their names not be released through fear of reprisals. They alleged major violations of numerous World Bank policies, including requirements for environmental assessment and protection of indigenous peoples.[10]

China treated the criticism as an outrageous impingement on its sovereignty, motivated by purely "political" machinations of the "Dalai [Lama] splittist clique." It threatened to withdraw from the World Bank if the board did not approve the loans, and informed the ambassadors of major Western donor countries that future investment prospects in Chinese markets were tied to their support of the Qinghai project.

Wolfensohn and the Bank were under extraordinary pressure. After all, China had become the biggest ongoing borrower from the World Bank,[11] and no one knew whether the Chinese were really bluffing; the Bank stood to lose its biggest client. Even though the executive directors representing the United States, Germany, France, Canada, the Nordic countries, and Austria/Belgium all refused to approve the loan, the board majority nevertheless did approve it. But there was an unprecedented condition: the $40 million for the Qinghai component of the $160 million total was to be withheld until the inspection panel could complete its investigation and the board could review the panel's findings.[12] The Chinese government did not publicly object to the investigation and even agreed to host visits to the project site, claiming that "we are in favor of transparency. . . . Transparency brings to light facts and scorches rumors."[13] But what resulted was a government-supervised trip for selected foreign press that was designed to inhibit frank discussions with local people.[14]

Meanwhile, two researchers—an American, Daja Meston, and an Australian, Gabriel Lafitte—traveled to Qinghai to learn more about the affected people's real opinions. They were both arrested, denied any contact with their embassies for days, interrogated, subjected to sleep deprivation, and threatened. Meston had formerly worked with Republican congressman Frank R. Wolf; Wolf wrote to President Clinton urging that the United States seek Meston's immediate release. On August 19, 1999, Meston fell from the third-story window of the building where he was being interrogated; he apparently was trying to escape. He suffered a broken back and serious internal organ damage before regaining consciousness in a hospital room, surrounded by interrogators and armed guards. Lafitte and Meston's alleged crimes were the misuse of tourist visas and "illegal" photography.[15] The Chinese government, it appeared, had a rather unusual interpretation of transparency.

The inspection panel released its investigation report on April 28, 2000. It was damning, finding major violations of seven different Bank environmental and social policies.[16] It revealed the dynamics of what was actually occurring on the ground with respect to the Wolfensohn organizational reforms. Perhaps the most important finding was that although the project would transform the ecology of more than 20,000 hectares of land, senior staff in the Bank's China region nevertheless insisted—against the recommendations of an environmental consultant they had hired for the project—that it not be subjected to a full environmental assessment.[17] From senior management down to working-level professionals, many Bank staff involved with China loans seemed to view Bank environmental and social protection policies as optional; the frequent refrain was "'in China things are done differently'" (emphasis in original source).[18] Here one could clearly see the effects of "Matrix management," which required staff to sell their services to country directors and project managers on the "internal market." One senior Bank official told the panel, "Frankly, they don't want to bite the hand that feeds them . . . by taking a hard-line view."[19] The result was that the Bank's largest country-lending department routinely ignored environmental and social requirements that might slow down a loan.

Wolfensohn tried to thread the needle, submitting the panel's report and the Bank management's reply for consideration at a July 6 board meeting. Management had come up with a belated plan to conduct full environmental and social assessments, and to carry out the ensuing mitigation measures—all of which, as required by the Bank's own policies, should have been undertaken before the loans were approved.

By an ironic quirk of fate, in the first week of July 2000 the annual Smithsonian Folklife festival was taking place on the National Mall in Washington. That year, Tibetan culture in exile was the highlight, attracting visitors, including Tibet activists, from around the world. Crowds of protesters surrounded the World Bank, chanting against the Qinghai project. The European Parliament passed a resolution condemning it. On the eve of the board meeting, the *New York Times* published a lead editorial entitled "A Misguided World Bank Project," calling upon the Bank's directors "to reject this poorly designed project."[20]

The board meeting was contentious. U.S. executive director Jan Piercy (who had been Hillary Clinton's roommate at Wellesley) declared the project "non-compliant," contending that "Bank staff has no consistent understanding of basic policies that have been in place for years."[21] On July 7, the U.S., Japanese, Canadian, Australian, and all the European members of the board rejected Wolfensohn's proposal to proceed. Before any board consensus could be reached, China announced that it was withdrawing its proposal for the $40 million of the loans that would have gone to the Qinghai project and would continue on its own without the World Bank.[22]

The Chinese did proceed with the project, but scaled it back to resettle 17,000 people rather than 58,000. Moreover, the Chinese decided to cut back on costs by moving the 17,000 into the existing housing facilities of a former "reform through labor" prison camp, which gave Tibet activists hope that the impact on the indigenous population would be lessened.[23] At least the World Bank was not giving an international stamp of approval to such a scheme.

The outcome was a victory of sorts for those who were pushing for greater accountability in the Bank, but perhaps a Pyrrhic victory only. It was becoming clear that full implementation of the Bank's environmental and social policies could involve scrutiny and transparency that many borrowing, developing countries would find uncomfortable. Business constituencies and their allies in donor countries as well sometimes found the safeguard policies to be an obstacle to their conventional, cozy, and not always transparent ways of doing business in the developing world. The inspection panel report revealed just how widespread resistance remained among some Bank staff and management to Bank environmental policies and accountability procedures.

Wolfensohn himself didn't seem to take to heart the inspection panel's disturbing findings. He maintained that the Qinghai project was a good one that "would help both Chinese and Tibetans, mainly very poor people wanting to live a better life." In his memoir, written several years later, he appears much more upset that "Congress was on our back, and so was the general public. Harrison Ford and his wife, screenwriter Melissa Mathison, friends of ours from Wyoming, stood at the front of the protests. Nancy Pelosi, another good friend and subsequently the Speaker of the House, gave me hell. Among her constituents in California were the groups that were most pro-Tibetan and anti-Chinese, and none of them would listen to our explanations."[24] He had begun to internalize the last defense always proffered by Bank management for misconceived projects: "The Bank's expulsion from the project left Beijing free to do as it liked without any of the safeguards and planning that accompanied all our work. . . . In the end the real losers were the farmers earning 20 cents a day."[25]

The growing reaction was to ignore the message and scapegoat the messengers, which were most often civil-society organizations, the Bank's own Independent Inspection Panel, and the Bank environmental staff who might risk career suicide by pushing for rigorous implementation of policies. Wolfensohn himself appeared to be tiring of the fight. He told representatives of civil-society groups in a 2001 meeting, "I have recently met with 22 African heads of state and most of them have complained that the bank has gone too far in working with civil-society organizations and allowing unrepresentative NGOS to influence government decision making."[26]

Meanwhile, the evidence grew that the McKinsey-inspired reforms had exacerbated the organizational dysfunction. A July 2001 "OED Review of the Bank's Performance on the Environment" documented a marked deterioration in the Bank's environmental performance, linking this directly to Wolfensohn's 1996–98 reorganization. OED itself belatedly concluded what NGOs had warned Bank management about from the beginning: the creation of the networks and the budgetary weakening of the technical departments had the direct—and completely foreseeable—consequence that "the quality of the EA [environmental assessment] process deteriorated."[27] Wolfensohn's botched decentralization changes "diminished the Bank's capacity both to mainstream the environment into country programs and to implement its [environmental and social] safeguard policies effectively."[28] The EAs still had little or no impact on project design, the Bank's failure to deliver environmentally sustainable results worsened, and the responsibility started at the top:

The findings of this evaluation [July 2001] are not new. Many are based on internal and external studies done over the past decade. . . . The structure of incentives, priorities, and direct processes of accountability from senior management down the line have not been supportive of strategic inclusion of the environment, of adequate monitoring and evaluation, nor of positive recognition of activities and staff in this area.[29]

Despite such findings, the backlash continued to grow against further efforts to internalize sustainability in the Bank. Perhaps the most flagrant example was the refusal of the Bank to accept and endorse the recommendations of a pathbreaking three-year series of consultations and reports that it cosponsored to resolve the international controversy over the financing and construction of large dams—the World Commission on Dams.

Temples or Tombs?

In the 1980s and '90s, no issue was more contentious than Bank support for large dams. (The standard working definition of a large dam is one 15 meters or higher, or with a reservoir of more than 3 million cubic meters.[30]) These projects, with or without international financing, had provoked massive protests not just for years, but for decades. In India, according to political scientist Sanjeev Khagram, "by the 1980s practically every big dam across India faced some form of organized resistance."[31] By the 1990s, "conflicts between proponents who viewed big dams as temples and opponents who saw them as tombs reached unprecedented levels."[32] In Brazil, by the 1970s hundreds of thousands of people had been forcibly displaced by various dam projects (some financed by the World Bank), and in 1991 various regional associations of "development refugees" formed the Movement of Dam-Affected People.[33] Most of the controversies involved the displacement of poor people, but sometimes local residents were simply voicing environmental concerns.

Already in 1994, on the 50th anniversary of the founding of the World Bank, some 326 civil-society organizations from 44 countries called for a moratorium on all new funding of large dams until there was reform. They demanded that the Bank strengthen its policies concerning forcible displacement, set up a reparations fund to compensate those already dispossessed, and establish an "independent, comprehensive review of all Bank-funded large-dam projects." This appeal was called the "Manebelli Declaration," named after a remote Indian village that was to be inundated by the Sardar

Sarovar Dam, which at that time the Bank was still supporting.[34]

The Bank eventually responded to the mounting outcry by asking the Switzerland-based World Conservation Union (IUCN) to organize a multi-stakeholder meeting on large dams. In April 1997, 39 attendees gathered for a two-day meeting. They represented all of the major constituencies effected by the controversy: large engineering and construction companies; pro-dam industry professional associations; NGOs; governments and governmental agencies; and state power companies.[35] Industry representatives were just as eager as NGOs for such a meeting, since it was becoming clear that grass-roots political opposition to big dam projects was resulting in enormous delays and cost overruns in many parts of the world.[36]

The World Commission on Dams that emerged from the meeting would have two main purposes: first, to review the effectiveness of large dams and assess alternatives for water and energy development; and second, to develop standards for all phases of dam development, from planning to decommissioning.[37] The commission would have 12 members, who were to represent a wide variety of viewpoints and backgrounds.[38] Four were supposedly dam critics—such as Medha Pakter, the fiery leader of the India Narmada Bachao Andolan (Struggle to Save the Narmada River). Four were chosen as well-known dam proponents, including Göran Lindahl, the president and CEO of the Swedish-Swiss engineering and construction company ABB. The other four were supposed "moderates" on the issue, including Achim Steiner, the secretary-general of IUCN, who subsequently went on to head the United Nations Environment Programme.

The commissioners formulated a two-and-a-half-year program to gather research for the final report. The program included a survey of the performance of 125 large dams; detailed case studies of eight individual dams in eight different countries; public hearings in four major regions of the world, which reviewed 947 submissions and presentations; and 17 "thematic reviews," issue papers on critical governance, institutional, social, environmental, and economic issues.[39] A budget of nearly $10 million was raised from 53 different sources: governments, aid agencies, industry, private foundations, and NGOs.[40]

It was arguably the single most serious international effort since the 1992 Rio Earth Summit to try to reconcile development, environmental conservation, and social equity. Wolfensohn's World Bank could take substantial credit for playing a constructive role in making it happen—attempting to find a way forward from the acrimony that its own negligence in earlier projects had provoked.

"The Commission Has Shown Us the Way Forward"

So it was that on November 16, 2000, in a glamorous gala in London, former South African president Nelson Mandela gave the opening address welcoming the release of the final 404-page report of the WCD, *Dams and Development: A New Framework for Decision Making*.[41] Echoing the report, Mandela noted that while dams "have delivered significant benefits for many," their "overall performance and impacts present us with a more complex and often bleak picture, especially for the unspoken minority and for nature." The Commission had "shown us the way forward for dealing with such complex issues," Mandela declared.[42] The Commission found that while large dams had "contributed significantly to human development," they also had forcibly displaced 40 to 80 million people worldwide. Those most grievously harmed were often indigenous people, ethnic minorities, and women.[43] A full 60 percent of the world's river systems had been fragmented by dams and water-transfer schemes, species and ecosystems had been irrevocably lost, and valuable land had been damaged by salinization and waterlogging.[44] The report also found that large dams contributed significantly to global warming, mainly through the release of methane from decaying plants in large reservoirs.[45]

The WCD found that large dams—even when analyzed on their own terms, without counting the environmental and social costs—had a clear record of underperformance. There appeared to be a widespread industry practice of purposely underestimating costs to push projects through and win contracts; the average cost overrun of the large projects surveyed was 56 percent (138 percent in South Asia!).[46] Nearly half of the irrigation projects failed to achieve their targets, and some 70 percent of the water-supply dam projects failed to achieve their supply goals.[47]

The WCD drew some conclusions of great importance not just for large dam projects, or for large development investments in general, but for governance in a globalized world. It noted that traditionally, lending agencies like the World Bank assessed the economic risks of projects like large dams to investors, lenders, and governments. These were "voluntary risk takers": people and entities who were directly involved in the project design and decision making, and who could decide what kind of risk they wanted to take. But there were far more people who had risk imposed on them—people who had no power to make decisions about the project, even though it might have dramatic consequences for their health, livelihoods, or even their very survival.[48] These "involuntary risk bearers" were the millions of poor people forcibly displaced by the dam reservoirs and the millions more whose livelihoods were undermined by the downstream environmental impacts (such as the collapse of fisheries). It was imperative, the WCD concluded, that these groups have the legal right to negotiate with the voluntary risk takers who also had the decision-making power.[49]

It could be argued, moreover, that there is also an even larger class of indirect, involuntary risk bearers, namely the poor in large developing countries for whom overly expensive and suboptimal infrastructure investments could crowd out fiscal space for more effective and equitable alternatives. This was what Martin Karcher, after 29 years at the World Bank, felt so deeply about with regard the proposed Nepal Arun III Dam project (discussed in chapter 3).

This WCD analysis, now more than a decade old, appears more relevant to the inhabitants of the United States and the industrialized world today than it might have done in 2000. The 2008–12 world financial crisis showed how most of the working-class and middle-class populations of the Western world had huge economic risks imposed on them involuntarily—risks managed by others in untransparent decisions over which they had no say, indeed affecting their health and sometimes very survival. The prevailing globalized economic model, with its deficits in transparency, accountability, and equity, reduced hundreds of millions of people to "involuntary risk takers."

The WCD's analysis had lasting social and political implications beyond large dams, and so did its prescriptions. The report set out five "core values" for decision making and planning: equity, efficiency, participation, sustainability, and accountability. It was easy for development agencies and governments to pay lip service to these abstractions. More specifically, the report articulated Seven Strategic Priorities for guiding future decision making on large dams. Two priorities were of particular importance: gaining "demonstrable" public acceptance and undertaking a comprehensive assessment of alternatives and options.

In the case of indigenous and tribal peoples—whose cultures and livelihoods are especially vulnerable—such demonstrable acceptance is indicated by "free, prior, and informed consent achieved through formal and informal representative bodies."[50] That free, prior, informed consent should be a precondition for projects and activities involving resettlement of indigenous peoples was already a principle of international law, enshrined in Article 16, Section 2, of the 1989 United Nations International Labor Organization (ILO) Convention Number 169 on Indigenous and Tribal Peoples.[51]

Concerning analysis of options, experience showed that frequently there were less-expensive and less-risky alternatives to massive dam projects that planners and government officials failed to consider. Energy-efficiency investments and rehabilitating existing dams, for example, had been neglected for decades in the economic-appraisal of alternatives to new hydroelectric projects. Other priorities emphasized the need to ensure compliance and crack down on corruption. Most importantly, the WCD laid out 26 specific good-practice recommendations for putting the priorities into action on the ground.

As might be expected, many NGOs welcomed the WCD report and its recommendations. The United Nations Environment Programme and the World Health Organization strongly supported it.[53] The German and Swedish government aid agencies adopted the recommendations and initiated programs to work with their developing-country partners and dam developers to help carry them out.[54] On the other hand, most major industry associations were critical of the findings, though some individual companies, such as Sweden's Skanska, and the British HSBC and French DEXIA banks, endorsed them. The South African government endorsed the report, but many other Southern governments were critical, and China and Turkey rejected it outright.[55]

Unfortunately, the WCD triggered the same old North–South knee-jerk reactions on development issues. The Indian government argued, for example, that the recommendations would result in hypocritical conditions on aid—ones the rich countries hadn't followed when they built their own dams. India alleged that it was a North-driven attempt to hinder the national development of poor countries. Yet the impetus for the WCD had been the protests of affected people in the South, and six of the twelve commissioners represented developing-country interests; the chair had been South African Minister of Water Resources.[56]

More importantly, the recommendations were not a top-down, academic formulation to be imposed on governments, but a reflection of decades of efforts within developing countries to come up with standards to prevent development tragedies from repeating themselves. India, in fact, was a prime example. In 1989, civil-society groups and academic researchers in India created a prototype National Policy on Developmental Resettlement of Project-Affected People, which anticipated the key WCD priorities and recommendations.[57] The Indian government's rejection of the WCD did not go without strong domestic condemnation. In the words of one Indian commentator, "two decades of slow emergence of enlightened

[India domestic] thinking were washed out in the flood of rhetoric against what was perceived as an international conspiracy to prevent India from developing."[58]

Still, the initial bunker-like reaction of the Indian government was followed by progress. In 2007 the Indian government approved a National Rehabilitation and Resettlement Policy that reflected many of the elements of the 1989 prototype and the WCD guidelines. Most of the 2007 Indian government recommendations were not legally binding, but they were nevertheless a major step forward. The WCD's role was to serve as an "international anchor" and present a restatement of proposed norms and procedures that had been circulating in the Indian domestic arena for the previous decade and a half prior to 2000, norms that eventually found their way into national policy.[59]

So what role would the World Bank play?

High Risk, High Reward

Bank management claimed that the WCD core values and strategic priorities were "consistent with Bank policies," but they refused to comply with the 26 good-practice recommendations.[60] Of course, the core values and priorities were generalities that were hard to dispute. The devil lay in the details—details that were the key to avoiding more Bank-financed dam disasters like Narmada Sardar Sarovar, Yacyretá, and the proposed Arun III project.

More disturbing were indications that some senior World Bank water-project staff actively tried to sabotage acceptance of the WCD by borrowing governments. Eighty-five nongovernmental groups from 30 different countries wrote to Wolfensohn on March 19, 2001, copying all the executive directors of the Bank, asserting that "we learnt from various sources that Bank representatives are misinforming or even lobbying governments and other institutions so that they reject the WCD report. Some institutions which expressed positive views about the WCD recommendations reported that they were strongly criticized by Bank representatives for doing so."[61]

The Bank also developed an approach, the 2003 Water Resources Sector Strategy, that was a declaration of independence from the WCD, from rigorous implementation of Bank environmental policies, and, above all, from the accountability of the Bank's own Independent Inspection Panel. The principal author was John Briscoe, a South African water engineer who had met with developing-country governments behind the scenes during the preparation of the WCD. The Strategy rejected the principle of "free, prior, informed consent" for indigenous peoples, arguing that it constituted a "veto right that would undermine the fundamental right of the state to make decisions in the best interests of the community as a whole."[62] More broadly, it called the WCD recommendations impractical, claiming that they "would virtually preclude the construction of any dam."[63]

Instead, the Bank would reengage with what it called "high-risk/high-reward" projects in the water sector. But based on the record of Bank dam projects, it was not clear what the Bank understood by risk and reward. The whole point of the WCD was that millions of some of the poorest and most vulnerable people on Earth had been deprived of their livelihoods, and that the "rewards" often ranged from mediocre to disastrous.

The Bank's brave new water strategy made clear what its recalibration of risk did entail: attacking the precautionary principle, widely accepted for years in many countries, including all the countries of the European Union. The precautionary principle requires that for activities with potential risks to human health and the environment, the burden of proof is on the proponents to show that the risks can be prevented or avoided. The new water proposal declared: "Most [development] practitioners, however, believe that the application of the precautionary principle would be a recipe for paralysis, and that few development projects would ever be undertaken if such an approach to risk were taken."[64]

The strategy urged that the high-risk/high-reward approach be extended to other areas with major environmental and social impacts, such as forestry and extractive industries (mining, oil, and gas). The costs of policy compliance in these fields had become too high compared to costs in other Bank projects; even worse, "the probability of such projects going to the Inspection Panel is rapidly approaching certainty."[65]

The bottom line was that by shying away from controversial projects, the Bank would be taking an even greater risk of not fulfilling its mission to promote development and help the poor, since such projects also entailed "high [development] rewards." Except that they didn't. The high reward part of the equation was an a *priori* theological assertion, contradicted time and time again by bitter experience.

Bujagali: Private Rewards, Public Risks, and Corruption

The Bank did not wait for the new water-resources strategy to finance projects that ignored the principles of the WCD. In fact, already in December, 2001 the board approved a $225 million IFC loan to the American energy company AES for construction of the 200-megawatt Bujagali Dam in Uganda. The project would affect some 8,700 people, of whom more than 600 would be involuntarily displaced.[66] It would submerge the Bujagali waterfalls, near where the Nile flows out of Lake Victoria. Bujagali Falls is area of great spiritual importance for some 2.5 million Busoga people in Uganda, who believe that the spirits protecting their communities inhabit the waters of the falls and rapids.

Five months before the board approved the project, two Ugandan organizations filed a complaint with the Bank inspection panel. There were concerns about resettlement and environmental impacts, but the biggest problem was economic. AES had demanded a 30-year power-purchase agreement that bound the government to pay a fixed price for all the power the plant could potentially produce, whether or not all the power was actually produced or needed. The contract was secret; not even the Uganda parliament had access to it, and the Bank also kept the agreement secret—a not uncommon practice with private-sector projects, since companies often invoked the principle of commercial confidentiality to avoid sharing information with their competitors. In such cases the Bank sided with the companies, even though it was subsidizing them with public international funds.[67]

The inspection panel released its report to the Bank's board on May 30, 2002. But before even discussing the panel's report, the board approved another $250 million for a MIGA guarantee of AES financing for the project on June 4. The board minutes for that date report that "a number of speakers commended Bank Group management and staff for their willingness to engage in such a complex and high-risk project at a time when there was a temptation to become risk-adverse because of outside criticism."[68]

The panel's approach was balanced, giving the Bank credit where credit was due. It ultimately found violations of several Bank policies, but it also noted that most of the affected people received adequate compensation and that the environmental assessment was generally sound. Above all, though, it found that the economic analysis appeared to be seriously flawed: the cost of electricity for the project was around 40 percent higher than the average cost of electricity for 20 other independent power projects it examined.[69] The Bank's analysis was dismissive of all alternatives, including geothermal power, which a 1999 Bank internal report recommended be analyzed in plans for expanding Uganda's power capacity. The price of electricity for geothermal production would have been less than half the price that would result from Bujagali.[70]

The Power Purchase Agreement finally became public despite the

Ugandan government's and World Bank's refusal, after Uganda environmental groups won a ruling in November 2002 from the Uganda High
Court that the Ugandan constitution required the Power Purchase Agreement to be disclosed.[71] A subsequent independent analysis of the Power
Purchase Agreement by an Indian energy research group was damning:
the covert deal between parts of the Ugandan government and AES would
subject the Ugandan people to needless extra electricity costs of over $20
million a year compared with similar hydroelectric projects in other developing countries. The World Bank had "given poor advice to the Ugandan
government, and . . . misled the public about the cost of the project."[72]

The Bank's handling of the project was a scandal—high rewards for AES
subsidized and guaranteed by the Bank, unconscionable risks for Uganda,
key information withheld by AES, the Ugandan government entities involved in the negotiating, and by the Bank itself. How could this happen?

Things became clearer when allegations of widespread corruption in
the Bujagali project began to appear in 2002, leading to simultaneous investigations by the governments of Norway, Uganda, the United Kingdom,
the United States, and the World Bank. Norway withdrew its support when
the Norwegian engineering contractor Veidekke admitted that its UK sub-
sidiary had bribed a Ugandan government official. The official in question
was the energy minister; he subsequently became Uganda's representative
to the executive board of the Bank.[73] The U.S. Department of Justice com-
menced an investigation of AES for violations of the Foreign Corrupt Practices Act in Bujagali.[74]

AES itself had much more serious problems, since it had lost enormous amounts of money in connection with the notorious Enron energy-
trading and price-manipulation activities in California in 2000–2002. AES
became the target of several class-action lawsuits and was subject to simultaneous investigations by the California state attorney's office, the California Public Utility Commission, and the U.S. Federal Energy Regulatory
Commission.[75] Ugandans were not the only people turned into involuntary risk takers by AES.

AES's share price collapsed, losing more than 95 percent of its value,
and to stave off bankruptcy it withdrew from Bujagali and a number of
other foreign energy projects in August 2003. AES had done a lot of business with the World Bank and IFC—in fact, prior to its financial implo-
sion, it had benefited from some $800 million in IFC loans and guarantees
since 1995.[76] The Bujagali Dam project, for the time being, collapsed. In
later years the Bank would revive the project with other participants, and

with more controversy—a story which we shall examine in more detail in chapters 7 and 9.

Concurrent Government and Market Failure

The high-risk–high-reward approach was not just limited to water projects—it extended to other areas where Bank lending had become inhibited by past environmental and social disasters. The notorious tropical-forest-colonization schemes the Bank had financed in the 1980s had left a traumatic aftermath, leading to a 1991 ban on Bank lending for logging in primary tropical forests.[77] The 1991 policy, inspired also in part by the pending 1992 Rio Earth Summit, emphasized conservation and attempts to expand forest cover. In the 1990s Bank forestry experts experienced underemployment for involvement in logging ("forest management") projects, similar to that of the big-dam proponents.

Unfortunately, a 2000 study by the Operations Evaluation Department (OED) concluded that the ban on Bank support for logging did nothing to reduce deforestation in tropical countries, which accelerated dramatically in the 1990s; by stepping back the Bank had had simply lost any influence to improve forest management.[78] Conservation projects were dwarfed in comparison to far more powerful macroeconomic forces—forces the Bank had actually fostered through its other lending. "The powerful forces of globalization and economic liberalization have intensified pressures for forest production and land conversion, challenging the goal of 'sustainable development.'" The Bank estimated that in many countries there was as much illegal logging as legal production, or even more.[79]

The growth of illegal logging in particular made it "pointless for entrepreneurs to invest in improved logging or tree planting. This is *a classic case of concurrent government and market failure*" (emphasis added).[80]

There were also revealing insights into the "big ideas" and technical fixes quite popular in mainstream development thinking. The 1991 forest policy assumed that intensifying agricultural production (which in practice included the use of genetically modified crops) was a solution that, besides increasing crop yields, would relieve pressure to deforest more land for food and commodity production. Who could argue with such a win–win solution? But a decade's experience had shown that "no universal principles" could be applied; whether agricultural intensification reduced pressures on forests, or actually increased them, was "highly location-specific." In very densely populated countries like China and India, productivity increases did reduce pressure to convert forests. But in Brazil and other countries with large land surpluses, increases in agricultural productivity *increased* incentives to chop down still more forests for farmland, again "a phenomenon [further] reinforced by globalization and the liberalization of markets"[81]

In Brazil, Indonesia, and Cameroon, forest conversion for agricultural exports was especially widespread. Currency devaluation, a standard Bank "structural adjustment" loan policy, had further driven agricultural and forest exports in all three countries.[82] Devaluation meant that more had to be exported to obtain the same amount in hard foreign currency, and the relative cheapness of the exports in turn fostered increased external demand.

The OED thesis that the global model of economic growth, free markets, and trade liberalization was the most important driving force behind forest destruction was something that one had heard from left-wing antiglobalization groups, but this was almost astounding to find in a World Bank evaluation report. It was also a thesis that ecological economist Hermann Daly had long espoused. In a cover article for *Scientific American* in 1993, he observed that the push for unregulated global commerce and growth probably "increase[ed] environmental costs faster than benefits from production—thereby making us poorer, not richer." Countries were irreversibly depleting their ecosystems, and ultimately the carrying capacity for all life in exchange for short-term trade income.[83] (Well-known trade economist Jagdish Bhagwati argued the opposing case in the same issue, reiterating the argument often proffered by economists, finance ministries, and, of course, the World Bank: Rising incomes brought about in developing countries through free trade would eventually generate more income that could be used to protect the environment. If some immediate environmental concerns reflected important and universally shared values, protections could be enforced by mutually agreed-upon international treaties—but this would entail trade-offs with economic growth.)[84]

The Bank's OED could hardly bring itself to question the entire global economic model promoted for years by the Bank and its most powerful member governments. So it recommended raising more cheap money (i.e., grants, such as from the GEF) to compensate countries for protecting forests; trying to fight illegal logging; creating incentives within the Bank to reengage in forestry management (improved logging) projects; and doing more to help poor people in forest areas.[85] In reality this was a policy punt. If the financial incentives for forest products were as great as the OED report maintained, and if indeed both markets and governments had failed to stop the destruction, the Bank's efforts would be akin to bailing out the sinking *Titanic* with buckets. Of course it was a good idea to promote good governance and law enforcement, but the stronger forces at work in major developing countries were not interested in the pious formulations of the Rio '92 Earth Summit, or even in "sustainable logging":

> In Brazil the government has viewed the Bank's focus on saving forest cover in the Amazon as an unnecessary interference in Brazil's domestic affairs. . . . In Indonesia the domestic plywood industry, working closely with the forest department, has resisted reform. In Cameroon the powerful foreign-owned [logging] industry working with the parliamentarians has resisted reform. . . . [86]

Bank management took the study as a green light to discard the ban on supporting commercial logging. A new 2002 forest policy allowed logging projects as long as they were certified as sustainable harvesting by an independent authority and did not result in "significant" conversion of "critical habitats" or "critical forests."[87] These limitations did not reassure many outside observers, given the flexibility of the language and the record of past World Bank projects. Most importantly, the policy did not address the Bank's macroeconomic prescriptions. The Bank continued to push for market liberalization and economic "structural adjustment," which emphasized exports.

Even members of the Bank's executive board were concerned. What was the sense of lending more money for "sustainable forestry" if the Bank's economic policies were contributing to greater pressures to deforest? So management promised it would deal with the problem in a new policy on "development policy lending," a promise which it mostly ignored in substance when the policy was issued in 2004. The policy stated that the Bank would examine and describe the borrowers' lack of capacity to address negative impacts on the environment and the poor in the case of structural adjustment / development policy loans, and would describe "how such gaps or shortcomings would be addressed . . . as appropriate."[88] There was no clear commitment to actually remedy such shortcomings. Moreover, since non-project adjustment and "development policy" loans are typically very large and fast-disbursing, the Bank effectively washed its hands of any responsibility for what actually happened on the ground.

In any case, the real impacts of the new forestry approach can be seen in the projects that were approved during Wolfensohn's second term. Unfortunately, most of the world's richest tropical forests lie in countries with massive problems of corruption and governance, such as Indonesia, Cambodia, Papua New Guinea, the Democratic Republic of the Congo, and other Sub-Saharan countries. The main exception—a very important one—is Brazil. The underlying quandary remained: even with the best of intentions, outside efforts to improve resource management would probably fail in areas of near total "concurrent government and market failure."

The Race for Logging Concessions in the Congo

One of the Bank's most risk-fraught forays into supporting logging took place in the Congo. In the early 2000s the Democratic Republic of the Congo (DRC) was emerging from a horrific civil war in which as many as 5 million people may have perished—one of the worst human rights atrocities since the Second World War. Governance was in a shambles; much of the civil war had been fueled by the efforts of various factions, war lords, and semi-criminal armies to gain control of natural resources such as timber and minerals. In 2002–3 a transitional government was established, and the Bank, together with other Western donors, worked with the government to promote a new Forest Code, as well as a system for managing forest concession contracts. In 2002 the Bank conditioned the release of $15 million of a structural adjustment credit on the new government's adopting the revised Forest Code.[89]

Under the old Mobutu regime, the Congo's official, taxable forest industry greatly declined. In 2002 a Bank Mission to the Congo suggested that production could be increased *60- to 100-fold* in a new "favorable climate for industrial logging." To this end, the Bank promoted a zoning system for the country's forests in which an area larger than France, some 60 million hectares, would be designated as "production forests."[90] The total area of tropical moist forest in the DRC was estimated at the time to be between 80 and 100 million hectares.

In August 2003 the Bank approved more funds for an "emergency" economic and social-support program, part of which went to finance the forestry zoning. Although the Bank's project documents paid lip service to securing rights and access to the forest for all stakeholders, as well as to environmental protection, the principal indicators it chose to measure the success of the forestry component were the conversion of old forest-concession contracts into new concessions under the new Forest Code, and the number of new concessions that were granted.[91]

The Bank's plan alarmed numerous communities of hundreds of thousands of Pygmies who lived in the prospective logging areas. In February 2004, some 51 Congolese organizations called for the traditional lands of the Pygmy populations to be respected,[92] but while the Bank assured the groups it shared similar concerns, the zoning went ahead unchanged.[93]

In addition to violating the rights of indigenous populations, scaled-up logging, given the post-conflict chaos continuing in the Congo, would threaten environmental disaster. The amount of money involved was relatively small, but the project would set parameters for the future development—or destruction—of one of the world's largest last-remaining tropical rain forests. The U.S. Agency for International Development (USAID) warned that the DRC qualified as a failed state unable to control much of its territory, let alone enforce laws or rules in that territory. Both Congolese and foreign logging companies would have every incentive "to employ the most aggressive strategies to log timber in their concessions as rapidly as possible."[94]

The Bank's logging concession goals appeared to be recklessly, dangerously detached from on-the-ground realities, given that

> . . . it is not simply a question of restoring governance systems and restarting a dormant economy, but rather the much more difficult challenge of totally reforming existing, ill-adapted governance and economic systems. This will involve doing away with criminal and corrupt systems and replacing them with transparent, equitable, and democratic systems and institutions.[95]

The growing concerns over the Congolese forestry situation percolated up to Wolfensohn, and on July 8, 2004, he participated in a videoconference involving various NGOs in the Congo, Europe, and elsewhere, together with World Bank officials, to discuss the Bank's role. The discussion starkly illustrated the difficult challenges in addressing not just forest management, but many environmental, conservation, and related social issues in quite a few developing countries.

Simon Counsell of the United Kingdom–based Rainforest Foundation observed that the new Bank-promoted forestry code was quite similar to what the Bank had instituted a few years earlier in Cameroon and the Republic of the Congo (Congo-Brazzaville)—with poor results. Large-scale industrial logging "probably perpetuates and even deepens poverty of some of the poorest people in those countries, the forest communities. . . . We see . . . the logging industry providing a potent vehicle for corruption, economic mismanagement, resource mismanagement."[96] The representative of an organization representing various Pygmy communities expressed their alarm that the Bank was promoting an approach that had already failed elsewhere, noting that "we met our colleagues the indigenous peoples of

Cameroon: they are suffering. They have not benefited one bit from the system which has been put in place."[97]

A leading researcher at the Center for International Forestry Research (CIFOR) in Jakarta said that forestry colleagues he talked with at the Bank claimed they were not promoting logging in the Congo, but believed it was going to happen anyway and what the Bank could do was promote measures to encourage that it be done in a more sustainable fashion.[98]

The researcher, David Kaimowitz, had indeed identified a key premise that repeated itself in much Bank thinking in financing environmentally controversial projects. The rationale that conversion of tropical forests was going to happen anyway had also been promoted in other disastrous Bank interventions in tropical forests, namely the Bank-financed agricultural settlement programs in Indonesia and Brazil in the 1980s. The whole point of the critics was that Bank involvement and support had actually accelerated such ill-conceived schemes and given them an international stamp of approval that attracted other funders, both development agencies and private banks.

A member of Greenpeace France pointed out that the Bank needed to clean up its own act first, since even a high-level, Wolfensohn-led partnership with the CEOs of major forest companies (the "CEO Forum on Forests," created in 1997 and co-chaired with the World Wildlife Fund) itself was indirectly tarnished with corruption and illegal logging through one of its founding members.[99] (The company in question was Danzer, a German-Swiss concern with over 4 million hectares of logging concessions in the DRC and the adjacent Republic of the Congo (Brazzaville).[100]

Wolfensohn exclaimed that he had "heard about this German company" and agreed that its behavior was "terrible." But he claimed that that the Bank had tried to change the company's practices, obviously with disappointing results.[101] As for Cameroon, yes, "the experience in Cameroon has been very difficult for everybody, and the question is what would it have been without intervention? But that is history; now the question is what is going to happen in this enormous country the size of Europe." Wolfensohn continued that the Bank wasn't trying to encourage industrial logging, it was trying to stop "irrational logging."[102] And yes, corruption was absolutely central to the issues the Bank faced, and it was embedded in a broader fabric of poor governance. But who had the solution? "I just want to say to the gentleman from Greenpeace," Wolfensohn continued defensively, "that I've spent nine years understanding the issues of corruption. And if he has any magic formulas that I can have to help eradicate corruption in ways that we are not doing then I would be more than happy to receive them."[103]

Simon Counsell replied that the Bank posed a false choice between, on the one hand, continued, rapacious illegal logging, and on the other hand, if the Bank's improbable plans actually worked, better managed, large-scale logging for export. Instead, the real choice was between the current scheme and an approach that would make the needs and livelihoods of tens of millions of rural poor and indigenous Pygmies in the Congo the priority. Such an approach would strengthen the informal economy of millions of forest dwellers. It would look at the way non-timber forest products were used and marketed, and based on that knowledge it would scale up activities that would finally benefit the rural poor.[104]

Such a choice implied a totally different economic model, one that really would focus on poverty and sustainability. It was not to be.

At the end of November 2005, Congolese groups filed a complaint with Bank's inspection panel reiterating their concerns that the Bank's logging-concession support violated major environmental and social policies. One week later, the Bank approved another $90 million for an IDA "Transitional Support for Economic Recovery Operation" (TSERO) grant, a substantial portion of which pumped more money into the ongoing forestry and logging-concession reform plan. The TSERO grant, which was disbursed in its entirety to the Congolese government three weeks later, was technically a budget-support, "Development Policy" operation, and thus was not subject to the Bank's environmental and social safeguard policies that applied to projects.

The panel took over a year and a half to complete its investigation, and its final report in August 2007 was even more damning than the NGO allegations. It concluded that the Bank had financed commercial logging at the expense of sustainable use and conservation, with most of the benefits going to foreign companies rather than local populations.[105] The documents presented to the board for loan approval "contained virtually no information or analysis on critical social and environmental issues and risks that would inevitably arise in connection with a Bank project involved with tropical forest concession operations." This was an oversight of dramatic proportions, given that in the aftermath of years of civil war and disintegration of governance, "the current rural population of about 40 million people relies heavily on the forest for subsistence."[106]

The omission of an environmental assessment for the Bank's "forest reform" financing was particularly alarming, given that "DRC forest lands are home to rare species such as bonobos, lowland gorillas, okapis, and many other species. In Africa, DRC ranks first for mammal and [other faunal] diversity and third for floral diversity." The DRC's forests contain around 13 to 15 billion tons of carbon, but that wasn't factored either into the Bank's plans for expanding logging concessions.[108]

In response, Bank management prepared an action plan that emphasized "staying engaged in the DRC forest sector, continuing to monitor a moratorium on future logging concessions, and strengthening forest law enforcement." Sixty-four million dollars in new financial commitments for the forest reforms were already in the works. The vice-president for the Africa Region declared: "We will continue to work closely with the DRC Government and development partners to help poor, forest-dependent people, including Pygmies, have a greater voice in decisions that affect them."[109] This was not entirely reassuring, since the emphasis seemed to be on "continuing" the approach of the past several years.

In 2009 and 2011, the Bank's Congo staff submitted reports claiming progress: more was supposedly being done to help the Pygmies, including "scaling up support" for community-based forest management.[110] Other observers were not so optimistic. From 2007 through 2011 Greenpeace International published several investigations documenting continuing corruption, illegal logging, and violence against local people by major European logging companies with vast timber concessions in the DRC, especially Danzer. The irony, of course, is that these same European countries were, and are, major funders of development assistance in Africa, including of course the World Bank.[111]

CHAPTER FIVE

The Logic Was Textbook Perfect

CAJAMARCA IS A PICTURESQUE colonial town in the northern highlands of Peru. Near the central square, travelers can visit a very old one-room house, built on the foundations of an Inca edifice, where the conquistador Francisco Pizarro held the last Inca emperor, Atahualpa, prisoner for several days in November 1532. William Prescott, in his classic *History of the Conquest of Peru*, describes what happened next: "It was not long before Atahuallpa [sic] discovered, amidst all the show of religious zeal in his Conquerors, a lurking appetite more potent in most of their bosoms than either religion or ambition. This was the love of gold. He determined to avail himself of it to procure his own freedom."[1] Atahualpa told Pizarro that he would fill the room—some 22 by 17 feet—up to where he could point (around eight feet high) once with gold and twice with silver, if his life would be spared.

Though the Incas valued gold and silver for ornamentation, they found the single-minded avarice of the invaders beyond their understanding. "The greedy eyes of the Conquerors gloated on the shining heaps of treasure, which were transported on the shoulders of the Indian porters. . . . They now began to believe that the magnificent promises of the Inca would be fulfilled. But, as their avarice was sharpened by the ravishing display of wealth . . . they became more craving and impatient."[2] The promises of Pizarro and the other conquistadors to spare Atahualpa were worthless; after the treasure was delivered, they murdered the Inca emperor. So began the history of foreign extraction of the mineral resources of Peru.

Nearly half a millennium after Atahualpa's murder, gold is still being extracted from the region: 18 kilometers outside of Cajamarca is the largest gold mine in Latin America. Seventy percent of Cajamarca's water supply comes from streams flowing through the mining site, which extends across 160 square kilometers, including six open pit mines, five leach pads, and various processing facilities, covering four distinct watersheds.[3] The huge open-pit excavation is run by Yanacocha, S.A. (Yanacocha means "black lake" in Quechua), a joint venture between the U.S. firm Newmont Corporation and Condesa, Peru. But not entirely: the World Bank International Finance Corporation is a 5 percent equity investor, and the IFC provided some $150 million in loans through 2000 to support the project. When mining operations began in the early 1990s, many inhabitants of the region were optimistic, hoping for jobs and improved roads.[4]

That hope had largely evaporated by 2000, when a truck traveling from the mine spilled 330 pounds of mercury along a stretch of road that ran through several villages. More than a thousand people were poisoned, including many children who tried to play with the unusual liquid metal. The company delayed reporting the accident and allegedly paid villagers to gather up the mercury without protective clothing.[5] The accident was only one of a number of incidents that led to protests from local residents. They complained about water contamination, coercion and displacement of local farmers, and greatly increased violence, crime, and prostitution associated with the influx of outsiders seeking employment. The mining operation created jobs—an estimated 2,200 long-term positions (and 6,000 short-term temporary jobs)—and was an important taxpayer to the Peruvian government.[6] But the region actually became poorer on a relative basis after the mine opened, sinking from the fourth poorest to second poorest district in Peru from 1993 to the early 2000s.[7]

In response to growing protests and formal complaints to its compliance advisor/ombudsman (CAO) office, the IFC set up a "roundtable dialogue" in 2001 to address the local concerns. The roundtable led to several studies, including one that found that Yanacocha indeed failed to have in place and carry out basic hazardous waste and emergency-response procedures.[8] But many local communities felt little was changing. They viewed the CAO and the roundtable as an alibi for the company to continue its practices, particularly since it was well known that the IFC was a co-investor in the project. The CAO seemed to be more concerned with process than results.[9] The roundtable's failure become clear in 2004, when Yanacocha attempted to open a new mine. For two weeks, thousands of protestors blocked the road to the mine; staff and provisions could enter only by helicopter. A regional strike ensued and 10,000 people mobilized on the main square of Cajamarca, yards from the former prison room of Atahualpa. Ultimately, Yanacocha was forced to abandon the expansion.[10]

Yet the conflict spread to other areas in Peru, where existing and proposed mining operations were increasingly questioned, with support from NGOs and the Roman Catholic Church.[11] In 2011, Yanacocha proposed new expansions, leading to weeks of violent protests. The president of Peru declared a state of emergency in Cajamarca District, dispatching hundreds of army troops to restore order. Newmont and Yanacocha suspended temporarily their expansion requests, as the government sought to prepare new review procedures.[12]

Love Is Repaid with Love

In the midst of massive protests, the IFC not only seemed remarkably unconcerned with environmental and social damage—it also looked the other way when it came to corruption. In 2001, secret videos revealed extensive scandals involving the administration of Peruvian president Alberto Fujimori. One showed Fujimori's intelligence chief, Vladimiro Montesinos, pressuring a judge to rule in favor of the U.S. firm Newmont in a dispute with a French company over ownership rights to Yanacocha.[13]

A joint PBS *Frontline / New York Times* investigation uncovered a tale of corruption and covert political pressure that extended well beyond Peru, involving the highest levels of the French and American governments. The number-three executive at Newmont at the time, Lawrence Kurlander, had received word from U.S. embassy and State Department officials that the French government, starting with President Jacques Chirac personally, was attempting to influence Peruvian officials to win the legal battle over Yanacocha. Kurlander told the *Times* that Fujimori's office instructed him to see Montesinos, whom he acknowledged "was an extremely bad man." Indeed he was; besides being the regime's fixer-in-chief, Montesinos was its head torturer and oversaw death squads.[14] His intelligence agency was also on the payroll of the CIA to the tune of a million dollars a month. A taped recording of Kurlander's meeting with Fujimori and Montesinos reveals the Intelligence Chief discussing "the lawyers and judges who may need to be influenced." At the end of the meeting, Montesinos tells Kurlander that *"amor con amor se paga"*: love is repaid with love.[15]

Kurlander repeatedly asserted that Newmont was not involved with bribery or illegal activity; on the contrary, he and the U.S. government were only trying to ensure a level playing field and to counter French pressure. "If the French were to be stopped, he [Montesinos] was the only one in Peru who would dare to do it." Unsurprisingly, the French denied the allegations and claimed that it was Newmont that was handing out bribes. The U.S. Department of Justice launched an investigation into possible Newmont bribery of

Peruvian officials, but dropped the case because of lack of cooperation from Peru's government and the expiration of the statue of limitations.[16]

Kurlander subsequently returned to Peru in 2004 to head up an environmental review of the mine. Following the audit, he wrote to Newmont's chief executive, Wayne Murdy, that the environmental violations were so grave that they could endanger the future of the entire undertaking, and that management could be subject to "criminal prosecution and imprisonment."[17] Apparently, Newmont kept the audit secret, never sharing the information with the public, its shareholders, the people of Cajamarca, or the Peruvian government. Kurlander, now in retirement, acknowledges the blindness of the company, writing, "We have come to this because we have been in denial. . . . We have not heeded the voices of those most intimate with our mine—those who live and work nearby."[18]

A local priest, Father Marco Arana, a son of school teachers from the Cajamarca District, was a key negotiator for the long-suffering community groups. Father Romero finally met Newmont's CEO, Wayne Murdy, in the spring of 2005 at a Newmont board meeting. Murdy told him, he recounted, that he always remembered what his mother told him, that we are given one mouth but two ears to listen—apparently an attempt to show that the company was finally open to dialogue. The good priest told Murdy, "In the Bible there is a saying about some people having eyes that don't see and ears that don't hear."[19]

The lesson of Yanacocha is that big extractive projects require a "social license to operate," which increasingly has been defined in terms of the requirement of "free, prior, informed consent," not just for indigenous peoples, but for all affected communities. The consequences of not obtaining this consent has become increasingly costly for businesses and companies around the world.[20]

A Most Curious Curse

Yanacocha was no exception for the IFC. In fact, it was emblematic, and far from the worst extractive project in which the Bank was involved. During Wolfensohn's tenure, controversies over IFC and MIGA support for large mining and oil- and gas-extraction projects proliferated.[21] By 2010 extractive projects accounted for over 40 percent of CAO complaints.[22]

Despite all their problems, the World Bank Group rationalized that these projects generated large revenues that could be taxed for the benefit of local governments, and thereby help finance new infrastructure such as roads, and support education and health budgets. The projects also generated some local employment. The Bank maintained that it could promote higher environmental and social standards, and ensure more benefits to the poor, than would come about otherwise. As with many other Bank undertakings, at a certain level of abstraction the reasoning was plausible. Such projects were certainly high risk; perhaps the Bank could help improve the likelihood that the poor would share more of the rewards, and fewer of the negative impacts.

Yet there was a troubling quandary with the Bank's support of extractive industries in poor countries: the so-called resource curse, or paradox of plenty: a country's dependence on revenue from extractive resources is almost always directly correlated with substandard economic growth and poor, declining indicators of human welfare. A well-known 1995 Harvard paper by Jeffrey Sachs and Andrew Warner noted that the "resource curse" was a "constant theme of economic history," concluding that during the 1990s and '80s the perverse relation held true in a "robust" way even after researchers controlled for a whole gamut of other variables, including initial GDP (gross domestic product), trade policy, investment rates, etc.[23]

Many studies, including those of the World Bank, confirmed these findings. A 2002 Bank mining department study found that during the 1990s developing countries had an average annual GDP growth rate of 1.7 percent, but in eight countries where mining accounted for more than 50 percent of exports, GDP declined at a rate of –2.3 percent a year. In 22 countries where mining accounted for between 15 and 50 percent of exports, the rate of decline was –1.1 percent annually, and in another 18 countries where mining provided between 6 and 15 percent of exports, the rate of decline was –0.7 percent annually.[24] The mostly middle-income, oil-exporting members of OPEC (the Organization of Petroleum Exporting Countries) underwent an average annual per capita income decline of –1.3 percent a year between 1968 and 1998, while lower- and middle-income economies as a whole grew at a rate of 2.2 percent a year.[25]

These negative growth figures don't tell the full story of growing inequality, massive corruption, suppression of democracy and human rights, and declining health and education.[26] Oxford development economist Paul Collier (a former World Bank research director) identifies the fundamental issue as one of governance, namely that large resource revenues in poorer countries undermine democracy, the rule of law, and investment in the poor. Corrupt autocrats use this revenue to seize and maintain power; there is no need to build popular support for a legitimate state that can raise money from taxing its citizens or other sources. Multinational mining and oil companies have often been accomplices in cutting deals with such autocrats. The inequality is further exacerbated by destruction of ecosystems on which the rural poor depend. Finally, the allure of rich, unaccountable sources of revenue often provokes political conflict and civil war.[27]

The "resource curse" also often diminishes investment in other manufacturing and service sectors that would diversify the economy and create more jobs. There are a number of explanations for this effect, a classical one being the so-called Dutch disease, a phenomenon whereby the rise in exports associated with extractive industry development results in a more highly valued, expensive currency for the exporting country, which then leads to the decline or even collapse of its other exports. (The phenomenon was first analyzed with respect to the impacts on the Dutch economy of development and export of North Sea oil.)

Unfortunately, more and more such cases came to light, raising questions about whether Bank involvement in extractive industries made any positive difference, or, by supporting extractive operations in high-risk areas where private international banks refused to lend, actually made things worse. For example, in 1995 the IFC approved $40 million in financing and a MIGA $45 million loan guarantee for a Canadian company to develop the Kumtor gold mine at an altitude of more than 4,000 meters in the Tian Shan mountains of Kyrgyzstan. The Canadian company, CAMECO, had experience in uranium mining but had never operated a gold mine before, let alone one in a poor, unstable country in a technically challenging mountain environment at over 13,000 feet. Without IFC and MIGA support, it is unlikely that CAMECO could have received sufficient private financing for the mine, given its lack of experience and the high political and operational risks involved in the project. The World Bank Group was certainly looking out for CAMECO's financial risk, but was it looking out for the risks to local people and the natural environment?

In May 1998 a CAMECO truck spilled over two tons of cyanide and sodium hydrochloride, contaminating the Barskoon River that runs into one of the natural marvels of Central Asia, the beautiful, mile-high Lake Issyk-Kul, surrounded by the 16,000-foot-high Tian Shan mountains. Issyk-Kul is the second-largest mountain lake in the world after Lake Titicaca. In the wake of the spill, several people died and hundreds sought medical treatment. Lake Issyk-Kul had been a prestige tourist site in the Soviet era, and high-level party dignitaries and Soviet celebrities such as the cosmonauts had villas there. Newly independent Kyrgyzstan had hoped to revive the tourist industry, which continued with visitors from other Central Asian countries and some adventure tourists from the West.

The cyanide disaster unleashed a mass panic in the local press, which referred to the accident as Kyrgyzstan's "Chernobyl." (One could imagine what kind of tourism and press reaction that a two-ton cyanide spill in Lake Tahoe or Lake Geneva would provoke.) Although the initial damage was significant, some of the reaction was exaggerated—it was hardly a Chernobyl—since cyanide, after killing everything in its wake, dissipates relatively quickly; but the secretiveness and arrogance of CAMECO compounded local mistrust. Just weeks later, in July 1998, there was another spill of 70 liters of nitric acid, followed by another CAMECO truck accident releasing over one and a half tons of ammonium nitrate. Nevertheless, in 2001 MIGA approved an additional loan guarantee for nearly $40 million.[28] In 2002 a 200-meter-high wall in the mine collapsed, killing a worker. In 2004 the IFC sold its interest in the project at a profit, divesting itself of future responsibility for its involvement.[29] For years afterwards, disputes continued among the locally affected people, CAMECO, and the government over compensation for the spills.

Unfortunately, example after example has shown that by supporting extractive operations in high-risk areas where private banks refuse to lend, the World Bank may have actually done more harm than good.

Help!

South African Archbishop Desmond Tutu was very upset with the World Bank. At first his ire might have seemed strange, since he was angry about the World Bank Group's single largest investment in Sub-Saharan Africa, which in turn made possible the largest private-sector investment in the region. And no one could doubt that the region needed investment and development. "The Chad-Cameroon project is not the help we asked for or needed," he publicly declared in 2002. "In the absence of the rule of law and respect for human rights and the environment, financing of large-scale oil development is destroying the environment and us. Help!"[30]

Of all the extractive industry projects that proceeded in the Wolfensohn years, the Chad-Cameroon oil and pipeline project was paradigmatic. It revealed the flaws, dysfunction, and hubris that led the World Bank to repeat, this time in new, more ambitious variations, the same mistakes as in risky big projects in the past, with disastrous consequences for both the environment and the poorest people on Earth.

Bank management had been involved in planning discussions for the project since the mid-1990s; the Chad-Cameroon project was seen as a prototype for the World Bank Group's involvement in private-sector financing deals around the world. The original idea was to use $250 million in IFC loans and about $120 million in IDA credits to develop a huge oil field in the Doba Basin in southern Chad, finance a 1,100-kilometer pipeline through Cameroon to the sea, and fund storage stations and road upgrades along the pipeline.[31] Three of the world's largest oil companies, Exxon, Royal Dutch Shell, and Elf-Aquitaine, were to form the consortium running the project. The IDA low-interest loans would go to the governments of Chad and Cameroon to finance their participation in two national pipeline companies that would be more than three-quarters-owned by the three oil companies. Exxon project documents stated clearly that World Bank involvement was essential for mitigating risk and generating over a billion dollars in cofinancing through public export credit agencies and commercial banks.[32]

But the use of scarce IDA funds for such purposes was unprecedented. The project would consume a considerable portion of the low-interest IDA loans available for Chad and Cameroon for several years, crowding out alternative investments in health, education, and development—all to subsidize the largest oil companies in the world. The Bank argued that oil was by far the most profitable investment—the revenue would be much greater than what it could lend to Chad and Cameroon directly. The governments could then use that money to fund poverty alleviation, public health, education, and environmental protection.

Yet there were considerable risks. Chad had suffered from intermittent civil war between its largely Muslim North and its Christian and Animist South for the better part of 30 years. The Doba area in particular had been the main center of resistance to the northern-controlled government, and informed observers worried that the project could reignite the conflict. The *Economist* Intelligence Unit estimated in 1996 that if oil development were to take place in southern Chad, the odds were 50–50 that a civil war would be reignited.[33] In 1998 Amnesty International documented massacres of unarmed civilians in the Chadian oil-producing region.[34]

From the outset, the likelihood of Chad's proposed development fund and Cameroon's pipeline royalties helping the poor did not appear to be very great. World Bank attempts to create similar development funds in Africa had not had much success. In the late 1990s and early 2000s, a development fund fed by revenues from a huge Bank-financed water-diversion project to supply South Africa, the Lesotho Highlands Project, failed to benefit local people affected by the project.[35] In the autumn of 1996, labor unrest on the Bank-funded dam site led to protests in which the police shot dead five workers and seriously injured 30 others. Some 1,000 other workers sought refuge on the grounds of a nearby Catholic church.[36] Moreover, the Chadian government was so corrupt that the national treasury had been controlled for several years by a Swiss company (COTECNA) at the insistence of foreign aid donors.

International concern built over the Bank's plans, including the use of IDA funds. So the Bank switched gears, using mostly IBRD loans rather than IDA credits. This meant much higher interest rates for Chad and Cameroon, but the extra costs of the loans could be paid out of the oil revenues and pipeline charges. Shell and ELF, however, had growing doubts about the project's risks, and in November 1999 they both pulled out of the consortium.[37] They were replaced by Chevron and the Malaysan state oil company, Petronas.[38] Exxon-Mobil led the new oil consortium with 40 percent of the shares; Petronas's cut was 35 percent, and Chevron's 25 percent.[39]

Deal of the Year

If the oil companies were concerned, the Bank appeared not to be. Management plowed ahead, approving in June 2000 nearly $350 million in loans and credits.[40] The Bank's involvement convinced the European Investment Bank to contribute a loan of 133 million euros (around $200 million), and the export credit agencies of the United States and France to loan $200 million each—after all, their companies would benefit from the investment.[41] It was Sub-Saharan Africa's largest private-investment project; total costs were estimated at over $3.7 billion in 2000, but rose to some $8 billion by 2011.[42] Project Finance magazine called the Chad-Cameroon project the "Africa Oil and Gas Deal of the Year" for 2001, and, from the perspective of ExxonMobil or Chevron, who could deny it?[43] There could be no stronger example of the leverage and multiplier effect of World Bank finance, for better or worse.

But even as the lending package was approved, a number of Bank executive directors expressed concerns about whether the project could deliver on its promise to alleviate poverty. They recognized that they would be under the microscope. The U.S. director called the project "a defining moment in World Bank history" as well as "a prism through which the world views the institution and, it is likely, development assistance more broadly. The stakes could not be higher."[44]

The whole project was premised on the Chadian and Cameroon governments using the oil revenues to benefit the poor. Bank staff assured the board that this would be no problem because Chad not only had put in place democratic institutions, but also was "determined to implement participatory mechanisms concerning the articulation of development policies, decisions on the allocation of public resources, and execution of public expenditures."[45] Human rights reports in 1999 and 2000 from the State Department suggested otherwise. They detailed a disturbing record of forced labor, child enslavement, and restrictions on free speech and assembly; as well as beatings, rapes, torture, and extrajudicial killings by state security forces.[46]

The rosy anticipation of Chad's blooming democracy notwithstanding, the Bank did take precautions. The oil income would not go directly to the Chadian government, but first to a so-called transit bank account from which the IBRD and the European Investment Bank would immediately take out interest payments. The remainder would be held in a special escrow account at Citibank in London. Ten percent was to be set aside for a so-called Future Generations Fund and the rest would go to Chad's central bank. The profits were to be managed under a new revenue management law for various poverty-alleviation, public-health, environmental, and educational purposes.

The project also set up an oversight committee and an international advisory group to monitor the use of the oil money.[47] Cameroon, too, was supposed to use its revenue for poverty alleviation, but because of its already high indebtedness, the money could not be set aside in an off-shore escrow account—its international commercial creditors would want access to the funds. Instead the Bank charged a 10 percent premium as a kind of risk insurance.[48]

The Bank's involvement also resulted in more environmental and social precautions than would otherwise have taken place. The pipeline was rerouted to reduce harm to critical forests and to minimize displacement of indigenous Pygmy people. Cameroon was to establish two new national parks to offset environmental damage and a foundation was planned for the benefit of the Bakola Pygmy people.[49] The Bank also analyzed the project's carbon emissions, but, in the end, argued that if the oil wasn't produced in Chad, it would be produced elsewhere. So there were no carbon offsets or other efforts to mitigate the project's contribution to global warming.[50] The climate risk was one more "free externality," to use the economists' jargon.

If the Bank took some precautions to protect the environment and local people, it took more to protect the oil consortium. As was typical in cases of IFC loans involving the private sector, the Chad and Cameroon governments legally guaranteed that they would not take any action that would increase the consortium's costs. If there should arise any conflict with domestic law, or with international human rights or environmental treaties, the contract with the oil companies would prevail. Many observers found such one-sided agreements to be unconscionable. Amnesty International denounced this state of affairs, and in 2005 the organization published a lengthy report censuring the legal agreements between the oil consortium and the governments of Chad and Cameroon.[51]

Already in April 2000, before the World Bank finance was approved, the Dutch government financed a symposium, organized by the Netherlands Committee for the World Conservation Union, on who would bear the liability for environmental damage in the project.[52] Poring over the legal agreements, the participants were disturbed and sent a letter to the World Bank and its executive directors, expressing concern that the legal arrangements raised issues of

> the lack of predictability and liability as a result of non-applicability of national laws, the non-applicability of international treaties, wide powers of the [oil] consortium to act as an official state organ: violating the rule of law, the lack of predictability and liability as a result of ambiguous articles, absence of the right to an effective remedy through a fair and public hearing by an independent and impartial court and the lack of appropriate enforcement mechanisms.[53]

"In the lack of any meaningful legal accountability for the companies involved in the pipeline project," the symposium participants continued, "the only source of normative regulation for the behavior of the companies involved comes from the World Bank's Guidelines."[54]

The Bank wrote back that "it is undisputed in international business that the parties to an international agreement enjoy the freedom to choose the applicable law governing their business-related relationships."[55] One would not want to infringe on the freedom of the poor of Chad and Cameroon, through their dictatorial and kleptocratic rulers, to negotiate with ExxonMobil their right to bear the full responsibility and costs for environmental and social harm that might ensue from the project. In the name of poverty alleviation, the Bank was subsidizing with more than a third of billion dollars in international public funds project agreements that set up the oil companies as an unaccountable law unto themselves. And this was not an exception, but business as usual—indeed, it was the model.

The Unraveling

Just a few months after the Bank approved the financing, things began to unravel. In January 2001, a $25 million signing bonus, which by way of exception was not escrowed in the Citibank account in London, flowed to the Chadian central bank. President Idriss Déby immediately used the first $4.5 million to buy arms. James Wolfensohn, who had staked his personal reputation on the project, personally called Déby and threatened to pull the plug on the project if the money was not returned—so it was.[56] In April 2001, Ngarlejy Yorongar, a member of Chad's parliament who represented the region where the oil fields were located, filed a complaint with the Bank inspection panel on behalf of more than 100 inhabitants of the oil-producing area. The claim asserted various environmental and economic damages, as well as human rights violations.

A month later, violent civil unrest erupted in the wake of a fraudulent presidential election—naturally Déby was declared the victor—delaying the panel's visit. Meanwhile, the election stolen, Déby arrested his opponent Yorongar, together with other opposition members, and subjected them to systematic beatings and torture. Wolfensohn only heard of the Chadian parliamentarian's imprisonment through Korinna Horta, a development economist then with the Environmental Defense Fund; the Bank Chad-Cameroon project staff hadn't told him a thing about Yorongar's plight. Once again, Wolfensohn called Idriss Déby and told him the project was off unless Yorongar was released immediately—as he was. Thanks to Wolfensohn, Bank funds helped him to be flown to a Parisian hospital specializing in the treatment of torture victims.

The Bank had minimized the implications of Chad's politics—problems that were clear to anyone familiar with the country or who had read the State Department human rights reports. President Déby's own ethnic group, the Zaghawa, predominated in northern Chad and held key government posts, but the oil was located in the south. So the ruling party maintained power by suppressing other groups and siphoning off the oil revenue for their own benefit. The Chad-Cameroon oil project only made things worse. A European Union–financed study noted that "the system to maintain Déby in power consists of patronage, clientism, and co-optation, based on . . . corrupt practices surrounding the distribution of state revenues—which originate to a huge extent from the oil sector."[57] Where co-optation failed, torture and terror would have to suffice. It was a theme repeated with variations in the history of other resource conflicts in Africa and elsewhere.

In the face of these dynamics, perhaps no fiscal management scheme would succeed. But the Bank's plan seemed to invite corruption. Professor Peter Rosenblum, in the early 2000s director of the Human Rights Program at the Harvard Law School, engaged Harvard Law students to study the project and its novel revenue-management provisions and mechanisms. In a 2002 hearing of the U.S. House of Representatives, Rosenblum was generous in his praise of some of the Bank's efforts, but went on to state that the protections in the revenue-management scheme were "substantively weak" and that the project would fail without major changes. For example, the plan allowed the president to unilaterally modify the allocation of use of the revenue every five years by decree—and the criteria for the allocation of the revenue, despite the developmentally correct purposes of poverty alleviation and environment, were extremely vague.[58]

For over two years, Rosenblum and his students analyzed the project and tried to come up with constructive suggestions. Bank staff and management reacted in a way that demonstrated just how pervasive a culture of arrogance and hubristic ignorance remained entrenched in parts of the institution. He told the House International Relations Committee that

> we at Harvard had a taste of Bank defensiveness when we submitted the Harvard Memorandum that analyzes the Revenue Management Plan. A number of Bank officials . . . called the office of the dean of the Law School to complain. Three officials came to Harvard personally to discuss the matter. One of them, a senior official in the legal department of the Bank, told us, essentially, that Africa "didn't need a group of Westerners parachuting in to tell them what to do." I introduced him to the students who had worked on the project, one-third of whom were from Sub-Saharan Africa.[59]

Sure enough, five years and a few months after the loans were approved, in October 2005 Déby told World Bank officials that it was time to abolish the "Future Generations Fund," supposedly "to respond to the aspirations of the present generation," as well as double the government's general budget.[60] In reality much of the extra money would go for arms purchases and beefed-up military security to keep Déby in power. The Bank responded by freezing the oil revenue escrow accounts in January 2006. Déby threatened to halt oil production, and the Bank caved in, unfreezing the accounts in April and acceding to most of Déby's demands for more unsupervised funds. By May the situation deteriorated further, when rebels originating in the Darfur region of Sudan stormed the capital, N'Djamena, and attempted to overthrow Déby.[61] Meanwhile, Déby had changed the constitution to allow him to run for a third term and become, in effect, president for life.

Chad's military budget expanded from $14 million annually in 2000 to

$315 million in 2009, made possible by the oil project. Arms imports in-
creased five-fold. By 2006 the country ranked 27th in the world in percentage of GDP reserved for the military—at 4.2 percent ahead of the United
States.[62] Meanwhile, infant, child, and maternal mortality steadily rose. In
2009, UNICEF reported that Chad had the third-highest mortality rate for
children under five in the world—only Sierra Leone and Afghanistan were
worse.[63]

The growing authoritarianism was accompanied by increasing unrest,
and another rebel attack on the capital in early February 2008 caused more
than 250 deaths, leading the Bank to evacuate its office in N'Djamena.
Shortly thereafter, Déby issued a decree suspending the revenue-management agreements, allowing him to use as much as he wanted for still more
military and arms expenditures.[64] In September 2008 the Bank finally pulled
the plug, requesting that Chad repay the IBRD loan and IDA credit. Money
intended for hospitals, schools, and the environment had been diverted to
save Idriss Déby's dictatorial regime. "Regrettably," the Bank statement
read, "it became evident that the arrangements that had underpinned
the bank's involvement in the Chad/Cameroon pipeline project were not
working."[65] The project's legacy was that "life has gone from bad to worse"
in Chad, wrote the *New York Times*. Antoine Berilengar, a Chadian Catholic
priest and member of the project's oversight commission, declared: "We
knew from the very beginning how this would end . . . the government
simply enriched itself."[66]

But the International Finance Corporation did not withdraw, and remains involved to this day.

The Debacle

In 2009 the Bank's Independent Evaluation Group reviewed the debacle. Its
conclusions are unequivocal: "The logic was textbook perfect—except for
the revealed weakness of every link in the chain." The billions in oil revenue
only led to "a resurgence of civil conflict and a worsening of governance."
Bank and IFC involvement "had *no discernible positive effects* on governance
development in Chad" (emphasis added).[67] Peter Rosenblum and his law
students were right: "The flaws in the design of the oil revenue and expenditure management arrangements adversely affected the impact of the
whole program."[68]

The oil development scheme was a technical and financial success; in
fact, the pipeline was completed and oil was flowing ahead of schedule.[69]
Fueled in part by the Chadian oil bonanza, ExxonMobil reported record

profits in 2006 and 2007. The huge revenues gave Chad one of the highest economic growth rates in the world in 2004, over 31 percent.[70] The country also enjoyed more paved roads and an improved system of water supply.

But much of the infrastructure budget went to the capital city, with a priority on repairing government buildings damaged by rebel attacks. Little was spent on rural areas. Funding of primary education and health was not only rife with corruption, but there was a serious disconnect between expenditures and actual needs: schools were built where there were no teachers, no supplies, and no demand, and were not built where they were needed. Some communities had empty classrooms while others were forced to build straw shelters. The situation was even worse with public health: some clinics and hospitals were actually constructed—but there was no money for doctors, equipment, or medicines.[71]

The project's environmental record was plagued by major failures, despite an extraordinary investment of Bank/IFC staff time and resources. The two pipeline companies had complied with most environmental and safety standards, but as of 2009 neither country government had developed an oil-spill response plan, and monitoring was "weak to nonexistent." In Chad, increased drilling threatened local livelihoods.[72] In Cameroon, the protection of two new national parks and a plan to help indigenous Pygmy peoples fell apart because of lack of funds and mismanagement.[73] Incredibly, even with the multibillion-dollar oil bonanza and the provision of nearly a billion dollars in public money to subsidize the project, not just from the World Bank Group, but also the European Investment Bank and the government export credit agencies of the United States and France, as well as the world's richest multinational corporation—yes, incredibly, the foundation set up by the Bank to fund the environmental and indigenous peoples' protection for the areas most affected by the pipeline was collapsing because of lack of money.

Despite the extraordinary failures, all involved in the project were at first eager to claim success. In 2002 the United Nations convened a special conference in Johannesburg, South Africa, to assess global environmental progress since the 1992 Rio Earth Summit—the United Nations World Summit on Sustainable Development (WSSD). The conference put a major emphasis on "public-private partnerships," i.e., governments and international agencies working with, and cofinancing, private-sector investments that putatively would promote "environmentally sustainable development." Some NGOs criticized the United Nations for letting multinational corporations hijack the conference, with charges of greenwashing and corporate welfare. The United States under the Bush administration touted the Chad-Cameroon project in Johannesburg as a model for Africa.[74]

Just in time for the 2002 environmental summit, the United Nations Environment Program (UNEP) published a report entitled "Industry as a Partner for Sustainable Development: Oil and Gas," written by the International Association of Oil and Gas Producers, and a so-called International Petroleum Industry Environmental Conservation Association, of which most of the major oil companies of the world were members. It singled out the Chad-Cameroon scheme as model of "community engagement and participation," highlighting the (subsequently failed) funding arrangements for the national parks and indigenous peoples' plan in Cameroon.[75]

James Wolfensohn defended the scheme to the end, asserting in 2005, "I am 100 percent convinced that it is a good project." The world isn't Holland or the United States, he noted—400 million people live in what are virtually failed states. Do you just abandon them? Do you wait for years or decades until they have better governance and less corruption?[76]

It was a patently false dichotomy. In terms of the actual welfare of the people, a civil war in Chad would be worse than doing nothing. Moreover, brave environmental and human rights organizations in Chad and Cameroon—led by courageous individuals such as Samuel Nguiffo of the Centre pour l'Environnement et le Développement in Cameroon, and Delphine Djiraibe of the Association Tchadienne pour la Promotion et la Défense des Droits de l'Homme in Chad—had argued from the beginning not against the project per se, but for a different sequencing of project components. If the key risk was very weak government capacity to manage the oil development, revenues, corruption, and environmental and social impacts, then, they argued, it would be much better for the Bank to use its funds to *first* build up this capacity through much more ambitious programs of technical assistance. The prospect of the oil project and its future revenues could serve as an incentive for the government to strengthen institutions and capacity. Time and time again, experience had demonstrated the failure of attempts to rush ahead with extractive projects (and many big infrastructure projects in general), while simultaneously trying to remedy weak governance and capacity. Inevitably, the infrastructure and hardware got built and revenues started flowing, but governance was further weakened and undermined.

Ironically, as the Chad-Cameroon project pressed forward, the Bank was beginning a formal review to reexamine its role in extractive industries, and whether it should support them at all.

CHAPTER SIX

Backwards into the Future

I T WAS THE LAST WEEK OF September 2000 and the streets of Prague were mobbed with thousands of anti-globalization protesters; many were Czechs, but others had come from all over Europe. Thirteen thousand Czech security forces mobilized, reinforced by busloads of police from the provinces. In the ensuing pitched battles the protesters' Molotov cocktails were met with teargas by the police. The World Bank and International Monetary Fund had come to town for their 55th Annual Meeting.[1]

Roads into the city and the city transport system were shut down, delegates told the press they were afraid to leave their hotel rooms, and 65 demonstrators, 61 police, and 25 delegates were injured; the Bank-Fund meeting was forced to end earlier than scheduled. Before they all left town, James Wolfensohn told a gathering of bankers and finance ministry officials from scores of countries that "Outside these walls, young people are demonstrating against globalization. I believe deeply that many of them are asking legitimate questions, and I embrace the commitment of a new generation to fight poverty. I share their passion and their questioning."[2]

Inside the meeting halls, representatives of NGOs such as Friends of the Earth and the Eastern European Bankwatch Network approached Wolfensohn, urging him to launch an independent review of the Bank's financing of extractive industries, analogous to the World Commission on Dams. This was before the Bank had rejected the WCD's recommendations, so there was much hope that such a review could actually change Bank lending for mining, oil, and gas projects. Wolfensohn agreed.

In the following months, however, Bank management became wary of allowing another "World Commission on Dams" to take place. In fact, it was the "independent" part of the review they most feared. The proponents of big dams felt that they had lost control of the WCD, allowing it to make recommendations that interfered with business as usual. The Bank had been put in the embarrassing situation of partially repudiating an exercise that it had cosponsored.

This time it would be different. The Extractive Industries Review (EIR) would be structured to ensure more control by the Bank and its focus would be narrower. Recommendations would concern only the Bank's practices rather than those of an entire worldwide sector, as was the case with the WCD. Still, Bank management prided itself on setting standards in international development, and the EIR would necessarily influence investment in the sector by other development and financial agencies.

The EIR was headed by an "Eminent Person," Emil Salim of Indonesia, who reported directly to Wolfensohn. Salim had been Indonesia's first environment minister, but earlier in his career he also was the CEO of the country's national coal company. He was to lead a four-person secretariat, which was initially housed in the International Finance Corporation Bank building, right down the hallway from the Mining Department. The secretariat staff were all employees and former employees of the World Bank Group; there would be no independent commission as there was with the WCD. Salim did not have control of the budget: the Bank administered and allocated half of it, and he had to get the Bank's sign-off on the use of the rest of it. Salim was over 70 years old, and he had other time-consuming duties such as heading up the preparations for the 2002 United Nations World Summit on Sustainable Development, which he chaired. There was little risk then, of a report that the Bank would find embarrassing.

Salim turned out to be feistier than some in the Bank anticipated; the day after New Year's 2002 he wrote Wolfensohn to complain, ever so politely, about the EIR's lack of independence and to request full control of the budget. He wanted most of the secretariat to be moved to Jakarta, where he still lived, and he asked for the report's time frame to be extended a year, until after a key performance report on extractive industries by the IEG was completed.

Wolfensohn agreed to most of Salim's requests, but emphasized the need for Bank staff to be involved—after all, this could ensure better buy-in, compared with what had happened with the World Commission on Dams. Salim also mentioned the problems of the Chad-Cameroon project in his letter, and Wolfensohn replied somewhat touchily: "I am surprised by the preliminary and cursory nature of your comments. . . . The Bank and IFC have been instrumental in ensuring transparent utilization of revenues flowing to the Government of Chad. . . ."[3]

Over the next year the EIR held numerous consultations with industry, affected communities and community groups, indigenous peoples' organizations, labor unions, academics, international organizations, and Bank staff. It visited project sites, conducted regional workshops in several developing countries, and commissioned studies. In January 2004 Emil Salim delivered the final EIR report to Wolfensohn.[4]

It was a pathbreaking document that once again put the Bank in an uncomfortable position, since a number of its recommendations would indeed require radical changes.[5] The EIR reiterated damning conclusions about the alleged benefits of extractive-industry investment in developing nations. It noted that from 1990 to 1999, dependence on these industries actually impaired economic growth for *all WBG borrower countries*.[6] EIR research in Peru, Indonesia, and Tanzania revealed that revenue often failed to reach affected communities, and the projects exacerbated social conflict. Widespread environmental despoilment from contaminated air and polluted rivers was responsible for ruined grazing grounds and felled forests, worsened poverty, and a host of health problems. In other words, the resource curse was alive and well. The stated goal of poverty reduction was almost entirely a fiction.[7]

Yet the EIR recommendations began with a finding that should have pleased the conservative elements of Bank management: yes, the World Bank Group should stay involved in financing extractive industries, but only under conditions that would allow it to "contribute to poverty alleviation through sustainable development."[8]

First, and most important, finance should be based on a "sequenced" approach: fundamental governance structures had to be in place first. Minimum conditions included basic rule of law; the absence of armed conflict or of even a high risk of armed conflict; and respect for labor standards, human rights, and indigenous peoples.[9]

Second, the Bank Group had to both improve and better implement its safeguard policies. For example, the (conservation of) Natural Habitats Policy should be strengthened in order to identify categories of "no-go" zones for mining, oil, and gas development, such as officially protected areas.[10]

Third, the Bank Group needed to address human rights head on. It should set up a central Human Rights Unit with regional counterparts (analogous to the organizational structure established for environmental issues in the late 1980s), which would develop an institution-wide policy. The unit would ensure that the Bank and its clients complied with international law, including previously ignored basic labor standards such as the right to collective bargaining.[11] And the Bank should finally insist that every project obtain Free Prior Informed Consent (FPIC) from indigenous communities before extractive industry investments proceeded.

Fourth, none of the policy changes the EIR recommended would amount to much unless the Bank finally changed its internal culture and incentives: "Instead of putting an emphasis on quantitative lending targets, staff should be rewarded for contributions to ensuring compliance with Safeguard Policies and maximizing poverty-alleviation impacts."[12] For well over a decade, this point had been repeated by reformers both inside and outside the institution: would Bank management ever listen?

Finally, the Bank had to reorient its energy priorities to reflect the singular threat that climate change posed to the poor in developing nations. It should help countries eliminate subsidies for fossil-fuel consumption, continue what was already a de facto moratorium on lending for coal mining, and phase out all investment in oil development by 2008. Bank support for fossil-fuel energy amounted to 94 percent of its energy portfolio, and renewables only 6 percent. The Bank should commit immediately to increasing its lending for renewables by 20 percent a year.[13]

Thus, the EIR eloquently addressed key elements of sustainable investment in the developing world—indeed, in the world at large. The issue of extractive industries highlighted the challenges in a particularly stark fashion, and at the core of these challenges was governance, including transparency and community acceptance—the so-called social license to operate. The need to phase out support for fossil fuels was an increasingly urgent issue. And the Bank could not play a truly constructive role until it changed its "loan approval culture."

In the first months of 2004 the Bank was swamped by letters arguing for and against the EIR reforms. African mining companies, the governments of a number of developing countries, and private international banks all weighed in against the EIR. In particular, 16 of the Equator Principle banks, including Citigroup, ABN Amro, and Barclay's, wrote the Bank urging it to reject key EIR proposals such as the phase-out of oil and coal finance, and the insistence on basic governance before handing out loans for extraction projects. (The banks did support, however, increased transparency concerning extractive-industry revenues.)[14]

The EIR's proponents were just as vocal. Six Nobel Peace Prize Laureates, including Archbishop Desmond Tutu, wrote Wolfensohn urging the adoption of all the EIR proposals. Seventeen major U.S. ethical-investment funds weighed in, emphasizing that the reforms would strengthen "our voice as shareholder advocates." There were dozens of letters of support

from legislators from 15 different nations, including the United States and
the United Kingdom, Japan and Morocco, Brazil and Bolivia. The European Parliament passed a resolution urging the adoption of the EIR's
recommendations.[15]

Bank management's response was mixed.[16] It adopted some of the recommendations, committing, for example, to increase renewable energy
lending by 20 percent a year and recognizing the principle of no-go zones
of critical biodiversity. But it strongly rejected phasing out support for oil
and coal, based on the rationale that they would "inevitably continue to
be major fuel sources for the world's poorest peoples for the foreseeable
future."[17] This was a disingenuous argument, given that oil development
investments tended to subsidize production for export, as in the case of
Chad-Cameroon; indeed, many of the Bank's large-scale coal-energy projects provided electricity to fuel urban and industrial growth rather than to
benefit the rural poor.

Management rejected any requirement for Free Prior Informed Consent, arguing that it could be interpreted as giving communities a "veto
power" over proposed investments. Instead it proposed "free, prior, informed *consultation*."[18] Indigenous-rights advocates were not happy with
this formulation; it seemed to only promise that communities would be
informed about what would happen to them but would have little real say
in the outcome.

On the most important recommendation, putting governance first, the
response was vague, indeed evasive: there was no specific commitment to
minimal standards of the rule of law and respect for human rights. Instead,
"where we make judgments in favor of involvement we will disclose our
rationale," and "for significant projects we will require risks be mitigated."[19]
It was an affirmation of business as usual, on, at best, the Chad-Cameroon
project model, i.e., continuing in risky cases to concurrently finance major
extractive projects while trying to build up governance capacity.

There would be no human rights unit nor Bank-wide human rights
policy, since "the World Bank draws on the values of human rights in all
its work." Concerning changing staff incentives, management maintained
that most Bank employees "do not work in posts where quantitative financing targets are relevant."[20] No, the internal culture did not need changing—
and it wasn't going to change.

The Bank framed all these decisions as part of the effort to grow economies and alleviate poverty. Magically, as in a fairy tale, the resource curse was
lifted. Yet the Bank wasn't acting in isolation, but in line with many of its

constituents: most developing-country governments, particularly those with extractive resources; mining and oil companies that were partners and clients for the IFC; and major international banks, even those that had shown leadership in adopting the Bank's safeguard policies in the Equator Principles.

Marlin

In the aftermath of the EIR, the World Bank's extractive projects showed little improvement. Rather than becoming more selective, the Bank Group actually increased its lending for risky investments. There is some evidence of slightly more attention to environmental concerns, but on the ground, the projects remained an international scandal. Disastrous cases proliferated, from logging in the Congo to mining in Ghana—but one, a mine in Guatemala, stands out.

Six months after the release of the EIR final report, the IFC lent $45 million to support the development of the Marlin gold mine in Guatemala by a Canadian mining company, Goldcorp. Over 95 percent of the population in the area surrounding the mine were indigenous Mayans. Local groups together with the Catholic Church opposed the project, which in its first phase either displaced or damaged the livelihoods of nearly 10,000 people. Protestors blockaded the mine, and in January 2005 the Guatemalan government occupied the area with 700 troops, resulting in one death and several wounded.[21] The local people's fear had to be understood in the context of the decades-long Guatemalan civil war, in which the military killed nearly two hundred thousand of the indigenous population, with massacres in 626 Mayan villages.[22]

In September 2005 the IFC's compliance advisor/ombudsman (CAO) found systematic failures in the IFC's due diligence in the project at large. The IFC didn't assess adequately whether the environmental management plan would be completed and carried out. It failed to take into account major social and political risks: the project was embedded in a pervasive climate of mistrust, conflict, violence, and intimidation, including death threats to opponents of the mine, the presence of the military at the mine, and overflights by military helicopters and reconnaissance planes.[23] Despite these findings, the CAO at first took a curiously upbeat perspective, simply encouraging the company and local communities to talk together more. After a follow-up visit in 2006, the ombudsman's office became aware that the social and political culture of violence and mistrust was even greater than it had originally judged, and it concluded that the conditions did not exist at the time for a dialogue among the communities, the mining company, and the government. The one thing that everyone did agree on was that "the Government of Guatemala does not have sufficient capacity to supervise and regulate the impacts of the mine."[24] Later that year Goldcorp repaid the entire IFC loan, thus making the CAO's belated revelations, as far as the World Bank Group was concerned, irrelevant.

Around the same time, an Italian specialist working with a local NGO conducted a hydrological study that found that heavy metals from the mine had already exceeded World Bank specifications. The pollution threatened one of the main water sources for the indigenous population in the region. The Italian researcher received death threats, his case was taken up by Amnesty International, and he finally had to flee Guatemala.[25]

For the next five years, allegations of pollution, violence, and human rights abuses continued. In 2010, 12,000 people demonstrated against the mine in the nearby city of Huehuetenango. The United Nations International Labor Organization called for suspension of the mining operations because of the lack of adequate consultation and approval by the indigenous population, as did the United Nations Special Rapporteur on the Human Rights of Indigenous Peoples.[26]

By the next year, Marlin had distinguished itself as one of the most widely condemned extractive investments on the planet, mobilizing not just the Catholic Church, but such peaceful souls as the Canadian Central Mennonite Committee and the Unitarian-Universalists.[27] The abuses spurred over a dozen film exposés, as well as a number of international studies of the contamination and health threats.[28] Researchers from the University of Ghent in Belgium, commissioned by the Catholic Church in Guatemala, found levels of arsenic in the groundwater used by local communities 26 times higher than allowed for by World Health Organization standards.[29] Another Catholic Church study, this time conducted by the University of Michigan School of Public Health, found alarmingly high levels of mercury, copper, arsenic, and zinc in the urine of people living near or downstream from the mine, as well as elevated blood levels of aluminum, manganese, and cobalt.[30] All of this and more had been missed by the IFC's environmental due diligence.

Even Goldcorp, under pressure from a shareholder resolution, commissioned a human rights assessment. The Goldcorp study belatedly found that the consultation in advance of the project had been seriously inadequate, a situation that was compounded by major gaps in the social and environmental assessments. The mining company study admitted that the Guatemalan government was not prepared for such a project.[31] Much more

should have been done to strengthen the government's capacities and institutions, ideally before the mining operations began.

One could hardly find a better example to vindicate the recommendations of the Extractive Industries Review report, particularly the one concerning "governance first."

Yet despite devastating cases like Marlin, the Bank Group continued to
argue that extractive projects were better with its support than without. Its
safeguard policies and commitment to poverty alleviation provided some
level of protection; comparable projects not funded by the Bank often had
even worse environmental and social records. There was some truth in this
assertion, albeit a half-truth. Certainly IFC-supported projects were supposed to conform to higher standards, and these did receive more international attention. In the Marlin case there is evidence that Goldcorp did
undertake more comprehensive environmental and social assessments than
it might otherwise have done because of IFC involvement—but these assessments were nevertheless grossly deficient in critical areas.

There was also some local support for the mine: it did employ people
from the surrounding area—according to Goldcorp over 60 percent of the
mine workers were from neighboring communities; some roads were improved; and there was some local improvement in educational infrastructure.[32] Marlin became the government's largest single taxpayer, though this
was not the unadulterated contribution it might appear, since a majority of
the population mistrusted the government.

In the final analysis, though, the IFC had helped finance, and had given
a stamp of approval to, a project that became internationally notorious for
human rights abuses and environmental negligence. The IFC seemed to
have an uncanny gift for finding and financing extractive projects that had
especially destructive ecological and social impacts. The Marlin project was
embedded in legacies of social and political conflict, and in fact it fueled this
conflict. It was a situation that required extraordinary attention to social
and environmental assessment, to risk mitigation, and above all to required
capacity and prior institution building in the Guatemalan government.
None of this took place. One would have thought that the IFC would have
better foreseen the risks, given the growing history of human rights and
environmental controversies in its mining projects, as well as the findings
of the Extractive Industries Review. But it appeared to make the same mistakes, to consistently and systematically underestimate the social, political,
and environmental threats, and to fail to ensure that its safeguard policies
were adequately carried out.

Whom to Blame

Unfortunately, there was a proliferation of other cases, each of them demonstrating the just how right the EIR analysis had been, and how in practice the Bank and IFC had difficulty following even their existing procedures. Besides promoting expanded, "sustainable" logging in the Democratic Republic of the Congo, the Bank Group also financed expanded mining beginning in the early 2000s, both through the Bank's non-project policy loans and IFC/MIGA equity investments and guarantees. Along with increased export production, the ostensible goals were to promote privatization and to improve governance and management in the mining sector. The results were not promising. In late 2006 internal Bank documents leaked to the *Financial Times* revealed that as the Bank increased support for increased mining, three multinational mining companies took over 75 percent of the mineral assets, worth billions of dollars, from Gécamines, the Congolese state mining company, in a totally untransparent, corrupt fire-sale deal with the government. Bank staff warned the Congo country director that the institution could be seen in the role of "perceived complicity and/or tacit approval" of the deals.[33]

"Blame the Congolese government," wrote author John le Carré and Jason Stearn of the International Crisis Group; "but also blame the international officials who were fully aware of the deals when they were struck. The World Bank may not control Congo's mining sector, but it has invested millions in resurrecting the industry, and it regularly meets with government officials and advises them on how best to run it. . . . Who were the [World Bank] document's authors talking to, if not themselves?"[34] It was as trenchant a statement as any of the Bank's role: yes, weak and corrupt governments often bore a prime responsibility, but time and time again the Bank was an enabler and accomplice. The pressure to move money, the imperative to be a player whatever the risks, reinforced institutional self-deception, a willful amnesia of lessons painfully learned and reiterated in countless internal and external studies, of which the EIR was only the most recent and incisive.

The IFC went on an extractives roll: it increased its lending and investment in extractive industries by 50 percent in 2006 and in 2007 announced it would double its lending and investments in mining in Sub-Saharan Africa.[35] In 2006 it approved some $280 million to subsidize three new mining projects in Sub-Saharan Africa alone: $5 million for an ore facility in Guinea, $150 million for a platinum mine in South Africa, and $125 million for still another operation of Newmont Mining, this time in Ghana, despite Newmont's controversial record in Peru.[36]

The Newmont Ghana Ahafo mine was an open-pit, cyanide-processing operation in the midst of the country's key agricultural region. The mine physically and economically displaced nearly 10,000 subsistence farmers, threatened contamination of water supplies, and operated within a protected forest reserve.[37] Before the loan was approved, more than 1,200 inhabitants of communities to be affected by the mine presented a petition to the Bank/IFC executive directors calling for measures to rectify these risks, but their plea was ignored.[38] Shortly before IFC Board approval of the Ahafo loan, a U.S. Environmental Protection Agency report blasted the IFC-required Newmont environmental assessment, stating that it did not meet either international or U.S. testing standards and that it lacked proper monitoring measures at mine waste disposal sites. As a result of the concerns of civil-society organizations and the EPA, the United States abstained from approving the IFC loan, though of course this did not in practice prevent the project from going forward.[39]

In October 2009, a major cyanide spill occurred at the mine, contaminating water supplies and resulting in a fish kill; the Ghanaian government demanded $5 million in compensation.[40] In 2010 civil-society groups in Ghana called for a government investigation of 15 deaths that had taken place in connection with the mine's operations. They cited continued environmental and human rights violations, and demanded that the mine comply with the IFC's performance standards on health and safety.[41] In 2011 WikiLeaks released cables from the U.S. embassy in Ghana that accused Newmont of a cover-up in the 2009 spill, and of using unsafe procedures that violated international mining standards.[42]

And Yet . . .

Yet the Bank's argument that projects of a similar nature without Bank Group support often showed even worse environmental and social performance was not untrue, but this simply begged more important questions about what kinds of development projects the Bank should support. Two University of Ghana law professors conducted a comparative study of the IFC-Newmont Ahafo project and of another Ghanaian gold mine, the AngloGold Ashanti Obuasi project. Commercial bank loans and equity financed AngloGold's investment. They concluded that IFC involvement did indeed result in the Ahafo project being subject to higher, "and probably preferable" standards of environmental, social, transparency, and human rights compliance. But they concluded with a critical caveat: "Whether this form of PF [project finance] . . . generates better compliance is still questionable."[43]

The more important question was whether not just extractive industry finance, but much of the IFC's subsidization of large, multinational corporate investments in developing countries was a good or optimal use of scarce public international finance that was supposed to alleviate poverty in an environmentally sustainable way. The unsoundness of such an approach was particularly true in cases like Chad-Cameroon and Kyrgyzstan Kumtor (see chapter 5), where the projects would not have proceeded without Bank support. Subsequent studies of the IFC portfolio by the Bank's Independent Evaluation Group (IEG) would call into question the poverty benefits and development "value added" of the entire IFC portfolio—an issue we will discuss in greater detail in chapter 10.

The Mallaby Effect and the Cost of Doing Business

In the autumn of 2004 a remarkable article appeared in *Foreign Policy*, one of the leading foreign affairs journals in the United States. Written by Sebastian Mallaby, an Englishman working at the *Washington Post*, "NGOs: Fighting Poverty, Hurting the Poor" in parts was redolent of Rupert Murdoch– or Rush Limbaugh–style journalism, albeit with a more sophisticated patina. "A swarm of media-savvy Western activists has descended upon aid agencies, staging protests to block projects that allegedly exploit the developing world. The protests serve professional agitators by keeping their pet causes in the headlines," but hurt the poor "who live without clean water or electricity." What was the motivation of the agitators? "If they stop denouncing big organizations, no one will send them cash."[44]

The threats posed by the professional troublemakers were no doubt underappreciated by most *Foreign Policy* readers: "Time after time the Western public raised on stories of World Bank white elephants believe them. Lawmakers in European Parliaments and the U.S. Congress accept NGO arguments at face value, and the government officials who sit on the World Bank's Board respond by blocking funding for deserving projects."[45] NGO criticism of World Bank projects was one of the most successful conspiracies in modern times: somehow a Bolshevik-like cohort of Lilliputian nongovernmental groups, motivated by publicity and personal gain, had managed to hoodwink not only the public and parliaments of the entire Western world, but the executive directors of the World Bank and the finance ministries to whom they report.

The reaction against Bank environmental and social safeguard policies, and indeed even against Wolfensohn's anti-corruption efforts, had found an eloquent outside spokesman, indeed a champion. Some staff and officials within the Bank, as well as among executive directors from some major borrowing countries, cited Mallaby's writings to justify weakening the Bank's environmental and social safeguard policies and to dismiss concerns of civil-society groups.[46] The "Mallaby effect" spread to other institutions, such as the Inter-American Development Bank, where some officials invoked his arguments to counter an attempted revision and updating of the IDB's environmental policy—a policy which had not changed since 1978.

The *Foreign Policy* article was based on Mallaby's provocative new book on the Bank's Wolfensohn years: *The World's Banker*.[47] The book itself was in part a well-written and engaging account of Wolfensohn's oversized, mercurial personality and his energetic efforts to revamp the Bank. Some of the assertions were credible and already widely acknowledged by observers of the Bank—the institution was trying to do too many things simultaneously, and James Wolfensohn's management style, while well-intentioned, too often exacerbated this "goal congestion" and "mission creep."[48] But the essence of Mallaby's argument, repeated in numerous public appearances in late 2004 and 2005, was that development was being hindered by *too much accountability* to the World Bank's "oppressive" board of executive directors and, worse, by "social, environmental, and anticorruption safeguards [that] require all manner of time-consuming precautions." The Bank must "*face down* the activists who have forced the bank to adopt [these] excessive rules . . ." (emphasis added).[49]

It was a bizarre thesis, not just because of the presumed Svengali-like ability of NGOs to "force" the executive directors on the Bank's board to adopt counterproductive policies, but also because in the Bank's entire 60-year history up to 2004 (in fact 68 years through 2012), the board had never formally turned down a loan. In just a handful of cases the United States and some donor countries had abstained from approving projects to register concerns, but the projects always went through with a majority of Bank directors' voting shares.

Mallaby not only ignored this basic fact, but grossly exaggerated the costs of the safeguards to both borrowing countries and the Bank itself. In one of the few studies or documents referenced in his work, he mis-cited a 2001 Bank paper on "The Cost of Doing Business," claiming that safeguard policies inflated costs by $200–300 million annually.[50] In reality, the additional annual costs for borrowing countries of doing business with the Bank (additional, since "all borrowers incur costs for public procurement, financial reporting, and safeguards work even if no Bank financing is involved") to comply with the safeguards and fiduciary requirements for borrowers was $71 to $129 million annually.[51] Of this, the yearly incremental costs to all the Bank's borrowing countries for dealing with all the Bank's environmental and social safeguards was only between $17.8 million and $26.3 million.[52] Financial audits and reporting, as well as procurement procedures—necessary to prevent corruption and to comply with the Bank's charter, which required it to ensure that the funds it lent were used for the purposes intended—were between three-quarters and four-fifths of the total costs. Given the mixed performance of Bank projects in the environmental and social arena, as documented in countless OED and IEG reports, one could argue that, on the contrary, more investment was particularly needed in safeguard policies and implementation.

The attack on the cost of anti-corruption measures was particularly ill informed. Earlier, in May and July 2004, the U.S. Senate Foreign Relations Committee held widely publicized hearings on corruption of World Bank and other MDB lending; according to then Foreign Relations Committee chairman Richard Lugar (Republican from Indiana), evidence presented in the hearings indicated that between 5 and 25 percent of annual World Bank lending was being illegally diverted from its intended purposes—as much as $100 billion or more had been stolen over the past several decades.[53] Here too, whatever the Bank was spending on anti-corruption, if anything, was not enough.

Mallaby condemned the guidelines of the World Commission on Dams as "appalling," as well as the Extractive Industries Review. "Thankfully," he wrote, "the Bank's management rejected the Commission's [he was referring to the EIR] recommendation" that the Bank pull out of lending for coal and oil, since the developing world's need for energy "has to be satisfied somehow."[54]

Most revealingly, in his book and articles Mallaby tried to make his case by highlighting three Bank operations which were supposed to be examples of the kinds of "deserving projects" that the professional agitators were succeeding in blocking or delaying: the Uganda Bujagali hydroelectric dam, the China Western Poverty Alleviation (Qinghai) Project, and the Chad-Cameroon Oil Development and Pipeline Project. He described Bujagali as a worthy project that was somehow being delayed or blocked by the

Berkeley, California–based International Rivers Network, which had raised concerns about environmental and social impacts. "This story is a tragedy for Uganda," he wrote. "Clinics and factories are being deprived of electricity by Californians whose idea of an electricity crisis is a handful of summer blackouts. But it is also a tragedy for the fight against poverty worldwide, because projects in dozens of countries are similarly held up for fear of activist resistance."[55] The collapse of the project, of course, had nothing to do with NGOs, and everything to do with governments and companies withdrawing in the face of revelations of corruption on the part of the company the Bank was supporting, AES. AES itself withdrew when it financially imploded into near bankruptcy in the wake of California and U.S. government investigations of its complicity with Enron in manipulating California energy prices. Ironically, there was indeed a connection between the California summer blackouts and Bujagali: AES machinations were involved in both.

Mallaby repeatedly claimed that criticisms of the proposed World Bank project to support the resettlement of nearly 60,000 mainly ethnic Han Chinese into a traditionally Tibetan region in Qinghai Province China "had no basis in fact whatsoever" and "were flat wrong on the facts,"[56] and had been made "on the basis of no evidence."[57] Since the Bank's Independent Inspection Panel found major violations of seven of the ten key Bank social and environmental safeguard policies, he attacked the panel and its head, James MacNeil, a distinguished 76-year-old (in 2004) former Canadian ambassador and an official of both the United Nations and the OECD. MacNeil sent a withering rebuttal to Foreign Policy, castigating Mallaby's "shoddy research and unremitting failure to get his facts straight."[58]

The World's Banker cited Chad-Cameroon as exactly the kind of high-risk/high-reward project the Bank should promote—again the logic being for a desperately poor country like Chad it was the only hope, and the risks had to be taken. When the executive board approved the loans for Chad-Cameroon, "the Bank had shown that, with some help from the might and muscle of an oil company it could stand up to its critics; it could defy the Rainforesters [sic—he was referring to the Rainforest Action Network] and the Environmental Defense Fund and all the other antis, and it could do so despite the rising tide of antiglobalization protests."[59] The bullied, beleaguered World Bank, heroically allied with the world's largest oil company, could finally defy the Rainforest Action Network and the Environmental Defense Fund and their ilk.

Backwards into the Future

Mallaby crystallized the backlash against the safeguard policies and Wolfensohn's reforms in general, but he was far from alone. By the summer of 2005, when Wolfensohn left the Bank after two full terms, his tenure had become a source of debate and controversy. Only Robert McNamara had influenced the institution more, and no one could doubt the sincerity, indeed what appeared to many the idealism, of Wolfensohn's intentions. But during his second term in the 2000s, Bank insiders pushed to revert to business as usual and weaken or ignore the safeguard policies and the independent inspection functions. And they were relatively successful—why?

Part of the explanation lies in the McKinsey-led reforms, which, in the words of one former Bank professional (who after 14 years inside the Bank left and wrote a scathing book on the Wolfensohn reorganization), were not only "deplorable," but a "debacle."[60] The whole approach was an unintentional parody of every business-school and consulting-company fad that had also failed in many mainstream American corporations and larger nonprofit organizations: "The *redefinition of objectives* toward the *knowledge bank*, the *matrix*, the *networks*, the *internal market* . . . the *decentralization*, the *budget cuts*, the *redundancies*, the *skill mix restructuring* . . . the *new information system* . . ." (emphasis added)[61] resulted in a situation where, by 2001,

> top management lacking in institutional knowledge reported to a CEO uninterested in operational results who reported to a board lacking in both experience and inside knowledge, which was in turn under the oversight of governors who were not able to pay attention.[62]

The net result was to empower the die-hard old guard in the Bank who wanted to turn the clock back. The way to deny much of the experience and knowledge the Bank had acquired, too often at the cost of the people it was supposed to help, was to reframe marching backwards into the future as "high-risk/high-reward." In the immediate years after Wolfensohn's departure, the IEG found that "matrix management" and the pooling of staff in the "networks" actually "impeded interaction among staff across sectors," with the result that the work and analysis of staff in one part of the Bank with relevant experience or knowledge was often ignored in the preparation of loans in a different sector.[63] What this could mean in practice was that the knowledge and expertise of the central environment department was increasingly ignored in the preparation of many new loans.

Outside criticism did not go away, the "Mallaby effect" notwithstanding. Although the Wolfensohn reorganization resulted in some internal budget cuts and redundancies, one area that expanded greatly in his tenure was public and external relations, which he elevated into a vice-presidency.

There was one more trend in Bank lending that would gather momentum both during Wolfensohn's tenure and following his departure: the increasing proportion of Bank loans that went to general support of governments rather than to specific projects, so-called structural adjustment and development policy loans. These loans flew in the face of the Bank's charter, which explicitly required it to lend for specific projects, "except in special circumstances."[64]

The prohibition was a response to practices in the 1920s and 1930s when such lending by private banks had led to government defaults and massive misuse of funds. In the Bank's first years, everyone involved agreed that such mistakes had to be avoided. In the Bank's internal newsletter of June 1951, the fifth anniversary of the Bank's first loan, Kyriakos Varvaressos, a founding executive director, who had represented Egypt, Ethiopia, Iran, Iraq, and Greece (i.e., developing-country borrowers), wrote the following:

> Very often countries defaulted because they over-borrowed or because they had misused the funds borrowed and had derived no benefit from them. . . . To avoid the wasteful utilization of foreign loans which had been frequent in the past the Bank was enjoined to lend only for the financing of specific projects and to exercise close supervision of the funds it lent.[65]

But that term *special circumstances* opened a loophole, and in the 1980s, non-project, adjustment lending began in order to alleviate the Latin American debt crises. It soon became a standard feature in Bank operations since it both permitted the Bank to promote (some would say impose) neoliberal reform measures for entire economies—privatization, reduction of government expenditures, opening up sectors for foreign investment—and was also a godsend to ambitious staff wanting to build up impressive country-lending portfolios. Such loans required much less preparation and supervision per dollar lent then conventional project finance.

The Bank's safeguard policies did not apply to adjustment and development policy operations, even though these might in fact finance a whole series of specific projects such as dams or coal plants. There was an internal Bank policy guiding this lending, but its environmental and social due diligence requirements were minimal in comparison with the safeguards (see chapter 5).[66] Since the safeguard policies did not apply, the inspection panel was for the most part out of the picture, too. During Wolfensohn's second term, non-project lending for the IBRD and IDA averaged around a third of all Bank loan commitments; in 2002 it was fully half of all lending.[67]

The IFC followed a similar pattern, lending more and more for general support of banks and other financial institutions that in turn would lend for specific investment projects. These so-called financial intermediary loans averaged more than a third of IFC lending during Wolfensohn's second term. IFC policy only required an examination of the environmental management capacity of the financial institutions that these loans funded; the institutions themselves were not subject to the IFC's environmental safeguards and performance standards, nor was their performance for the specific investment projects they supported accountable to the CAO.[68]

The hard-won lessons about the risks of such non-project lending that so preoccupied the founders of the Bank had been forgotten.

The return to lending for big, environmentally and socially risky infrastructure and extractive projects, as well as the increase in non-project lending, had one other major risk, the full extent of which was only becoming more and more apparent: massive, pervasive corruption. It was an issue that the incoming new president of the Bank, Paul Wolfowitz, was all too aware of—he had been the U.S. ambassador to Indonesia in the late 1980s when the Suharto family corruption machine was in its heyday.

Coda on the Wolfensohn Era: The Smile on a Child's Face

The Wolfensohn era was plagued with contradictions largely because reforms ran afoul of the wishes of the Bank's real clients: namely, borrowing governments, or more exactly, particular constituencies within those governments, whose principal interest was to receive as much money with as few restrictions as possible, as quickly as possible. As the role of the IFC and MIGA increased, as well as the use of IBRD and IDA funds to guarantee or promote private investment, large companies also became a growing constituency, and they also had a major interest in profiting from the World Bank Group's financial support and quality stamp of approval with as few conditions as possible.

On one level, this reaction reflected simply the fundamental interest of any borrower. Most ordinary people, for example, would rather not take out a loan from a local bank that required them to provide quarterly reports on their expenditures or to manage their household according to certain environmental rules. But of course borrowers do not get everything they might want. At least in the past, private banks would investigate a borrower's credit, assets, debts, job security, and salary, etc., before giving larger loans—a due diligence which evaporated in the first decade of the 2000s. Of course, in the United States the resulting lending frenzy led to a housing bubble that ended in the near collapse of the international financial system.

But the World Bank is a public institution whose loans are supported by the taxpayers of the richer countries; it supposedly offers financial support for agreed upon public international purposes. A visitor to its headquarters during the Wolfensohn era would be greeted in the main lobby by large banners proclaiming: "Our Dream Is a World Without Poverty." The donor governments increasingly entrusted additional resources to the Bank to address so-called global public goods—fighting climate change, financing public health initiatives, etc. Japan set up a major Bank-administered trust fund to provide extra money to help borrowing countries prepare environmental assessments. When the Bank went to its donors for increased financing, it emphasized both its role in helping the poor and the environment, and also its supposed reliability in managing funds rigorously to ensure they were not stolen.

Near the beginning of his tenure, in the famous, or infamous, March 12, 1996, session between Wolfensohn and 300 senior managers, a Bank manager identified the fundamental contradiction in the entire internal "cultural change" that Wolfensohn announced he would promote:

> Mr. President, the second-most recurrent theme in your appeals, after today's theme of cynicism and lack of trust [of Bank staff vis-à-vis management], is client responsiveness, which can be rephrased as "Why can't we be more like merchant banks, which are quick in providing what their customers ask. . . . We keep assuming the client is the government. . . . [But] we can't have our cake and eat it too. We have to make a choice. *Either we treat our governments as clients and we behave like merchant banks, in which case we owe it—again, to ourselves, in the first place, and to our counterparts, second—to stop talking about the environment, about women in development, about poverty alleviation, and so on, as priorities.* . . . If the government is not our client . . . [then] the client is the people of the countries we work with, and the governments are agencies, instruments, with whom we work to meet our clients' needs.[69] (emphasis added)

Wolfensohn did not have a coherent rejoinder, because the contradiction is real, and in some cases perhaps insurmountable:

I, obviously, have perceived the task of moving from investment banking to development banking in a too-simplistic fashion. . . . There are no generalizations about governments and their relationships with people. . . . We have a legal client that is the government. . . . By law the Bank can lend only to governments. . . . We're ultimately serving the people. Ultimately. But our instrument is to work with government. . . . So it is a process of persuasion, of discussion, of cajoling, of advice and, in some cases, agreeing not to agree and doing no lending . . . to help a government and not help the people is not going to come through, in terms of economic stability, political stability, social stability. . . . And I still go back, as I said before . . . I judge our effectiveness by the smile on the child's face in the village. I would extend it to the mother.[70]

CHAPTER SEVEN

The Brief, Broken Presidency
of Paul Wolfowitz

A S SPRING CAME TO Washington in 2005, the World Bank once again was a cynosure of controversy, indeed outrage. The outrage was directed not at the Bank per se, but at U.S. President George W. Bush's nominee to replace James Wolfensohn, none other than Deputy Secretary of Defense Paul Wolfowitz, a major architect of the Iraq war. It was, according to the London-based World Development Movement, a "truly terrifying appointment."[1] Some 1,650 NGOs around the world protested the nomination, and internal polls of Bank employees found 90 percent opposed to the prospect of Wolfowitz as their new boss.[2] Wolfowitz seemed to personify the unilateral arrogance of the George W. Bush administration; among other things, under his aegis the U.S. Defense Department had banned countries that opposed the Iraq war (many of them U.S. allies) from bidding for contracts for Iraqi reconstruction.[3] Nobel economics laureate Joseph Stiglitz, who had served under Wolfensohn as the Bank's chief economist, feared that the Wolfowitz appointment would again make the Bank a "hated organization," and potentially lead to "street violence and demonstrations" against its policies.[4]

Few were willing to admit that Wolfowitz was arguably more qualified to lead the Bank than his predecessors, all of whom also had little or no professional background in international development. The Bank's first president, Eugene Meyer, had been the publisher of the *Washington Post*; many of his successors, including James Wolfensohn, had been Wall Street bankers. One, Barber Conable, was a Republican congressman from upstate New York who had chaired the House Ways and Means Committee; he was chosen to head the Bank during the Reagan Administration for one reason only: to cajole a recalcitrant U.S. Congress to approve World Bank funding replenishments. And of course Wolfowitz was not even the first high-ranking U.S. Defense Department official who went from managing a controversial war to head the Bank, though the Iraq fiasco was a small-scale affair compared to Robert McNamara's Vietnam.

Unlike all his predecessors, Wolfowitz had actually lived in a developing country, Indonesia, for an extended period of time: three years while he was U.S. ambassador there. Critics argued that he could have done more to speak out against human rights abuses and corruption during his time in Jakarta, but in this respect he was no different from any of the other envoys from major countries to the Suharto regime. In fact, he was remembered as one of the more competent of all Western representatives, and he also had an understanding of, and liking for, the country's moderate Muslim culture. He was the only World Bank president who spoke fluently a non-Western, developing-country language—Bahasa Indonesia. Also unlike his predecessors, Wolfowitz did have credible academic familiarity with development issues, since he had been the dean of the Johns Hopkins University School of Advanced International Affairs, a graduate institution that was a feeder school for positions in the Bank and other international-development institutions.

Over the course of his first year in office, Wolfowitz gradually made anti-corruption the hallmark of his administration, halting loan disbursements for projects in several countries, including politically powerful borrowers such as India and Argentina.[5] James Wolfensohn had broken the Bank taboo on even mentioning the "C word" (Corruption), creating an internal anti-corruption unit and flagging the issue in numerous speeches. But in reality, Wolfensohn's Bank had not gotten tough with borrowing governments that were flagrantly stealing from Bank loans, nor did it stop doing business with large multinational corporations that were bribing governments to secure Bank contracts. Instead, the operational heart of the Bank's anti-corruption strategy was to lend still more money to corrupt governments for programs to improve governance.

The $100 Billion Bank Heist

The corruption attracted attention on Capitol Hill. Beginning in 2004, as we noted in the previous chapter, an unprecedented series of hearings in the U.S. Senate Foreign Relations Committee revealed the gravity of the problem, James Wolfensohn's reforms notwithstanding. The hearings continued through Wolfowitz's tenure.

At the first hearing, on May 14, 2004, Northwestern University political science professor Jeffrey Winters testified that 20 to 30 percent of World

Bank loans, roughly $100 billion, had been stolen by borrowing-country officials and contractors. The World Bank issued an angry denial, but there was very credible evidence for the allegations. Foreign Relations Committee staff had interviewed a number of former World Bank professionals, including Steve Berkman, who had been a project director for over 100 World Bank loans, and had served as one of the Bank's chief anti-corruption investigators between 1998 and 2002. Among his firsthand observations was that the Bank's Nigeria country team already in the 1990s estimated that fraud on Bank projects in that country was as much as 40 percent.[6] Theft on this scale had already been suggested by Bank officials internally in the leaked Indonesia corruption memos of the late 1990s.[7]

The committee inquired about specific cases of corruption, including Bank lending to Cambodia (where corruption in the forestry sector was endemic) and Bank support for the Yacyretá Dam on the Argentina-Paraguay border, where even in 2004 project costs had escalated from $2 billion to over $10 billion.[8] In July 2004 a separate hearing delved into a massive Bank-financed water project in the Southern African country of Lesotho.

The Lesotho Highlands Water Project (LHWP) was a prime example of how large infrastructure projects seem to invite fraud—and a test case of how serious the Bank was about preventing it. The project dated back to the apartheid era, when the South African regime proposed the construction of five large dams in its mountainous neighbor (completely surrounded by South African territory), for the purpose of supplying water to South Africa's richest industrial areas, including Johannesburg and Pretoria. The World Bank helped to finance the project, and its involvement attracted lending from the African Development Bank, the European Union, and several export credit agencies and private international commercial banks. Total costs for the first phase were about $3.6 billion.

From the beginning, Lesotho—where the poorest rural people earned less than two dollars a day, the average life expectancy was 36, and the HIV-positive rate was 30 percent—got the short end of the bargain. During construction, workers rioted for better wages, and police opened fire, killing five. Resettlement plans were poorly carried out, leaving many of the 27,000 people affected by the project dispossessed. Thousands of hectares of farm and grazing land were lost, adding to an already ecologically stressed situation in a country where only 9 percent of the land was arable. A 1999 World Bank–commissioned study concluded that the complete project would result in Lesotho's rivers losing 90 percent of their water, reducing the arid country's river systems to "something akin to waste-water drains" with risks of increased pollution and public health threats for an estimated 150,000 people living downstream.[9] The only benefit to Lesotho's government was $40 million per year in sales of water to South Africa, while the financial stakes for the multinational contractors totaled in the billions.

Starting in the mid-1990s, investigations by the Lesotho government revealed that the chief executive of the project authority had received millions of dollars in pay-offs from companies in leading industrialized countries. The head of the authority was convicted of bribery and sentenced to 15 years in jail. In 2002 the Lesotho High Court handed down bribery convictions for two of the companies that had procurement contracts from the World Bank loans: Acres International, a leading Canadian engineering firm, and Lahmeyer International, a major German Firm. In 2004 a French company involved in the World Bank–financed part of the project, Schneider Electric, S.A., pleaded guilty to bribery.

Guido Penzhorn, chief prosecutor for the Lesotho government, told the Senate Foreign Relations Committee that Lesotho, faced with its own economic and social problems, such as a frightening AIDS pandemic, nevertheless thought it critical to prosecute corruption in the project. What surprised him and his colleagues was how little help they received from rich-country governments and donor agencies, including the World Bank.

Penzhorn's testimony revealed the Bank's lackadaisical response to corruption in its own projects. One of the Bank's main tools for discouraging bribery was to debar offending companies and individuals from future contracts for a given period of time, usually from a year up to several years. Despite the Lesotho court convictions, the Bank hadn't debarred a single company.[10] Nor did it follow through on vague promises to help the impoverished Lesotho government defray the costs of prosecuting the corruption it had enabled—costs that ran several millions of dollars.

Penzhorn was also critical of the EU countries and agencies, which, unlike the Bank, were not even helpful in sharing information. From his own experience, he testified, their main interest seemed to be "whitewashing EU spending," concluding that "there is a lingering impression in Lesotho, as well as in South Africa, that the interest of first-world countries in the present prosecutions lies not so much in the successful outcome of these prosecutions but rather in protecting the interests of its companies that are involved."[11]

The July 2004 hearing did produce a result: two days later the Bank officially debarred Acres from doing any business with it for three years.[12] But inexplicably—or perhaps all too explicably—Lahmeyer, a major company from a much bigger aid donor, Germany, continued to do millions of dollars in business with the Bank for two more years. Shortly after Paul Wolfowitz began his tenure, in August 2005, the Bank reopened its investigation of Lahmeyer; in November 2006 it finally debarred the company from doing business with the Bank for seven years. Wolfowitz himself went out of his way to praise Lesotho for its "courage and leadership in successfully prosecuting its own officials and several large foreign companies for corruption. . . . Institutions like the World Bank, and the governments of rich countries, should support the bold stance of poor countries like Lesotho which are working to make sure that precious public resources go to help the poor, for whom they are intended."[13]

But would they?

Trying to Make Corruption History

"If you want to make poverty history," Wolfowitz is reported to have said, "you have to make corruption history."[14] In his first year, Wolfowitz halted loans totaling nearly $2 billion to a variety of governments where theft from Bank lending was rampant: $265 million in Kenya, hundreds of millions more in Congo-Brazzaville, Uzbekistan, Argentina, Bangladesh, and Yemen.

He made his most politically courageous decision in July 2005, when he halted over a billion dollars in public-health loans to India because of suspected corruption.[15] He subsequently resumed much of the lending after agreements were reached with the Indian government to rectify the fraud, but such actions were unprecedented. Investigations completed two and a half years later showed that his suspicion was well justified, and that in fact, the loans may have been reinstated too quickly: hospitals that were supposed to be funded by bank loans were crumbling or entirely abandoned; a malaria project was found to involve bid-rigging by major international companies like Bayer; and bribery and fraud were rampant throughout the health projects.[16]

Yet many viewed Wolfowitz's hard line on India's health sector as the beginning of his downfall.[17] India had considerable clout in the Bank; it was the largest cumulative borrower, and Indian Bank staff represented nearly a sixth of the total. Moreover, Wolfowitz's action embarrassed the British government, which was funneling large amounts into the same projects through its own aid program. Wolfowitz was making the entire aid establishment look bad.

Transparency International praised Wolfowitz's efforts, but high-level Bank officials protested his approach. One of the executive directors warned that "the bank should not become a world policeman pointing its moral finger," and a recently retired Bank vice-president told the *New York Times* that it "should not emphasize its anti-corruption policies at the expense of other policies required for development."[18] The Bank's executive directors and much of its management seemed quite nonchalant about ensuring that its loans were used for the purposes intended—that is, about fulfilling the most basic fiduciary duty of any financial institution.

What the World Bank Learned about Infrastructure

As Wolfowitz tried to tamp down corruption, the Bank was ramping up its lending for the types of "high-risk/high-reward" projects that had, at least in past, bred the most flagrant abuses. An "Action Plan" to increase infrastructure lending in the period 2004–7 was very successful—growing IBRD and IDA loans for such projects by 50 percent, to $33 billion, and those from the entire World Bank Group from $28 billion to $41 billion. More impressive still, the World Bank Group financial support was able to catalyze another $70 billion from other aid donors, official export credit agencies, and private banks during the same period.[19] Already in Wolfowitz's first year (2005) infrastructure accounted for 41 percent of new Bank lending.[20] Quantity was not a problem, but would the Bank finally place an equal emphasis on quality? Had it learned anything from the previous two decades of controversy over large infrastructure projects?

One chronic problem was the Bank's bias (which it in turn blamed partly on borrowing governments) for new projects in preference over support for maintenance of existing infrastructure, compounded by its lack of attention to credible plans for generating domestic funds that would keep the new infrastructure functioning.[21] The poorer the country, the more acute the problem: in Sub-Saharan Africa, countries indebted themselves for more loans for new roads, dams, and power projects as existing roads washed away, dam reservoirs and irrigation channels silted up, and power plants fell idle. Meanwhile, corruption raked off as much as half of the new funds.[22]

The problems with the Bank's big projects were not, to say the least, new. In fact, a 2006 internal review of "Infrastructure: Lessons from the Last Two Decades of World Bank Engagement" conveys the perversity of a seemingly timeless bureaucratic culture. Decades pass and new generations of Bank staff discover the same fundamental institutional failings, make recommendations and issue policies similar to those of decades before, with the same ensuing failures and lack of accountability for failure. For example, the review notes that *as far back as 1977* the Bank had recommended that all investment projects include monitoring and evaluation ("M&E") systems. Yet the 1991 Wapenhans Report "found systematic weaknesses in M&E, and recommended specific actions to remedy these." Then, in 1995, yet another review found that more than half of the Bank's infrastructure projects still did not have effective M&E measures. Despite the endless reports, throughout the 1990s the problem *grew worse*, not better.[23] A decade later, the Bank vowed once again to make M&E a priority.[24]

The Bank's 2004–7 action plan coupled increasing finance for high-risk/high-reward projects with continuing to promote privatization of infrastructure. Yet the 2006 "infrastructure lessons" review describes with apparent puzzlement nothing less than a full-on revolt against Bank privatization policies among the very poor in whose name these policies were promoted:

> Even where private infrastructure appears to be working well to economists, it has not always gained public acceptance. In Latin America, the region with the most experience of private participation in infrastructure, a survey of public opinion in 2002 found two-thirds of respondents strongly disagreeing with the statement that privatization "has been beneficial" for their country. In all surveyed countries, negative opinions had increased. . . . *Public dissatisfaction does not show up simply as bad polls, but sometimes as public riots.* The Bank is now making an effort to understand whether this disparity occurs because the economic appraisals are somehow faulty, or whether non-economic factors play a large part in shaping public opinion.[25] (emphasis added)

This growing hostility was linked to widespread public awareness of corruption.[26] But rather than questioning the fundamental approach, the review timidly notes, "Going forward, a major effort *is planned to deepen our knowledge* of the infrastructure-corruption interface, *with the goal of developing and implementing an effective anti-corruption program* for the infrastructure sector" (emphasis added).[27]

Like an alcoholic in his latest bout of promised recovery, the Bank's infrastructure staff proclaimed to the world that it had learned its lessons and this time would get it right: "Infrastructure is complex, controversial, and often risky. We know, because we've seen it, and we've been on the wrong side of the equation at times, making some mistakes along the way." They swore, once again, to address access for the poor. Moreover, they acknowledged that in the bad old days "projects were designed first, and the mitigation of their environmental and social impacts was handled as an afterthought." Now, though, in 2006—more than a quarter century after the Bank's initial environmental and social assessment policies were promulgated, and a decade after these being strengthened into the Safeguards— now, finally: "We learned. Environmental and social dimensions should be integrated into project preparation, appraisal, and supervision." A decade after Wolfensohn launched his anti-corruption efforts, they finally realized that "infrastructure is particularly vulnerable to corruption." From now on, they determined, "we should fight it all levels—in the projects we finance, in the sectors we engage, and in the countries we support."[28]

"We know . . . we learned. . . . "

Did they?

Fostering Failed States

Indeed, in some cases the Bank's penchant for pumping new money into high-risk infrastructure projects had contributed not only to needless environmental and social harm, coupled with widespread corruption, but also to long-term destabilization of whole societies.

Pakistan was a case in point. The Bank had been involved for decades in helping to shape Pakistan's Indus Basin Irrigation System, the world's largest irrigation scheme. From the 1950s through the mid-2000s, Bank lending totaled around $20 billion (in 2005 dollars), profoundly influencing the country's water policies and institutions. The Bank's approach favored investment in a top-down, capital-intensive irrigation infrastructure system that reinforced a semi-feudal hierarchy and caste-based tribal politics. The masses of rural poor were excluded from control of irrigated land, and the new investments in infrastructure strengthened the power, riches, and influence of rural landed elites. Both the civil bureaucracy and the military gained power through the control of irrigation management and land distribution. The whole system weakened already-weak political institutions, and it fostered personalized informal hierarchies of bribery, corruption, and influence peddling.[29] Meanwhile, over 200,000 poor were displaced by these initiatives, and many of them were never adequately compensated. A 2005 Bank-commissioned report pointed out that forced resettlement in

Pakistan, coupled with corruption, continued to create "extreme hardship for people."[30] World Bank internal documents flatly observed that bribes to Pakistani government officials to ensure the delivery of water were "routine and endemic," such that "water availability clearly depends on efforts to bribe irrigation officials."[31]

The same corrupt system resulted in massive environmental mismanagement that entailed the loss of over 60 percent of the water before it reached crops. Sedimentation associated with poor watershed management seriously depleted the capacity of dam reservoirs. Blocking the normal water and sedimentation flows of the Indus River resulted in the downstream destruction of thousands of square kilometers of once-fertile farmland, the intrusion of saltwater 100 kilometers upstream in the Indus, and the destruction of floodplain forests home to hundreds of thousands of people.[32] Poor drainage and overuse of irrigation water resulted in widespread rise of water tables in irrigated areas, with the result that over 40 percent of the total irrigated land area of Pakistan was threatened by waterlogging and salinization.[33] Salt was accumulating in the irrigated soils of the Indus Basin at a much greater rate than it was being discharged, posing a growing threats to the future environmental and economic sustainability of most of Pakistan's agricultural economy.[34]

Of course, the Bank was not the origin of the complex problems in Pakistani society, but arguably its approach compounded and reinforced social and political weaknesses that were undermining the country's entire ecology and its very viability as a state.

As the Bank prepared a new water strategy for Pakistan in 2005, a background paper it commissioned observed that the model of "large and capital-intensive water infrastructure projects, mostly funded by international agencies" would have to change if the abuses of the past were not to be exacerbated:

> A more balanced view would recognize that interventions have impacts both on ecology and communities. . . . A more socio-centric approach would incorporate these wider interests. It would entail sensitivity to community concerns and impacts, the acknowledgment that traditional forms of water utilization can also have value, and readiness to involve localities and communities in water-sector management reforms and infrastructure development.[35]

Yet the Bank ignored the lessons it claimed it had learned. The new strategy reiterated that "Pakistan has to invest, and invest soon, in costly and contentious new dams," despite the fact that the IEG had found that renovating the existing irrigation infrastructure could provide more irrigation water for one-fifth the cost of new dams.[36] The strategy neglected urgent needs for more investment in maintenance and stronger measures to address and mitigate the grave environmental and social impacts of large water infrastructure. There was virtually no input from civil-society organizations or local communities.[37] Months later, in early 2006, Pakistan military dictator Pervez Musharraf announced that Pakistan would go ahead with the construction of two huge new dams, Bhasha and Kalabagh, for a cost of over $20 billion—dams which the Bank's water strategy had highlighted as prospective new investments.[38] The projects would entail the forced resettlement of over 160,000 rural poor.[39]

Both projects encountered growing controversy and protests.[40] Financing was delayed for several years, but in early 2012 the Bank expressed renewed interest in funding Bhasha, in part due to U.S. interests in pushing still more money into Pakistan for large projects to ameliorate strained relations with the Pakistani government. The Bank also reiterated its recommendation that Pakistan proceed with the Kalabagh project.[41]

The Political Economy of Corruption

In the summer of 2006, as the new Pakistan water strategy entered into effect, the Senate Foreign Relations Committee continued with a hearing on corruption in major infrastructure projects such as the Chad-Cameroon Oil Development and Pipeline scheme.[42] One of the witnesses, Manish Bapna, then head of the Washington-based NGO Bank Information Center, succinctly summarized the problems with the Bank's approach. His testimony illustrated why the kinds of assurances made in the infrastructure-lessons-learned review (and those made in 1977, 1991, 1995, and on many other occasions) ultimately proved hollow.

No one could dispute the need for better infrastructure to promote development, but what was needed was "smart infrastructure," focusing on providing services to the poor, typically smaller in scale, decentralized, and more attuned to local conditions, including investments to upgrade efficiency in existing infrastructure. The multilateral development banks (MDBs) had funded such projects on a limited scale, including smaller run-of-the-river hydroelectric projects (which do not involve dams that create significant reservoirs behind them, thus avoiding the flooding of natural habitat and human settlements), renewable energy and off-grid electrification, rural access roads, and traditional water-harvesting and irrigation systems.[43]

Yet the World Bank insisted on increasing investments in large, high-risk/high-reward projects. Why? Bapna argued it was not a matter of efficiency, but of politics—indeed the political economy of big international development projects.[44] Large projects fed professional advancement for Bank staff, major contracts for private firms, political goals for borrowing countries, and healthy kickbacks for many bureaucrats and politicians. Senior Bank management and the board of executive directors, said Bapna, were mostly keen to lend large amounts of money in large tranches—what else is a World Bank for?

Bapna's argument was echoed by prominent economists and former officials at the Bank, including William Easterly, who had spent 17 years there as a senior economist and researcher. In March 2006 he testified in still another hearing before the Senate Foreign Relations Committee that the Bank's approach was basically hopeless and counterproductive: "Giving aid to corrupt autocrats just props up gangsters in power to stay longer in power." The aid community had been struggling with the issue for 50 years, and now the evidence of failure was overwhelming—yet amazingly there was little real change or learning on the part of the Bank. Easterly cited as one of numerous examples the dictator of Cameroon, Paul Biya, who had been in power for decades and whose government's budget received most of its funds from foreign aid, despite the fact that Cameroon also had oil revenues (and indeed pipeline revenues as well, thanks to the Bank's support for the Chad-Cameroon project).[45] Yet Cameroonians were no better off, and the Bank's attempts to promote environmental measures in the Chad-Cameroon project in Cameroon were largely a shambles.

The way out of the conundrum, Easterly suggested, was to find ways to bypass corrupt governments and instead support projects that would directly help the poor, developing, for example, education and better roads.[46] Of course, there was another unspoken conundrum in Easterly's suggestion, namely that elementary and secondary education and road building in most countries have been public, state functions. Even if roads and schools are built without state involvement, maintaining these public goods still typically involves functioning state institutions—exactly what was largely lacking in many of the poorest countries. Sooner or later, it is impossible to avoid the problem that longer-term economic and social development is not possible without a decently functioning government and the rule of law.

These more general debates over the effectiveness of aid, and particularly of the World Bank's role in disbursing aid, were critical for evaluating efforts to address international environmental problems. Since the 1992 Rio Earth Summit, both richer donor governments and some international environmental NGOs had looked to aid generally and the Bank specifically to be the conduit for funds and programs to deal with climate, biodiversity conservation, and other global environmental issues. Yet much of the mainstream, establishment international environmental community often seemed to play the role of naïve bystanders in the increasingly visible debates over governance, corruption, and the viability of aid—and of the World Bank.

High-Risk/High-Reward: Too Big to Fail

By halting major loans for projects suspected of corruption, even for politically sensitive programs of major borrowers, Wolfowitz was showing that the Bank was getting serious about governance. But the lending portfolio and re-engagement in high-risk/high-reward cruised ahead, a bit like a 747 on autopilot, or—to use the metaphor so often chosen to describe the blind momentum of the Bank—the proverbial supertanker so large that changing course at best was a slow, cumbersome affair. In fact, that was an optimistic metaphor; perhaps the Bank under Wolfowitz could better be compared with a supertanker hobbled by a defective steering mechanism, and with key members of the crew ready to mutiny against any change in direction.

On April 1, 2005, three months before Wolfowitz assumed the presidency, the Bank's board of directors, after many years of delay and international controversy, approved $250 million in private-sector loan guarantees, as well as a $20 million grant, for the $1.25 billion, 1,070-megawatt Nam Theun 2 Dam in Laos. Like the Chad-Cameroon pipeline project, the Bank viewed Nam Theun 2 as a prototype, claiming that the extra environmental and social measures the Bank incorporated into the project could become a model for mitigating risks in future big-dam projects in poor countries. Like Chad, Laos was one of the most corrupt countries on Earth, with extremely weak governance and institutions.

The funding would support a multinational consortium of power companies led by Électricité de France, which would generate electricity not for local use, but to export to Thailand for profit. Thailand itself already had developed much of its hydroelectric capacity, and a burgeoning social movement had mounted increasingly successful protests against new dams. In Laos, with a small, relatively unsophisticated rural population (5.6

million compared to Thailand's 67 million), and an autocratic communist government, there was no risk of large-scale local protest.

The dam reservoir would flood 40 percent of the Nakai Plateau, one of the most richly biodiverse areas in Southeast Asia and of truly unique international significance. The Nakai is home to over 400 bird species, including eight species that are globally endangered. It is also home to 14 globally endangered large mammals, including two large mammals formerly unknown to science until the 1990s: the saola, or so-called Asian Unicorn, and the Giant Muntjac deer.[47] It would also displace 6,200 poor farmers upstream, and over 100,000 rural poor living downstream would see their subsistence livelihoods disrupted or destroyed. The main source of protein for the downstream populations was riverine fish resources, which studies showed would be greatly reduced or destroyed by dam-induced radical changes in river flows.

The promised payoff was modest: if all worked well, the government would receive over a 25-year period around a 5.2 percent boost to its expected revenues.[48] But upfront, *nearly 2 percent of the population of the entire country*, one of the poorest in the world, would have their already-meager livelihoods diminished by the project—in the name of poverty alleviation. Imagine a hugely expensive scheme in the United States to export resources abroad, justified in the name of the poor, which would begin by impoverishing over 6 million people.

Given the controversy over the project, the Bank did plan significant social- and environmental-mitigation measures and better monitoring than for most infrastructure investments. But there were serious doubts about the capacity of the Laotian government and of the World Bank to ensure these goals, particularly concerning the impacts on the large downstream population. The project's anti-corruption measures were a major step backward from what had been attempted in the Chad-Cameroon venture. There would be no independent financial oversight or separate bank accounts to ensure that profits actually went to poverty alleviation and environmental programs. The Bank did not require the use of any external independent financial auditors. Instead, the revenue to the Laotian government from the dam funds would be treated just like any other government income.[49]

Yet just weeks before the project was approved, in December 2004, the Bank's Country Economic Memorandum on Laos warned that even compared with other low-income countries with weak governance, Laos rated poorly, especially by measures of accountability of officials and control of corruption. The memorandum strongly cautioned that "failure to improve governance substantially **upfront**—*before* resources start to flow—all but guarantees that the resources will *not* translate into good development outcomes" (emphasis in original).[50] In plowing ahead with Nam Theun 2, the Bank ignored the painful lessons of the World Commission on Dams (WCD), the Extractive Industries Review—and its own evaluation of the country's economic prospects.

David Hales was outraged. The former professor of natural resources management at the University of Michigan had directed environmental policy and sustainability programs at the U.S. Agency for International Development in the Clinton administration, representing the United States in numerous international environmental negotiations. In a series of articles in the *New York Times* and elsewhere he denounced the project as "exactly the kind of . . . proposal that the safeguard procedures of the World Bank . . . are designed to prevent." He noted that studies of the Thai energy sector showed that there was no need to import extra power from Laos, even though Thailand was the only prospective purchaser of the power. The Nam Theun 2 electricity would be sold "at a price higher than other sources of power for the purposes of producing profits for a French corporation and a government [Laotian] that is resolutely unaccountable to its own people."[51]

At least as far as private-sector risk was concerned, the mantra of high-risk/high-reward was the World Bank's version of "too big to fail": let the risks to the environment and poor fall where they may. The vast majority of the Bank's financial support was to mitigate risk to foreign investors, not to the Laotian people, who were truly "involuntary risk takers." The quarter of a billion dollars of World Bank guarantees for the Nam Theun 2 consortium companies were as a matter of course counter-guaranteed by the Lao government, exposing it to a huge financial vulnerability in relation to its meager resources. The U.S. executive director alone on the Bank's board refused to approve the project, both because of its social and environmental risks and because of the financial burden of the project in relation to the size of the Laotian economy.

The Bank's own analyses also revealed that the rationale of poverty alleviation for Nam Theun 2 was a sham, since other investments would provide greater direct benefits for the poor. The December 2004 Country Economic Memorandum concluded that the most important sector for investment in poverty alleviation, and for development in general in Laos, was agriculture, not natural resource (including energy) extraction and sale.[52]

In December 2010, a gala ceremony marked the inauguration of the

Nam Theun 2 Dam. Among those gathered were the prime minister of Thailand, a representative of President Sarkozy of France, and officials of the World Bank and Asian Development Bank. The French minister of state for foreign trade enthused that the construction of the dam had been a high political priority not just for Sarkozy, but also for his predecessor, Jacques Chirac. France had played an important role "at every stage of the project, from concept to completion."[53]

Meanwhile, dozens of environmental and development groups from around the world urged the Bank to address the plight of the rural poor living downstream. The project had already led to flooding, declining fish catches, riverbank erosion, illegal mining, poaching, and contamination of drinking water.[54] As Nam Theun 2 began its first full year of operation in 2011, it was too early to judge whether any of these harms would be counterbalanced by the poverty-alleviation programs supposed to be funded by dam revenues. Meanwhile, governance in Laos deteriorated in relative rankings by Transparency International: in 2010 it was ranked as the 19th-most corrupt country on Earth, worsening from 26th-most corrupt in 2008.

The respected U.S. journal *Science* reported that both the critics and the World Bank agreed "that a major experiment in hydrology and ecology is now under way," the results of which were still to be seen. It quoted at length a U.S. water-development expert working in Laos (whose identity *Science* kept anonymous because of fears of retaliation by the Laotian government), who strongly maintained that the mitigation measures were insufficient. "The World Bank," the expert added, "will, I expect, regret ever getting involved in this project."[55]

Take Me Back to Bujagali

As Nam Theun 2 proceeded, the Bank rapidly scaled up its investments for extractive industries and big private-sector high-risk/high-reward infrastructure in Africa. New IFC mining finance increased in Africa sixfold, from $50 million in 2006 to $300 million in 2007. In March 2007 a high-ranking IFC official announced that the IFC planned to further double its mining investments in the continent.[56] The Bank also revived its interest in subsidizing private-sector investment in the Bujagali Dam in Uganda.

This time, behind the companies that would build and operate the dam stood none other than the Wall Street private-equity goliath Blackstone Group, which was the main owner of the Bujagali's consortium's lead participant, the U.S. power generation firm Sithe Global.[57] On April 26, 2007, the Bank Group approved a total of $360 million in financial support for the consortium.[58]

Bank management and the board went ahead with the project despite a complaint lodged with the Bank inspection panel seven weeks earlier, on March 5, 2007, by the Ugandan National Association of Professional Environmentalists (NAPE).[59]

The inspection panel, after a 17-month investigation, released its findings in August, 2008. Incredibly, "Bujagali II" was even worse in some environmental and economic respects than the corruption-ridden earlier proposal involving AES. The panel found that the new power purchase agreement backed by the Bank between the private investors and the Ugandan government put so much additional financial risk on the Ugandan power utility and government, with guaranteed high profits for Sithe Global and Blackstone, that together with the underestimation of the hydrological risks, there was an increased possibility of default. Financial risks were minimized for the private investors, whereas there was no limit to the capital costs and other project expenses the Uganda government would be burdened with. Moreover, the panel was concerned that the expense of the project would siphon off resources for other social- and economic-development programs offering more tangible benefits to the country's poor.[60]

The Bank seemed to be gripped with an ideological fervor in pushing forward with subsidizing large private-sector infrastructure projects without adequately examining alternatives. The panel found that that the Bank had violated its own economic-appraisal policy concerning the need to analyze alternatives, asking why, in a poor country where only 5 percent of the population was connected to the electric grid, more attention had not been "paid to small and/or distributed generation options (not only hydro) which might in theory more directly address local and rural poverty." Such alternatives would include biomass generation from municipal solid waste, wind, and solar. Moreover, much of the expected benefit of the project in its initial years would be enjoyed by already-better-off urban households.[61]

Many in Uganda were well aware of this, but they felt powerless. "During its visits to the Project area," the panel reported, "[we] heard strong expressions of concern from local people and their representatives that they will not benefit from the Project but will, nevertheless, have to bear its social, economic, and environmental costs."[62]

Meanwhile, the IFC boasted that *Euromoney Project Finance* magazine awarded Bujagali the coveted distinction of "Africa Power Finance Deal of the Year" for 2007.[63]

Abolishing the Vice-Presidency for Environmentally Sustainable Development

Apart from the attempted corruption crackdown, Wolfowitz himself seemed at times more to be surfing the powerful waves of long-standing currents in the Bank rather than changing course. He backed the abolition of the Bank's central environmental unit and the vice-presidency for environmentally and socially sustainable development (ESSD) in June, 2006. The staff of the former environment unit were merged with the Bank's infrastructure and energy departments, creating a new "Sustainable Development Network" headed by the infrastructure vice-president. The new unit would be a bank within the Bank, overseeing nearly half of the institution's lending.

Unfortunately, the separate environment unit was the only semi-independent voice left in the Bank to address critical issues such as biodiversity, climate change, indigenous peoples' rights, and resettlement, to name only a few. In a neo-Orwellian twist, giant oil-extraction and pipeline projects, mining operations, and large dams would now all fall under the rubric of the internal "Sustainable Development Network."

Bank officials, including Wolfowitz himself, claimed that the reorganization did not weaken environmental and social goals; on the contrary, it meant that these concerns would be truly "mainstreamed" into the Bank's main lending operations. Mainstreaming the environment, of course, was a claim that the Bank had already been making for over 15 years, but each new internal report revealed that such assertions were as empty as ever.[64]

Avoiding Irrelevance

During Wolfowitz's tenure other long-brewing trends emerged as public challenges to the Bank's future. One of the greatest quandaries was posed by the growing economic clout and international credit-worthiness of newly prosperous nations such as China, Brazil, India, Mexico, and South Africa, middle-income countries that borrowed from the oldest part of the Bank, the International Bank for Reconstruction and Development (IBRD). The IBRD, as we recall, lent at higher interest rates, as opposed to IDA, which provided mostly very-low-interest "credits" to the poorest economies.

By 2006–7, many of these countries could borrow all they needed from commercial banks. (This situation would temporarily change for several years after the 2008 global financial crisis, a matter that will be discussed in chapter 10.) They no longer had to put up with the hassle of the Bank's environmental, social, and anti-corruption conditions—even though, as we have seen, these measures were often bent or ignored in order to keep the loan pipeline flowing. Already in 2000 a bipartisan commission convened by the U.S. Congress to examine the future of the multilateral development banks (the so-called Meltzer Commission, named for its chair, Carnegie-Mellon University economist Alan Meltzer) recommended that Bank lending for middle-income countries, and thus the IBRD, be phased out, arguing that it had outlived its useful role and now served principally as a subsidized source of competition to private international banks.[65]

In 2007, a critical IEG internal evaluation concluded that for the IBRD to avoid irrelevance in middle-income countries it should become a "beacon" of best environmental, social and anti-corruption practice. The review argued that IBRD loans to these 86 countries (which accounted for nearly two-thirds of the World Bank Group's total lending from 1996 through 2007) had probably contributed somewhat to economic growth.[66] But how much was questionable: many of the largest of these economies were already experiencing strong growth, regardless of the Bank's relatively modest (and decreasing) lending.

More importantly, the evaluation found that the IBRD's efforts to reduce economic inequality, fight corruption, and address environmental challenges were mostly failures. In client surveys of people in its borrowing countries, *only 2 percent* of those interviewed rated the IBRD's work as "highly effective."[67] The same surveys found that in reducing corruption, two-thirds of the clients interviewed found the Bank's efforts to be "moderately ineffective or worse."[68] Over half of those interviewed found that the Bank's impact on addressing inequality was "moderately ineffective or worse." The Bank's environmental performance in middle income countries was mostly "problematic," with widespread poor performance compared to projects in other sectors.[69]

If the Bank was ineffective in addressing these matters in countries accounting for two-thirds of its lending, countries which did not need its money, what was the rationale for the IBRD's continued existence?

The IEG concluded that the best rationale for continued Bank involvement in middle-income countries would have to be for its projects to be world-class examples of best practice in critical areas like environment, fighting corruption, and promoting social equity—"beacons of performance that encourage replication and scaling up." The Bank should be more selective in the future in choosing which projects it would finance, a recommendation that echoed both the World Commission on Dams and the Extractive Industries Review.[70]

The same middle-income countries, particularly China and Brazil, were also becoming competing sources of foreign assistance themselves, often offering finance for large infrastructure and extractive projects in other developing nations and having few scruples about environmental impact, poverty alleviation, or corruption. From 2001–10, for Sub-Saharan Africa alone, the Chinese Export-Import Bank became the largest foreign public lender, a cumulative $67.2 billion compared to the Bank's $54.7 billion.[71]

Brazil's national public development bank, BNDES (National Bank for Economic and Social Development) also surpassed the World Bank in lending, growing to $85.5 billion annually in 2010.[72] Most BNDES loans funded projects in Brazil, but an increasing portion of the BNDES portfolio in the 2000s went to help finance the participation of Brazilian companies in projects abroad, particularly in the rest of Latin America and in Africa.[73]

Brazil and particularly China came under increasing attack for low environmental and social standards in their lending.[74] In October 2006 Wolfowitz publicly lambasted China for its conduct in Africa.[75] He accused the Chinese of ignoring the Equator Principles, the 2003 agreement of leading commercial international banks to adhere to the Bank's environmental and social safeguards when they financed big projects. A notorious example was massive Chinese support for oil development in Darfur, which was contributing to the Sudanese dictatorship's genocidal actions against rebel tribal groups.

It was a paradoxical and revealing development. Since the early 2000s, many Bank officials had argued that environmental and social safeguards were hobbling the Bank's lending, as countries could increasingly borrow elsewhere. They were backed, as we have noted, by some developing-country executive directors on the Bank's board. This was at first true for middle-income countries, but now, because of Chinese investments, it was becoming true even, or especially, for Sub-Saharan Africa. Wolfowitz realized that in the face of this competition, the main justification for the Bank was its relatively high environmental and social standards. Rather than a hindrance, the safeguards provided the central argument for the Bank's future role in setting the development agenda. The Chinese were quickly showing they could shovel out money to poor African countries with few strings attached in much greater quantities than the Bank could ever equal.

The Chinese government showed Wolfowitz no respect, despite being the World Bank's largest current borrower. In Beijing, within hours of Wolfowitz's statements, the foreign ministry denounced his criticisms as "groundless" and "unacceptable."[76]

The Carnival of Hypocrisy

The pushback from member countries against Wolfowitz's anti-corruption agenda only intensified with each month of his tenure. Not just the developing countries, but even the United Kingdom publicly attacked him at the Bank's October 2006 annual meeting in Singapore, withholding 50 million pounds it had pledged to IDA in protest.[77] The U.K. international development minister, Hilary Benn, argued: "Why should a mother be denied healthcare . . . just because someone or something in their government is corrupt?"[78] Clearly Benn had not been following the actual consequences of the corruption of Bank lending to the health sector in India: it was precisely this corruption that denied healthcare to countless poor Indian mothers.

The Bank's executive board had demanded that Wolfowitz prepare a new anti-corruption strategy, both to help it "see the method in Wolfowitz's meddling," in the words of the *Economist*, and to launch a process whereby there would be greater board oversight of his efforts. In a sense he was being set up, since the draft strategy was greeted in Singapore by opposition from the Europeans and major borrowers such as China and India; only the United States and its loyal acolyte, Japan, fully backed the Wolfowitz agenda.[79]

Several months later, in March 2007, the Chinese unleashed the coup de grace, threatening to immediately halt borrowing from the Bank if it did not let up on anti-corruption.[80] By this time the Wolfowitz anti-corruption strategy was in its fourth draft, and opposition had grown despite its being watered down. Governments and other aid donors piously invoked the harm that would be done to the poor if the Bank's anti-corruption agenda actually led to decreased aid, and borrowing governments pointed out that the Bank itself had governance problems.[81]

The Chinese actually challenged the very legitimacy of the Bank's governance and anti-theft measures: "International experience suggests a positive correlation between corruption and countries at earlier stages of development. . . . The level of corruption in a country should not be used as a tool to deny or reduce assistance," Chinese government officials told the Bank. Mexico questioned, "How can the World Bank talk about governance when its president broke international legality with the Iraq war?"[82]

So Wolfowitz watered down his proposals still further: he agreed that the Bank would not withdraw from even the most corrupt borrowers and would seek board approval to halt loans on the basis of corruption. He also backed off from the suggestion that the Bank would circumvent corrupt governments by engaging more directly with those more supportive of reform—nongovernmental organizations, parliaments, and the private sector.[83]

Meanwhile, Wolfowitz himself was slowing sinking in what appeared to be his own governance scandal. His political and bureaucratic obtuseness had given the rapidly growing number of his enemies inside and outside the Bank more than enough ammunition to move in for the kill.

"Wolfowitz Agonistes"[84]

The web of corruption was so widespread that confronting it would expose any Bank president to major political risks. Wolfowitz, unfortunately, added recklessly to his already heavy political baggage. He brought in as his closest advisors colleagues from the Bush administration and Republican Party with little or no experience in international development, and whose presence was deeply resented by many Bank staff.[85]

He appointed Dick Cheney's communications director, Kevin Kellems, to head the Bank's public relations office; Kellems had relentlessly promoted the U.S. invasion of Iraq, claiming that Saddam Hussein and Al Qaeda had collaborated in the 9/11 attacks. He also hired Robin Cleveland, who had been a key player in post-invasion Iraq planning. Characterized by one prominent Washington blogger as "one of the few genuinely monstrous personalities among Congressional staff" when she worked for Republican senator Mitch McConnell,[86] Cleveland proffered financial estimates based on the notion that the Iraq war would pay for itself through the United States skimming off the country's oil revenues.[87] At the Bank, Cleveland reportedly drove a Hummer to work, which some saw both as her statement on fighting climate change and an all-too-telling symbol of the finesse with which she approached her job.

Wolfowitz further antagonized Bank staff and some members of the executive board by pushing aggressively to involve the Bank as quickly as possible in Iraq reconstruction during the U.S. occupation. Moreover, corruption was rampant in Iraq but the Bank's anti-corruption measures did not apply, on the grounds it was a post-conflict, emergency situation.[88]

All of this paled in comparison to the scandal exposed by a Washington-based nongovernmental organization, the Government Accountability Project (GAP). In late March 2007 GAP released a document leaked from the Bank on the salary history of Wolfowitz's girlfriend, Shaha Riza. Riza, born in Libya, was a graduate of the London School of Economics and had worked at the Bank as a specialist in promoting gender equality and women's issues in the Middle East. When Wolfowitz assumed the Bank's presidency she was the acting external-relations manager for the entire Bank Middle East and North Africa region. The Bank's Ethics Committee insisted that Riza would have to leave the Bank to avoid a conflict of interest with Wolfowitz, who would technically be her ultimate boss. After consulting the board, which directed him to decide Riza Shaha's arrangements himself, Wolfowitz arranged for her to be seconded to the U.S. State Department, where she would work under the direction of Liz Cheney, Vice President Cheney's daughter.[89]

The leaked Bank document revealed that Riza, just weeks she before she moved to the State Department, received an extraordinary pay increase, from $132,660 to $180,000, and then again to $193,590, tax free— some $40,000 more than the after-tax pay of Secretary of State Condoleeza Rice. And the Bank continued to pay Riza while she was working at State. The amount of the increase violated Bank rules, and it appeared that Wolfowitz had personally pushed through the pay raise.[90]

After the *Washington Post* publicized the leak, the World Bank Staff Association erupted in outrage, calling for an investigation. The Bank's board formed a special committee to look into the matter, and a cascade of other allegations poured in: Wolfowitz had also hired and paid his inner circle of advisors such as Cleveland and Kellems in violation of Bank personnel rules. He had hired a right-wing politician from El Salvador, Juan José Daboub, as one of the two managing directors of the Bank. Daboub insisted that all references to family planning be eliminated from the Bank's assistance strategy for Madagascar, and he also attempted to remove all references to climate change from the Bank's energy investment strategy.[91]

Over the next several weeks over 40 former Bank vice-presidents and directors, the Bank's Independent Evaluation Group, the European Parliament, hundreds of NGOs worldwide, numerous leading world newspapers such as the *Financial Times*, the *New York Times*, and *Le Monde*, all called for Wolfowitz to step down.[92] His fate was sealed when, in early May, the investigative committee appointed by the board issued its findings: Wolfowitz had indeed broken the institution's personnel rules, and he had violated the high ethical standards expected of all Bank staff, let alone the president. He defended himself before the board, claiming he was the victim of a smear campaign, and pointed out that there were literally hundreds of Bank staff who earned more than the U.S. secretary of state. He claimed he was acting on the vague indications the board had given him to set the terms himself for Shaha Riza's seconding away from the Bank. But his position had become untenable; on May 17, 2007, he announced his resignation, effective at the end of the Bank's fiscal year on June 30.[93]

Some argued that Wolfowitz, for all his faults, was really pushed out for other reasons, particularly his aggressive anti-corruption agenda, which threatened the careers of quite a few well-ensconced officials both inside and outside the Bank. Robert B. Holland III, the U.S. executive director on the Bank's board from 2002 through 2006, wrote in the *Wall Street Journal* that "those interested in the success of the World Bank should be under no illusion as to what is really motivating the staff revolt. . . . Many are opposed to Mr. Wolfowitz's anti-corruption emphasis."[94] Steve Berkman, a veteran manager with 20 years at the Bank, was more blunt: "The stuff about his [Wolfowitz's] girlfriend was all contrived. It was a mini-scandal people at the Bank used to nail him."[95]

Indeed, there were numerous conflict-of-interest situations involving couples in the Bank in which, as a matter of course, action was never taken. Shaha Riza pointed out that two managing directors (the next-highest-ranking officials after the president) appeared to have conflicts of interest regarding the simultaneous employment of their wives at the Bank.[96] The Bank's internal intranet staff-communications board posted various comments along the same lines. One staffer, remaining anonymous for fear of reprisals, wrote that at least at the IFC where he or she worked, "the Board should not be shocked that this is not an isolated incident. This behavior is prevalent and pervasive. . . ."[97]

The Wolfowitz Interregnum: Postscript

Paul Wolfowitz submitted his resignation only 22 and a half months after his first day of work at the World Bank. Many longer-term trends in the Bank that had begun in the early 2000s continued, indeed gathered momentum, under his administration. These included the reaction against environmental and social safeguards, the re-engagement with so-called high/risk–high/reward big-infrastructure and extractive projects, and the increased focus on subsidizing private-sector investment for development purposes, with the Bank promoting the shifting of financial risk from the private sector to borrowing governments and their populations.

Yet Wolfowitz recognized that all development efforts were dependent on governance, and he was a strong advocate of the safeguard policies, in addition to fighting corruption. Months after his departure, Wall Street icon Paul Volcker vindicated Wolfowitz's anti-corruption drive, blaming many of its shortcomings on the hypocrisy of substantial numbers of Bank staff, on management, and last but not least, on the Bank's member countries as represented by the executive directors on the board.

The Bank's board had requested in February 2007 that Volcker lead an independent review of the Department of Institutional Integrity (INT) in response to widespread staff complaints that under Wolfowitz, INT was unfairly prosecuting Bank personnel. The anti-corruption campaign, some Bank staff maintained, was a politically motivated effort to undermine the Bank on behalf of Wolfowitz and the right-wing advisors he brought in from the Bush Administration.[98]

In September 2007 Volcker released his findings. The charges of unfairness and political motivations were baseless, he concluded, but he did note that relations between INT and other Bank employees had led to a "siege mentality," with widespread mistrust among staff. There were some problems in the organization of INT, but the underlying issue, Volcker told the *Financial Times*, was "ambivalence in the bank as to whether they really want an effective anti-corruption program or not." "The board," he added, "itself has been ambivalent."[99]

Many on the board, as well as in the Operations staff, feared that "a strong anti-corruption effort would somehow be anti-development." Indeed, though "the bank does not lack for units reviewing and evaluating its varied operations . . . a strong focus on managerial and institutional accountability is absent."[100]

The new president of the Bank, Robert B. Zoellick, found the Volcker report "excellent," adding that "stealing from the poor is not acceptable."[101]

Indeed.

CHAPTER EIGHT

The Carbon Caravan

O NCE AGAIN, a new president of the World Bank assumed office faced with an institution in crisis. The unprecedented forced exit of Wolfowitz left a bitter aftermath, and a new chief executive would have to tread carefully. Robert Zoellick proved himself equal to the challenge. By 2010 he was widely praised in the mainstream Washington press for turning the institution around, praise which only grew through the end of his tenure in June 2012. Writing in the *Financial Times*, Sebastian Mallaby lauded Zoellick as "the quiet revolutionary who saved the World Bank."[1]

Just who was Robert Zoellick?

Though often thought of as a quintessential technocrat because of his former role as chief U.S. trade negotiator, much of his ascent had highly politicized overtones. Zoellick, along with Paul Wolfowitz and other right-wing, hawkish Republican policy experts, known popularly known as the "Vulcans," served as foreign-policy advisor to George W. Bush in the 2000 presidential campaign. George W. Bush's campaign director, former Secretary of State and Secretary of the Treasury James Baker, brought in Zoellick as second in command in the political fight over the contested 2000 election results in Florida, an effort which successfully blocked efforts to recount votes that could have decided the election in favor of Democrat Al Gore. Zoellick was also part of the small group of Wall Street financial leaders whom many would hold partly responsible for the excesses that led to the global financial crisis: he had served as a vice-president of Fannie Mae and also as managing director of Goldman Sachs. Finally, during the 2008 presidential campaign, he was also considered a candidate for secretary of state in a Republican administration, had the McCain-Palin ticket won.

Certainly such a résumé could, in different circumstances, have been almost as controversial as Wolfowitz's. But Wolfowitz had done Zoellick a great, if inadvertent, favor by creating an atmosphere at the Bank that would welcome anyone who would replace him. The two men certainly had different styles. Whereas Wolfowitz's office was adorned with menacing Indonesian daggers, Zoellick preferred paintings and photos of tigers and other large, predatory cats.[2]

"Developing countries will bear the brunt of the effects of climate change," Zoellick wrote in 2009. *"We must act now"* (emphasis in original).[3] Under Zoellick, Mallaby asserted, "the Bank became "probably the most innovative player in the struggle against climate change."[4]

Increasingly the Bank's environmental role, especially with regard to climate change, would be the prism through which the critical, interrelated issues of governance, corruption, social inequality, finance, and the fate of the project of sustainable development itself would be played out. Let us examine, then, the putative successes of the Zoellick period in this light.

The Defining Human Development Issue of Our Generation

The climate crisis, in the words of the United Nations Development Programme (UNDP), is "cumulative, urgent, and global," and is, indeed, the "defining human development issue of our generation."[5] Unfortunately, as Zoellick entered office in 2007 greenhouse-gas emissions were rising at an accelerating rate, beyond even the most pessimistic scenarios of a few years before. The projected warming in less than a century would be greater than the cumulative warming since the end of the last ice age, nearly 20,000 years ago, giving both ecosystems and human societies little time to adapt. In its flagship 2010 World Development Report, the Bank itself warned that unchecked global warming could condemn more than half of all species to extinction. Sea levels could rise by one meter by the end of this century, threatening more than 60 million people and $200 billion in assets in developing countries alone. Agricultural productivity would likely decline throughout the world, resulting in over 3 million additional deaths from malnutrition each year.[6]

The Bank declared that fighting climate change was not just an "environmental" issue, but a challenge to the future of economic development itself, that required "decisive and immediate action."[7] The Bank accepted the consensus of scientists and of the International Energy Agency (IEA) that global warming of more than 2° Celsius above pre-industrial levels was intolerably dangerous, and indeed, "from the perspective of development . . . simply unacceptable."[8]

The Bank was arguably the main international institution that could catalyze needed changes because of its role in energy investment in developing countries. Energy-related emissions account for over three-quarters of all global warming gases, and if no action is taken, 97 percent of the increase in those emissions will come from the developing nations.[9]

"Coal Plants Are Factories of Death"

According to the IEA, most of the acceleration of greenhouse-gas (GHG) emissions came from a growing "re-carbonization" of world energy production since the 1990s, linked mainly to the rapid growth in coal-fired energy production in developing nations.[10] Coal is by far the most carbon-intensive of fossil fuels: for equivalent amounts of energy produced, coal combustion releases double the amount of carbon dioxide (CO_2) found in natural gas, and 40 percent more than oil.[11] Global coal use, mainly for power production in developing countries and economies in transition, grew at 4.9 percent between 2000 and 2006, faster than any other fossil fuel, and faster than the use of renewable-energy technologies (wind, solar, geothermal), which grew at an annual rate of 3.1 percent.[12]

This trend was particularly worrisome since every new investment in a coal-fired plant locks in future CO_2 emissions for as long as a half century. Of all energy infrastructure, coal plants, after large hydro projects, have the longest projected operating life, 50 years—longer than nuclear power plants (45 years), combined-cycle gas-turbine plants (around 25 years), and longer by far than wind- and solar-power infrastructure (20 years).[13] The climate consequences of this long lock-in period are further exacerbated by the accumulating CO_2 in the atmosphere. Fifty-eight percent of the CO_2 in the atmosphere released over the past 50 years is still there; even after 1,000 years a significant amount of CO_2 emitted today will remain, on the order of around 17 percent to 33 percent; and after 10,000 years 10–15 percent.[14]

Thus, NASA climate scientist James Hansen wrote President-elect Obama in December 2008 that "Coal plants are factories of death. It is no wonder that young people (and some not so young) are beginning to block new construction."[15]

Hansen was referring to campaigns against coal plants in the United States, but in reality the future threat was from the huge growth in coal-based power production in newly industrializing countries. The message of the IEA was bleak: *If the trend of increasing carbonization of new energy sources in developing countries is not reversed, the richer industrialized countries could reduce their CO_2 emissions to zero by 2030 and the entire planet would still overshoot irreversibly past the point of no return for climate disaster.*[16]

How did the Bank confront this challenge?

A Political Double Bind

The Bank encountered formidable political obstacles to greening (i.e., decarbonizing) its energy lending, opposition which mirrored the large North–South conflicts that had effectively stalled the United Nations climate negotiations for many years. Since the Rio Earth Summit in 1992, international agreements to reduce climate change have placed the main responsibility with industrialized nations, given their larger historical and current per capita carbon footprint. (Nevertheless, larger developing nations such as China and India have already caught up in terms of total, rather than per capita emissions.) Under the 1992 United Nations Framework Convention on Climate Change (UNFCCC) and the1997 Kyoto Protocol, the developing nations' only obligation was to report their emissions.

The very engagement of developing nations in the whole UN climate-negotiation process was predicated on money: morally and politically justified bribes. The poor countries still needed to rise out of poverty with the least-expensive energy investments, which in the case of many nations— South Africa, Botswana, China, India, Vietnam, Bangladesh, and Indonesia to name a few—happened to be coal. If these countries were to pay more to invest in climate-friendly alternative energy, then the rich countries had the duty to absorb the extra costs.

But the costs were daunting. One of the more modest United Nations estimates was that $119 billion in *additional* funds would be needed annually to reduce energy-related CO_2 emissions (in the power sector) in the developing world to avoid greater than 2°C—that is, "dangerous"—global warming. This was nearly double the net annual amount of all foreign aid for all purposes from the industrialized nations (some $65 million) in the mid-2000s.[17]

These amounts would not be forthcoming, though the industrialized countries did promote three more-modest programs to fund clean energy in poor nations: the Global Environment Facility, the Kyoto Protocol Clean Development Mechanism, and the Climate Investment Funds. Throughout the 1990s and 2000s, the Bank became heavily involved in the finance and management of these programs.

As we saw in chapter 2, the Bank administered the investment projects of the Global Environment Facility (involving three-quarters of its funds), which was created in 1991 to help poor countries fund environmental projects. But over the next 19 years, the GEF provided an average of only $162 million annually for climate mitigation—a pittance in comparison with the

Bank's main energy portfolio, which approved $12 billion in new loans in 2010 alone.[18] In the end, the GEF did little or nothing to help "green" this broader energy lending; in fact, on occasion the Bank misused GEF funds to subsidize carbon-intensive projects.

As we also noted in chapter 1, in 2008 the industrialized countries, led by the United States, the United Kingdom, and Japan, chose the World Bank to manage several climate investment funds (CIFs) totaling $6.7 billion to provide grants and low-interest loans to developing countries for clean-energy investments and other programs to address climate change. The CIFs were supposed to be transitional arrangements, to be replaced by a new, larger United Nations "Green Climate Fund" for which the World Bank would be the interim trustee. At the December 2011 climate negotiations in Durban, South Africa, the industrialized countries promised that the Green Climate Fund would by 2020 transfer $100 billion annually to developing nations, but it was totally unclear where these funds would come from.[19]

Finally, the Bank became a key player in the global carbon market that evolved in the 2000s. This market grew out of the Kyoto Protocol, under which wealthy countries agreed to reduce their greenhouse-gas emissions by an average of 5.2 percent below 1990 levels. But to make the deal more affordable, the industrialized countries were allowed to meet their domestic targets in part by investing in emission reductions in developing countries—the idea being that it was cheaper to, say, fund a wind farm in China to replace a CO_2-belching coal-fired power plant in that country, than to do the same thing in Europe. From the standpoint of atmospheric physics, there is no difference between a ton of CO_2 not being emitted in China or India as opposed to it not being emitted in Germany—if the CO_2 reductions in China or India are real. The Kyoto Protocol set up an entity to approve and help establish a market for the carbon credits for reducing GHG emissions for these projects in developing countries—the Clean Development Mechanism (CDM).

The CDM-approved methodologies were intended to show which projects were "additional"—i.e., which ones truly replaced more carbon-intensive alternatives, and would not be built but for the financial subsidy of the CDM carbon credits (known as Certified Emission Rights, CERs). The CDM was also set up to approve (register) the specific projects that showed they had met the requirements of the methodologies, and to issue the CER carbon credits, a CER equaling one metric ton of CO_2 or CO_2e (CO_2-equivalent for reduction of other greenhouse gases). Carbon-intensive industrialized country industries would buy the credits—and help thereby fund green energy in poorer countries—once it became cheaper for them to do so than to make more-costly investments in reducing their GHG emissions at home.

Though in theory the CDM would not reduce overall GHG emissions—it is basically a zero-sum game in terms of extra GHG reductions beyond what countries had already committed to do at Kyoto—superficially the idea was seductive, an apparent win-win for everyone involved.

Starting in 2000, the Bank established with the contributions of donor countries some 13 carbon funds whose main purpose was to jump start the CDM by purchasing and reselling CDM carbon credits. The main market for CDM carbon credits was the European Union, which allowed its member countries to meet up to 13 percent of their emission-reduction targets under Kyoto through the purchase of CDM CERs, which were traded across the European Union as part of the EU carbon market (known as the European Trading Scheme).

The result of this influx of new climate money from donors, combined with the resistance of borrowing countries to pay more themselves for clean-energy investments, was that the Bank was happy to seek out new funds for climate-friendly energy, but took the path of least resistance in continuing to finance huge investments in new fossil-fuel projects, especially coal.

But extra investments in low-carbon, climate-friendly energy are irrelevant to the problem of global warming if the growth in high-carbon energy generation, particularly coal, continues unabated. A thousand megawatts of extra new solar power in India or additional wind farms in China do not save us from dangerous global warming if a new 1,000-megawatt coal plant is still built in these countries every 10 days, which indeed was the case.

So what energy investments did Zoellick's Bank propose to finance?

The World Bank Proclaims a Climate Strategy

In 2008, 16 years after the Rio Summit, the Bank finally unveiled its first overall institutional climate strategy, the "Strategic Framework on Climate Change and Development."[20] Bank management emphasized—counterintuitively to say the least—that "a simplistic approach of withdrawal from 'carbon-intensive' sectors, such as thermal power or transport, will not serve either climate change or the development agendas."[21]

The new climate strategy instead proposed designing climate adaptation and resilience into Bank operations, particularly in agriculture and water projects. It committed the Bank to expanding the carbon markets and raising money for the Climate Investment Funds.[22] And it promised to increase finance for energy efficiency and what it called "new" renewable energy (wind, solar, small hydro, geothermal, biomass—large hydro was excluded from this definition) by an average of 30 percent a year.

The strategy also announced that the World Bank Group would begin to develop a system of greenhouse-gas accounting for projects that could be used by borrowing countries requesting such assistance. Greenhouse-gas accounting could be a major solution to the Bank's flawed decision-making process in financing fossil-fuel projects because they were supposedly a cheap source of power. Once the GHG emissions of proposed power investments (as well as other industrial, transport, and agricultural projects) were calculated, then a so-called shadow price could be assigned to the tons of CO_2 that would be emitted annually by a proposed project, and incorporated into the economic analysis for choosing among alternatives. If the Bank would simply internalize the cost of carbon in analyzing new investments, it would never finance giant new coal plants, which, as we shall discuss below, it did in 2008 and 2010. But of course the key was not just calculating the GHG footprint, but also costing it and weighing it in the economic decision-making process.

The Bank had used the technique of shadow pricing—that is, assigning a hypothetical market price to goods for which market demand was absent or deficient—ever since the time of Robert McNamara in the 1970s to provide economic justification for its health and education loans. In 2004 the Extractive Industries Review recommended that it adopt the same shadow-pricing technique to incorporate the external costs of carbon and climate change in its project-appraisal process.[23]

But the climate strategy emphasized that GHG accounting would only be an "analytical exercise" and would not play any role whatsoever in decision making about projects.[24] The tone of extreme caution reflected the reluctance of the Bank's developing-country members to accept any conditions that would limit their borrowing for fossil-fuel projects.

The Bank also claimed that 40 percent of its energy lending was already "low-carbon," and that it would increase this proportion to 50 percent by 2011. Incredibly, its definition of low-carbon included large, new, coal-fired power plants, provided they were of the more efficient "supercritical" variety.[25] The Framework also suggested that the largest component of the Climate Investment Funds, the $4.8 billion Clean Technology Fund, could be used to support new supercritical coal-fired power plants.[26]

Coal Like There Is No Tomorrow

Coal plants might be factories of death for James Hansen, but for the Bank they were a compelling lending opportunity.

So it was that, even as the Bank was promulgating its new climate strategy, it went on a coal-plant financing binge. Massive loans over the next two years totaling some $6.75 billion were dished out for coal plants and associated infrastructure in the Philippines, Chile, Botswana, India, and South Africa.

Two of these World Bank Group–financed plants, one in India and the other in South Africa, aroused widespread international controversy. In 2008 the IFC approved a $450 million loan to help fund the Tata Power Company's proposed supercritical coal-fired Tata Mundra power plant in India. Tata Power is one of 80 companies in the $100 billion Tata Group, India's biggest and richest family-owned multinational conglomerate, with over 100 operating companies in more than 80 countries. Tata Mundra will be one of the largest new sources of greenhouse gases on Earth, emitting 26.7 million tons of CO_2 a year for the next 40 or 50 years. Two years later the Bank approved one of the largest energy loans in its history, $3.75 billion to help the South African power utility Eskom build the Medupi power plant, which will be the fourth-largest coal-fired plant on Earth. Medupi, as well as Tata Mundra, will emit more carbon annually than 115 countries.[27] Four hundred and ten million dollars of the Medupi loan also went to finance a railroad to transport coal to another coal power plant, which the Bank's appraisal report described as an energy-efficiency sub-project, since it would replace truck transport.[28]

The Bank not only provided funds, but also advised both Tata Power and Eskom to seek carbon credits from the Clean Development Mechanism. On the carbon market, these credits would be worth tens of millions of dollars annually. According to one account, Eskom was seeking CDM carbon credits for 10 years for a putative 6.5 million tons of CO_2 a year that Eskom claimed would be "saved" through the construction of the supposedly more efficient Medupi plant.[29] This would be worth nearly $125 million a year at mid-October 2010 CDM CER prices of around $19.18 U.S (13.70 euros) per CER. If approved by the CDM, Eskom would get more than a billion dollars over a decade for building one of the 50 biggest point sources of CO_2 emission on Earth. Large coal-power utilities and other carbon-intense industries in Europe who would pay for the credits could then pump an extra 6.5 million tons of CO_2 a year into the atmosphere, which they otherwise would be constrained from doing under the Kyoto Protocol. All this would be ultimately financed by taxpayers and consumers in Europe in the name of fighting global warming.

When the Bank reported that "low-carbon" finance was more than 40 percent of its energy funding for 2009, the London-based Bretton Woods Project questioned its definitions of low-carbon. More than half of the Bank's total combined lending portfolio for energy efficiency and renewable energy—critical components of "low-carbon" energy production—in 2009 consisted of additional finance for coal-fired and other fossil-fuel energy sources for modernization, efficiency improvements, and life extension. The Bank puffed up its low-carbon figures further by including not just its own energy lending, but the finance provided for renewable energy and energy efficiency of the Global Environment Facility, the Climate Investment Funds, and its Carbon Funds. In fact, 40 percent of what the Bank claimed was its lending for renewables in the period 2003–9 was actually funded through the GEF and the Bank's carbon funds. Moreover, since the carbon funds finance offsets that allow increased emissions elsewhere, even in the best of cases they do not result in any net reduction of global-warming gases. The GEF, the CIFs, and the carbon funds are technically separate, independent entities, managed by the Bank, with separate financial and governance structures.[30]

"An Example of the Type of Project the GEF Should Not Support"

A 2009 $180 million IBRD loan and $45.4 million Bank-administered GEF grant for coal-plant modernization and life extension in India is a remarkable example of the Orwellian gymnastics that Bank staff went through to inflate the Bank's claims of increasing its "low-carbon," energy-efficient, climate-friendly lending.[31] The project involved the rehabilitation and life extension of three coal-fired power plants with a total capacity of 640 megawatts. To justify the use of over $45 million of scarce GEF grant funds, the Bank claimed that the increased efficiency of the renovated plants would result in a direct reduction of 3.69 million tons of CO_2 equivalent over the seven to ten years of the project's implementation.[32]

For the average rational reader, these claims might produce skull-splitting cognitive dissonance, since the Bank's investment, though it was supposed to improve efficiency in the coal plants so that they would release 15 percent less CO_2 for a given amount of energy produced, also extended the lifetime of the plants by an average of at least 10 years.[33] Not only that, the old coal plants were real clunkers, suffering breakdowns and long main-tenance periods. The Bank project would tune them up to operate at full capacity, meaning they would consume more coal annually after their new "efficient" rehabilitation than before. So the net result of the Bank's project would be that the three plants would burn more coal annually, and do so for a period of 10 years longer than if the Bank had done nothing. It was like building three new coal-fired plants that would have a lifetime of 10 years.[34]

Moreover, the India coal-plant rehabilitation project was supposed to be a prototype, the first in a possible series of Bank projects for life-extension and modernization of numerous other aging coal plants in India—with 27,000 megawatts of generating capacity—that also awaited a new lease on life.[35]

Wouldn't it be better to let the aging, inefficient plants die their natural death, and instead use Bank loans, and especially GEF grants, to invest in true new low-carbon energy, such as wind or solar? In fact, a United Na-tions technical paper called in 2008 for a major *disinvestment* through 2030 in future fossil-fuel power production in developing countries if the world was to avoid dangerous global warming.[36] In 2010 the IEA concluded that more-radical measures were needed: to avoid the 2°C-warming scenario the world would have to shut down one-third of existing coal plants *before* the end of their existing technical lifetimes.[37]

At the GEF Secretariat, the United Nations Environment Programme—as the only GEF-implementing agency whose core business is the environ-ment—was supposed to bring scientific advice and review to decisions approving GEF projects.[38] When the GEF Secretariat reviewed the World Bank India coal-fired power-plant rehabilitation project proposal, the UNEP representative protested that the project would "favor the use of coal over other fuels. . . . Global impacts will be negative on the long run." UNEP added that *"these proposals be set as examples of [the] types of projects GEF should not support"* (emphasis added).[39] The protest was in vain: the Bank used the GEF funds for the coal plants.

"Why Would Anyone Want to Invest in a Coal Project?"

The underlying rationale for all of the Bank's coal financing, as well as for topping off this financing with carbon credits, was that without subsidies, new plants would be built using less-efficient and more-polluting technol-ogy in cheaper "subcritical" rather than "supercritical" facilities. Supercriti-cal coal plants burn coal at a higher temperature and emit 15–20 percent less CO_2 for the same amount of power produced. But the Bank's rationale was bogus. David Wheeler, who served as lead environmental economist in the World Bank for 17 years, denounced the Bank's justification in articles and blogs as well as in Congressional hearings. In 2008, as Tata Mundra was being considered, he pointed out that in India, for example, most of new coal plants already planned were supercritical.[40] Coal prices had more than doubled in recent years, meaning that the extra capital cost for a supercritical plant was increasingly compensated in financial calculations by reduced operating costs and reduced fuel use. Wheeler's critique was confirmed in 2010 by the Bank's own Independent Evaluation Group, which found that for Tata Mundra and several other new Bank-financed supercritical coal plants, the coal-burning "technology was largely or entirely predetermined by project sponsors before WBG [World Bank Group] involvement."[41] The Bank, then, was squandering scarce resources on coal projects that did not need international subsidies.

Wheeler also attacked the Bank's claims concerning the supposed low cost of new coal: "Power from Mundra will never be sold at the rate advertised on IFC's website (5.6 cents/kWh), because this would guarantee bankruptcy in short order."[42]

How right he was. Once again a familiar story began to repeat itself: a huge project with massive environmental impacts, justified on bogus economic assumptions, began to unravel. Tata Mundra sourced its coal not from India but from Indonesia, where the government sold it for export at subsidized prices. As coal prices soared in world markets, the Indonesian government halted its coal-export subsidies. In 2011 Tata Power appealed to the Indian government to allow it to double the rate it would charge for its electricity, claiming that otherwise the plant would become a non-performing asset. Bloomberg News India reported that even after doubling the electricity tariff, the project could still be financially unviable.[43]

In March 2012 Tata Power's Executive Director announced that henceforth the company, in its quest for profits and growth, would only invest in wind and solar, both domestically and abroad. Such clean-energy investments are smaller and less risky, the plants can be built more quickly, and costs tend to be less variable and more predictable. "Why would anyone want to invest at this stage in a coal project?" he exclaimed.[44]

Why indeed?

The Bank's last-ditch justification for the new coal plants was that they would provide needed energy for the poor. But for Tata Mundra, only one-tenth of 1 percent of its electricity was allocated to households without power.[45] Similarly, the power generated from Medupi in South Africa would go mainly to multinational companies, many of which enjoy highly subsidized electricity rates formalized in agreements dating back to the apartheid era. On the other hand, to help pay for the massive plant Eskom secured a tariff that would double household electricity bills.[46] Activists pointed out that a full 20 percent of the South African population was not even connected to the electricity grid, and 10 million people had been cut off because they could not pay.[47]

These projects highlighted the question of whether Bank energy lending was really aiding the 1.4 billion people on Earth living without electricity. A 2011 study conducted by several international nongovernmental organizations found that only 9 percent of the Bank's energy lending in 2009 and 2010 targeted increasing energy access for the poor. Not a single new fossil-fuel energy project in that two-year period, when Bank lending for coal and fossil fuels set records, promoted greater access for the poor. On the other hand, of the few Bank energy projects that did explicitly try to increase electric power for the impoverished, 76 percent were in the areas of new renewable energy (solar, wind, geothermal) and energy efficiency.[48]

An Energy Strategy to Nowhere

Against the background of North–South conflicts in the UN climate negotiations, and the growing protests against its coal and other fossil-fuel lending, the Bank began in 2009 to develop still another new energy strategy. The fundamental quandary remained: should developing countries bear any of the costs for fighting climate change?

After nearly two years of consultations with governments, civil-society groups, and the private sector, the draft strategy was ready to send to the Bank's board in the spring of 2011. Given the underlying conflicts, it was no surprise that the document was expansive in its stated objectives, but timid and evasive with respect to specific, measurable benchmarks. No one could question its purported goals: increasing energy access for the poor, and promoting the shift to climate-friendly, low-carbon energy.[49] But the Bank had already made similar claims for some time, for example in its 2008 Strategic Framework on Climate Change and Development. The strategy in detail read a like a laundry list of Bank commitments to continue everything it was doing in the past, and on a bigger scale, but supposedly more "selectively." The laundry list included continued investments, made more "selectively," in oil and gas extraction for export, supposedly to help finance poverty alleviation. The Chad-Cameroon debacle had left no lessons.[50]

The Bank stated that in any case the entire energy strategy risked failure if certain "external factors" did not materialize: an international climate agreement that would set a high and stable world price for carbon, and the availability of large amounts of additional concessional financing (i.e., grants or very low-interest loans) to compensate developing countries for the costs of lower-carbon energy (no, the World Bank would not do this on its own).[51] This, of course, was the global climate deal that visibly was not happening. In other words, don't count on the World Bank to show any leadership if no one else will.

But all of this became moot, for there was one proposed major change that sabotaged the whole undertaking. In the future, the strategy stated, the World Bank Group would not finance new coal plants in middle-income countries but would continue to do so in the poorest countries for efficient plants that increase energy access. So no more Bank finance for new coal plants in India or South Africa, but Bangladesh and poorer Sub-Saharan African countries, for example, could qualify—the rationale being it would be particularly unfair to deprive the poorest nations of finance for what might be their cheapest option for new power development. In one sense this reasoning was understandable, but in a broader sense it was surrealistic: since the Bank, along with many other agencies, had reiterated that the poorest countries would suffer the most from climate change, the Bank's new draft policy promised it would continue to subsidize new coal plants within their borders, helping them contribute to their own future climatic calamities, whether from drought or inundation.[52]

In mid-April 2011 a subcommittee of the World Bank board of directors, the Committee on Development Effectiveness (CODE), met to discuss the draft strategy. Directors representing developing countries, particularly China, India, and Brazil, and also high-income oil producers Saudi Arabia and Kuwait, rejected it, vociferously objecting to the proposed ban on coal lending to middle-income countries. The Brazilian executive director said it was like banning the rich members of a club from smoking, but not the poor. The Chinese representative directly attacked Western nations for their political pressure on the issue, stating "this is an institution of 187 members. We should not be listening to just a few of them." The developing nations also criticized the Bank's growing emphasis on the private sector and markets, and did not agree on the need for greenhouse-gas accounting for more bank projects. The Europeans criticized the Bank's vague definition of what it claimed was "clean energy."[53]

The North–South divisions on the board were becoming more divisive and chaotic, mirroring the larger impasse in the international climate negotiations. The Bank's brave new energy strategy was stillborn, consigned to bureaucratic limbo, where it remained through 2013.

The Road Not Taken

In reality, the path to simultaneously reducing global warming emissions and increasing energy access for the poor was quite clear. In 2010 the International Energy Agency argued that new investments in efficiency and renewable energy could provide 89 percent of the CO_2-emissions reductions needed by 2020 to avoid dangerous global warming of greater than $2°C$. The reductions would be split roughly evenly between efficiency and renewables.[54]

Decentralized renewable energy was also key to increasing access for the world's 1.4 billion poor without electricity. The majority of these people live in rural areas in Sub-Saharan Africa and South Asia; linking them up to a centralized electricity grid with power provided by large dams and coal plants is often more expensive than off-grid, or so-called mini-grid (village- or district-scale) local connections to renewable energy sources such as wind, solar, and biogas.[55]

A major advantage of efficiency investments is that they *more than pay for themselves*. The consulting company McKinsey has estimated that for every dollar invested in efficiency, developing countries would save three dollars in forgone energy-generating expenditures.[56]

Another huge economic and climate win-win entails the reform and redeployment of some $250 billion in annual subsidies for fossil fuel prices by governments of developing countries. The scale of these subsidies is huge—over $10 billion a year in India, Indonesia, Egypt, Ukraine, and Russia. Government fossil-fuel subsidies range from one and a half to seven and a half times larger than public expenditures on health in India, Bangladesh, Pakistan, Angola, Nigeria, Cambodia, Egypt, Ecuador, Venezuela, Turkmenistan, and Yemen. Moreover, these fossil-fuel subsidies are socially regressive, accruing much more to the benefit of the better-off whose energy consumption is much higher than the poor, not to speak of those with no access to electricity whatsoever.[57]

These figures are striking, since much of the impasse in the North–South climate debate hinged on demands of developing nations to be compensated for the extra cost of investing in green energy. Perverse fossil-fuel subsidies are far more than the extra $100 billion a year they were demanding from the Global Green Fund, money that appeared less and less likely to materialize as the global economic crisis worsened. In contrast, the IEA estimates that it would take $36 billion per year to provide universal energy access for the world's poor by 2030.[58] Moreover, according to the Bank's own IEG, providing electricity for the planet's unconnected households only would increase world GHG emissions at most only one-third of 1 percent, and "much less" if the focus were to be on renewable energy and energy efficiency.[59]

The Bank then had a clear energy agenda already mapped out for it: Focus on investments in efficiency and renewables, and help countries redeploy existing fossil-fuel subsidies to help finance this agenda. But this was not a political priority for the Bank's borrowers or donors, the Bank lacked the will to pressure its members to reconsider those priorities, and time and time again it demonstrated its inability to reform its long-dysfunctional "loan approval culture."

A Quarter Century of Failed Promises on Energy Efficiency

The full environmental and economic failure of the Bank's dysfunctional organizational culture can be seen in the failed promises to scale up energy-efficiency investments it had been making for a quarter century. The assembly line of hollow policy commitments and strategies included the 1992 Bank World Development Report, which emphasized the importance of fighting climate change, and win-win policies such as investing in energy efficiency. The Bank's 1993 policy paper, *Energy Efficiency and Conservation in the Developing World: The World Bank's Role*, proclaimed that the Bank would *"continue its efforts* toward increasing lending for components to improve energy efficiency . . ." (emphasis added).[60] In 2000 the Bank's environmental strategy for the energy sector proposed "mitigat[ing] the potential impact of energy use on global climate change," noting that since 1992 progress on environment and climate had unfortunately lagged, both because borrowing countries were not committed, and because "the strength of the [World Bank] Group's commitment to energy efficiency and the environment is not what it should or could be."[61]

In fact, concern by the Bank's donors that it was neglecting the win-win economic and environmental opportunities in energy efficiency and renewables *preceded* the 1992 Rio Earth Summit. Every year from 1985 through the early 1990s the U.S. Congress enacted legislation and report language instructing the U.S. World Bank executive director to promote end-use efficiency and conservation. The 1990 IDA Donors' Agreement, the legal document that accompanied the ninth three-year funding replenishment of the Bank's International Development Association, called upon the Bank to "expand its efforts in end-use energy efficiencies and renewable energy programs and to encourage least-cost planning in borrower countries."[62]

World Bank financial commitments for energy efficiency averaged only 5 percent of its energy finance from 1991 to 2007. The IEG attributed this underemphasis on win-win efficiency investments to the deep-seated perversities in the Bank's unwritten internal incentive structure: "Internal Bank incentives work against these [efficiency] projects because they are often small in scale, demanding of staff time and preparation funds, and may require persistent client engagement over a period of years."[63] Yet the tragedy—in terms of the economic and environmental needs of developing nations—is that *"much of the demand for energy services over the next 30 years can be provided more cheaply through increased efficiency [rather] than through increased generation"* (emphasis added).[64]

The Bank's evaluation department described a grotesque situation in which, within the institution, "a small group of dedicated enthusiasts has pursued energy-efficiency projects, despite an incentive structure that does not favor small, staff-intensive projects requir[ing] sustained, long-term engagement with [borrowing-country] clients." The language almost evoked a group of amateur hobbyists, who could just as well have been "enthusiasts" for collecting stamps or butterflies. The efficiency projects that did go forward depended heavily on extra grant money *outside* the Bank's main energy-lending portfolio, for example from the GEF.[65]

The IEG recommended in 2009 that the Bank develop internal incentives to promote energy efficiency such as specific metrics and indicators of progress in achieving efficiency that would be linked to country strategies and project decisions. Bank management replied that "management is not prepared to agree with establishing new metrics that focus solely on energy efficiency."[66]

Trustee of the Climate?

So it was that as the planet warmed and international climate negotiations slogged along, the Bank's fossil-fuel lending became a global scandal for many nongovernmental groups. In answer the Bank would point to the increasing investments in climate-friendly projects it helped administer through the nearly $7 billion in Climate Investment Funds. The Climate Investment Funds (CIFs), as we've noted, were trust funds managed by the Bank, under the direction of a separate governance structure. As with the GEF, the Bank Group shared responsibility for the implementation of lending programs and projects with other public international financial institutions, in this case four other multilateral development banks. The Clean Technology Fund was by far the largest of the CIFs, with $4.8 billion pledged.[67] It was overseen and approved by a CTF Trust Fund Committee of 16 country members with equal representation from developing countries and donor countries. This was a step forward in the view of some NGOs that had also been critical of the "one dollar one vote" governance structure of the World Bank and other MDBs.

Financing renewable energy was, in theory, central to the Clean Technology Fund. Yet at the prodding of China and India, who sat on CTF's Trust Fund Committee, the definition of clean technology initially included new, more efficient, "ultra- and super-critical" coal-fired power plants, modernization and life extension for existing plants, and new hydroelectric projects. Protests from nongovernmental groups led the U.S. Congress to refuse to fund the CTF in 2009, though in subsequent years, revenue was approved.[68]

By 2011 most of the CTF funds had been committed for future "clean technology" investment plans in 15 countries. On their face, most of the plans appeared to favor energy efficiency and renewables. For example, in 2009 the CTF board approved $750 million to catalyze a $5.6 billion portfolio for new concentrated-solar-power projects in Algeria, Egypt, Morocco, Jordan, and Tunisia. This was the kind of leveraged investment that critics of the Bank's energy lending had hoped for: the projects would double global concentrated-solar-power capacity.[69]

But why did donor countries have to give still more money to the Bank to get it do what it should have been doing in its main energy lending portfolio? In a single year, 2010, the Bank lent almost as much for fossil fuels ($6.6 billion, of which $4.4 billion was for coal) as the total funding of the portfolios of all the CIFs, funding which was to support at least four or five years of CIF investment commitments.

It was almost as if the donor countries were rewarding the Bank with still more money to promote clean energy when it had demonstrably failed to deliver on previous commitments to do so for decades. Finance ministers and economists were fond of the term "moral hazard," which referred to bailing out countries, financial institutions, or individuals for reckless behavior and failure (often accompanied by promises that behavior would change): the moral hazard being that the bailouts would in reality perversely encourage more of the same behavior in the future. Given the Bank's record, giving more money to it to fight climate change was a global warming moral hazard that put everyone on the planet at risk.

There were also questions of conflict of interest. The World Bank served as trustee of the CIFs' money, housed the administrative CIF Secretariat, and also, along with other multilateral development banks, implemented the loans. There was the danger of the Bank commingling CIF funds to top off Bank lending operations and general administrative costs.[70] The history of the GEF, where the Bank had similar multiple roles, showed how, all too often, GEF grants were used to sweeten or even greenwash already-planned loans—the $45 million GEF grant to subsidize the Bank's India coal-plant-rehabilitation and life-extension loan described above being a case in point.

Plus, the CIFs favored heavy involvement of the private sector, raising familiar questions about the main beneficiaries of Bank lending—the poor in developing countries or well-heeled corporations. The relative lack of transparency and accountability for the social and local environmental impacts of projects financed in this way was a matter of growing concern for many civil-society groups. The CTF required MDB managers to sign a lengthy nondisclosure agreement concerning the financial terms and conditions of private-sector projects they supported.[71]

Some asserted an even more far-reaching critique, maintaining that the CIFs were subverting the entire United Nations climate-negotiation process. Developing countries and some NGOs had argued for years that climate finance should be managed in new institutions separate from development banks controlled by the rich countries. Moreover, the same critics argued, the developing countries should have direct access to new funds for climate mitigation and adaptation, and should not have to negotiate through an intermediate World Bank–managed bureaucracy.[72]

Others objected to the fact that much of the CIF money would be in loans rather than grants. The rich industrialized nations were historically responsible for the problem of global warming; it was inequitable and outrageous, so the argument went, to then require that poorer countries indebt themselves still further to address a problem they did not cause. Moreover, the various climate trust funds were not truly "additional" foreign aid, as the developing nations demanded in the United Nations climate negotiations. Instead, the donors were simply reallocating existing aid away from other purposes to one that better served their self-interest. This was a charge that the Bank's own IEG partly concurred with—at least there was no clear evidence that increasing use of trust funds by donors was associated with any net increase in aid.[73]

But most developing countries, not to speak of NGOs, had little traction in how climate finance would be managed. The big donors, led by the United States, the United Kingdom, and Japan, were calling the shots, and the CIFs largely reflected their preferences: management by an institution they controlled, the World Bank; greater priority to subsidizing the involvement of the private sector; and sequestering the money in trust funds where they didn't have to pay much attention to monitoring.

Given the poor environmental and climate performance of much of the Bank's main energy portfolio, and the North–South political impasse that characterized board deliberations on lending for fossil fuels, one could argue that the CTF offered a marginally more promising alternative. The argument could certainly be made that the North African CSP projects, with all the caveats, were still a sign that the Clean Technology Fund could do what critics of the Bank's energy lending had urged for years: help to scale up investments in renewable energy quickly.

Carbon Accomplice or Instigator?

The Bank was hardly alone in its carbon potlatch: other public financial agencies supported by the rich industrial countries—particularly other multilateral development banks and bilateral export-finance agencies and export-import banks—provided even more money for fossil-fuel projects. A study by the Environmental Defense Fund found that between 1994— when the United Nations Framework Convention on Climate Change became legally binding—and spring 2009, 30 public financial agencies provided over $37 billion for 88 coal plants in developing countries. These plants will generate around 791 million tons of CO_2 emissions annually for decades, more than 72 percent of the 2008 emissions of all coal-fired power in the European Union. Health experts estimated that between 6,000 and 10,700 additional deaths per year—just from cardiovascular diseases and cancer—would be attributable to the 88 coal plants.[74]

Together, the major export-credit agencies (ECAs) and export-import banks of the rich countries played a bigger role in financing new coal plants than the World Bank Group or any other multilateral organization. They were, of course, often involved in cofinancing Bank projects, as in the cases of Medupi and Tata Mundra. But on their own they were also setting their own carbon-binge records. Japan's ECA, the Japan Bank for International Cooperation (JBIC), together with its government foreign-investment insurance agency, Nippon Export Insurance (NEXI), stood at the top of the list, with over $10 billion in loans, guarantees, and insurance for 21 new coal plants, mainly in Asia. The export-import banks and government-backed investment-insurance agencies of the United States (the U.S. Export-Import Bank—US EXIM—and the U.S. Overseas Private Investment Corporation) and of Germany were also major players. So the World Bank Group was more an accomplice of the leading industrialized nations, who hypocritically preached the need for carbon reductions while subsidizing carbon emissions through government-subsidized export finance.·

The coal-finance binge actually accelerated after 2009. In May 2010 US EXIM approved a loan of $900 million for the 3,960-megawatt Sasan superthermal coal plant in India.[75] Sasan will emit over 25 million tons of CO_2 a year, making the plant a new addition to the list of the world's 50 biggest point sources of greenhouse-gas emissions. Particularly disturbing, and illuminating, is the political process in the United States through which an initial refusal in June 2010 by the board of directors of EXIM to finance Sasan, on environmental grounds, was reversed because of political pressure just weeks later.[76] Later in 2010, the Chinese Export-Import Bank, together with the China Development Bank, the Bank of China, and the British private bank Standard Charter, provided another $1.1 billion for Sasan. Like Tata Mundra, Sasan subsequently encountered financial difficulties because of the increase in the price of coal.[77]

In December 2009 the French ECA, COFACE, and the German ECA approved government guarantees for loans of 1,185 million and 705 million euros ($1.71 billion and $1.02 billion), respectively, for a giant companion coal plant to Medupi in South Africa, the 4,800-megawatt Kusile plant. Kusile will emit 36.8 million tons of CO_2 a year, increasing annual South African greenhouse-gas emissions by nearly 10 percent with a single investment.[78]

No, there was no stopping the coal caravan.

In early 2011, Sasan, which belonged to the Indian firm Reliance Power, succeeded where Tata Mundra had failed: its application for Kyoto Protocol carbon credits was approved by the Clean Development Mechanism. Reliance executives estimated that the plant would receive around 33 million euros a year for 10 years at the then-prevailing carbon credit (CER) prices, i.e., around $45 million annually, or a total of $450 million in grant money for its supposed role in fighting global warming (i.e., enabling carbon-intensive companies in Europe to buy offsets from Sasan). The Indian business press reported that the Reliance stock market price was doing well, "perhaps in expectation of money coming in from carbon credits."[79]

Were there other equally dubious CDM projects? The Bank, as we have seen, encouraged the sponsors of the supercritical coal plants it supported to apply for carbon credits from the CDM. The Bank was proud of its role in promoting the CDM through a dozen or so of the "carbon funds" it managed. The Bank bragged that it had helped the CDM develop 40 percent or more of its methodologies for approving carbon credits. The Bank hoped thereby to catalyze global carbon markets, no mean ambition. So let us look at this curious and extraordinary story.

CHAPTER NINE

A Market Like No Other

ISTORY MAY WELL JUDGE the Bank's role in subsidizing global carbon markets as an ill-advised and quixotic foray into the early-twenty-first-century equivalent of the seventeenth-century speculative bubble in tulip-bulb futures. Here the seductive lure was not to purchase a whole house in Amsterdam for the price of a single rare tulip bulb (as was the case at the peak of the infamous Dutch financial bubble in tulip futures), but to unleash a global carbon market whereby businesses in developed countries would pay tens of billions of dollars a year for activities in poorer countries to offset rich-country greenhouse-gas (GHG) emissions. Superficially, it seemed plausible enough; after all, major industrialized country governments were pushing the scheme, and they gave the Bank still more money to help catalyze it.

The Clean Development Mechanism, and the much smaller Joint Implementation mechanism (or JI, established under the Kyoto Protocol to buy carbon offsets in post-communist economies in transition), were the only global carbon trading offset mechanisms officially recognized by any governments, namely by the governments of the European Union. We noted earlier that the Bank's carbon trust funds were financed by new, additional contributions from the governments in the industrialized countries, particularly the Europeans, who clearly had an interest in the success of CDM and JI, as a way for them to meet their emissions-reduction targets more cheaply. In 2000 the Bank set up the Prototype Carbon Fund (PCF), to be followed by 13 other funds over the next 11 years. Some focused, for example, on smaller GHG offset projects that supposedly would help community development or forest conservation, and others were separate carbon funds financed by individual countries—the Netherlands, Spain, Denmark, and Italy. The largest was the Umbrella Carbon Facility, launched in 2006 with a final capitalization of over 914 million euros (nearly $1.2 billion). By the end of its fiscal year 2011, the Bank claimed it was managing some $3 billion in its various carbon funds.[1]

CDM projects, we recall, were allowed by the Kyoto Protocol to help achieve GHG reductions less expensively by allowing rich countries to meet part of their requirements in poorer nations, but Kyoto also required that the projects bring local sustainable-development benefits.[2] Unfortunately, the CDM turned out to be a major failure in terms of both goals, and the Bank's carbon funds played a significant role in contributing to that failure.

The central concept of the CDM was climate "additionality," i.e., that a project really was reducing emissions that otherwise would have taken place in the recipient developing country, and that the project would not have been built without the extra subsidy. In practice it was extraordinarily difficult to prove whether a particular CDM subsidized project, say, a wind farm in India or a hydroelectric project in China, would or would not have been built but for the CDM subsidy, and whether it would displace a cheaper, climate-unfriendly investment, such as a coal plant. Indeed, the major developing countries that would host most of the CDM projects were rife with state manipulation of energy investment and markets, not to speak of corruption. The underlying operational concept of the CDM was arguably an exercise in futility, and an invitation to both gaming the system and outright fraud.

The U.S. Government Accountability Office (GAO) examined the lessons of the CDM for U.S climate policy in 2008 and again in 2011. The GAO concluded that there was growing evidence that many CDM projects were not "additional" in their GHG reductions, and that, indeed, "it is nearly impossible to ensure that projects are additional."[3] The Bank itself in a 10-year review of its experience with its carbon funds was compelled to admit that showing a project's additionality was "very challenging" and "constantly subject to questioning."[4]

This was not a mere technical issue, since the Bank rightly emphasized that "environmental integrity" is essential for the entire global climate regime, i.e., that emissions reductions are real and not bogus, and that it is also critical for confidence in the development of carbon markets. Environmental integrity for the CDM was a synonym for additionality.[5] And the CDM was the engine of the whole global carbon market, since even so-called voluntary markets (whereby companies would buy and trade carbon offsets outside the official, UN- and EU-government-recognized system), based their methodologies on the CDM.

An examination of the CDM project pipeline over its first decade (through 2010) brings home the enormity of the "environmental integrity" problem. As of 2010 China accounted for 40 percent of CDM projects, and 55 percent of total prospective CDM emission reductions.[6] But there was substantial evidence that China was submitting virtually *every* new wind, hydroelectric, and gas power project to the CDM, even though most of these projects were already planned and many were actually under construction. This was also the case for other countries, such as India, but China obtained by far the largest number of CDM carbon credits.[7]

It was no wonder that some Chinese sardonically referred to the CDM as the "China Development Mechanism."

Climate-Neutral Sustainable Charcoal Burning

Through July 2012, the homepage of the Bank's Carbon Finance Unit highlighted as a model the Plantar pig-iron forest-plantation project in Brazil. Plantar was one of the first projects financed through the Bank's Prototype Carbon Fund; from 2002 through 2012, also using other carbon funds (one is called the "Biocarbon Fund"), the Bank purchased carbon credits from Plantar totaling about $57 million. This money supported the establishment of 23,100 hectares of eucalyptus plantations that the Bank claims produce "sustainable" and "climate-neutral" charcoal that is burnt in pig-iron production.[8] But eucalyptus monocultures are notorious for draining water tables and depleting soil, and obviously chopping down trees and burning the charcoal made from them contributes significantly to GHG emissions. In the Alice-in-Wonderland world of the carbon funds, the project reduced CO_2 emissions that otherwise would have taken place: Plantar claimed that without millions of dollars in CDM grants, it would make its pig iron by burning coal coke, which is even more carbon intensive.

One hundred and forty-three Brazilian NGOs wrote the CDM board protesting Plantar's application for CERs, arguing that the company was simply using the threat of coal coke "to claim carbon credits for continuing to do what they have been doing for decades—plant unsustainable eucalyptus plantations."[9] The point was apt: Plantar already owned 180,000 hectares of rural land used mainly for eucalyptus for charcoal, and it provided management services for another 590,000 hectares of tree plantations used by Plantar itself and other Brazilian companies.[10]

In Brazil, Plantar operations were subject to numerous protests, legal actions, and congressional investigations. The project was accused of having illegally dispossessed local people, of polluting local water supplies, destroying livelihoods, depleting local soils, and "exploiting labor under

appalling conditions." Local farmers, whose land was affected by the eucalyptus plantations, alleged that the company had orchestrated death threats
against those who opposed them.[11] Some of the World Bank–sponsored
Plantar carbon credits were purchased by British Petroleum to offset the
CO_2 emissions from an oil refinery in Scotland, a refinery whose pollution
also threatened the health of local children. The Bank's effusive praise of
the Plantar project was not shared by Scotland's leading newspaper, the
Scotsman, which called the offset deal "Scotland's gift to Brazil: drought and
despair."[12]

A New Way to Subsidize Dams

As we saw in chapter 7, the Bank also encouraged the owners of hydropower projects it financed to apply for carbon credits. These projects could
enjoy a substantial windfall for—supposedly—fighting climate change. But
did the carbon-credit subsidies really support any hydro projects that would
not otherwise have been built? And were these projects actually benefitting
local communities or simply destroying natural habitats and livelihoods?

Once again, the IFC-financed Uganda Bujagali Dam erupted in the news
as a grotesque prototype for innovative finance of unsustainable development. In March 2012, Bujagali got the green light from the CDM board
to receive between $8 and $16 million annually for 860,000 tons a year of
supposedly foregone CO_2 emissions that the dam's construction made possible.[13] Industrial facilities in the Netherlands were the purchasers, enabling
them to discharge 8.6 million tons of CO_2 over a decade that they otherwise would not have been able to emit.[14] Bujagali was already operating;
to maintain that it would not be built without the 2012 carbon credits was
preposterous. And it was not an exception: the vast majority of hydro projects that received CDM credits were already fully financed and well under
construction.

Bujagali received CDM approval without Bank carbon finance, but in a
number of instances the Bank used carbon credits to top off projects it had
financed earlier. The Allain Duhangan Dam in the Indian Himalayas was a
case in point. The IFC provided $53 million for the project during 2004–6,
and then in 2007, with the help of the Bank-managed Italian Carbon Fund,
secured credits worth up to $13.4 million annually. Several Italian firms,
including two cement companies (cement companies have high CO_2 emissions) would pay as much as $134 million over a decade to allow them to
emit 5.1 million tons of CO_2 more than they otherwise would have done, a
cost that would be passed through to European consumers.[15]

Indian activists protested that the granting of the CDM credits was a blatant fraud, since the project had already been approved by the Indian government as economically viable in 1996, and the IFC had approved finance for it in 2004–6. How could anyone maintain with a straight face that the dam would not be built except for the carbon credits? Worse, the IFC had gone ahead with its initial support in 2004 despite the protests of hundreds of local villagers and an ongoing investigation of the IFC CAO. The project involved diverting most of the water from the Duhangan stream, where the villagers lived, and from the Allain stream, into underground tunnels where the combined flow would generate 193 megawatts of power. The villagers feared that the diversion of most of their water supply would destroy their livelihoods.[16]

Eventually, in 2010, the Bank's Independent Evaluation Group confirmed the lack of additionality—"environmental integrity"—not only for hydro projects supported by the Bank's carbon funds, but also for wind power and geothermal projects. These investments, and the economic returns from them, were on a much larger scale than Bank's relatively modest carbon-credit purchases; the Bank's use of carbon-fund money to top them off made no appreciable difference in whether the projects would go ahead or not.[17]

But all these findings and criticisms had no impact: through 2011 and 2012 the Bank continued to push for credits for projects that had been financed years earlier.

There was a shameless duplicity in many Bank-promoted CDM deals: at the time loans are approved for projects, the Bank claims they are financially viable, but it purports the opposite when it subsequently lobbies for carbon credits for the same projects, which most often are already fully funded and under construction.[18]

The China Syndrome

One category of projects accounted for nearly two-thirds of the carbon credits the Bank contracted to purchase through 2010, and three-quarters of all CDM-approved credits (CERs, Certified Emission Rights): industrial gas projects, mainly factories in China and India that produce HCFC-22, or chlorodifluoromethane, a gas used as a refrigerant and plastic feedstock.[19] HCFC-22 factories also produce the super–greenhouse gas fluoroform, or HFC-23, as a byproduct. One ton of HFC-23 is the equivalent of 11,700 tons of CO_2 in its global-warming impact. The Bank boasted of its pioneering role in jumpstarting the global carbon market for HFC-23 reductions.

Because of the super-GHG effects of HFC-23, under the rules of the CDM huge quantities of tons of supposed GHG reductions—and of corresponding CERs—could be generated in a single project. According to the Bank, this was low-hanging fruit, a "black and white" choice: without carbon credits, there would be no incentive to destroy HFC-23 in the production of HCFC-22.[20]

So it was that in 2006 the Bank's Umbrella Carbon Facility agreed to purchase over a billion dollars in carbon credits from two Chinese plants for the destruction of HFC-23.[21] It was the centerpiece of the Bank's carbon-fund investments, both in terms of size and the claimed climate-abatement benefits. It was also a major contribution to, and catalyst of, what some called the "Biggest Environmental Scandal in History."[22]

The Bank's (and the CDM's) reasoning was bogus: the cost of destroying HFC-23 was so little that since the 1990s, most producers in industrialized countries did it voluntarily as a matter of course—without extra financial incentives.[23] In fact, the CDM created huge perverse incentives to *increase* HFC-23 production, since the value of the carbon credits was between 45 and 75 times the actual cost of abatement. Thanks to the CDM, the profits from the climate-destroying byproduct were multiples of the profits of selling HCFC-22—in effect, HCFC-22 became the byproduct, and superpotent global-warming gases the product. After the Bank started purchasing credits from the two Chinese factories, they substantially increased their production of this most powerful of GHGs in view of obtaining massive carbon-credit windfalls for its abatement.[24]

Under growing international pressure, in August 2010 the CDM board suspended credits for the two huge World Bank HFC-23 abatement projects and three others without Bank involvement.[25] In January 2011 the European Union banned the use of CDM credits for HFC-23 abatement programs after April 2013.[26]

The Bank was faced with an embarrassing financial problem: it had committed over a billion dollars for credits that the CDM was now questioning, making them virtually unsalable; by 2011 they were described by the financial press as "junk carbon credits."[27] Other holders of the dubious HFC-23 CERs included major Wall Street firms such as Goldman Sachs, CitiGroup, and JPMorgan Chase—their interest, of course, was in trading the carbon credits for profit. The Bank actively lobbied the CDM board and the European Union to continue to credit the HFC-23 offsets.[29] European Union Climate Change Commissioner Connie Hedegaard (who also chaired the 2009 Copenhagen Climate Summit) declared that "it ought to be clear to everybody" that there was "a total lack of environmental integrity" in the Chinese HFC-23 carbon credits.[30]

The Bank succeeded in a perverse way: in the period up to 2009 it indeed helped catalyze the CDM to issue over $6 billion (4.7 billion euros) in HFC-23 CERs. This money would pay a handful of HCFC-22 factories in China and elsewhere in Asia to destroy HFC-23: but the actual cost of destruction was under $130 million dollars (100 million euros). Even if one were to assume that the HCFC-22 and HFC-23 production had not been jacked up to gain this financial windfall, it was a grotesque squandering of scarce international finance for fighting climate change.

Experts pointed out that a much more rational approach to destroying HFC-23 would be to set up a separate fund, based on the real cost of abatement, in an existing international treaty framework, such as the Montreal Protocol. The Montreal Protocol had successfully employed just such a mitigation-cost approach to compensate companies for phasing out chlorofluorocarbons (CFCs), industrial gases that were destroying the Earth's protective atmospheric ozone layer. (Ironically, HCFC-22 was the relatively ozone-safe industrial gas that replaced CFCs; no one at the time was thinking about the global-warming impacts of HCFC-22 and HCF-23.)[31]

The HFC-23 scandal illustrated another fatal flaw in the economists' utopia of global carbon-market trading: the market was set up to put a uniform price on a ton of GHG emissions (CO_2-equivalent) anywhere in the world, but the actual cost of abatement varied wildly according to the sector concerned, with perverse effects.

As if the scandal were not already sufficiently grotesque, in late 2011, in advance of the Durban, South Africa, global climate negotiations, the director of China's CDM national fund threatened that if the HFC-23 credits were not forthcoming, the Chinese factories would vent their super–greenhouse gases without constraints, a threat that was widely condemned as global climate blackmail. The Chinese had actively blocked proposals in 2009 and 2010 at meetings of the Montreal Protocol to pay the *real* price of the destruction of HFC-23 to developing-country HCFC-22 plants, which of course was a tiny fraction of the inflated windfall prices provided by the CDM and World Bank.[32]

There was another systemic problem in the carbon markets and associated World Bank carbon funds: pervasive fraud. Independent verification of carbon reductions was vested in private companies approved by the CDM.

The U.S. Government Accounting Office pointed out that these companies, along with every major financial stakeholder in the CDM system (sellers and buyers of the carbon credits), had a perverse incentive to ignore "environmental integrity" (i.e., whether real reductions in GHG emissions were actually taking place).[33] The profits are in getting carbon credits approved, selling them, buying them, and trading them. That the underlying commodity was bogus made no difference so long as it could be traded. Market incentives were working here, but not in the way CDM proponents intended.

A handful of companies soon cornered the CDM verification market. By 2008, for example, the Norwegian firm Det Norske Veritas (DNV—ironically the company's name means "The Norwegian Truth") was responsible for nearly half of all the CDM-successful project verifications, including such gems as Allain Duhangan, in which a Norwegian dam-building company also had a major interest. The CDM suspended DVN in 2008 when it was found to be verifying some projects without even making the requisite site visits to ascertain if they physically existed.[34] It wasn't alone: over 2008 and 2009, a total of four companies that accounted for more than two-thirds of CDM project verifications were suspended.[35] But after several months all were reinstated. In 2009 and 2010 the World Wildlife Fund and the German Oeko-Institute released annual reports rating the top five companies responsible for 80 percent of CDM project verifications on a scale of A to F (criteria included adequately trained personnel, proving additionality etc.). For both years the average grade was E+.[36]

The major developing countries, particularly China and India, that received the majority of CDM carbon credits (and of Bank purchased CERs) were equally cynical participants in gaming the system. Just how cynical was revealed in 2011 when WikiLeaks released a cable from the U.S. embassy in New Delhi that documented a 2008 meeting sponsored by the embassy. The meeting included an agent of the U.S. Government Accountability Office, representatives of various Indian companies and CDM project developers, a representative of Det Norske Veritas, and the then chairman of the Clean Development Mechanism executive board. The Indian officials admitted that none of their projects were additional and none should have received credits according to the Kyoto Protocol. Yet Indian projects accounted for over 20 percent of the CDM's approved carbon credits, which allowed 112 million metric tons of extra CO_2 to be emitted in Europe. Parts of the meeting read like a parody of a convocation of second-rate mobsters. A Mr. Somak Gosh, a senior official at the Yes Bank (!) observed that the project proponents typically kept two sets of books—one for the banks in order to obtain loans, and another, for the CDM, that would present figures purporting to show the need for CDM finance.[37]

Flawed at the Creation

There was no question that the problems in the CDM, and in the Bank's carbon-fund projects, were linked to fundamental flaws in the whole concept of a global carbon market. The offsets were politically created, virtual notions—they represented *something that supposedly would not happen*, i.e., a quantity of GHG emissions that otherwise would be emitted. But the business-as-usual scenarios (and hence the profits) were calculated—or fabricated—by people who had a clear financial stake in these transactions. A carbon credit was a new step in what many critics called the financialization of nature. Of course global markets in agricultural commodities have existed for a very long time. But in the case of carbon credits, to cite the pithy characterization of one critic, "unlike traditional commodities, which sometime during the course of their market exchange must be delivered to someone in physical form, the carbon market is based on the lack of delivery of an invisible substance to no one."[38]

Thus the Bank was not the origin of the problems in the CDM; but it was an accomplice and enabler of its defects. The major priority—which the Bank itself at times proclaimed—was pumping up and buying carbon credits quickly to jump start the markets. The single most important contribution of the Bank was to aggressively catalyze the global HFC-23 offset market, which still at the end of 2011 accounted for over half of the tons of claimed CO_2 reductions that the Bank carbon funds had promoted. The Bank pushed just as intensely for CERs for new supercritical coal plants and hydroelectric projects, sectors that also competed with the HFC-23 offsets as scandalous examples of lacking environmental integrity in the carbon markets. Since there was also neither any financial incentive whatsoever nor any common methodology to show that CDM projects fulfilled the other Kyoto Protocol requirement—local sustainable-development benefits—local benefits fell by the wayside in the vast majority of CDM/World Bank carbon-fund projects.[39]

Still, the Bank's 2011 draft energy strategy called for scaling up carbon markets, and in particular a new market in offsets for forest conservation, with no indication of any lessons learned from the CDM debacles. Officials at Interpol warned governments of growing systemic corruption risks in the carbon markets, including money laundering by international mafias. In 2011 most of the European carbon-market trading scheme was shut down for weeks after criminal mafias engineered the cybertheft of over $65 million worth of credits. Transparency International researchers suggested that "bribes and kickbacks" were common among CDM participants.[40] In the words of one Interpol official, who was surprised to find himself the only law enforcement professional at a climate-change meeting in Indonesia about the prospective carbon market for forest offsets: "In [the] future, if you are running a factory and you desperately need credits to offset your emissions, there will be someone who can make that happen for you. Absolutely, organized crime will be involved."[41]

Indeed, both Transparency International and the U.S. Government Accountability Office warned that efforts to create markets in forest carbon offsets were even more prone to risks of corruption than the CDM.[42] But again, backed by its donors, the Bank plowed ahead.

Just Forest Governance, for Sanity's Sake!

As we noted in chapter 4, in 2000 the Bank identified destruction of tropical forests as a prime example of "concurrent government and market failure." The accelerating forces "of globalization and economic liberalization have intensified pressures for forest production and land conversion," pressures that were overwhelming Bank efforts at conservation.[43] More than a decade later, an internal review of World Bank Group lending for forests through June 2011 reached similar conclusions, namely that global commodity prices for agricultural products and wood continued to drive destruction of forests at an unsustainable rate. Bank efforts to re-engage in "sustainable" forest management had been a major failure. In Cameroon and Gabon, forest operations were "causing substantial environmental and social harm." Bank-supported timber concession programs in places like the Democratic Republic of the Congo and Cambodia faced massive problems of corruption and poor governance. Above all, Bank lending for forests was failing to help the poor, even in cases where some environmental goals were achieved.[44]

The Bank finally pulled all its lending from Cambodia in 2011, after a particularly egregious scandal in which officials used a Bank-financed program to forcibly evict 20,000 people from a park in the center of the capital, Phnom Penh, to make way for corrupt private-sector land speculation. The abuse of the Bank loan was part of a larger pattern in which the country's rulers sold off much of the nation's arable and protected land to Chinese and Vietnamese investors for undertakings such as rubber plantations, large-scale logging, and gambling resorts.[45] Cambodia's leading activist for forest protection, Chut Wutty, was murdered in April 2012, followed a few months later by the murder of one of the country's leading environmental journalists.[46] The Bank's belated action resulted in partial restitution of land and compensation for some of the evicted families, but the larger amounts of funds available from Chinese investors for extractive and speculative projects meant that the Bank's leverage over the government was limited.

Cambodia was another sad example that led many to believe that without countervailing economic incentives, the world's tropical forests could not be saved. The siren allure of huge amounts of money that might be generated from future global carbon markets had seduced many: if standing forests could be conserved for their value as carbon sinks, then perhaps an international market could be established to pay people in tropical forests for not selling them or chopping them down. But as we saw, the future of carbon markets was dependent on industrialized countries committing to reduce further their greenhouse-gas emissions through a new international climate agreement; the Kyoto Protocol would expire in 2012.

Indeed, the Kyoto Protocol and the Clean Development Mechanism, whatever their other failures, excluded the conservation of existing, standing forests as a carbon offset for GHG emissions in rich countries. At the time (1997), measuring forest carbon appeared too difficult scientifically, and the problems of assuring "additionality" (i.e., that payment would go for a preserved forest area that otherwise would be threatened), "permanence" (i.e., that a payments would go to preserve a forest area that would not be burnt down or deforested later), and preventing "leakage" (i.e., that preserving one area would not just drive logging and agricultural expansion into other unprotected areas both within a country and outside it, resulting in no net gain of protected forests) appeared too daunting.[47]

In the 2000s, forest nations like Papua New Guinea pushed to include in a prospective new climate agreement a program to pay developing countries for preserving existing forests. So it was that in the international climate negotiations the concept of REDD—"Reduced Emissions from Deforestation and Forest Degradation"—was endorsed in December 2010 at the meeting of the UN Framework Convention on Climate Change, held at Cancún, Mexico.[48] What was endorsed at Cancún is actually called "REDD+" (REDD-plus), which also included finance for "sustainable management of forests" and "enhancement of forest carbon stocks."[49] Nongovernmental groups feared that these generic terms, having no technical definition, could be interpreted to provide finance—either through direct funding or carbon credits—for commercial logging operations that purported to be "sustainable." The agreement did not even have a clear definition of "forest," which created the risk that even palm-oil plantations—a major driver of destruction of primary tropical forests in Indonesia and elsewhere—conceivably could receive REDD+ finance.[50]

Cancún approved a framework for developing REDD+ as national programs, with interim sub-national pilot projects, but it postponed for future work any agreed-upon definition of the key technical parameter for determining additionality—a baseline of historical deforestation against which future reductions could be measured, and compensated for.

The baseline issue is hugely political: there is the danger of rewarding countries with high deforestation rates, since it would be easier to achieve larger reductions, and effectively punishing countries that had been successful in limiting their deforestation.[51] In fact, similar to the problem with the HCFC-22 plants, there was a risk of creating perverse incentives for countries to *increase* their deforestation rates in the short term, in anticipation of receiving REDD+ compensation for reductions in the future. Inclusion of so-called sub-national programs opened the door for leakage within countries—i.e., logging and agriculture simply being pushed from one newly protected area to other, unprotected, forests.[52]

There was no agreement on how the program would be funded. Many hoped that an eventual global carbon market could provide as much as $30 billion annually for REDD+ projects, but an international agreement to succeed the Kyoto Protocol was not materializing. Without the massive long-term funding that a global carbon market could provide, a *Financial Times* article concluded, "REDD is worthless."[53]

At Cancún, Bolivia and various environmental and indigenous peoples' organizations protested the "commodification of forests" that REDD+ could entail. They maintained that the political creation of this new commodity of forest carbon would be similar to the discovery of other internationally tradable commodities on indigenous forest land—gold, other minerals, and oil and gas—which, historically, frequently led to land grabs and despoliation.[54] Of particular concern was the lack of a strong commitment to social and environmental safeguards, especially for indigenous and community land rights, starting with the principal of recognizing Free, Prior, Informed Consent.[55]

Still, many viewed the vague agreement as an evolving process to save tropical forests and fight climate change, a signal that in the future preserving tropical forests would pay enough to counteract the huge market pressures to destroy them.[56]

Following Cancún, REDD+ proceeded with about $5 billion in aid to help some 44 developing countries undertake "REDD+ readiness," i.e., build technical capacity and create plans for the day when additional funding would allow for their implementation.[57]

As with the CDM, donors contributed extra money to two new World Bank trust funds to jump start a new carbon market (this time for forest carbon) and to help shape the rules of the evolving REDD+ program.[58] The first was the $435 million Forest Carbon Partnership Facility (FCPF), which began operations in June 2008.[59] In 2009, as part of the Climate Investment Funds, a new "Forest Investment Program" (FIP) was established under World Bank trusteeship to leverage additional finance for "REDD+ readiness."[60] By 2013 donor countries had pledged some $639 million to the FIP.[61]

Among the founding funders of the FCPF were not just governments, but also BP—British Petroleum. Environmental campaigners noted that BP would do better to use the money to improve its safety procedures, which were clearly negligent in causing oil spills in the Gulf of Mexico and elsewhere. But BP recognized a leveraged investment: its contribution could be repaid many times, since a forest carbon market would allow the company to purchase cheap emissions offsets in tropical-forest countries while continuing to pollute elsewhere.[62]

Nongovernmental critics argued that the Forest Investment Program didn't take into account the governance and management capacities of countries in its planning, and that its terms of reference were vague enough to allow financing of standard Bank forestry management, "sustainable logging," and plantation programs that had failed in the past.[63]

The REDD+ national proposals often emphasized the wrong priorities: they tended to focus on the technical complexities of measuring forest carbon while ignoring impacts on indigenous peoples.[64] When the plans did acknowledge governance and land-tenure issues, it was still unclear how these problems would actually be addressed.[65]

In 2011, a major European Commission and UK government–sponsored study concluded that REDD national strategies in Indonesia, Ghana, Mozambique, Tanzania, and Vietnam were on the wrong path with "overhasty, formulaic, and barely credible plans that *could do more harm than good*" (emphasis added). In fact, "all" of the REDD strategies were "based on the idea that with enough money over two to four years, a top-down, government-led process will impose governance and give forest-based practitioners what they need to guarantee emissions reductions and qualify for REDD payments."[66] The study's title—"Just Forest Governance—for

REDD, for Sanity," summarized neatly the central challenge for any program to conserve forests.

A State of Denial

The whole program seemed to be in denial about the intractable challenge of governance. The unprecedented complexity and novelty of the proposed framework for developing and monitoring REDD+ projects posed even greater challenges than the legions of forest-management and conservation projects that had failed in the past.

The vast majority of countries eligible for REDD+ ranked in the bottom half of Transparency International rankings for corruption in 2011.[67] Already in October 2010 Interpol found (in a study supported by the World Bank) that "it has become very apparent . . . that there is an inescapable nexus between emissions trading, illegal logging, and organized crime." Interpol warned that "as globalization continues, the demand for timber and land increases, [and] as the resource base continues to shrink, and unless there is a revolutionary change in the quality of forest management policy," forests in developing countries will attract growing international criminal activity. "It can already be seen that criminals are targeting the REDD markets. . . ."[68] Around the same time, one of the main authors of Indonesia's REDD+ program, who also helped lead Indonesia's delegation to the climate negotiations, became a suspect in several notorious corruption and bribery investigations.[69]

Interpol gives the example of an $80 million fraud in carbon credits: in an unnamed country, corrupt forest-carbon speculators purchased tracts of forests with nonexistent boundaries, sold them using fraudulent documents to their own shell companies, and then sold carbon credits from these illicitly obtained forest lands to a regional agency that bundled the carbon credits with others in "emission carbon bonds" for sale to rich industrialized nations. In this case the real owners of the forests (one could speculate that they were perhaps indigenous people or local forest-dwelling communities) were able to expose the fraud. The elements of this scheme were all too typical in tropical countries: forests in remote areas, disputed or unclear ownership, fraudulent documentation, criminal conspiracy motivated by the prospect of profits from a quick sale of the carbon credits—credits that would lose all connection with any physical location once they were bundled up with other credits for international sale and trading.[70]

The extent of the governance collapse for conserving forests in the face of global market forces exploited by criminal and local mafias can be seen in the following Interpol estimates: illegal timber harvesting in Indonesia is 70–80 percent of all timber marketed and exported; in Cambodia, 90 percent; in Papua New Guinea, 70 percent; in Vietnam, 20–40 percent; in Brazil, 20–47 percent; in Peru, 80 percent; in Cameroon, 50 percent; and in Ghana, 60 percent.[71]

For the Climate Itself, an Unqualified Disaster

In December 2011, international climate negotiators again met in Durban, South Africa. REDD+ was a sideshow in the broader negotiations, which concluded with a nonbinding commitment to negotiate a new climate treaty as a successor to Kyoto by 2015. But the new treaty would not go into effect until 2020. So there would be no further action for nearly a decade, and certainly no global carbon market, which was the financial cargo cult that had driven much of the early enthusiasm for REDD+.

Although some mainstream environmental groups tried to portray Durban as a partial "victory," since for the first time countries like China and India indicated that they would be open to limiting their GHG emissions, in reality it was a grotesque charade. One of the two leading scientific journals in the world, *Nature*, lambasted the Durban climate talks in an editorial worthy of Greenpeace—no, more scathing than Greenpeace—observing that

> the mask of political rhetoric has now slipped so far, to reveal the ugly political reality underneath. . . . It takes a certain kind of optimism—or an outbreak of collective Stockholm syndrome—to see the Durban outcome as a significant breakthrough on global warming, as many are claiming . . . for the climate itself, it is an unqualified disaster. It is clear that the science of climate change and the politics of climate change, which claims to represent it, now inhabit parallel worlds.[72]

At Durban the REDD+ negotiators, with uncanny bad timing, formally endorsed carbon markets as a potential funding source, including vague suggestions to include REDD+ in a possible revivified and extended CDM. But the money was drying up. By 2012 global carbon markets were collapsing, starting with what had been the most robust market extant, the CDM itself.[73]

The World Wildlife Fund sounded the alarm, noting that in the absence of an international climate agreement the private sector had no incentive to play a large role in financing REDD+ implementation. Such funding as there was, for REDD+ readiness, came from traditional foreign aid, with the Bank's carbon finance in the vanguard. But the complexities of trying to "prepare for REDD+," while disagreements dragged on for years in the REDD negotiations, undermined the whole scheme. These problems also slowed actual disbursement of the approximately $5 billion in REDD+ readiness funds: in the summer of 2012 only 5 percent had been distributed after more than four years of operations. Why, WWF concluded, would forest nations and communities commit to a 30 year or longer activity, where at best "the rewards beyond year 2 or 3 are completely unknown."[74]

An Ultimately Useless Forest-Carbon Market?

REDD+ exemplified the "parallel" world of climate policy and politics. The process of "REDD+ readiness" had gone on for so long that the participants suffered from the climate-negotiation Stockholm syndrome that *Nature* caustically denounced in its highly unusual polemic. If the ultimate justification was fighting global warming, participants seemed to forget that even in the most wildly optimistic scenario of a successful, scaled-up program, the net result would be no overall reduction in GHG emissions: REDD+ carbon sequestration offsets would be paid for by emitters in other parts of the world to allow them to release more global-warming gases than they otherwise would.

The irony is that REDD+ was an overly complicated, untested, proposed "solution" that largely ignored existing successful efforts in developing countries to conserve and manage forests. In Latin America in particular there have been a growing number of success stories in community-led forest conservation and management.

Mexico is often cited as a model, with some 8,000 square kilometers of forests under community management. Many of these areas engage in low-intensity, selective logging that has indeed been shown to be sustainable. Although some community forests in Mexico have been subject to corruption and illegal logging, studies have found that they have performed as well, or in some cases even better, than protected areas in conserving forest cover. In Brazil and Bolivia, community forestry has a shorter history, but local management of non-timber sources such as rubber and Brazil nuts has a 20-year history of evolving local forest governance.[75]

Thus there are some forests in Mexico and elsewhere that embody all the successful outcomes that REDD+ is supposed to promote. But as one academic expert on community forests observes, "as most REDD+ proposals assume a baseline of deforestation it is not clear how communities that are already doing the 'right thing' (in terms of sustainably managing and conserving their forests) can be rewarded."[76]

In fact, the same point can be made at the national level. For example, Brazil achieved a remarkable record of decreasing its deforestation in the Amazon between 2004 and 2011 by 78 percent and the associated carbon emissions by 57 percent. In 2012 Brazilian Amazon deforestation fell again by 23 percent more.[77] Although some of this decline was probably associated with the global recession, it was nevertheless a testament to Brazil's political will and effectiveness in improving governance, enforcement, and the technology of monitoring. A bright spot on the Bank's forest record was its support for these efforts through two large environmental policy loans in 2005 and 2009.[78] But for the most part Brazil did this on its own, not because of any external financial incentives. The difference that REDD+ would make, if it ever takes off, would appear questionable.

Meanwhile, the huge, quixotic investment of time and effort to set up new institutions in places like Congo and Cambodia to commodify forest carbon appeared senseless in light of the collapse of global carbon markets.

Would it not be better to abandon the focus on commodifying forest carbon and instead reconfigure REDD+ into an aid program that could help to empower local communities? Already groups in Peru and elsewhere had made just such a proposal for an "indigenous REDD": use actually existing, modest REDD funding to regularize land tenure and promote community forest management.[79]

But that would be too simple. In the aftermath of the global financial crisis and Great Recession, as people and governments around the world renounced market fundamentalism, faith in the economic utopia of future global carbon markets remained alive in the World Bank carbon funds. After all, the future carbon market was the very reason for their existence.

So it was that, in 2011, 11 donor countries contributed some $75 million for a 14th carbon fund at the Bank—the Partnership for Market Readiness. The optimistically named fund has the mission of helping middle-income countries "explore market instruments," build up "[carbon] market readiness," and build up capacity to set carbon baselines, collect data, and monitor and evaluate emissions in order to create carbon credits that can be traded nationally or internationally.[80]

This foray into the carbon market was one more voyage to an alternative planet, a planet of climate policy and politics increasingly divorced from the natural world—and, one might add, from the actually existing economic one. In September 2012 the price of the gold standard of international carbon credits, a Clean Development Mechanism Certified Emission Right, representing a ton of CO_2/CO_2-equivalent, sank in the European Trading Scheme below 1.50 euros, and Barclay's Bank issued a note predicting that the price of CERs would never rise above three euros—not even with a bail-out of carbon prices by EU governments.[81] Barclay's was over-optimistic: by January 2013, a CER was worth around 50 euro cents.[82]

Yes, after the rocky tenure of Wolfowitz, Zoellick succeeded in giving the Bank a more reassuring image, as long as one did not look too closely into what was actually going on—climate finance being a case in point. Below the surface, corruption festered and worsened.

CHAPTER TEN

Financializing Development

R OBERT ZOELLICK WAS PROUD of his achievements at the World Bank. In 2012, in his last months on the job, he wrote in *Foreign Affairs* that under his leadership the Bank had made progress in promoting good governance and fighting corruption. He reiterated that "at times the bank must say no to clients that refuse to meet standards on and safeguards regarding corruption, the environment, and governance."[1]

The Bank had succeeded in meeting the challenge of lending to middle-income countries, he wrote, by treating them as clients and partners rather than by prescribing overly detailed conditions—"the World Bank should be a seeker of solutions, not a purveyor of prescriptions." In response to the global financial crisis, the Bank quickly disbursed more than $200 billion to developing countries between 2008 and 2010—more than the IMF—to stanch the threat of international financial collapse.

He noted his success in obtaining from the Bank's donor countries the largest funding increases in history: the triennial replenishments of IDA in 2007 and 2009 together totaled more than $90 billion, and in 2010 he secured the first funding increase for the IBRD in 20 years, a "General Capital Increase" of $86.2 billion.[2]

But there were discordant notes to this panegyric of success, both within and outside the Bank.

Two years before Zoellick took the helm in 2007, in preparing for their triennial refunding of IDA the Bank's major donors demanded that IDA— and thus also the IBRD, which shared the same management systems— take stock of itself. They asked the IEG to oversee a comprehensive study of the Bank's management controls and procedures concerning its lending, compliance with its own policies, and the requirements of the Bank's charter, particularly concerning the institution's fiduciary duties.

In April 2009 the Bank finally released a massive, five-volume report to the public: the "Review of IDA Internal Controls." Given the findings, it could be argued that it was a mistake to trust the Bank with another $42 billion without some real changes—which unfortunately is exactly what the donors did before the report was even completed.[3] Internal controls to prevent fraud and corruption were so weak as to constitute a "material weakness," i.e., a threat to the Bank's ability to accomplish its objectives and fulfill its fiduciary duties as required by its charter. Let us recall that the charter requires that the Bank ensure that the money it lends "is used for the purposes intended," i.e., is not stolen or diverted.[4]

The Bank's "culture, management priorities, staff incentives, and HR (Human Resources) practices" did not make preventing fraud, theft, and corruption a priority. Integrity and ethical values were "not well reflected in staff's performance evaluation. . . . Incentives do not link to ethical behavior." Management often failed to follow up on reported improprieties, as well as on findings of internal audits, investigations, and evaluations.[5]

Worse, "[Bank] staff fear reprisal for reporting infringements [of policy and of fraud and corruption] and unethical behavior." And where was there the greatest fear of reprisals in the entire World Bank? Where else but in the Bank's anti-corruption investigative unit—the Department of Institutional Integrity (INT)![6]

The IEG also found a partial explanation (beyond the culture of loan approval) for why the Bank violated in practice so many of its own policies: half of the Bank's supposedly mandatory operational policies "were not directly linked by Management to any key controls or business processes."[7] This was in practice an incentive for staff to disregard many of the Bank's requirements, including a critical one governing the supervision of operations in the field. So it was hardly a surprise that IEG found that only 37 percent of existing projects were rated as "substantial" or better for monitoring and supervision, a situation that had persisted not just for years, but decades.[8] The system was actually designed so that, in most cases, once the Bank pushed the money out the door it was not too concerned with following up on what actually happened.

The Bank's move toward non-project lending, which generally involved massive transfers of funds to governments accompanied by vague policy prescriptions, led to further corruption. These "Development Policy Loans" and "Poverty Reduction Strategy Credits," totaled 40 percent of new IBRD/IDA lending commitments in 2009 and 2010.[9] Yet they were not governed by the Bank's procurement policies, and local borrower-country controls were "often weak or nonexistent."[10] And, as we noted before, the

Bank's environmental and social safeguard measures for projects also did not apply.

In response to these findings, the Bank undertook an "Action Plan," purportedly to address the most serious problems. In 2010 the IEG found that there had been some improvement: the so-called material weakness in dealing with corruption was now only a "significant deficiency," a term implying that the Bank might eventually stop violating the fiduciary requirements of its own charter.[11]

The U.S. Senate Foreign Relations Committee, which by this time had been following corruption of lending by the World Bank and other multilateral development banks for nearly six years, strongly disagreed. In March 2010 the committee urged the United States and other major donor countries "to be firm in demanding that needed reforms are secured before committing additional funds" for the IBRD capital increase.[12] The committee denounced the continuing "pressure to lend," noting the Bank's "inertia and a reluctance to reform."[13]

But in the end, Congress approved the money.

Useful Expenditures

In justice to the Bank, it was hardly the only international institution struggling to get a handle on how to fight what appeared to be growing corruption in the international system; indeed, many looked to it as a leader.

There was growing evidence that some of the biggest engines of corruption were not just elements in the governments of many developing countries, but some of the largest and most respected multinational corporations, many of them major procurement customers of the Bank. One of the greatest corruption scandals of the past 60 years involved none other than Siemens, the 165-year-old German company (founded in 1847) that played the role of a leader, like its rival General Electric in the United States, in green energy, corporate social responsibility, and anti-corruption efforts.

Siemens was a member of the United Nations Global Compact, of the German Business Ethics Network, the World Economic Forum, and last but not least, Transparency International.[14] For the uninitiated, the UN Global Compact is, in its own words, a "strategic policy initiative for businesses that are committed to aligning their operations and strategies with 10 universally accepted principles in the areas of human rights, labor, environment, and anti-corruption." Siemens was one of its more illustrious members, and like the other members, it reported on, inter alia, its anti-corruption efforts in the Compact's "transparency and accountability policy."[15]

Through most of the first decade of the 2000s Siemens orchestrated a worldwide corruption machine that in scores of countries paid over $1.4 *billion* dollars in bribes in over 4,280 separate transactions, with the goal of winning contracts from its competitors. Bribes were typically at least 5 or 6 percent of the value of a contract, sometimes as high as 40 percent in the more corrupt developing countries. The individual bribes were the size of smaller World Bank loans—$40 million for a $1 billion contract in Argentina for national identity cards, $16 million in Venezuela for a "green" urban-rail project, $14 million in China for a medical-equipment contract.[16] Internally, the Siemens bribe slush funds were called *nützliche Aufwendungen*—"useful expenditures."[17]

During this same period, Siemens reaped around $140 million every year, on average, from World Bank–financed contracts.[18]

Investigations by German prosecutors in 2006, followed by separate inquiries by the U.S. Department of Justice and the Securities Exchange Commission, led to the exposure of the Siemens corruption web. As the investigations were echoed in headlines around the world, a shame-faced Transparency International revoked Siemens' membership in December 2006.[19] In 2008 Siemens paid one of the largest fines in corporate history to U.S. and German authorities—$1.6 billion.[20]

A year passed after the time of the initial investigations and Transparency's ouster of Siemens, and then another year, and then another six months, while hundreds of millions of dollars for Siemens contracts continued to flow through the World Bank lending pipeline. Only in July 2009 did the Bank announce that it had found that Siemens had paid $3 million in bribes in a single Bank project in Russia in 2005–6; obviously the scale of Siemens corruption in Bank projects must have been much larger. The Bank banned any further business with Siemens for two years, and Siemens could not bid on Bank contracts in Russia for four years. And Siemens admitted past (but unspecified) misconduct and agreed to contribute $100 million over a 15-year period to support international anti-corruption work. The Bank presented the settlement as a "groundbreaking" advance in its governance and anti-corruption agenda.[21]

Truth

In reality, the "Review of IDA Internal Controls" study greatly understated the extent of corruption at the very core of the Bank. For example, it found that "lack of information-technology security in certain areas" was a "significant deficiency."[22] What did this vague bureaucratic language refer to?

More than a decade after the Bank launched its anti-corruption efforts, the story of Satyam and the Bank, which extends from 2000 through the beginning of 2009, is exemplary, and profoundly unsettling.

Satyam was the name of the wildly successful Indian computer-services company that the World Bank contracted to manage its information technology (IT) and many of its most critical financial-accounting systems. It was surprising choice, since in 1999 Satyam was a small, little-known family firm in Hyderabad. The Bank's IT director, Mohamed Vazir Muhsin, a Sri Lankan accountant, set Satyam on its path by first awarding it contracts to address the Year 2000 scare. (In the late 1990s there was widespread concern that the turn of the millennium could cause widespread computer-network breakdowns because most computer code had not been written to deal with the date change.) In 2003 the Bank awarded a five-year contract to Satyam that, together with subsequent contracts and deals, was worth hundreds of millions of dollars. The company would eventually help manage many of the Bank's most important financial operations, including financial accounting for its 1,000-plus trust funds, such as the GEF, the Climate Investment Funds, and the various carbon funds.[23]

Satyam's World Bank contracts gave it the credibility to subsequently seal IT deals with several governments and more than 150 Fortune 500 companies, including General Electric, General Motors, Microsoft, Citigroup, Merrill Lynch, Cisco, Sony, Nestlé, as well as the United Nations and the U.S government. Satyam's clients often entrusted the company with their most critical and confidential computer services.[24] It was the kind of outsourcing triumph that Tom Friedman had been raving about in paeans to the wonders of globalization in his *New York Times* columns.

In early 2005, growing suspicions about Bank IT director Muhsin's financial lifestyle and his connections with Satyam led to an internal investigation—which, according to one account, was in danger of going nowhere until Paul Wolfowitz arrived as president in midyear.[25] It turned out that Muhsin had for years maintained close financial ties to the company's owners and was offered company shares at huge discounts before he awarded Satyam the series of contracts that literally made its fortune. In October 2005 Muhsin was expelled from the Bank with two hours' notice, just days before his scheduled retirement. In January 2007 the Bank debarred him from ever doing business with the institution again. Besides accusing Muhsin of having a secret economic interest in Satyam, the Bank also charged him with having orchestrated deals that allowed Satyam to become the beneficiary of 32 separate, so-called sole-source contracts and purchase orders.[26] In fact, by the mid-2000s Satyam was controlling virtually all the World Bank's computer software and codes; the Bank in a very real sense had lost control of its own information system.[27]

In 2007 and 2008, massive computer breaches attacked the World Bank's most confidential financial information. The Bank first learned of the intrusions when the FBI notified it, indicating that the Johannesburg South Africa office of the IFC was compromised. Subsequently, many of the Bank's servers, as well as its entire e-mail system, were compromised. It then emerged that Satyam had implanted spyware in the Bank's most sensitive computer systems, including the Bank's Treasury, which managed all of its money as well as another $57.5 billion in the trust funds. It was not clear who was behind the intrusions: some of the Internet Provider (IP) addresses were in Macao, but IP addresses can easily be disguised. Some speculated that Satyam had played a critical role, but the Bank and Satyam at the time denied it.[28]

The Bank had a lot of confidential inside information on governments and companies that could be profitable to hackers. One fear was that contractors, and even governments, wanted information on prospective Bank anti-corruption investigations, and also wanted to know what the Bank knew about corruption in member-country governments, which in some cases was a lot.[29]

When informed about the Satyam spyware, Robert Zoellick was apoplectic: he is reported to have exclaimed that he wanted Satyam "off the premises now." But it was not so easy: the Bank had lost control of its own information system, and that knowledge was in the heads of Satyam employees. The Bank would have literally closed down. Instead, it undertook a seven-month process of transferring the knowledge from Satyam employees to noncompromised staff and contractors; in fact part of the so-called process of knowledge transfer involved simply moving the contracted Satyam personnel to new Indian tech companies, where they would continue to work for the Bank's IT services.[30]

In February 2008 the Bank suspended Satyam from bidding for future contracts, and in September formally debarred the company from doing business with the Bank for eight years. But even in the autumn of 2008, the Bank had made nothing about the Satyam issue public, nor had it breathed a word to the United Nations committee that kept track of corrupt contractors. In the meantime, the UN signed a new $6 million contract with Satyam. Rather than warning the world, the Bank stayed silent. It subsequently claimed that around 2007 it did notify the U.S. Department of Justice about Satyam's fraudulent practices, but this action appeared to have no effect. It was only a Fox News report that finally forced the Bank to acknowledge the fraud.[31]

A few weeks later, the full extent of Satyam's corruption exploded as one of the greatest corporate scandals in modern history—"India's Enron," in the terms of the Indian Press. It started on January 7, 2009, when Satyam's founder and chairman, Ramalinga Raju, announced to the world that he had systematically falsified the company books, assets, and profits for years; about $1 billion in assets did not really exist. On January 20 Indian prosecutors announced that about a fifth of Satyam's employees, some 10,000, did not exist either, though they were very profitable, since Satyam charged its clients for their services, and substantial amounts of this money may have ended up in secret bank accounts for Raju and his relatives and friends. Disappointingly for those who might believe in the reforming power of confession, Raju could not be trusted even when he publicly declared he was coming clean; he even lied about the extent of the fake assets. In November 2009 the Indian FBI, the Criminal Bureau of Investigation, announced that the fraudulent assets amounted to still another billion dollars—a bogus billion here, a fraudulent billion there, for a company whose reported net worth was in the $4–5 billion range—ironically, it was adding up to real money.[32]

Meanwhile, during all those years the Bank was proclaiming its fight against corruption and bad governance. It was certainly an opportunity for lending more: between 2000 and 2009, from 15 to 34 percent of its yearly lending—$4 billion to nearly $7 billion annually—was going to support "governance related themes."[33] Internally, during the same period, Bank administrative budget expenditures to help carry out its governance work averaged over $140 million annually, padded by an additional more than $30 million a year from the Bank's trust funds.[34] Of course, all this money was kept track of and administered, at least from the information technology standpoint, by Satyam.

While some people in the Bank, particularly the IT department and highest levels of management, had increasing knowledge of Satyam's corruption culture, the deception reached grotesque proportions. In 2008, of all years, Satyam won the prestigious "Golden Peacock Award for Excellence in Corporate Governance," presented annually by the United Kingdom–based World Council for Corporate Governance, with Dr. Ola Ullsten, the former prime minister of Sweden, as the presiding judge. In 2006 and 2007, Investor Relations Global Rankings (IRGR)—using "proprietary research of publicly traded companies based on a clear and transparent methodology that is supported and backed by key global institutions, including Arnold & Porter, KPMG," etc., according to its website—rated Satyam as the company with Best Corporate Governance Practices.[35]

Some Bank staff not in the inner management loop were tragicomically clueless. In 2006 the World Bank's Sustainable Development Network published a report, "Beyond Corporate Social Responsibility: The Scope for Corporate Investment in Community-Driven Urban Development" that cited Satyam as a model case study, praising its Corporate Social Responsibility (CSR) efforts, which involved investments in environment, education, and health care in urban areas. Satyam, the Bank study proclaimed, made "the business case" for CSR. (In the 2000s "making the business case" became a favorite catchphrase of all kinds of organizations, from NGOs to universities, eager to show they were tough minded and serious.) The company went beyond mere charity by "using Satyam's management experience to turn each of its developmental projects into an economically sound business venture to build employment opportunities for the poor."[36]

Daniel Kaufman, a Brookings Institution scholar who led work on global governance and anti-corruption at the World Bank training academy, the World Bank Institute, for many years, wrote of "the illusion of CSR and codes of business integrity." He noted that the "whole politically correct mantra on CSR and voluntary corporate codes" was a common theme in both the Siemens and the Satyam scandals: both companies put themselves forth as leaders—and were in fact recognized as leaders—in socially responsible behavior. The whole value of such approaches, Kaufman observed, needs to be revisited.[37]

And what ever happened to Mohamed Muhsin, whom the Bank supposedly banned for life from ever doing business with it again? He joined a Sri Lankan company, John Keells Holdings, as one of its directors. In February 2008, 13 months after the Bank issued Muhsin's lifetime ban, John Keells Holdings received a $75 million loan from the International Finance Corporation, the biggest investment the IFC had ever made in the Sri Lankan services and manufacturing sector.[38]

In this saga there was one final irony, and a warning: *Satyam* means "truth" in Sanskrit.

Wolfowitz's . . . and Wolfensohn's Ghost

Paul Wolfowitz had left one positive legacy: greater awareness of the centrality of good governance and fighting corruption in the Bank's work. Weeks before his departure, the Bank's board finally approved his proposal to help borrowing countries improve financial management and accountability. But after four years, it was not faring well. Pressure from the board had resulted in a pitifully diluted "Governance and Anti-corruption Strategy," ensuring that even countries with deteriorating governance received loans—in the name of the poor of course, "not making the poor pay twice" for the corruption of their rulers.[39] The Independent Evaluation Group found in 2011 that the Bank's efforts focused more on trying to protect its own reputation and resources rather than on the institutional problems faced by its borrowers. And once again, the Achilles heel in the whole strategy was the Bank's lending culture.[40]

Many Bank staff and, outside the Bank, government officials, academics, and NGOs, told the IEG that the Bank's culture of lending imperatives conflicted directly with anti-corruption and good-governance goals.[41] The Bank was showing more attention to preventing corruption in some specific investment projects, but the corruption risks in the growing volume of policy- and budgetary-support lending were still not being addressed.[42]

The more things on the outside appeared to change, the more they remained the same.

Who to Trust

The Bank's trust funds were rife with even more governance risks, less supervision, and a greater likelihood of fraud and corruption than its main lending operations. Over the years, major aid-donor countries increasingly preferred setting up specific trust funds for political purposes to target specific countries and/or specific issues. Some trust funds had a single country donor, others several donors. The growth of trust funds in the international aid architecture didn't mean more aid; aid budgets in most countries were fixed, and putting more money into trust funds meant generally less money for other programs. The Bank was the biggest manager of these aid trust funds. Between 2002 and 2011 donors contributed some $67.8 billion to 1,075 different funds managed by the Bank, and by 2010–11 trust fund disbursements averaged over 8 percent of its total annual disbursements. The trust funds paid for a disproportionate amount of the Bank's internal administrative budget, around a quarter. The largest Bank-managed trust funds by far were for so-called global public goods, i.e., environment, climate, and public health.[43]

This was not good news for the environment. As we noted, most of the new money that rich countries contributed for global environmental purposes went to Bank-managed trust funds: the Global Environment Facility, the growing number of Bank carbon funds, the Climate Investment Funds, and even the prospective Green Climate Fund that the 2011 Durban climate negotiations endorsed.

The Bank's information gathering and monitoring of much trust fund finance appeared be in a semi-shambles. It was "extremely difficult," the IEG reported, to gather reliable information on fund use. Bank managers complained that they didn't receive enough information on the trust-fund monies to make adequate decisions, but they had to make decisions anyway. A Bank manager in Indonesia observed, "Eighty percent of the . . . approvals in my in-box each day have to do with trust funds—and often I don't really know what I am approving."[44] The Bank's executive directors, the IEG warned, were so poorly informed about the Bank's management of trust funds that they could not exercise governance over their administration. Bank management maintained that it had no responsibilities concerning reporting on "results related to development effectiveness" in trust-fund expenditures, since that was the job of the separate governance structures of the trust funds.[45]

Internal surveys found that about half of all Bank managers thought oversight of trust-fund activities was inferior to other Bank activities. They stated that staff felt a lesser degree of accountability for the use of the money, and the donor governments themselves "don't value supervision."[46]

The political propensity of rich countries to channel more and more money into trust funds—led by the United States, the United Kingdom, and the European Union—was certainly as responsible for this state of affairs as the negligence of high-level Bank management. But the Bank was an accomplice in a new aid model that was fraught with corruption and governance risks.

Once again the IEG had sounded the alarm. But were the donor countries and the Bank's management listening?

Go Directly to Jale

Zoellick himself faced problems trusting his own staff. In 2009, when he learned just how systematically some Bank staff had lied about an environmental project in Albania, he publicly called the Bank's actions "appalling."[47]

The Albanian "Integrated Coastal Zone Management and Clean-Up Project" was a typical example of how the Bank could leverage more money from other donors for environmentally and politically correct plans. The project's goals included "enhancing regulatory policy and governance of the coastal zone . . . and institutional capacity. . . ." It would "improve environmental conditions, enhance cultural resources and encourage community support for sustainable coastal zone management. . . ."[48] In 2005 the Bank succeeded in topping off its own $17.5 million loan for the project with a grant of nearly a million dollars from the Global Environment Facility, plus $2.2 million in grants from a Japanese trust fund, $5.2 million from the European Commission, $3.1 million from the Netherlands, and $2.6 million from Austria.[49]

Once again, if it hadn't been for the Independent Inspection Panel, and the refusal of Albanians displaced and impoverished by the project to keep quiet, the outside world might have never been any the wiser. After all—coastal-zone management, environmental cleanup, encouraging community support—who would question such an investment?

The reality on the ground was different. The project coordinator in Albania was the son-in-law of the prime minister; in fact he got the coordinator job shortly after his father-in-law took over the reins of power.[50] The project was supposed to support environmental management in the small coastal Albanian town of Jale, with the goal of developing a privately owned tourist resort. Most of the people in Jale were nobodies—poor and elderly. One fine day in April 2007, the villagers received a notice that their houses were illegal and would be demolished. They tried to appeal to Albanian courts, but just two weeks later police arrived in the town, the houses were bulldozed, and the inhabitants were evicted. One witness recounted that the police "surrounded the village like we were in a state of war . . . snipers in watching positions, for three days the road was blocked and no one could bring even food." The police were reported to have said, "Don't worry, you will be eating with silver spoons soon as this is part of a big World Bank project."[51]

The demolitions caused an uproar in the Albanian parliament; the prime minister and his son-in-law were accused of pushing the demolitions through in order to benefit their business interests in the tourist resort.[52] The villagers, homeless and practically destitute, appealed to the Bank's Independent Inspection Panel.

That there might have been abuses and corruption in a Bank-financed project was not so unusual. What was unusual was the reaction of Bank management and staff to the inspection panel's work, which was met by internally coordinated cover-ups, lies, and misrepresentations that went on for years.

Back in 2005, when the Board first considered the loan and expressed concern about the residents of Jale, Bank staff claimed that the Albanian government had agreed to provide humane resettlement and compensation, in accordance with Bank policies. Such an agreement never existed—it was fictitious. As this became evident in the panel's investigations, Bank management then presented fake documents, which supposedly corrected the original lie.[53] Then they claimed there was no connection between the project and the forced evictions, even in the face of letters from the project coordinator to the Albanian police requesting demolition of the houses.[54]

The panel reported management's clumsy lies to the board in no uncertain terms, citing an "omission of critical facts during staff interviews, and seemingly unusual lack of recollection of crucial Project events by some of the interviewed staff . . . instances of reluctance to provide or even identify relevant Project documents . . . a systematic effort to fend off the Panel's access to the necessary information . . . some staff gave the impression that there had been pre-interview 'coaching' . . . both at Headquarters and in the field. . . ."[55]

In this case, the Bank under Zoellick's leadership responded strongly, suspending loan disbursements until the project could be restructured and promising legal and other aid for the villagers. Zoellick declared: "The Bank cannot let this happen again."[56] It was the closest to a full mea culpa the institution had ever publicly admitted in recent memory.

Unfortunately, the villagers never received full redress for their misfortune. The Bank claimed that the Albanian government, not itself, was responsible for the abuses, and the Albanian government admitted no wrongdoing, even going so far, according to one press account, as to spread the rumor that the inspection panel was really linked to an "unnamed-land mafia."[57]

The international publicity over the project put a spotlight on two long-simmering issues: poor supervision of Bank operations and blatant lies by Bank employees about controversial projects. The critical importance of the inspection panel was reaffirmed more than ever. The *Economist* suggested that the panel should be strengthened so that it could also investigate corruption.[58]

Safeguards at Risk

The Inspection Panel and its homologue at the IFC, the Compliance Officer/Ombudsman (CAO), were set up to ensure that the Bank carried out its environmental and social safeguard polices, as well as the IFC's Performance Standards. But after more than two decades these protections were under siege as never before.

The increase in non-project policy- and budget-support lending was a major threat to the relevance of the Independent Inspection Panel and the CAO. Since the Safeguards and Performance Standards did not apply to these loans, complainants in borrowing countries could not call on the inspection panel or CAO to investigate abuses. Part of this increase in non-project lending was a temporary response to the global financial crisis, whereby the Bank helped to pump large amounts of money to critical developing-country governments. But the longer-term growth in non-project lending was also a response to increasingly vocal client governments, which preferred such loans because they were quick disbursing, and came with fewer strings attached.

Perverse pressures and incentives hampered carrying out environmental safeguards and performance standards for the half of the Bank Group's operations where they still applied. Too often the safeguards were treated as add-ons, and the Bank's environmental and social specialists had inadequate resources to do their jobs and weren't integrated into project teams. The Bank did not reward efforts to improve environmental and social quality. In the words of one Bank manager, "The incentives are not there. Nobody wants to work on safeguards."[59]

One of the most striking examples of how the Bank had regressed concerned resettlement. The first policy on involuntary resettlement dated back to 1980, preceding many of the subsequent environmental policies. For an institution that proclaimed its mission as poverty alleviation, one would think that a safeguard not to make the poor poorer would be one of the highest priorities. The policy provided that for Bank-financed projects involving forcible resettlement of populations—most often big infrastructure operations such as dams—a resettlement and economic-rehabilitation plan had to be prepared and carried out so that the affected population was, preferably, put in a better economic situation, or at least was left no worse off than before.

During the 1990s the Bank regularly updated its information on how many people were being displaced by its projects; this was prerequisite data for assisting resettlement-affected populations. In 1994 a Bankwide Resettlement Review found that in early 1994, 146 ongoing Bank projects were responsible for forcibly resettling and/or adversely affecting 2 million people.[60] In late 1999 another internal Bank inventory recorded 223 projects displacing or harming the livelihoods of more than 2.6 million people.[61]

In 2010 the IEG found that 30 percent of Bank projects involved resettlement. But in contrast to a decade before, Bank staff and management were unable to provide any information on the number of people adversely affected or displaced. A Bank manager years ago in the then-existing Environment Department had decided that gathering such data was not a useful employment of staff time.[62] The IEG had to estimate the figure, which it very conservatively calculated at over one million poor that at any given time were involuntary resettled or harmed in World Bank projects.[63] Experts on resettlement thought that the real number was probably much higher, at least double.[64] In one of its classic understatements, the IEG observed that "the resettlement impact of Bank-financed activities is nontrivial and merits careful monitoring to ensure it does not lead to impoverishment of affected persons."[65]

The Safeguards and the Performance Standards, whatever their weaknesses, were the core of the Bank's slow and reluctant move, over the past two decades, to become an ecologically and socially responsible institution. If the environment and its services, on which the poor in developing countries were especially dependent, were needlessly destroyed through Bank negligence, if the poor were further impoverished through Bank-financed projects, if indigenous societies were pushed further into social and economic disintegration by Bank-supported operations, the slogan that greeted every visitor to the main lobby of the Bank in Washington—"Our dream is a world free of poverty"—was a grotesque and cynical charade.

Thus, the continued erosion of the effectiveness of these policies during the Zoellick era was a scandal. It was true that the safeguards and performance standards imposed a minor cost in terms of time and money, but what was the cost of not applying them?

Despite its sizeable research apparatus, the Bank had never really attempted to weigh the benefits and costs of its environmental and social safeguards and standards. The IEG undertook a modest effort in this direction, examining the benefit/cost ratios of the safeguards and performance standards in several hypothetical, archetypal World Bank Group projects. One was a road project in Sub-Saharan Africa that would have traversed primary tropical forests and protected habitat areas, catalyzing illegal logging, threatening to involuntarily resettle 400 people, and negatively affecting 1,600 members of an indigenous tribe. The safeguards involving environmental assessment (identifying a less disruptive route for the road, for example), protection of forest habitat, reduction of illegal logging, protection of indigenous peoples, and addressing involuntary resettlement cost an extra $12.2 million, but benefits over the project life were estimated to be $335.5 million—a benefit/cost ratio of 27.3.[66]

Another hypothetical example involved an IFC-financed gold mine in West Africa employing 500 people. The IFC performance standards would help reduce accidents and deaths at the mine, reduce spills of toxic substances such as cyanide, and handle resettlement concerns involving people displaced from the mine site. The benefit/cost ratio for the IFC standards ranged from 1.5 for community health and safety, 3.6 for pollution prevention and abatement, and 4.4–6.5 for resettlement.[67]

In 2010 Bank management pushed to eliminate individual safeguards in favor of a single, simplified social- and environmental-sustainability umbrella policy. Supposedly the key elements of the old safeguards would be maintained, but the new policy would be streamlined, easier to use, and emphasize greater reliance on the borrowing country's own approaches rather than Bank prescriptions. The new policy would be less specific and more a statement of general principles and goals. All this was part of a far-reaching program to "modernize" the Bank. The details of the safeguard "reforms" were to be circulated in an initial draft in the latter half of 2012, with the goal of board approval by the end of 2013 or early 2014.[68]

Certainly in the Bank, as in any other large institution, there was a periodic need to update and streamline policies. But it was clear to many observers that the "Safeguards Reform" was one more step, in the words of Vince McElhinny of the Washington-based Bank Information Center, in a "shifting balance of power" where what was at stake was to what "extent the World Bank will remain a rules-based lending institution or dilute hard-won development standards in order to sustain lending to its largest clients."[69]

The Bank had proudly pointed to its safeguards as a model for export credit agencies and private international banks. Now the long-embedded loan-approval culture appeared to have finally triumphed as Bank management embarked on a path to undermine this achievement.

A Program for . . . Results?

Other, more far-reaching decisions under Zoellick would push the Bank toward even less accountability, as well as further undermining the inspection panel. The fact that half the Bank's lending was still going for projects ("investment lending" in the Bank's jargon) was still too much for management.

In 2009 the Bank proposed a dramatic shift away from project lending, which it claimed was "created for a different era." In a note to the Bank's board, managers characterized the Bank's safeguards as "one of the critical bottlenecks that slow delivery and increase preparation costs," a view shared by client governments. Preparing projects was excessively "rule-based," which meant spending too much time on "fiduciary and other demands," supposedly at the expense of work in and with borrowing countries.[70] One had to read such assertions twice: enforcing rules to protect the environment, the poor, and public money was just too much of a "bottleneck" that wasted the Bank's time?

Instead, Bank management argued that it was time to provide broader financial support to governments and to eliminate "direct accounting linkages between disbursements of Bank resources and expenditures by the client." Push the money out the door, and supposedly "the client's accounting and reporting system would demonstrate that resources are being used in the program."[71] The logic was tortured: the Bank's environmental and financial safeguards had been put in place precisely because, for many countries to which it lent money, one could not rely on the capacity and integrity of local practices. And evidence showed that in many of these nations, corruption had only gotten worse over the past two decades. The proposal was one of the most dramatic in Bank history: to eliminate the founding principle of its own charter: to "lend for specific projects, except in special circumstances."

Thus, much if not most project lending was to be replaced by something called "P4R," "Program for Results": i.e., loans to support borrowing-government development programs. The Bank's environmental assessments, safeguards, and financial management policies would not apply. Instead, it would rely on the borrowing country's approaches, evaluate the risks involved, and provide "implementation support," supposedly to help the country carry out the program once the money started flowing.[72] There would be a "shift [away] from an emphasis on supervision and compliance. . . ."[73] P4R was supposed to usher in a brave new world of "development results," which apparently Bank management had decided was not being achieved through continued lending for mere projects with more specific rules and monitoring of the use of the Bank's money.

Such an approach ignored the previous two decades of Bank experience with pushing money out the door without ensuring *first* that adequate capacity was in place to enable borrowers to manage it. This was the "sequencing" issue emphasized in the Extractive Industries Review: it was necessary to build technical and institutional capacity *before* lending large amounts in situations with weak governance, which was the situation of many of the Bank's borrowers. The Bank had learned nothing from the Chad-Cameroon debacle, or numerous other similar cases, or from recent IEG studies, which emphasized that the risks of fraud and corruption were greater in the Bank's non-project, "flexible" lending, because of "weakened safeguards" and greater reliance on "country systems," which, the IEG observed, "are often weak or nonexistent."[74] The fiduciary and safeguard systems of recipient countries needed strengthening, but to achieve this outcome, the Bank would have to redouble rather than relinquish its efforts in supervision and compliance.

Leading up to the approval by the Bank's board of the Program for Results in January 2012, many nongovernmental organizations protested what they perceived as a major dismantling of the Bank's remaining environmental and social commitments.[75] Over 200 civil-society organizations from 51 countries wrote the Bank in October 2011 calling P4R "the most radical development" in the Bank's march to dilute the Safeguards.[76]

Thanks in part to pressure from the U.S. Congress and Treasury Department, the initial P4R loans could not be used to support operations with high or irreversible environmental and social risks. Moreover, for the first two years, no more than 5 percent of Bank lending could be P4R, and both Bank management and the Independent Evaluation Group would conduct evaluations of the two-year pilot phase, with input from both civil-society organizations and the private sector.[77]

Still, the implications remained alarming. For one thing, eventually as much as a third of Bank lending could be channeled through P4R operations, and, combined with nearly 40 percent development-policy lending, conventional projects could account for less than 30 percent of Bank operations in the future.[78] The P4R operations could also be a mechanism for pooling Bank money with funds from both public and private creditors, including eventually from institutional investors, hedge funds, and sovereign wealth funds—sources which Zoellick hoped to tap.[79]

The IFC Über Alles?

The whole first decade of the 2000s brought to a paroxysm what many characterized as the "financialization" of Western economies: whereby the real economic activity of societies—producing and trading goods—became increasingly dominated by abstract financial instruments and intermediaries. Under Zoellick these same values became more prevalent at the Bank; some called it the financialization of development. The Bank's priorities appeared more and more to be finding novel new instruments, be it carbon trading or P4R, to move larger and larger amounts of money—and not just its own money—more quickly. Given Zoellick's background on Wall Street, it was an approach he understood. Thus it came as no surprise that the role of the International Finance Corporation in the World Bank Group became increasingly influential during the Zoellick years. On occasion, some disgruntled Bank staffers would describe what was happening as the "IFCi-zation" of the World Bank.

Zoellick himself admired the efficient, businesslike approach of the IFC, which owed as much to investment banking as to traditional development work. He reportedly contrasted the quicker, more deal-oriented IFC culture with that of the IBRD and IDA, which more resembled a think tank or a university—an observation some Bank staff did not take as a compliment.[80] In any case, the IFC's new annual financial commitments increased from a level of $3–4 billion in the early 2000s to around $15 billion in 2008 through 2010, and nearly $19 billion in 2011.[81] In 2011 the IFC accounted for about 30 percent of World Bank Group annual finance.

At first sight, the IFC appeared to have moved more quickly than the rest of the Bank to improve its environmental and social policies. Over the 2000s the IFC's Performance Standards were gradually strengthened, and in some respects contrasted favorably with the IBRD/IDA safeguards. For example, in 2006 the IFC finally guaranteed the right of workers in projects it financed to organize, a right that was a "Core Labor Standard" of the United Nations International Labor Organization that had been part of international law since 1998.[82] In 2012 it finally required its clients to obtain "free, prior, informed Consent" from indigenous groups for activities that would impact their land and natural resources, something that the IBRD/IDA safeguards still did not endorse.[83] The IFC also initiated a requirement for its clients to annually report the greenhouse-gas pollution of projects with yearly emissions of over 25,000 tons of CO_2-equivalent, and to make public their contracts with governments for extractive industry projects.[84]

The IFC claimed to make progress too in finally increasing financial support for renewable energy and energy efficiency, ramping up investments in renewable energy and energy efficiency by 60 percent from 2009 to 2011, to around $1.6 billion annually. These figures had to be viewed with caution: some of what the World Bank Group characterized as efficiency investments and renewables, we recall, was dubious: investments in, say, modernization and life extension of coal plants could be counted as funding for efficiency, as well as, in the Eskom case, financing a railroad to replace truck traffic to transport coal to a coal plant. Large hydroelectric dams in the tropics, which could be significant sources of GHG emissions, counted as renewables. Nonetheless, the IFC could point to new investments in greenfield wind farms in Mexico, China, Bulgaria, and Turkey. In India it was doing more to support solar power and, on a very modest scale, to help develop off-grid renewable power to reach the poor.[85]

But the progress on the performance standards was all too often made only under pressure from outside civil-society organizations that, in specific cases such as labor or indigenous peoples' rights, were only asking the IFC to recognize what were already long-established principles of the United Nations and international law. Human rights groups continued to protest that IFC policies undermined already existing, stronger standards recognized in the United Nations, and the IFC continued to maintain an overall restriction on disclosure of any supposedly "commercially sensitive and confidential information" of its clients.[86]

In any case, these new and improved rules did not govern most of the IFC's lending. Even more so than other parts of the World Bank Group, the IFC increasingly focused on non-project finance, such as lending to other financial institutions (so-called financial intermediary lending) and "Global Trade Finance"—short-term loans and guarantees to promote trade in developing countries. The performance standards did not apply to any of this lending. By 2010 only a third of the IFC's new annual finance was for traditional projects.[87]

True, some of this non-project lending did go for environmentally positive goals. For example, in 2011 nearly half of the IFC's $1.2 billion for renewables was channeled through financial intermediaries.[88] But in the absence of the performance standards, the IFC did not necessarily know the social or environmental impacts of the specific wind-farm projects, or hydroelectric dams, or large concentrated solar arrays it would help finance.

The IFC's belated increase in climate-friendly investments was also counteracted by its continued support for highly problematic mining and fossil-fuel development. The IFC, we recall, took the lead in financing huge new extractive projects such as the Marlin and Yanacocha mines in Guatemala and Peru, as well as new mining development in Congo, Ghana, and other parts of Africa. These projects were characterized by human rights and/or environmental abuses that aroused international concerns.[89]

In 2008 the IFC approved a $300 million loan to support expansion of the Camisea project, a huge gas and oil export-development undertaking in the Peruvian Amazon that had already generated a history of environmental abuses and conflicts with indigenous peoples. Oxfam and other nongovernmental groups in Peru, North America, and Europe condemned the IFC's involvement for lack of economic and social due diligence and for not complying with its own performance standards.[90]

Camisea was followed in 2009 by IFC loans for $215 million to American and British companies for offshore oil development in the coastal waters of Ghana. Contrary to its claims of promoting "best international practice" for environmentally risky projects, the IFC had approved practices that were truly substandard: in contravention of International Maritime Organization recommendations, the use of a single-hulled tanker, rather than a double-hulled vessel, as an offshore production, storage, and offloading facility, and the dumping of drilling wastes into the ocean. The Ghanaian government did not have coherent plans to deal with oil spills, nor did it have the equipment; spills affecting fishing villages had already occurred from initial offshore operations, with no clean-up response from either the government or the companies involved.[91]

In 2010 the IFC accounted for around three-quarters of total new World Bank Group investment of around a billion dollars in extractive industries, including still more oil and gas development in India, Brazil, and Ghana, and a large gold mine in the Solomon Islands.[92] By 2011, around a third of all complaints to the IFC Compliance Officer/Ombudsman (CAO) concerned extractive projects.[93] Through 2012 the IFC still remained involved in the notorious Chad-Cameroon oil development and pipeline project, several years after the IBRD had withdrawn because of continual violations of environmental, social, and fiduciary requirements.

The other, junior, private-sector finance partner in the World Bank Group, the Multilateral Investment Guarantee Agency, was no slacker either when it came to risky extractive projects. In August 2010, MIGA issued a $208 million loan guarantee for a Japanese-French mining consortium to help finance engineering studies for the Weda Bay nickel and cobalt mine, and an associated ore-processing plant, on the island of Halmahera in eastern Indonesia. The project, involving one of the world's largest un-developed sources of nickel, would threaten thousands of hectares of tropi-cal forest in the buffer zone of a national park.[94] The mine would release treated mineral-processing effluent and waste water beneath the sea in an area with coral reefs. Local fishing folk protested that the mine would threaten their livelihoods. Given the environmental and social risks, the U.S. World Bank Group executive director abstained from approving the MIGA guarantee, but he stood alone in this position among the other executive directors.[95]

MIGA's support for the development of the Weda Bay mine raises a critical issue: at what point is an investment, in this case prospectively one of the world's largest nickel mines on a small tropical island whose popula-tion depends significantly on forest and marine resources, inherently unsus-tainable, even with "best practice" precautions? In 2012 MIGA highlighted its role in Weda Bay as a model of "advancing sustainable investments." MIGA's view was that it was playing a vital role in helping the investors at an early stage study and mitigate environmental and social risk.[96] But even in the best of circumstances, the scale of such projects often turns the local ecology into a national environmental sacrifice zone, for the benefit of the global economy, revenues to the national government, and relatively high-paying employment for outsiders and a minority of the local people.

The IFC Failed . . . and Greenpeace Succeeded

At times it appeared that the IFC and MIGA intentionally sought out inher-ently risky, environmentally dubious projects on the theory that Bank subsi-dies would somehow make them more sustainable. A case in point involved $150 million in IFC loans between 2002 and 2007 to help two of the larg-est agribusiness concerns in the world, the soybean multinational Amaggi and the beef-processing giant Bertin, expand their Brazilian production fa-cilities. The conversion of Amazon rain forest for cattle ranching and soy-bean production is a global environmental concern, and the IFC projects required that the soy and beef be traced through the supply chain to ensure that the products would not come from illegally deforested lands.[97]

But whatever the intentions, one had to wonder whether subsidizing multibillion-dollar agribusiness in the Brazilian Amazon was a good use of international development funds. It turned out that both Amaagi and Bertin were sourcing their products from Amazon farms that used slave la-bor.[98] Amaggi ensured that no new deforestation occurred through its own farms, but it did not keep track of where its suppliers got their soya. Bertin not only failed to ensure that its more than 600 suppliers were not providing cattle from illegally deforested lands, it also resisted paying government fines for illegal activities at its slaughterhouses and it opened new ones in the heart of the rainforest.[99] After learning of the abuses, the IFC cancelled the remaining disbursements of its loan to Bertin in 2009.[100]

Amaggi and Bertin were so huge that the IFC loans were relatively small change and not essential for their expansion plans. The companies were clearly not particularly interested in greening their supply chains.[101]

Meanwhile, Greenpeace Brazil launched an international campaign that forced the country's entire soy industry to agree to a "soy moratorium" in 2006. The moratorium avoids the complications of tracing supplier chains by requiring zero new deforestation, monitored by remote-sensing technologies of the Brazilian Space Agency.[102]

In 2008 Greenpeace also launched a report and campaign, "Slaughtering the Amazon," against beef and leather products produced in violation of Brazilian environmental laws. The campaign helped spur aggressive legal enforcement by Brazil's public prosecutors and environmental agency against numerous ranches and slaughterhouses. Brazilian NGOs organized nationwide boycotts of supermarkets that continued to purchase beef from Bertin and other illegally operating beef producers and processors.[103]

There were clear lessons here on how to promote greening of supply chains, which might be applicable to other commodities such as palm oil and tropical timber. The IFC thought its loans would help make the soya and beef industries more sustainable, but the strategy did not work. What finally succeeded was a combination of political and legal pressure, combined with improved monitoring technology. This was the way to fight destructive market forces and the companies that profited from them—not trying to create new economic incentives with limited means.[104]

The IFC, the Private Sector, and the Poor

All of these dubious undertakings of the IFC, as with the rest of the World Bank Group, were justified in the name of poverty alleviation. Private-sector-led economic growth was needed for the poor, and the IFC could promote it and ensure that it would be environmentally and socially more sustainable, or so the argument went. But what if the IFC was not really helping the poor, and most of its finance was nothing more than international corporate welfare, a charge repeated by many for decades?

A 2011 internal study of 486 IFC projects approved between 2000 and 2010 showed that only 13 percent even included any objectives that explicitly targeted the poor.[105] Instead, an increasing proportion of IFC support, 63 percent, went to financial institutions and financial markets.[106] Most IFC projects had satisfactory economic returns, but growth does not necessarily help the poor, especially in situations where political structures, market failures, and other social barriers work against them.[107]

The study (conducted by the IEG) concluded with a painfully obvious admonition: "An enhanced understanding of the intended beneficiaries is key to creating opportunities for them."[108] But who were the real, intended beneficiaries of the World Bank Group—that is, beneath the politically correct rhetoric, who were the real clients? That was the question discussed in Wolfensohn's "town hall" meetings with Bank staff 15 years earlier, and a question that constantly recurs the more one examines the Bank's operations.

In reality, the Bank's support of the private sector necessarily marginalized environmental, poverty, and social concerns. Its priority was to promote a favorable investment climate, and that meant in negotiations with developing countries, the Bank took the side of investors, and acted as their advocate. Often developing-country governments were pressured to shoulder more financial risk of private companies and banks than they otherwise would have done.[109]

Promoting a favorable investment climate meant lower taxes, government guarantees, freedom from regulatory burdens, and reduced costs of all kinds for the multinational enterprises. The strategy emphasized shorter-term financial returns for the companies rather than long-term environmental sustainability or poverty alleviation. The World Bank Group was not alone in pushing such priorities: they came from the rich-country aid donors, and were reflected in the private-sector finance of the other publicly financed multilateral development banks, such as the Asian Development Bank and the Inter-American Development Bank.[110]

Moreover, the World Bank Group, and particularly the IFC, habitually supported companies that used offshore tax havens such as the Cayman Islands and Bermuda.[111] In 2011 two Danish watchdog groups examined the IFC's entire portfolio of extractive industries operations, some 69 projects. Of the 49 investments for which they were able to find data, 28, or some 57 percent, used tax havens.[112] This hardly seemed consistent with the Bank's proclaimed focus on improving governance, transparency, and fighting corruption.

The World Bank Group argued that there were legitimate reasons for using the offshore financial centers—for example, to avoid double taxation in developing countries or supposedly to "provide legal infrastructure that a given host country lacks."[113] In response to the Danish report, the Bank claimed that it was "very unlikely" that host developing countries would suffer reduced tax payments, but conceded that it was "possible" that the taxes paid to the industrialized countries, where corporations were based, could be reduced or avoided. In other words, the Bank admitted that it was giving publicly backed subsidized loans to companies that were avoiding paying taxes in the Bank's donor nations.[114] In November 2011 the Bank issued a revised policy on offshore financial centers, stating it would do more to help its borrowers improve the transparency of their tax systems—but only if they so requested.[115]

NGOs and some governments found such rationalizations and half measures disingenuous, calling for the World Bank Group not to support companies using offshore tax havens.[116] The use of offshore financial centers over the past two decades by multinational corporations, banks, dictators, criminals, and mafias has played an immense role in promoting corruption and undermining governance in virtually every country around the globe—directly undermining "sustainable development" and the "dream of a world without poverty." Corrupt elites, officials, and companies in developing nations, operating outside the legal accountability of any nation, had secreted to offshore accounts an estimated $7.3–9.3 *trillion*, about double the total amount of developing-country debt.[117] In the words of former French president Nicholas Sarkozy, addressing the European Parliament in 2008, "If we provide banks with loans, can we have them working with tax havens?"[118]

The Financialization of Development and Its Risks

Under Robert Zoellick, the Bank not only become more and more integrated with Wall Street, the City of London, the Cayman Islands, and other international financial centers—its ethos increasingly resembled them. As the IFC became the new model for the rest of the World Bank Group, the historical emphasis of the IBRD and IDA on projects, rules, and compliance (however imperfectly carried out . . .) appeared obsolete to influential Bank managers in the go-go world of financial globalization.

If one were to believe the official Bank rhetoric, the whole point of moving money more quickly with fewer restrictions was to free up time and resources to help countries develop better systems for using the money.

But it wasn't working. In fact, "implementation support," or building up capacity and institutions in recipient countries, was failing across the board.

The IEG reported in 2011 that in the majority of evaluations of the Bank's country work in recent years, "efforts at promoting environmental sustainability were rated marginally unsatisfactory or lower." Recipient governments just didn't view environmental management and sustainability as a priority. Bank supervision continued to be undermined by both perverse internal staff incentives and the Bank's failure to predictably allot resources for oversight of implementation.[119]

Nor were the anti-corruption efforts doing any better. Seven of the ten most recent country evaluations of Bank anti-corruption work found that "the achievement of anti-corruption objectives was unsatisfactory. . . . The Bank has not yet found a way to make interventions to reduce corruption more effective."[120]

Of course, none of this should have come as a surprise. Since the time of the Wapenhans and Morse Commission reports two decades earlier, it required only the most banal kind of common sense to understand that the central problem in the Bank was a culture of loan approval, institutionalized in various perverse internal incentives. Creating still more incentives and mechanisms to push money out the door—ever more quickly, in ever larger volumes, with less overall oversight and accountability—would only make the development ("sustainable" or otherwise) performance of the Bank worse.

This was the major legacy of Robert Zoellick.

CHAPTER ELEVEN

Dying for Growth

A NEW PRESIDENT WOULD TAKE the helm at the World Bank Group on July 1, 2012. Robert Zoellick was preparing to join Mitt Romney's presidential campaign, hoping he would be considered as a potential secretary of state or secretary of the treasury. Speculation on likely candidates for Zoellick's successor at the World Bank included Susan Rice, U.S. ambassador to the United Nations, John Kerry, former presidential candidate and chairman of the Senate Foreign Relations Committee, and none other than Larry Summers, former secretary of the treasury and president of Harvard. Summers' nomination would certainly have sent a signal—20 years earlier, as chief economist of the Bank, he had argued that the only way to solve environmental problems was through more growth.[1]

Instead, President Barack Obama went in a very different direction. In March 2012 he nominated Dr. Jim Yong Kim, a physician and anthropologist who had bitterly criticized the effect of Bank policies on the poor and public health in the 1990s and early 2000s. Kim's nomination was controversial for a number of reasons. For one thing, developing countries were increasingly impatient with the cozy, unspoken rule that the United States always appointed the president of the World Bank, and the Europeans the head of the IMF. For the first time, the Bank's borrowers put up two of their own candidates, who in conventional terms were arguably better qualified than Kim. Both had distinguished records as economists and administrators: José Antonia Ocampo, a former finance minister of Colombia and head of the United Nations Economic Commission for Latin America, and Ngozi Okonjo-Iweala, a former anti-corruption-crusading finance minister of Nigeria and a managing director of the Bank from 2007 to 2011. At the Bank Okonjo-Iweala received, in the words of the London-based *Economist*, "rave reviews."[2]

In contrast, Kim's background was in international public health. He, along with Paul Farmer, was a founder of Partners in Health, the innovative nonprofit that worked in some of the poorest places and most difficult settings on Earth: treating HIV in Haiti and resistant strains of tuberculosis in Russian prisons. He had served as the head of the HIV / AIDS department of the World Health Organization, and more recently as president of Dartmouth College. Critics asserted that he was unqualified, especially compared with Ocampo and Okonjo-Iweala, since he was not an economist, and his expertise was narrowly limited to health.[3]

In 2000 Kim had been the co-editor of a forceful indictment, *Dying for Growth*, of the disastrous impacts on public health of the neoliberal, pro–corporate economic globalization policies promoted by the World Bank and other international financial institutions. The book's title was a macabre pun: the poor in developing countries were literally dying because of the policy prescriptions of the Bank and IMF. In the words of the introduction, which Kim co-authored: "The studies in this book present evidence that the quest for growth in GDP and corporate profits has in fact worsened the lives of millions of women and men . . . [and has] inflicted additional suffering on disenfranchised and vulnerable populations. . . . The main advocates of neoliberal policies—governments of wealthy countries, banks, corporations, and investors—are those who have profited most handsomely from their application."[4]

Even more damning was a case study on Peru in the 1990s, based on Kim's own experiences in the country. He lambasted the World Bank Group's support for private-sector mining and oil production, singling out the IFC-financed Yanacocha gold mine as an egregious example. Under Bank-promoted policies, "environmental laws shaped to encourage investments have led to significant ecological degradation from deforestation, oil spills, and poisoned waterways. In mining towns, villagers reported mass deaths of fish and livestock as a result of copper and sulfate stream contamination."[5]

And he argued that Bank supported "private-public partnerships" (the state assumes the financial risks, and a private corporation, usually foreign, is guaranteed a profit—think Bujagali, Nam Theun 2, Yanacocha, Marlin, Tata Mundra . . .) were also undermining health:

> In developing countries, the principles of privatization have been applied to health services with similar disregard for the health of the poor and marginalized. . . . The capriciousness of such policy shifts highlights the lack of accountability with which multilateral agencies have designed, disseminated, and implemented their models.

The penalties for failure have been borne by the poor, the infirm, and the vulnerable that accepted the experts' designs.[6]

So it was hardly a surprise when the *Economist* not only backed Ngozi Okonjo-Iweala as the qualified candidate ("a golden opportunity for the rest of the world to show Barack Obama the meaning of meritocracy"), but stated that Kim's views were more appropriate for leading Occupy Wall Street than heading the Bank.[7]

For admirers of Kim's iconoclastic, radical views in *Dying for Growth*, one of his first public statements after his nomination was not encouraging: "The Bank has shifted tremendously since that time (2000), and now the notion of pro-poor development is at the core of the World Bank."[8]

Really?

The Future We Want?

Meanwhile, just as Kim was preparing for his first day of work, some 50,000 people from 189 nations gathered in Rio de Janeiro from June 13 through June 22 for the Rio Plus 20 Conference on Sustainable Development—"Rio+20." Expectations were low to begin with, and they were more than fulfilled. The conference confirmed the pervasive failure of political will, as well as the brazen hypocrisy, of most of the world's governments in effectively addressing global environmental challenges. Unlike the original 1992 Rio Earth Summit, heads of state of major countries stayed away; even Secretary of State Hillary Clinton, the highest-ranking U.S. representative, only came for a few hours.[9] In fact, host country Brazil and the UN organizers gave up the pretense of even trying: to avoid the chaotic collapse that had characterized the climate negotiations, the Brazilian foreign ministry drafted in advance a final conference declaration that everyone could agree on, since it committed no one to do anything. In fact, it even backtracked on existing commitments.

The 49-page document," entitled "The Future We Want," omitted a proposed call for ending subsidies for fossil fuels—despite the commitment of the G20 (that is, the group of 20 of the most important economies, including China, India, Brazil, and the richer industrialized nations) to phase out such subsidies in 2009. In any case, the G20 had done virtually nothing to deliver on that commitment.[10] Proposals for green taxes and obligatory reporting on sustainability for large corporations also were swatted down.[11] Instead the document "reaffirmed" 59 times (more than once per page) earlier commitments—to international cooperation, to sustainable development, and to the be-all and end-all, economic stability—with no indication of what specifically, if anything, would be done, with what means, and when.[12] "The Future We Want" also reaffirmed commitments of the 1972 Stockholm Conference on the Human Environment, of the 1992 Rio Summit, of Agenda 21, of the Rio Declaration, and of the 2002 Johannesburg World Summit on Sustainable Development ("Rio Plus Ten"). Lest anything be left out, "We recall as well our commitments in the outcomes of all the major United Nations conferences and summits in the economic, social, and environmental fields. . . ."[13]

Unlike the World Bank, no one could accuse the United Nations of institutional amnesia; the problem was one of total impotence.

The developing countries, led by China and Brazil, predictably saw the conference as an opportunity to demand more money as well as rights to intellectual property from the aging industrialized nations. They proposed still another new global fund for sustainable development, which would hand out $30 billion annually to support climate-friendly energy, sustainable agricultural practices, and even—a bit of a financial non-sequitur here—the phase-out of fossil-fuel subsidies. For a few hours, developing-country negotiators staged a walk-out to protest the refusal of the richer countries to endorse such a fund. The irony of course is that the formerly rich countries were in many cases already debtors of newly industrializing nations such as China and Brazil, the new creditors in the international financial system. The older industrialized nations were happy to talk and make vague commitments so long as nothing substantial was involved, like large amounts of more money.[14]

Meanwhile, in the real, natural world, human-caused greenhouse-gas emissions had increased by nearly 50 percent since 1992, and 1.15 million square miles of forest had been cleared, an area nearly 40 percent of the size of the continental United States.[15] The director of the International Energy Agency warned that "the world's energy system is being pushed to the breaking point, and our addiction to fossil fuels grows stronger each year." Because of the failure of governments and markets, the world was on a path to 6° Celsius warming by the end of the twenty-first century. Rising sea levels, extreme storms, and the collapse of agriculture in many regions could promote mass migrations on a scale unprecedented in human history.[16]

The conference was a particularly grotesque example of the disconnect between the fantasy world of climate politics and the real, natural world—where critical ecosystems were unraveling. Even the more mainstream, normally circumspect groups had had enough: the director of

WWF International (the World Wide Fund for Nature) denounced "The Future We Want" as a "colossal failure of leadership and vision." CARE proclaimed that it "was nothing more than a political charade" and the head of Oxfam UK called the conference a "hoax:" "they came, they talked, but they failed to act."[17]

The Green Economy—or the Greenwash Economy?

But there was a counter-narrative, namely that Rio was a partial success because of various nonbinding agreements made outside the official negotiations. The United Nations claimed that more than 700 voluntary commitments had been made, mobilizing $513 billion to promote sustainable development.

After more than 20 years, "sustainable development" had become a shopworn and empty phrase, so many of the conference participants preferred the terms "green growth" or "green economy"—and indeed the "green economy" was a major theme of the meeting. But was this simply a public relations pitch for "a greenwash economy," another vapid effort to repackage business as usual?[18]

Microsoft proclaimed that its operations would be carbon neutral by 2030; Virgin Airlines mogul Richard Branson headed an effort that pledged to make the Caribbean island of Aruba stop using fossil fuels by 2020. Coca-Cola pledged $3.5 million to support "more sustainable water access in several African countries."[19] Walmart, Unilever, the giant Maggi soybean agribusiness group in Brazil, Lockheed-Martin, Anglo-American mining, China Merchants Property Development, ArcelorMittal mining, Clorox, and Dow Chemical, along with scores of other corporations and national governments, endorsed various declarations supporting natural capital accounting, i.e., quantifying and accounting for the impacts and costs of economic decisions on ecosystems and the environment.[20]

The UN proclaimed a "Sustainable Energy for All Initiative": the aim was to double, by 2030, the proportion of renewables in world energy consumption and the rate of improvement in energy efficiency, as well as to provide electricity to the 1.3 billion people in the world without it.[21] The goals sounded familiar, echoing reams of UN and World Bank documents from past years and decades. And the players were familiar, too: there were some prominent leaders and academics in the renewable-energy field, as well as renewable-energy companies. But the other participants, whose financial and political clout was greater, were not a particularly reassuring lot: the World Bank and other MDBs, and the South African power utility

Eskom, which we recall had recently embarked on a coal-plant building binge without equal. Siemens was there, committed to a prominent public role in corporate social responsibility, as well as the Norwegian state oil corporation, Statoil, the Brazilian minister of mines and energy, the head of the Russian energy agency, and the leaders of the Brazilian and Chinese development banks.[22]

The World Bank and seven other multilateral development banks also pledged $175 billion for public transport—trains, subways, buses, and cycling lanes—over the next 10 years. This was not new money; it was a promise to use a bigger portion of existing funds for lower-carbon transportation. The World Bank and other MDBs would still fund massive highway projects, but public transport would play a larger role in their future lending—or so they promised.[23]

Past experience dictated caution if not skepticism. For the past two decades, the Bank had been promising to promote efficiency and renewable energy—which it finally, modestly, began to do in the two or three years leading up to the Rio+20 Summit, but in conjunction with large increases in financing coal, oil, and gas.

Waiting for Sustainability

It required a peculiar suspension of disbelief, a conference-induced amnesia, or as *Nature* had proclaimed in its denunciation of the December, 2011 Durban climate negotiations, a UN-conference-going-induced "Stockholm syndrome"—to give serious credence to the overall impact of most of the commitments. Yes, in some cases, the voluntary public engagement might indeed result in more environmentally "good things" happening at the margin than otherwise might have taken place. But the optimists at Rio seemed to be in denial of what was clear once one exited the conference center: the intensifying failure of governance and markets around the world to avoid ecological unraveling.

Instead of the two hobos in Samuel Beckett's play endlessly talking, declaring their firm resolve to go finally and do something, and then sitting still, waiting for Godot, the tragicomic play of Rio involved 50,000 people talking about 700 commitments of suspect credibility, waiting for sustainability—as the world outside burned.

For the global climate, time had already run out. Governments were not moving slowly in the right direction toward sustainability—they were moving backwards, driven by much more powerful economic and political forces than 700 voluntary United Nations commitments.

Accountable to Nature?

The World Bank was a cynosure for some of these voluntary, nonbinding pledges. Rachel Kyte, the Bank's new vice-president for sustainable development—recently promoted from years in the IFC as a vice-president—declared that the Bank was "all about action in support of countries to achieve growth that is inclusive, and green." The Bank claimed in Rio that nearly half of its lending in 2011, some $24.6 billion of $57.3 billion in new commitments, was for "sustainable development."[24]

The Bank highlighted its own version of "inclusive green growth," which included a highly publicized event and declaration on natural capital accounting. "Massive Show of Support for Action on Natural Capital Accounting at Rio Summit," the Bank's public relations department trumpeted.[25] To help nervous heads of state and finance ministers understand what such a commitment might actually entail, the Bank's "Frequently Asked Questions" section on its website was reassuring: Question: "What does it mean 'to support the communiqué'" Answer: "Expressing support for the Communiqué on Natural Capital Accounting will mean that your country will be featured at the . . . initiative's launch event on June 20th in Rio, as well as on this website and subsequent communications, and that you will be invited to discuss and engage on the topic of natural capital accounting with other national governments and organizations. . . ."[26] On the last day of the conference, Kyte enthused that "natural capital accounting events filled the Rio Convention Center. . . . This new energy and emphasis around this issue may be the most important outcome of Rio+20."[27]

Unfortunately, nongovernmental groups, academics, and even some marginalized elements inside the World Bank had pushed for "natural capital accounting" for over 20 years, with absolutely no impact whatsoever on real market forces. Leading up to the original Rio Earth Summit in 1992, a small but dedicated group of environmental specialists within the World Bank desperately tried to promote this approach, only to be squelched by then–Chief Economist Larry Summers.[28] Think tanks like the World Resources Institute published reams of studies that called for factoring in the true cost of destroying ecosystem services—again with no impact.[29] Indeed, economic globalization, freer trade, and deregulation unleashed a system where longer-term concerns for conserving "natural capital" factored less and less into financial decision making.

The Bank itself had fled from numerous opportunities to put a price tag on the environmental impacts of its lending decisions. In 2004 the

Extractive Industries Review urged the Bank to develop greenhouse-gas accounting and, most important, give economic weight to the climate impacts of prospective investments in its decision making. Over the past year the Bank was finally expanding its GHG accounting, but went out of the way to emphasize it was an heuristic exercise—with no economic weight in lending decisions.

At Rio, the Bank touted new pilot programs to help a few countries over a number of years develop still another "policy framework" for analyzing the value of, and impacts on, natural capital in economic decisions. But what were the environmental and social-safeguard policies of the Bank, if not a painfully won policy framework for analyzing and weighing such impacts? True, the safeguards were not written in the language of economics; they had the virtue of serving as quasi-regulatory guidelines that, if enforced, actually prevented destruction of natural and social capital, as well as identifying necessary mitigatory measures.

The most ambitious of newer efforts at natural capital accounting were, in a broader sense, none other than the failed carbon markets promoted through the Clean Development Mechanism and REDD+ programs. But as we saw, each of these efforts was plagued by corruption and fundamental questions about the environmental integrity of internationally tradable climate offsets themselves.

The Bank asserted that "much of green growth is about . . . addressing market failures and 'getting the price right' by introducing environmental taxation, pricing environmental externalities (such as carbon pricing), creating tradable property rights, and reducing inappropriate subsidies." It acknowledged that putting these principles into practice is "an enormous challenge" because of failures of governance and the realities of political economy, i.e., "political and social acceptability issues," "missing markets or institutions," and "inertia and biases in behavior."[30] In other words, "green growth" meant getting prices right and creating new markets—the utopian goal of much neoliberal economic policy. But there were the sticky problems of the resistance of human societies, anti-market social values, the perversity of human behavior, and in many cases the embarrassing absence of actually existing institutions, and the even more embarrassing problem of actually existing markets failing—uncomfortable questions if more markets were supposed to be the solution.

In many countries, and not just the poorest developing ones, the growing criminalization and mafiazation of important sectors of the economy mocked the pretensions of natural capital accounting. In fact, corrupt, brutal, and dictatorial behavior, based on ruthless exploitation of natural resources, some political scientists maintained, was eminently the most rational and successful path for many a ruler and politician in countries with weak or failing governance.[31]

While the Bank babbled on about "inclusive green growth" and "natural capital accounting," many saw the initiatives as an attempt to quantify, commodify, and privatize nature.[32] The political foundation of the German Green Party, the Heinrich Böll Stiftung (Foundation), criticized the Bank for asserting that new investments in infrastructure were the "heart of green growth" without identifying the preconditions necessary to avoid the conflicts between local communities and investors that had increasingly plagued infrastructure in developing countries—most especially in World Bank projects themselves![33] Again, it was as if the World Commission on Dams and the Extractive Industries Review had never taken place.

Yes, at a certain level of generality, everyone could agree with the need to put a value on environmental externalities, i.e., the real costs of harming ecosystems. But rather than strengthening the political and social-policy approaches that decades of experience had produced, the good-practice approaches of the Safeguard policies and the collective learning experiences of the World Commission on Dams and the Extractive Industries Review, the Bank preached further development of market mechanisms at the very time when governments (with massive bailout lending for the private sector, including lending from the World Bank) were desperately trying to save the global economy from the effects of overreliance on markets. For the environment, the Böll Foundation warned that such an approach could unleash new forms of resource exploitation and human rights abuses. There had already been harbingers in projects financed by the Bank's carbon funds—for example, Plantar in Brazil, controversial dams, and growing protests by some indigenous communities against the commodification of forest carbon.

In the words of an eloquent counter-manifesto at Rio,

> instead of expanding the scope of markets to every domain of nature, creating a true green economy would start from the opposite; reversing the tide of commodification and financialisation, reducing the role of markets and the financial sector, acknowledging the limits of business versus other spheres of life, and recognising the collective responsibility of all people for, and strengthening the democratic control over, the worlds' ecological commons. Rather

than a Natural Capital Declaration we need more Nature without Capital.[34]

The whole Rio+20 spectacle was best characterized by one journalist as "tragedy, farce, and distraction."[35]

"We Have a Great Mission Statement"

The following month, Jim Yong Kim made his first public pronouncements as president of the World Bank. They were a far cry from the worldview of *Dying for Growth*.

Speaking at the Brookings Institution in Washington on July 19, 2012, he declared: "You walk in the door of the World Bank and it says on the wall 'Our dream is a world free of poverty.' Now, I was so moved by that slogan on the wall. . . . So, we have a great mission statement. We know what we're doing in the largest sense and it's really critical."[36] He reiterated that sustaining economic growth was the major priority, but naturally it would be growth that was "inclusive" and "sustainable." He praised the achievements of the Bank, especially its subsidization of the private sector, noting for example that "all across the developing world, the International Finance Corporation, our private sector arm, together with MIGA, the Multilateral Investment Guarantee Association [Agency], are leading the way in proposing innovative approaches to leveraging private sector investment. . . ."[37]

At times his language seemed to echo the more vapid of the canned press releases of the Bank's public relations department. Kim appeared reluctant to voice independent views; he may have been all too aware of the criticism of his appointment in establishment circles and in the conservative financial press.

Near the end of the event a representative of a nongovernmental organization in Pristina, Kosovo, asked Kim about the Bank's ongoing plans to finance a new 600-megawatt lignite (brown coal) power plant in her country. The Bank's prospective support for the coal plant had become a high-profile international controversy, building on years of previous protests against Bank funding for coal-fired power.

The Dirtiest New Coal Plant in Europe[38]

On its face, the Bank's support for the Kosovo project appeared scandalous: after all, lignite is the dirtiest of all fossil fuels, with even higher emissions of sulfur and heavy metals such as lead and mercury, as well as carbon, than conventional coal. There was, however, speculation that in the wake of previous controversies, the Bank was actually reluctant to support the Kosovo lignite plant: it was doing so because of strong political pressure from the United States, with support from most of the European Union countries.[39]

In fact, the project revealed how the U.S. government took strongly contradictory positions within the Bank. The United States had been quite aggressive in criticizing the Bank's continued lending for coal, refusing to approve, for example, the Bank's loans for the giant South Africa Medupi coal plant in 2010. But the United States had invested a great deal of political capital in leading NATO bombing attacks against Serbia in 1999 in an effort to force Serbian withdrawal from Kosovo during the civil war that followed the breakup of Yugoslavia. The U.S. State Department had pushed aggressively for Kosovo's independence. Now the country was an economic basket case, and one of its gravest problems was a chronic shortage of electric power, associated with two decrepit lignite power plants operating below capacity; they were in desperate need of renovation or replacement. The quickest solution, as proposed by a U.S. Agency for International Development study, would be to renovate one of the plants, bringing it up to European Union coal-plant-pollution standards, and close the other plant and replace it with a new 600-MW facility.[40]

The Bank claimed in January 2012 that that while there was some potential for developing renewable energy sources in the country, lignite was the only cheap, plentifully available domestic fuel.[41] Yet this was not the case.

None other than the first—and last—so-called renewable energy czar at the Bank, University of California–Berkeley professor Daniel Kammen, vociferously protested the United States' support for the Kosovo project.[42] Kammen was the founder and director of the Renewable and Appropriate Energy Laboratory at Berkeley. The Bank touted his appointment in October 2010 to a newly created high-level position of "Chief Technical Specialist for Renewable Energy and Energy Efficiency," where he would "provide strategic leadership on the policy, technical, and operational fronts."[43] Kammen lasted all of 14 months and then returned to academia as the Bank abolished his position.

Kammen pointed out that simply addressing Kosovo's huge power losses from inefficiency—some 40 percent of the electricity generated—would be much more economical than funding a new plant. Combined with investments in renewable energy, efficiency measures would also create more jobs. Indeed, 200 megawatts of private-sector wind projects were already waiting for approval from the Kosovo government.[44]

Moreover, the health impacts of the new lignite plant, even if it met EU standards, would expose the inhabitants of the nearby capital, Pristina, to pollution that in the United States, as Kammen pointed out, is responsible for the premature deaths of 30,000 people annually. If the proposed project were to proceed, it would leave "a devastating legacy for a young nation that we know can have a different path."[45]

Kim replied to the Kosovo activist that he thought that the Bank's member countries and Executive Board expected it to play a "very large role" in confronting climate change and other environmental issues. "We'll simply have to figure out over time the best mechanisms to do that. The commitment to it is there."[46] After 25 years of Bank declarations on its commitment to the environment, and 20 years after its initial commitments to address climate in its energy lending, the Bank's new president said the Bank was still trying to figure out "over time" what to do.

In fact, in his response to the question of the Kosovo lignite plant, Kim demonstrated exactly what the problem was. He first declared that "energy is a critical part of boosting prosperity and eradicating poverty," a statement that everyone could agree on but that did not clarify anything. He then added that there were differing views among the Bank's executive directors "about this tradeoff between our need to keep the environment clean and poor countries' need for energy."[47]

One might venture that Kim knew better than this, that this was a false tradeoff, but perhaps he realized that he was in the middle of a political minefield.

The IFC Marikana Nightmare

Kim's first major overseas visit to Africa on behalf of the Bank, in early September 2012, raised more disturbing questions. In South Africa Kim effusively praised the local staff of the IFC, but made no mention of the worse massacre of workers since the apartheid era at the IFC-supported Marikana platinum mine just three weeks before. In August, police opened fire on striking miners, killing 34. Most of the victims were migrant workers who lived in insalubrious shanties and shacks. As Jim Yong Kim arrived in South Africa, Archbishop Desmond Tutu denounced the massacre; "Marikana felt like a nightmare," the Nobel Peace Prize laureate declared.[48]

The Marikana project showed the hypocrisy of companies that proclaim their leadership in "corporate social responsibility" while catalyzing appalling social and environmental conditions. Through 2010 the IFC had committed $200 million in financing to the London-based Lonmin corporation, the world's third-largest miner of platinum. Lonmin in turn promised an ambitious community-development program for the Marikana mine workers, including workforce training, opportunities for women, and HIV/AIDS education. The program was highlighted on the IFC website with every catchword of politically correct sustainable-development-speak—including a clever PR slogan for the extractive industries: "Digging Deep for Development."[49]

During the whole period of IFC involvement with Lonmin, the Benchmarks Foundation, a South African NGO affiliated with the South African Council of Churches, conducted on-site visits and issued reports on the real conditions at the company's platinum mines at Marikana, as well as in the adjacent mines of the Anglo-American corporation. Anglo-American was one of the multinational corporations highlighted in the Bank's Rio+20 event as having committed to natural capital accounting. In 2006, as the IFC was appraising its prospective involvement in Lonmin, Benchmarks reported that the platinum boom in northwestern South Africa had huge negative environmental and social impacts on the 350,000 people in surrounding communities, "contrary to the popular myth that the benefits from mining trickle down to local communities." Benchmarks expressed hope, though, that the environmental, social, and poverty problems might be addressed by the mining companies.[50]

Five years later, just two days before the Marikana massacre, Benchmarks released an alarming report on the failure of "corporate social responsibility" of the mining companies in the region:

> We have seen very little improvement in the performance of the companies. . . . What we have seen, is a large increase in corporate advertising, large spreads in newspapers and billboards stating how responsible mining is, in particular by Anglo [Anglo-American] Platinum.[51]

For the Lonmin operations at Marikana, Benchmarks found a high, "unacceptable" level of fatal accidents; "appalling" housing conditions with a "proliferation of shacks and informal settlements, the rapid deterioration of formal infrastructure and housing;" drainage leaks and spills of sewage that resulted in chronic childhood illnesses, including bilharzia; asbestos-contaminated school buildings; and a failed, abandoned white-elephant hydroponics "'Corporate Social Responsibility' community project" in "wrack and ruin."[52] Indeed, "environmental degradation goes like a golden thread in the area; in fact, the situation seems even worse than more than five years ago."[53]

The "inclusive green economy" propaganda of Rio, and the pronouncements of the new Bank president, even as he visited South Africa, were totally disconnected from this stark reality. In a press conference in Pretoria on September 6, 2012, Kim emphasized that in South Africa the Bank's "largest efforts are through the International Finance Corporation, our private sector wing. So I would never dare to change a mission as powerful and clear as ending poverty and boosting prosperity. That's a wonderful mission to have."

Asked about the Bank's role in financing fossil fuels and coal, Kim maintained that South Africa "needed energy in order for the economy to grow—in order for the economy to grow and provide good jobs so that people can [unclear] poverty you need energy. And there was a very strong sense that this clean coal project was the way to go." He was referring to Medupi, which South African nongovernmental groups had convincingly shown was not going to provide power for the poor. Yes, the fourth-largest new coal plant on Earth, financed with over $3 billion from the Bank, was "clean coal." Kim added that, yes, we also needed to mitigate climate change, but he had to balance competing priorities.[54]

Dying for Growth

In fact, as Kim was extolling the IFC, conflict continued to spread to its other extractive investments.[55] When Kim took over at the Bank in July, protests against the expansion of the IFC-financed Yanacocha gold mine in Peru culminated with the police killing five people.[56] Though it would be unfair to expect Kim to keep track of every controversial project, he had singled out Yanacocha in *Dying for Growth*, we recall, as an example of non-sustainable, non-inclusive, environmentally harmful investment.

In late 2011 and mid-2012, there were also CAO complaints and mass protests against other IFC-supported mines in Peru (in this case an operation run by natural-capital-accounting leader Anglo-American) and Colombia—both charged with serious health and environmental damage. In the Colombian case, local community groups and NGOs protested risks from a Canadian-owned gold mine to downstream drinking water that supplied the city of Bucaramanga, with 1.2 million people, in an area that Colombia's environment ministry had prioritized for conservation and preservation. The IFC-supported the project despite an evaluation of Colombia's environmental ministry that it was "environmentally nonviable in the way its development and environmental management have been structured. . . ."[57]

The IFC continued its extractives binge in Sub-Saharan Africa, providing

$150 million in late June 2012 for multinational mining giant Rio Tinto's Simandou iron ore project in Guinea, a mine that was cofinanced by the Chinese mining company Chinalco. The IFC's action was described in the Australian press as "shoring up Rio [Tinto's] share" in the project, making the IFC a 5 percent minority shareholder in the mine. The U.S. executive director of the World Bank Group refused to approve the project, since the IFC had rushed in to participate before the requisite environmental and social assessments had been completed.[58]

In early 2013 the IFC was preparing to give up to $900 million in loans, and MIGA up to $1 billion in risk guarantees, to support Rio Tinto's development of a huge copper and gold mine, Oyu Tolgoi, in the Gobi Desert in Mongolia. The project would disrupt large areas of nomadic herders' pasture lands, divert much of the only underground river in a water-scarce arid region, and obtain power from a new 750-megawatt coal-fired electricity plant. It would be one of the three biggest copper-gold mines on Earth, would export mainly to China, and would account for over a third of Mongolia's GNP by 2018. The Sierra Club and other environmental organizations protested the Bank's "climate hypocrisy" of not requiring a consideration of lower-carbon alternatives to the project's coal plant.[59] Mongolian organizations representing the herders filed a complaint with the IFC/MIGA CAO. The view of the herders, some of whom had even tried working for the mine, was expressed by one who declared: "We don't need money from mining. . . . What we need is water and land."[60] In March 2013 the Bank's board approved the IFC's support for the mine, notwithstanding the abstention of the U.S. executive director, who cited critical gaps in the environmental and social assessment, as well as a lack of details on the cumulative impacts of the project, such as those associated the proposed coal plant. The U.S. representative also noted that, despite some recent improvements, Mongolia still lacked institutional capacity for mining regulation.[61]

The perspective of the Mongolian herders was backed up in a way by an unusual source, the Bank's own semiannual publication on Africa's economic prospects, *Africa's Pulse*. The October 2012 report asserted that not only were investments in extractive industries not benefiting the poor, the relationship of such investments to poverty alleviation was at times even inverse. Extractive projects did result in high apparent economic growth rates in quite a few Sub-Saharan African countries, but

> some countries such as Angola, Republic of Congo, and Gabon have
> actually witnessed an increase in the percent of the population living

in extreme poverty. Overall, the decline in poverty rates in resource-rich countries has generally lagged that of the region's non-resource-rich countries. . . . To a large extent, the benefits of growth have not reached the poorest segments of society.[62]

While more than half of the natural-resource-rich countries in Sub-Saharan Africa had middle-income status (a per capita income of over $1,000 annually), they often had lower levels of education and health than the regional average. Incredibly, "many of the resource-rich countries score at the bottom of the [United Nations Development Program] Human Development Index."[63] In fact, Gabon, with a per capita income of over $10,000, "has one of the lowest child immunization rates in Africa," noted the Bank's chief economist for Africa.[64]

It was particularly ironic that a high-ranking Bank official would single out Gabon as an egregious example of non-inclusive, unequal growth from mineral (in this case oil) extraction, since the Bank's signature "green inclusive growth" natural accounting event at Rio highlighted, along with several northern European prime ministers and various corporate bigwigs, none other than President Bongo Odima of Gabon. Bongo Odima had recently inherited the kleptocratic empire of his father Omar Bong, who had been the country's dictator for 42 years.[65]

The central problem, of course, was poor governance and its associated corruption, which the "resource curse" persistently made worse, despite (and sometimes because of) the efforts of the World Bank Group and other public international financial agencies. Oil-rich countries had the most perverse results of all; they, concluded *Africa's Pulse*, "systematically perform worse than other country groups in terms of voice and accountability, political stability, rule of law, and the control of corruption. . . . This pattern has persisted over time."[66]

The Solutions Bank?

The new president's contradictory positions were in full evidence at the World Bank/International Monetary Fund meetings in Tokyo in October, 2012.[67] Kim's statements reflected the conflicting political pressures in the Bank, what may have been his own ambivalent views, and perhaps his ignorance of the Bank's actual operations.

He emphasized in a "town hall" meeting with NGOs that he had spent most of his career as "part of civil-society [organizations] demanding social justice." "I can't end poverty without the deep engagement of CSOs." "I am very concerned on climate change—we will move forward on this," he asserted.[68] He claimed that the Bank had "absolutely no intention of diluting the safeguards," which he described as a "great accomplishment."[69] But the Bank needed to "get through the [safeguards] process more quickly."

He also claimed that Bank staff "agree that we are too focused on volume instead of results," and seemed to blame the Bank's executive board and member countries for the problem: "We want the board to stop paying attention to approval and volume."[70] The loan-approval culture in the Bank was a product of various pressures, but from the 1992 Wapenhans Report onwards, the first and foremost problem had been identified as a perverse internal incentive structure, reinforced by many who rose in management, that indeed rewarded staff for pushing money out the door. The Bank, he said, "needed to reward those staff who produce results for the poor." And what was the model for the entire World Bank Group for accomplishing this? The "IFC has moved in this direction and we need to move in this direction."[71]

This was an astounding and depressing statement; was Kim aware of the recent (2011) IEG evaluation of the IFC and the poor, which found that 87 percent of IFC operations reviewed had no explicit objectives relating to the poor; that, for the most part, the IFC didn't even bother to collect data on how its lending impacted the poor; and that in 2011 more than two-thirds of its financing went to the financial sector?[72]

His address at the meeting's plenary session was full of lofty rhetoric. He quoted Martin Luther King Jr. about the arc of the moral universe bending toward justice; he cited anecdotes that seemed to be a stock feature of World Bank Group presidential addresses, depicting poor peoples' aspirations (a 26-year-old woman in Honduras who wanted jobs for her community, a mother in India who wanted a clean neighborhood and clean air to keep her children healthy).[73]

"What will it take?" he asked. He then reiterated the changes that had been launched by Zoellick: the Bank had to become "faster, more innovative, more flexible," particularly with respect to middle-income countries, lending, for example, to "financial services in asset management and hedging." He praised the IFC again for "unlocking new investment funds for the private sector in frontier markets." The Bank had to focus on results, so "that's why I will work with the board to streamline our procedures, simplify our processes, and cut down project preparation time."[74]

Politically correct rhetorical flourishes aside, Kim's words seemed to reconfirm the further weakening of environmental and social safeguards, and the growing abandonment of project finance as the main business of the Bank.

Bank staff at the Tokyo meeting were decked out in identical T-shirts with the logo "What Will It Take?"[75]

More bizarre, but typical of the corporate sloganeering that increasingly permeated the Bank's rhetoric over the years, was his declaration that the "we must stake out a new strategic identity for ourselves. We must grow from being the knowledge bank to the solutions bank." This did not mean that the Bank had ready-made solutions, he explained, but that it would work with clients, partners, and local communities to identify them. The big problem was delivery—implementation. So a "relentless focus on the details of implementation" was required.[76]

Kim was restating the same contradictory goals of World Bank presidents past; he was almost channeling Wolfensohn's "strategic compact" and Zoellick's "modernization initiatives," just with a revised vocabulary. Speed up lending, simplify or marginalize all the pesky procedures, fiduciary rules, and environmental and social safeguards, but simultaneously improve results on the ground and implementation: that is, square the circle.

Of course, the World Bank Group didn't have the resources or expertise, let alone the political power, to "end poverty" or save the environment. But it *could* play a leadership role—setting a standard for other banks, export credit agencies, governments, and yes, the private sector. It only had to listen to the voices and criticisms of some of its own staff, whether in the environmental area or in many of the findings and recommendations of the Independent Evaluation Group. But throughout the Bank's management there was a persistent failure of leadership—part of a global failure of governance that was rapidly foreclosing the future of humanity. The initial public appearances of Jim Yong Kim, who had inspired much hope for change, aroused fears that this failure of nerve was highly contagious at the Bank—and that no one was immune, not even the president.

CHAPTER TWELVE

What Does It Take?

IN NOVEMBER 2012, the World Bank with great fanfare released a report entitled "Turn Down the Heat," urgently warning that the Earth was headed for 4° Celsius (7.2° Fahrenheit) warming in coming decades, with catastrophic impacts. The world, and particularly its poorest populations, faced the prospects of increasing droughts and food shortages, rising malnutrition rates, the flooding of coastal cities, and growing shortages of water in many regions. There was increasing uncertainty about the future of economic development itself. The Bank's president, Jim Yong Kim, declared that "it is my hope that this report shocks us into action."[1]

He proclaimed that "data and evidence drive the work of the World Bank Group" and that "the World Bank is a leading advocate for ambitious action on climate change." The Bank, Kim added, will "redouble" its efforts to support "national initiatives to mitigate carbon emissions and build adaptive capacity as well as support inclusive green growth and climate-smart development."[2]

No one could doubt Kim's sincerity, but there was a massive disconnect between his statements and, as we have examined, the history of the Bank concerning the environment and climate change. If the Bank's internal priorities did not change, there would be little likelihood that it would be more effective in the future than the past, not just in addressing climate change and environmental issues, but in achieving its newly proclaimed goal of "inclusive green growth."

The World Bank Group, as we have seen, had suffered for decades from a bureaucratic original sin: the loan-approval culture, coupled with a lack of political will to resist the contradictory, often hypocritical pressures of its donors and borrowers. Tens of thousands of pages of both internal Bank reviews and external studies had documented the implications of this conundrum, to very little effect. Poor performance of Bank projects, massive corruption of lending, and incoherence in promoting consistent environmental goals across its operations (of which its lending for fossil fuels combined with siphoning off new multibillion-dollar funds to fight climate change was an outstanding example, but hardly alone)—all were rooted in the Bank's dysfunctional internal culture.

This management culture was in large part the end result, and the mirror, of the political contradictions and hypocrisies of its member nations. The misguided decisions of senior Bank managers to push money more quickly with fewer controls also stemmed from a desire for the Bank to remain relevant in a world of growing private-sector and middle-income-country (e.g., China, Brazil . . .) international financial flows. These new sources of funds often did not bother very much with procedures or conditions related to social and environmental impacts of what was being financed.

Yet the Bank itself, at least its Independent Evaluation Group, had identified a clear solution. To avoid irrelevance, starting with middle-income countries that could find finance elsewhere, its operations should become "beacons of performance" of good and best practice in the areas of environment, social equity, and anti-corruption. If it focused on quality, rather than quantity, its projects would "encourage replication and scaling up." It would have to be much more selective in the future in choosing which projects it would finance.[3]

Another key lesson of the past two decades concerned "sequencing"—i.e., the need in many situations to build up governance structures and institutions first before showering Bank money on a proposed investment program, a sector (particularly extractive industries), or a country. Otherwise infrastructure gets built first, but the social, environmental, and fiduciary "software" that would improve the chances for an investment to actually benefit people, gets left behind. One could view the "resource curse" as just an extreme example of this more general principle of "governance first."[4]

As Kim assumed the presidency, the need for these fundamental reforms was greater than ever. If the Bank simply pursued its strategy of pushing out more money with less oversight, it would not only contradict its own avowed principles, it would become obsolete as an institution. The World Bank could never compete with, say, the Chinese Export Import Bank, which in 2011 approved $82.57 billion in loans—over $25 billion more than the entire World Bank Group for that year.[5]

Let us examine the ramifications of the Bank's dilemma, and what it would take to begin effective change.

★ ★ ★

We have seen many examples of the Bank's perverse lending culture. But it is useful to look at the straight arithmetic of the perverse incentives that are at work. Compare two projects: a $5.7 million Global Environment Facility energy-efficiency program in Vietnam, and a $335 million hydroelectric dam in Ethiopia, made possible by a $195 million IDA credit. The Ethiopian dam disbursed 35 times more Bank-managed money than the Vietnamese energy-efficiency project, yet it only involved 3.8 times the work in internal Bank preparation and supervision. The dam's total cost was 58 times that of the energy-efficiency project, yet only provided 20 times as much electric power as the efficiency investment would free up.[6]

From the standpoint of efficient use of scarce public resources, the math would appear to be overwhelmingly in favor of the efficiency project; but from the standpoint of the amount of internal Bank staff time involved to push money out the door, the dam wins hands down. Still more effective in moving money with less cost, from the Bank's internal standpoint, are non-project loans. Because the Bank's donors are unwilling to pressure the Bank to change its internal incentives, projects like the Vietnamese efficiency operation are typically financed through trust funds like the GEF or the Climate Investment Funds—while the main energy portfolio too often continues to lend for fossil fuels and other big projects that work at cross purposes with climate and efficiency goals.

Thomas Heller of Stanford Law School, who was asked by the Bank to participate in an external review panel on the Bank's energy and climate performance, concluded that the Bank's environmental failures were rooted both in the perverse incentives of the Bank's organizational culture, and in the equally perverse dynamics of political economy on the borrower side. (On either side there is a preference for moving large amounts of money to the detriment of environmental, climate, and economic-efficiency concerns.) He noted these problems had been known to the Bank since the early 1990s. "Are there systemic or institutional reasons that cause the persistence of these obvious and long-standing attributes of World Bank Group practice?" "The unanswered question," he noted, "is why outcomes should be different now and in years to come than they have been in the past."[7]

The incentives would have to change.

These perverse incentives also explained why many of the biggest Bank Group environmental and social scandals often turned out to be economic debacles: the litany of such projects began with the Argentina-Paraguay Yacyretá Dam, but also include more recent investments such as the India

Tata Mundra super-thermal coal plant. The Bank bore no financial account-ability for its lending decisions (its loans are guaranteed by the borrower countries and, in the last resort, by the donors), so it was the problem of the borrower governments and their populations (not the sometimes corrupt officials who negotiated the loans) if things went awry.

Dirty Money and Cleaning Up the World

We have seen that the corollary of the loan-approval culture was corruption of Bank lending. Corruption undermined every goal the World Bank Group set for itself. But without changing internal incentives, the Bank's anti-corruption efforts would remain marginal. Even Paul Volcker met his match in the resistance of the Bank's management and board to change this culture: "A strong focus on managerial and institutional accountability is absent," he wrote just before Robert Zoellick entered office. Under Zoel-lick the continued move away from project lending to general finance only exacerbated the problem.[8]

But the Bank's responsibility—and missed opportunity—to address corruption goes much further than simply reducing the "leakage" from its own lending. The World Bank (and its sister, the International Monetary Fund) have a key role in a corruption issue of an entirely different scale—corruption that dwarfs the theft from all forms of international aid. It is the issue of what former international businessman and Brookings Institution schol-ar Raymond Baker has called "dirty money," or illicit capital flight from developing nations (that is, the transfer of money and assets from countries with weak governance and high financial risk to more-secure jurisdictions).[9]

Baker estimates these losses at $723 billion to $844 billion annually in the first decade of the 2000s, around 5 percent of the entire gross national income (GNI) of the developing world in 2008. India lost a total of $128 billion during the period 2000–2009, Indonesia $145 billion, Nigeria $182 billion, Mexico $504 billion. Adjusted for inflation, this looting grew about 10 percent each year.[10]

How do you steal nearly a trillion dollars a year? About half comes from trade mispricing, the over- and underpricing of exports and imports, with Western banks and companies helping crooked officials and businessmen in developing countries to channel huge sums into offshore accounts and shell companies, and in turn, into bank accounts and investments in New York, Frankfurt, Zurich, or London. The other half of the dirty-money flows are the proceeds of bribery, kickbacks, outright theft and tax evasion. Major international banks have specialized in setting up elaborate chains of phony accounts and dummy companies in scores of offshore jurisdictions. Major Western companies have used the same offshore mechanisms, and a variant of mispricing within enterprises known as transfer pricing, to avoid paying taxes.[11]

The sagas of illegal capital flight and theft by notorious rulers have been well known for decades. But the World Bank and IMF not only continued to loan to these kleptocracies, but also studiously underreported and ignored these huge illicit outflows from their borrowers. Moreover, the growth in looting was directly associated with the market and trade-liberalization policies promoted by the Bank, the IMF, and other aid agencies over the past 20 years. In fact, we have seen that the World Bank Group itself became an increasingly profligate supporter of companies using offshore tax havens in the 2000s.

In the case of India, for example, Baker and his colleagues concluded that

> What is clear is that, during the post-reform period of 1991–2008, deregulation and trade liberalization have accelerated the outflow of illicit money from the Indian economy. Opportunities for trade mispricing have grown, and expansion of the global shadow financial system accommodates hot money, particularly in island tax havens.[12]

Thus, there exists a huge mass of invisible, financial dark matter in the development cosmos.[13] For every dollar of official development assistance flowing from rich to poor nations, around seven to eight dollars of dirty money flows from poor to rich ones.[14]

Moreover, corruption and illicit transfers of resources are most prevalent in sectors with particularly intense impacts on ecosystems and local communities, such as extractive industries (oil, gas, mining, logging) and large infrastructure.

The scale of these illicit financial flows is particularly relevant to the demands of developing nations in UN climate negotiations for an additional $100–200 billion annually to help finance lower-carbon, more-expensive energy production, and to help them adapt to climate change. These demands build on decades of pleas that the rich nations greatly increase overall foreign aid and forgive more of poor-country debt. The total amounts developing nations have asked for from the rich nations are only a fraction of what they lose to them through illegal flows of dirty money.

The World Bank and the IMF have largely ignored this larger issue of dirty money outflows, since their masters, the G8 finance ministries, and more recently the G20, have shown relatively little enthusiasm for getting a handle on the problem, even post 9/11, when it became clear that the same techniques that have allowed the corrupt rich in poor countries to stash their wealth out of country are also useful conduits for terrorists and international criminal syndicates.

At the Rio+20 Summit, the Bank and other participants would have been better served by making a real commitment not to natural capital accounting, but to *honest* accounting. The World Bank and the IMF could begin by undertaking a more realistic appraisal of work they do constantly—calculating national accounts and flows of trade and capital. Currently, "national accounts are all wrong," says Baker. "Mispricing, falsified transfer pricing, smuggling, and most forms of money laundering shift money out of developing and transitional economies, [contributing] hugely to poverty within these economies."[15] An attempt at estimating, calculating, and publicizing the real financial flows between rich and poor countries would in itself be a powerful spur for rich countries to assume their responsibility in the further impoverishing of the poorest.

After estimating the flows of dirty money for prospective borrowers, the Bank could promote in its policy lending specific measures for borrowing countries to stanch the outflow, measures such as curtailing trade mispricing and to requiring full reporting on beneficial ownership in all banking and securities accounts.[16] Conveniently ignoring the huge capital flight of dirty money, Bank adjustment and development policy loans have entailed measures to squeeze poor countries even further: controversial austerity measures and incentives to increase commodity and agricultural exports (putting greater stress on already unsustainably managed ecosystems). The macro-accounting behind these programs has been, in a gigantic, global sense, rigged. Changing this would require the full engagement and cooperation of Western finance ministries, banks, and corporations, since they are enablers and accomplices of the current state of affairs.

The disconnect is immense between the Bank's development rhetoric and these massive, untransparent, corrupt financial flows from the Bank's borrowers to its donors. In the words of dirty money expert Raymond Baker: "The borrowers stole the money and the lenders helped them steal it, and neither side can say so. In my judgment this is the ugliest chapter in international commerce since slavery."[17]

Unaccountable

Ironically, when the Bank called for natural resource accounting at Rio+20, it was abandoning the most basic elements of textbook economic evaluation and accounting, particularly the use of cost-benefit analysis in its investment projects. One of its most important mandatory policies, OP (Operational Procedure) 10.04,"Economic Analysis of Investment Operations," has required since 1994 that every investment project must be chosen to maximize "net present value" based on an economic analysis compared with alternatives. There is an exception for projects whose benefits cannot be measured in monetary terms, but even here the operation has to be justified as costing least to achieve the desired objectives.[18]

Traditional cost-benefit analysis had been criticized by environmentalists and some economists for decades because it did not quantify or weigh environmental and social costs, so-called externalities. The concept of "internalizing the externalities" was a hoary one, recognized in theory but mostly ignored in practice, dating back to its formulation by British economist Arthur Cecil Pigou in 1920. Moreover, the traditional approach discounted future economic benefits beyond a few years to a present value of almost nothing—i.e., the longer-term economic benefits of maintaining ecosystems and harvesting resources from them selectively also counted for nothing.

The Bank's 1994 policy would have been a major step forward toward correcting some of these defects, if only Bank management and the board had ever taken it seriously. It contains a requirement that a prospective project be sustainable in economic, institutional, and environmental terms over its lifetime, and that "externalities"—the costs of the external environmental and social impacts of the project domestically, and across borders of nations, be taken into account in the economic analysis.[19]

But over the 2000s the Bank virtually abandoned calculable cost-benefit analysis of any kind for most of its loans. The percentage of investment projects that included an economic cost-benefit analysis declined from 70 percent in 1970 to 25 percent in 2008.[20] Moreover, a 2010 IEG report found that the "weak points in economic analysis of bank projects are fundamental issues such as the public-sector rationale, comparison against alternatives, and measurement of benefits against a without-project counterfactual." In other words, the decision to approve a project only rarely gave full consideration to alternatives and whether that project would produce a public good.[21] Even when cost-benefit analysis was performed, it was typically completed *after* project approval. Further, there was a clear bias toward overly optimistic findings, since the cost-benefit analysis was typically done by project managers who benefited professionally from moving money out the door. Not that these findings mattered much anyway, since there was a "general lack of interest by senior management and, in some cases, active staff opposition to the use of cost-benefit analysis for decision making."[22]

And yes, a major internal study of the Bank on its use—and lack of use—of cost-benefit analysis nearly 20 years before—in 1992—found precisely the same problems as the 2010 IEG study: "lack of interest by higher management, low morale stemming from the belief that better evidence would not alter decisions, poor incentives, and lack of skills. . . ." The 1992 report made numerous recommendations that were ignored.[23] All of this took place in an institution that arguably had the greatest number of PhD economists of any single organization in the world.

Some members of the Bank's board were clearly chagrined by the 2010 IEG findings. After all, it was essential that the Bank assure both donors and borrowers that its resources were used in a cost-effective way. Worse, all this was going on, or more properly said, not going on, while the Bank declared itself "the knowledge bank" and as Zoellick's marginalization of project finance was relabeled the "Results Agenda." Minutes of a meeting of a committee of the board of eight executive directors that met to review the report record their exhortation that "as a knowledge institution, and in the context of the Results Agenda, the Bank was urged to continue to take the technical lead on how costs and benefits may be measured." Not only that, "they considered it unacceptable that Bank operational policies are simply disregarded. . . ." That the Bank was ignoring its own policies and procedures also raised "the issue of the Board's fiduciary responsibility. The need for clear policies for staff and both negative and positive staff incentives to follow the operational procedures were noted."[24]

Yes, once again "noted"—and again subsequently ignored.

False Solutions

There is no shortage of policy discussions concerning the future of the Bank—and of Bank internal documents about itself—that propose agendas for the Bank's future. But many proposed reforms are false solutions, distractions from addressing the deepest underlying problems crippling the Bank's effectiveness. The foremost problem is undoubtedly the persistent loan-approval culture that is furthered by the Bank management's lack of accountability for changing the culture. Second, even if the Bank were reformed to focus on quality, not quantity, it would still face the daunting issue of whether its interventions, and those of any aid agency, could make a real difference in countries with weak governance and institutions. Many proposals for the Bank's future tend to coalesce around several common themes while begging these more fundamental questions. Let us examine these false solutions and see why they cannot resolve the fundamental challenges facing the Bank.

More Involvement of the Private Sector and Private-Public Partnerships . . .
Greater involvement of the private sector has often been touted as a partial answer to the quandaries of aid, whether this private-sector involvement comes through privatization, public-private partnerships, deregulation, corporate social responsibility, or voluntary commitments. It was not just the Bank, but the United Nations itself, that, when faced with the failure of governments to agree on effective action and sufficient resources to deal with climate change and global environmental challenges, almost in desperation turned to multinational corporations as, at the very least, a stopgap. That in part was what Rio+20 was all about. And at the Bank, over the decade of the 2000s and beyond, we've seen the rise of the IFC as the model for the rest of the institution.

Yet in practice much of the IFC's record has been dismal; the list of extractive projects it supported that almost inexorably catalyzed environmental deterioration and social unrest is truly impressive. Its analytical engagement to even look at the poverty impacts of its investments, we saw, was startlingly absent. Its model projects that were supposed to show how private multinational corporation income would help the poorest were alarming debacles. Let us recall one more time the highly touted Chad-Cameroon project, from which once again the Bank Group appears to have learned nothing. In the words of two political scientists writing in late 2010, "The intervention of the World Bank has arguably done Chad's people irreparable harm. . . . The main things that have changed are that the benefits of retaining power are vastly higher, and that the government now has the money to buy arms."[25]

Yes, constructive, careful, selective engagement of the private sector can help the poor and the environment—but if the fundamental problems at the Bank are not addressed, much of the help from the IFC and MIGA will continue to do more harm than good.

The Knowledge Bank . . .

In 2012, Jim Yong Kim proclaimed that the World Bank Group should transition from being "the Knowledge Bank" to the "Solutions Bank." But how could it find solutions if it never remembered to stop committing the same mistakes?

If nothing else, the history of the Bank over the past 20 years has been a monument to the proposition, eloquently put forth in the late 1990s by the now-defunct internal Bank "Quality Assurance Group," that the corollary of the Bank's institutional optimism was institutional amnesia.[26] The Bank's internal evaluations constantly repeated findings and recommendations of similar reports dating back a decade or even two decades, findings and recommendations that were systematically ignored—the bureaucratic equivalent of the chorus in a Greek tragedy. The tragedy, of course, was not for the Bank, which did very well for itself in continuing to lend for the same mistakes, but for the poor and the environment—the supposed beneficiaries of its operations.

Moreover, academic researchers have raised major questions about the credibility of much of the Bank's intellectual work. For one thing, already by the early 2000s the Bank's public relations budget began to exceed research expenditures. David Phillips, a British economist who worked at the Bank for 14 years before writing a book on its failed reforms, noted with British understatement that the expanding PR budgets, while research expenditures remained stagnant in real terms, were "of questionable relevance" for improving operations.[27]

More importantly, at the Bank's own request, a distinguished group of economists from such institutions as Princeton (Angus Deaton), Harvard (Kenneth Rogoff, who had been director of research at the International Monetary Fund), MIT, and the United Nations Development Program evaluated Bank research from 1998 through 2005, coming up with some unsettling findings. During that period Bank researchers and consultants produced over 4,000 papers, reports, and books. While the economists praised some of the publications, they noted that the research was often used to "proselytize on behalf of Bank policy, often without taking a balanced view of the evidence." The Bank's leadership ignored internal research that was unfavorable to the Bank, and gave great prominence to more-favorable findings. It selectively touted "new and untested research as hard evidence that its preferred policies work," giving "unwarranted confidence in the Bank's prescriptions." Some past heads of the research department alleged that they were pressured by management and the PR staff to avoid generating information that could be used to criticize the Bank. Not infrequently they would be asked by Bank operations staff to come up in advance with a study that would show that a particular program or policy was successful. The pressure to lend was "tremendous."[28]

Five years later, in 2011, economists and development experts at the University of London concluded that the Bank mostly ignored the critique leveled by Deaton, Rogoff, and other distinguished economists.[29]

Other observers pointed out—in *Foreign Affairs*, for example—that it was nevertheless enormously valuable that the Bank made internal reports critical of the institution available to the public.[30] Yes, up to a point—but what if the reams of internally commissioned studies had no impact on the institution? Could transparency alone change the on-the-ground impact or quality of its operations? More broadly speaking, could transparency pressure authoritarian governments to democratize, and serve at least as a partial check against the massive corruption and kleptocracy that had increased faster than economic growth in the world (and not just the developing world) over the past two decades? This was certainly the hope of many both outside and inside the Bank.

Transparency Will Reform the Bank and Its Borrowers . . .
Everyone could agree that giving the public more access to information was a good thing. And indeed, the Bank was a leader among public international organizations in terms of transparency. Robert Zoellick had reinforced the trend by making public the Bank's voluminous data collections on every aspect of its work; for the first time, Zoellick emphasized, the information would be "freely available to anyone with an Internet connection."[31] The Bank also partnered with Google to create maps of public services in developing countries by using crowd-sourcing (input from citizens, communities, researchers . . .), something that could potentially be of use to anyone trying to promote development on the ground. When Google at first insisted that the information generated would be proprietary, the Bank did insist that it should be made available to all for free.[32] Washington pundits and development experts mused that Zoellick's "Open Data Initiative" could change the culture of the Bank "from inside out," creating a new, bottom-up, democratized development process.[33] Zoellick proclaimed that "the next step is to allow people to use handheld devices to let the Bank know, from any location, what is really going on with its projects."[34]

This leap into cyber-utopianism was timely, and indeed fashionable—after all, Hillary Clinton's younger cyber-advisers in the U.S. State Department thought that democratic, pro-Western, pro-market revolutions could be unleashed around the world by freer access to the Internet, cell phones, and social media such as Twitter. In reality, much of this was an illusion. For example, during the protests of Iran's rigged 2009 elections—protests alleged to have been catalyzed by Twitter users—Al Jazeera fact-checkers found that there were only 60 active Twitter accounts in Tehran, which dropped to six once the government cracked down.[35] Authoritarian governments from China to Russia and Belarus have proved themselves quite adept at manipulating the Internet for their own purposes, even by regularly paying thousands of government-sponsored bloggers, and using the blogosphere to whip up nationalistic sentiment.[36]

Evgeny Morozov, a Belarus émigré web expert and author, has cogently pointed out that the introduction of technologies like mobile phones into corrupt, dysfunctional social and governmental settings often simply turbocharges existing pathologies. In Kenya, for example, "who could have predicted that learning of the multiple money-transfer opportunities offered by mobile-banking, corrupt Kenyan police officers would demand that drivers now pay their bribes with much-easier-to-conceal transfers of air time rather than cash?"[37] The brave new world of globalized, interconnected, unregulated markets, combined with the power of the Internet, has energized the opening of new markets in endangered species, allowing corrupt mafias of poachers and potential buyers to connect and trade. Morozov cites the example of Kaiser's spotted newt, a species found only in Iran, as one of the first species that will be driven to extinction by the Internet: nearly a dozen companies are selling specimens online, and the endangered newt's population collapsed 80 percent between 2001 and 2005.[38]

In the case of the World Bank, there is a huge disconnect between the rhetoric of a developmental cyber-utopia, on the one hand, and recent trends in Bank operations, on the other. Under Zoellick, let us recall once more, the institution moved away from investment projects that can be monitored to less-transparent non-project loans to governments and the private sector. Where the Bank has made praiseworthy efforts to fight corruption through greater transparency, the results have been disappointing because of the unexpected strength of political and social pathologies. For example, the Bank supported the Extractive Industries Transparency Initiative, which required developing-country governments to publicize information on their revenues from extractive investments by multinational corporations. The hope was that this would help alleviate the "resource curse," but an IEG review found that the initiative had little impact on improving governance, improving management of income, and curbing corruption.[39]

The infatuation with new technology as a solution to what are political, institutional, and social problems not only postpones a final reckoning, it often exacerbates existing problems by ignoring their root causes.[40]

A New Mission as Financer and Provider of Global Public Goods . . .

As it entered the second decade of the twenty-first century, the Bank's crisis of mission became more and more apparent. Its relative importance as a source of public international finance had been declining for many years. Its soft-loan window, the International Development Association, continued to lend to the poorest countries, mainly in Sub-Saharan Africa, with mixed results and growing competition from newly emerging economic power-houses such as China and Brazil. The relevance of the other branches of the World Bank Group, the International Bank for Reconstruction and Development (IBRD), the IFC, and MIGA, faced growing questioning. The increasing number of countries that were achieving middle-income status could borrow from other sources than the IBRD. Although Bank management had been promoting a growing role for the IFC over the past two decades, critics of every ideological persuasion questioned the utility of this subsidization of the private sector, particularly of larger multinational corporations.

At the same time, we saw that the older industrialized countries preferred to use the World Bank to administer trust funds to address global environmental issues such as climate change. Climate was just one of a number of "global public goods," such as public health and ecosystem protection, that called for international collective action. Unfortunately, the nation-states of the world, with their short-term financial and political priorities, were failing to address these challenges with either the required economic policies or finance.

So the World Bank, as one argument goes, was a global institution in search of a new global mission, and the world needs a transnational institution with the financial and technical expertise to address the growing challenges of the so-called global commons. Certainly President Jim Yong Kim's resolve to reorient the Bank toward fighting climate change was congruent with this view.[41]

The Bank, it is alleged, has "the global reach," the "technical depth," and the "fiduciary strengths" to play a much more important role in saving the global commons, starting with climate. The older industrialized countries and the newly rich economies such as China should agree, for example, on establishing an ambitious new arm of the Bank to address global public goods on a much larger scale.[42]

This argument—put forth by the experienced head of the Center for Global Development in Washington—exemplifies much of the discourse around the Bank in official circles in Washington and other capitals: give the Bank more money to address new issues. Decades of experience and reams of Bank reports detailing institutional dysfunctions and project fiascoes have failed to disrupt this kind of thinking. Time and again, conventional wisdom ignores the fundamental problems of the Bank's internal culture and the challenges of governance in many of its recipients. Why should we pump still more resources for "global public goods" into an institution that manifestly cannot fulfill its existing mandate of environmentally sustainable economic development? In fact, as we have seen, it is precisely in the area of climate where the Bank's institutional dysfunction and contradictions, as well as those of its member countries, are most acute.

What then does it take?

Beacons of Good Practice

Real change would start with a reorientation of priorities and internal incentives that reward quality rather than quantity in the Bank's operations. Although Bank management prattled on about a "results agenda," in terms of attention to developmental quality they were moving in the opposite direction. A focus on quality would mean a renewed commitment to project finance that can be monitored, which is what the Bank's charter requires. This would mean a shift not only in internal incentives, but also in institutional accounting priorities. If a project's goals are better met through more staff time but lower loan amounts, then that approach should be pursued. Staff should be rewarded if, for example, they use more administrative budget to prepare and monitor a smaller loan for an energy-efficiency project that has better environmental and energy payoffs than a larger loan for a large hydroelectric dam, not to speak of a giant coal plant.

Bank management, we remember, characterized project lending as obsolete and rigid—too focused on safeguards and fiduciary requirements, and not suited to borrower needs.[43] Let us recall once more the observation made by one of the Bank's founding executive directors that "to avoid the wasteful utilization of foreign loans which had been frequent in the past the Bank was enjoined to lend only for the financing of specific projects and to exercise close supervision of the funds it lent."[44] With the growth of new forms of corruption and the increasing environmental and social risks of many large investments, this admonition is more urgent today than when it was uttered in 1951.

Since Rio 1992 the Bank *had* accumulated knowledge and identified measures that could help sustain the environment and improve the lives of the poor. The problem was that these approaches were often unpopular with management and borrowing countries. This neglected legacy includes the environmental and social safeguards and the recommendations of the IEG, the World Commission on Dams, and the Extractive Industries Review. The Bank's efforts in these areas are already promoting standards and processes that could serve as the evolving framework for good practice in major international-development finance, public and private, in the future.

These are real achievements, albeit often arrived at through external political pressure and the protests of civil-society groups in both borrowing and donor nations. In a world ever more urgently in need of leadership on the environment and social equity, the Bank has developed an invaluable intellectual capital and potential influence—if it were only more fully engaged to use it. It has been a tragedy, not for the institution, but for the future of a sustainable world order, that the Bank has retreated from these priorities.

The Independent Inspection Panel and the IFC Compliance Officer/ Ombudsman also represent important strides in making financial institutions more accountable for the impacts of their activities. The other multilateral development banks followed the World Bank Group's lead in setting up their own versions of an independent inspection function. Several publicly financed export credit agencies, including Canada's Export Development Corporation, the Japan Bank for International Cooperation, and the U.S. Overseas Investment Corporation, have also set up their independent inspection and compliance mechanisms.[45]

Accountability mechanisms like the ones pioneered in the World Bank Group not only provide redress for the intended beneficiaries of international development, but are very much in the self-interest of financial institutions themselves: when empowered, they can both improve the institution's reputation and help correct its mistakes. Their investigations identify important management and policy issues, and they illustrate that ignoring environmental and social safeguards is often more costly than compliance.[46]

If, rather than moving away from its safeguards and accountability mechanisms, the World Bank instead strengthened and promoted them, it could leverage its most important comparative advantage in a world where other financial institutions have more money and fewer scruples. The hard-won lessons of the Bank's experiences might then set influential precedents for good practice in other institutions and investments.

Instead of aiming for good and best practice, Bank management often thought it had to take risks to show it could make inherently unsustainable, socially and environmentally risky investments better—whether in extractive industries, large infrastructure projects, or speculative carbon-trading deals—resulting in many of the Bank's biggest and worst debacles. It ignored the warnings of the past two decades to be more selective in its investment choices.

Yes, in some cases the World Bank Group could legitimately argue that its involvement in such projects meant that they would be subject, in theory, to higher standards than those governing other equivalent projects. But also in such cases it was questionable whether the actual record in mitigating environmental and social impacts was substantially better.[47] The Bank's chronic underinvestment in monitoring and evaluation of ongoing investments, similarly documented for the past two decades by reams of internal reports, played a major role in these failures.

The more important question is whether the World Bank Group's subsidization of projects with inherently excessive environmental, social, and political risks is the best use of scarce public international funds.

Governance First

The other lesson of more than 20 years of World Bank Group efforts was governance first: even the best-conceived projects failed without proper institutional and legal capacity. In practice this means designing interventions in a sequenced fashion; where governance capacity is weak, it has to be built up first before large amounts of money can be pushed into ambitious schemes.

Unfortunately, the Bank's own experience has shown that attempts to build up local capacity were often swamped by much more powerful global economic forces. This was particularly true for the Bank's wildlife, biodiversity, and forest-protection projects, which were frequently overwhelmed by internationally driven demand and prices, and by highly organized cabals of investors and mafias that made poaching, illegal logging, and destruction of natural habitat for cash crops virtually irresistible. This is a challenge for which there appears to be no easy solution, or any solution at all without a major reorientation of the world economic order and national economic priorities.

There was no question that for many officials in the Bank's borrowing nations, corruption and bad governance were not only eminently rational in terms of self-survival, but wise politics. Achieving power and staying in power meant stealing from the poor and giving to the rich, and keeping the rich on one's side. In the words of political scientists Bruce Bueno de Mesquita and Alastair Smith, "absolute corruption empowers absolutely." In their trenchant analysis of global politics since the end of the cold war, *The Dictator's Handbook*, they cogently argue that "bad behavior is almost always good politics." The World Bank Group's loan-approval culture has been the handmaiden of such behavior for decades. And for decades successive Bank presidents have failed to change the Bank's internal culture while pushing new claims that this time aid will work for the poor—"a quest," Bueno de Mesquita and Smith observe," that is "phoenix-like in its ability to rise and rise again. Or come to think of it, maybe, like Sisyphus, we just keep climbing the same hill only to fall down again."[48]

The Bank cannot solve these conundrums, but its interventions and selective finance could help build up governance and democratic accountability at the local level. There are critical lessons, gained at great cost, on how to begin to do this contained within the recommendations of the World Commission on Dams and the Extractive Industries Review, the important precedents set through its independent accountability mechanisms, and many of the findings we have examined in over two decades of OED and IEG reports. Ignoring this experience has been hugely expensive in monetary terms, and immeasurably costly for the world's poor and for the global environment.

A World to Gain—or to Lose

The global financial crisis that began in 2008 was only the latest evidence of the folly that market forces and a deregulated private sector will lead the world along a path of "inclusive sustainable growth." Instead, this model of development has further marginalized hundreds of millions people—displacing them from the last asset they possessed, access to land and natural resources. India has been a case in point. In 2011 India was still by far the World Bank Group's largest cumulative borrower, and the Bank had been instrumental in promoting a partial deregulation of the Indian economy since the early 1990s.[49] Billionaires proliferated, as well as corruption.

At the same time, an underreported armed rebellion of India's poorest, led by Maoist-inspired communists, intensified across the remote forests of the country. The insurgency spread through the areas inhabited by India's more than 100 million tribal people, who are often outside the caste system and who endure deeply ingrained social and economic discrimination. By 2010 over 20,000 armed guerrillas controlled around 20 percent of India's forests, had killed over 6,000 police, soldiers, and other people, and were active from the south of India all the way northward to the Nepali border. Prime Minister Manmohan Singh called the insurgency the single biggest threat to the nation's security, and in 2009 he mobilized some 70,000 troops, including elite special forces, in "Operation Green Hunt" to fight the rebels across more than one-third of India's territory.[50]

The revolt was sparked by large-scale mining and industrial development on indigenous land, often driven by multinational investment. In the words of Booker Prize–winning author and activist Arundhati Roy,

> The real problem is that the flagship of India's miraculous "growth" story has run aground. It came at huge social and environmental cost. And now, as the rivers dry up and forests disappear, as the water table recedes and as people realize what is being done to them, the chickens are coming home to roost. All over the country, there's unrest, there are protests by people refusing to give up their land and their access to resources, refusing to believe false promises anymore.[51]

Most of this development is highly energy and carbon intensive, a less glamorous story than the much more publicized software and Internet service industries in the south of India. International security expert Paul Rogers has observed that the Maoist revolt in India may be an early prototype of the conflicts that will dominate the twenty-first century, which will be driven by growing inequality, environmental degradation, and lack of access of growing populations to ecosystem services. Climate change and environmental degradation will decrease the carrying capacity of large, densely populated tropical and subtropical regions. The spread of "more fragile and failing states with intense migratory pressures" rooted in growing "socio-economic divisions and environmental limits" already makes, Rogers writes, "a new definition of security essential."[52]

Will the Bank help address these challenges, or will it exacerbate them?

A Global Ethic

We might recall that the early reforms at the World Bank Group were driven by the protests of marginalized poor people, whose access to land and resources was threatened by large Bank-funded projects, of which the India

Sardar Sarovar Dam was prototypal. Indeed, it was the controversy over Sardar Sarovar that led to the creation of the Bank's Independent Inspection Panel.

Since that period of the early 1990s a world of growing environmental stress, increasing inequality, and spreading failures of governance has been the context in which Bank operations have taken place. All too often the Bank, driven by its loan-approval culture, has had a baneful attraction to investments that only compound these problems—the Bank's stated intentions notwithstanding.

The world is faced with a failure of global governance at a moment when good governance is needed more urgently than at any time in history. Since the original Rio Earth Summit in 1992, the World Bank Group has had a conflicted approach to its own rule- and accountability-based reforms, achieved in no small part during periods of intense public scrutiny and pressure. The Bank Group's retreat from safeguards and accountability, the fundamental incoherence of its energy and climate activities, and its flight from more-effective controls on corruption of its lending—all reflect the hypocrisy of its member governments and the contradictory political pressures they put on the Bank Group. Yes, the Bank is to blame, but the blame ultimately lies with governments around the world that are failing to meet the environmental and social challenges of living together on an increasingly crowded planet.

Contrary, perhaps, to what one would expect or hope, the richer our world becomes as an economic system, the more our collective imagination seems to atrophy, so that all common goals collapse into competitive efforts to increase production and trade. Even in a time of crisis, when economic fundamentalism appears to be failing on its own terms, there is a corresponding failure to imagine alternatives.

It might have been Aristotle who first noted this pathology, writing in his *Politics* that:

> while it seems that there must be a limit to every form of wealth, in practice we find that the opposite occurs: all those engaged in acquiring goods go on increasing their coin without limit. . . . The reason why some people get this notion into their heads may be that they are eager for life but not for the good life; so desire for life being unlimited, they desire also an unlimited amount of what [they think] enables it to go on . . . These people turn all skills into skills of acquiring goods, as though that were the end and everything had to serve that end.[53]

The pathology of which Aristotle spoke has its modern reformulation in the obsession with limitless economic growth—seeing the entire planet as a machine for producing and consuming more and more commodities. Of course, it is taboo for any politician, let alone the managers of international financial institutions like the World Bank, to question growth. A few ecological economists such as Herman Daly have done so, but they have been marginalized from mainstream economic discourse. Yet more recently, even mainstream figures such as Kenneth Rogoff, the former chief economist of the International Monetary Fund, have begun to ask uncomfortable questions: "Does it really make sense to take growth as the main social objective in perpetuity, as economics textbooks implicitly assume?"[54]

Thinkers as disparate as George Soros and Catholic theologian Hans Küng have had similar insights. Soros has warned that market fundamentalism is a greater threat to human society than any totalitarian ideology, noting that "the supreme challenge of our time is to establish a set of values that applies to a largely transactional, global society." In the words of Küng, "A global market economy requires a global ethic."[55]

It is important to remember that the founder of modern economics, Adam Smith, issued the same warning about prioritizing markets and economic production as the foundation of society. Smith, in his *Theory of Moral Sentiments* (less cited than the *Wealth of Nations* but equally critical to the underpinning of his thought) goes to great lengths to emphasize the moral values that are essential for social cohesion, and he levels a detailed attack on those who advocate the primacy of economic utility. Smith emphasizes that three values uphold the social order: justice, prudence, and beneficence. Justice is by far the most important; a society can exist without beneficence (magnanimity, compassion, public-spiritedness) though it will be "less happy and agreeable," based on short-term mercenary concerns whereby no man feels he has any obligation to society. "Justice, he emphasizes, "is the main pillar that upholds the whole edifice. . . . If it is removed, the great, immense fabrick of human society . . . must in a moment crumble to atoms."[56]

Many of the contemporary critiques of globalization are grounded in a shared realization that a global economy calls for a global project of justice. The reorganization of all social values around endless economic growth cannot hold together the 7 billion inhabitants of a small planet. On the contrary, we see how these priorities are driving societies apart while undermining the ecological foundations on which humanity depends.

The issues, the project examples, and the policy conflicts we have examined in the Bank are a microcosm of a wider battle that is going on in the world, a battle for the kind of global society that future generations will inhabit—if indeed there will even be a global society, rather than a world of dystopian, Hobbesian "mere anarchy." The basic question is whether global economic activity, and the forces that have been unleashed through liberalization, privatization, and deregulation, can be guided by standards and rules that are agreed upon and enforced. Such rules and standards would be founded on commonly shared ethical principles that human societies recognize as having priority over short-term, parochial economic goals and incentives. The proliferation of global and local environmental crises forces us to recognize that an ethic for long-term human well-being—indeed, an ethic for survival—will have to be grounded in respect for all life.

Such an ethic is a work in progress, but for the World Bank to make a greater contribution, it will have to learn from its experience rather than flee from it. The world can ill afford institutions that have built amnesia into their bureaucratic DNA.

Notes

All references that do not include full publication information are online resources. A complete set of these notes, including hyperlinks to all online resources, is available at www.foreclosingthefuture.com.

Chapter 1 Notes

1. World Bank Global Tiger Initiative Secretariat, Global Tiger Recovery Program 2010–2022 (Washington, DC: World Bank, 2011), iv.
2. Fred Weir, "Putin Praises DiCaprio as 'Real Man' after Harrowing Journey to Tiger Summit," *Christian Science Monitor*, November 24, 2010.
3. Shaun Walker, "DeCaprio, Putin, and the All-Star Plot to Save Tigers," *The Independent* (UK), November 25, 2010.
4. Ibid.
5. Ibid.
6. Jonathan Watts, "Putin May Be the Tiger's Champion, but China Will Decide the Species' Future: Premier Wen's Vague Words at the Tiger Summit Do Little to Inspire Confidence in the Country That Drives a Gruesome Trade," *Guardian*, Environment Blog, November 23, 2010.
7. Caroline Fraser, "As Tigers Near Extinction, A Last-Ditch Strategy Emerges," *Yale Environment 360*, November 15, 2010.
8. Wildlife Extra, "New $350-Million Plan to Save the Tiger—But Will It Work?" *Wild Travel*, n.d., wildlifeextra.com.
9. Technically the World Bank Group also includes a fifth institution, the International Center for the Settlement of Investment Disputes. As the name indicates, this is an arbitration panel, not a financial lending, insurance, or investment agency, as are the IBRD, IDA, IFC, and MIGA.
10. Voting shares differ, though, for the different affiliates, e.g., in the IBRD the United States has 16.09 percent, Japan 9.62 percent, Germany 4.41 percent, and the United Kingdom and France 4.22 percent each. In IDA the U.S. share is 11.09 percent, followed by 8.74 percent for Japan, 5.68 percent for Germany, 5.46 percent for the United Kingdom, and 3.86 percent for France. See: The World Bank, "Executive Directors and Their Voting Power, June 30, 2011,"*Annual Report 2011: Year in Review* (Washington, DC: The World Bank, 2011). At the IFC the United States has 24.03 percent of the voting shares, followed by Japan, Germany, France, and the United Kingdom with 5.96 percent, 5.44 percent, 5.11 percent, and 5.11 percent, respectively. See: International Finance Corporation, World Bank Group, *I Am Opportunity—IFC Annual Report 2011* (Washington, DC: IFC, 2011), 91.
11. See: World Bank Group website, worldbank.org.
12. World Bank, *Annual Report 2011*, 3–4.
13. "Rights groups say 19 journalists have been victims of contract killings in Russia since 2000, the year Putin was first elected president, and none of the masterminds of the

murders has been jailed." See: Timothy Heritage, "Analysis: Journalist's Murder a Test Case for Russia's Putin," Reuters, October 6, 2011.

14. Gary Peach, "Greenpeace Decries Russian PM's Environmental Record over Past Decade," Associated Press, June 4, 2010.

15. Claudia Dreifus, "Zoologist Gives a Voice to Big Cats in the Wilderness," *New York Times*, Science Section, December 18, 2007.

16. Patrick Barkham, "One Last Chance: Can We Save the Tiger?," *Guardian*, November 9, 2010.

17. Ibid.

18. Ibid.

19. Ibid.

20. Peter Foster, "Poachers Empty Indian Wildlife Park of Tigers," *Telegraph*, London, April 9, 2005; Fraser, "As Tigers Near Extinction."

21. Rachna Singh, "Illegal Mining Threatens Sariska," *Times of India*, October 13, 2010.

22. Kathy Lilly, "Members of Russian Summit Have Diverging Views but United Goal: Saving the Tiger," *Washington Post*, November 20, 2010.

23. Marwaan Macan-Marker, "World Bank Aims to Earn Stripes through Tiger Summit," *Online Asia Times*, January 26, 2010.

24. For more on the Operations Evaluation Department, see: Bruce Rich, *Mortgaging the Earth: The World Bank, Environmental Impoverishment, and the Crisis of Development* (Boston, MA: Beacon Press, 1994), 171–72.

25. Richard Carlos Worden and Colin Reese, *IEG Review of Twenty World Bank–Funded Projects in Tiger Landscapes*, Evaluation Brief 12 (Washington, DC: World Bank Independent Evaluation Group (IEG), 2011), x.

26. Ibid., 17. The three projects in question were so-called ICDPs—Integrated Conservation and Development Projects. The concept of combining rural development with conservation dates back to the mid-1980s.

27. Ibid., xi.

28. See, e.g.: Steve Berkman, *The World Bank and the Gods of Lending* (Sterling, VA: Kumarian Press, 2008). All of these issues will be discussed in greater detail in subsequent chapters.

29. World Bank *Annual Report 2011*, IBRD and IDA Cumulative Lending by Country / Fiscal 1945–2011.

30. Independent People's Tribunal on the World Bank in India, *Findings of the Jury* (New Delhi: Shivaam Sundaram, September 11, 2008), 2, 26–27. Two non-Indians were also on the jury: Alejandro Nadal, professor of economics and coordinator of the Science and Technology Program at El Colegio de Mexico, and the author.

31. Ibid., 11, 17, 23.

32. Herman Daly, interview with Martin Eierman, "We Need a Crisis, and a Change of Values," *The European*, September 5, 2011.

33. William Easterly, *The Elusive Quest for Growth* (Cambridge, MA, and London: MIT Press, 2011).

34. William Easterly, "The Failure of Development: In Spite of Billions of Dollars Spent on Aid to Poor Countries, There Has Been No Real Progress, says William E," *Financial Times*, USA Edition, July 4, 2001.

35. William Easterly, "The Ideology of Development," *Foreign Policy*, July–August 2007.

36. Quoted in Vincent McElhinny, "Troubling Implications for Investment Lending Reform," Bank Information Center IFI INFO Brief, October 2010.

37. Ibid.

38. UK Parliament, *House of Commons Environmental Audit Committee—Fifth Report: The Impact of UK Overseas Aid on Environmental Protection and Climate Change Mitigation and Adaptation* (London: UK Parliament, June 29, 2011).

39. Ibid., paragraph 44.

40. UK Parliament, Report Published on Impact of Overseas Aid on Environmental Protection," June 29, 2011.

41. World Bank *Annual Report 2011*, 11–12.

42. UK Parliament, *Environmental Audit Committee—Fifth Report*, paragraph 49.

43. Heike Mainhardt-Gibbs, "World Bank Group Energy Sector Financing Update," Bank Information Center, November 2010.

44. Ibid.

45. Zachary Shahan, "World Bank Approves $3B for World's 4th Largest Coal Power Plant," *Ecopolitology*, April 10, 2010.

46. UK Parliament, *Environmental Audit Committee—Fifth Report*, paragraph 60.

47. World Bank Independent Evaluation Group (IEG), *Annual Report of Development Effectivess: Achieving Sustainable Development* (Washington, DC: World Bank, 2009), xvi.

48. Ibid., xvii, 23.

49. Ibid., 27.

50. Ibid., 58.

51. Ibid., xvi, 43, 50, 51.

52. The actual increase in the voting share for borrowing, developing countries was modest: a shift of 4.6 percent in voting shares for borrowers in International Bank for Reconstruction and Development (IBRD), which lends to all but the poorest countries (concentrated mainly in Sub-Saharan Africa), to 47.2 percent; as in the past, rich country donors still control the voting majority. See: World Bank, *Annual Report 2011*, 28. But China's voting share rose to 4.42 percent, third behind the United States (16.4 percent) and Japan (6.84 percent). (Ibid., "Executive Directors and Alternates of the World Bank and Their Voting Power, June 30, 2011.") The political clout of China, India, and Brazil on the Bank's board is not just a function of voting shares, but of their fast-growing influence in the global economy and in other international fora such as the G20.

53. See, e.g.: Sebastian Mallaby, *The World's Banker: A Study of Failed States, Financial Crises, and the Wealth and Poverty of Nations* (New York: Penguin, 2004). These issues are discussed in later chapters.

54. The Bank's IEG examined a number of these issues in a 2011 report: World Bank Independent Evaluation Group, *Safeguards and Sustainability Policies in a Changing World* (Washington, DC: World Bank, 2010). This IEG report and others will be discussed in subsequent chapters.

55. World Bank and International Monetary Fund, *Global Monitoring Report 2008: MDGs and the Environment* (Washington, DC: World Bank, 2008), 5, 6.

56. Independent Tribunal, *Findings*, 23.

57. Ibid., 19. It is important to note that the charge is not that the Bank is bribing officials to make certain decisions, but that, from working at the Bank and IMF, they benefit personally and professionally by articulating and carrying out the policies of these institutions, so there are few incentives to raise doubts or questions. After five years as a full staff member at the World Bank or the IMF, an Indian official—or any other professional from a developing nation—vests in the institution's pension program, which pays a benefit for life that is oftentimes as great as or greater than their government salary when they return to their former jobs.

58. Fraser, *As Tigers Near Extinction*.
59. Watts, "Putin May Be the Tiger's Champion."
60. United Nations Secretary-General, "Twentieth-Century Model 'A Global Suicide Pact,' Secretary-General Tells World Economic Forum Session on Redefining Sustainable Development," SG/SM/13372, EC/186,ENV/DEV/1182 (New York: United Nations Department of Public Information, News and Media Division, January 28, 2011).
61. Ibid.

Chapter 2 Notes

1. The U.S. Government, during the administration of President Jimmy Carter, was a pioneer in identifying these global environmental concerns already in the late 1970s. Sadly, the Carter administration was perhaps the high point of American international environmental leadership.
2. Address of Barber B. Conable, President, World Bank and International Finance Corporation, to the World Resources Institute, Washington, DC, May 5, 1987 (printed version of the speech released to the press). A detailed description of the events leading up to the Bank's first wave of environmental reforms, and of major aspects of the reforms themselves, can be found in Bruce Rich, *Mortgaging the Earth: The World Bank, Environmental Impoverishment, and the Crisis of Development* (Boston: Beacon Press, 1994), 107–81.
3. World Bank, *The Forest Sector: A World Bank Policy Paper* (Washington, DC: World Bank, 1991), 21–22. See also: Uma Lele et al., *The World Bank Forest Strategy: Striking the Right Balance* (Washington, DC: World Bank Operations Evaluation Department, 2000), 2–4.
4. Robert Wade, "Greening the Bank: The Struggle Over the Environment, 1970–1995," in *The World Bank: Its First Half Century*, vol. 2: *Perspectives*, ed. Devesh Kapur, John P. Lewis, and Richard Webb (Washington, DC: Brookings Institution Press, 1997), 612. The figures on increases in Bank staff, funding for environmental projects and research, etc., are from Wade, 612.
5. Ibid., 711.
6. Ibid., 612.
7. Ibid.
8. Korinna Horta, Robin Round, and Zoe Young, "The Global Environment Facility: The First Ten Years—Growing Pains or Inherent Flaws?" report by Environmental Defense and Halifax Initiative, August 2002, 4.
9. Wade, 679.
10. Charlotte Streck, "The Network Structure of the Global Environment Facility," UN Vision Project on Global Policy Networks, n.d., 10. (See also: Charlotte Streck, "The Global Environment Facility: A Role Model for International Governance?" *Global Environmental Politics* 1, no. 2 (May 2001): 71–94).
11. Horta et al., 5.
12. See: Gareth Porter et al., *Study of GEF's Overall Performance*, First Overall Performance Study, OPS1 (Washington, DC: Global Environment Facility, 1999), 69.
13. RESOLVE, Inc., "Issues Assessment: Incremental Cost Determination for GEF-Funded Projects," in Global Environment Facility, GEF Council, Progress on Incremental Costs, GEF/C.12.If.4, September 14, 1998, 3, 4, 7; see also: Porter, *Study of GEF's Overall Performance*, 70–71.
14. Streck, "The Network Structure of the Global Environment Facility," 20.
15. The projects are discussed at length in Rich, *Mortgaging the Earth*, 178–80.

16. Susan George, quoted in Tom Athanasiou, *Divided Planet: The Ecology of Rich and Poor* (Athens, GA: University of Georgia Press, 1998), 283.

17. See, for example, Wade, 622.

18. See discussion in Rich, 243.

19. For a good description of the Bank's role in Stockholm and immediately afterwards, see Wade, 620–23.

20. Wade, 672.

21. Streck, "The Network Structure of the Global Environment Facility," 23.

22. See GEF website: thegef.org/gef/instrument.

23. See: Rich, *Mortgaging the Earth*, 261.

24. United Nations Conference on Environmentally Sustainable Development (UNCED), *Agenda 21*, chap. 33, paragraphs 13, 18.

25. International Monetary Fund, *IMF Survey*, vol. 29, issue 8 (2000), 172.

26. See, e.g.: United Nations Development Programme, "The Millennium Development Goals: Eight Goals for 2015"; the World Bank's commitment to the MDGs can be found on its website, worldbank.org.

27. Rich, 151, 250.

28. Arundhati Roy, "The Greater Common Good," April 1999, narmada.org.

29. *Sardar Sarovar: Report of the Independent Review*, Bradford Morse, Chairman; Thomas Berger, Deputy Chairman (Ottawa: Resource Future International, 1992), 226, 233–34.

30. Ibid., 53.

31. Ibid., 36.

32. Willi A. Wapenhans et al., "Report of the Portfolio Management Task Force, July 1, 1992" (internal World Bank document), 12, 14.

33. "Statement of E. Patrick Coady, U.S. Executive Director, to an Executive Board Seminar, May 4, 1993" (U.S. Treasury Department, typewritten document, 4 pages).

34. For example, action number 15—"produce report on Bank's environmental policies and activities"—referred to a public relations environment report the Bank had been already issuing for three years.

35. Action 85 was "provide leadership in implementing the reform plan" and action 86 was "assess implementation progress."

36. Willi A. Wapenhans, "Efficiency and Effectiveness: Is the World Bank Group Prepared for the Task Ahead?" in Bretton Woods Commission, *Bretton Woods: Looking to the Future* (Washington, DC: Bretton Woods Commission, July 1994), note 22, C-304.

37. Wade, 704.

38. For an in-depth discussion of the Morse Commission and the Bank's subsequent withdrawal from the project, see: Wade, 699–709; see also: Rich, *Mortgaging the Earth*, 249–54, 301–2; Maartje Van Putten, *Policing the Banks: Accountability Mechanisms and the Financial Sector* (Montreal, QC, and Kingston, ON: McGill-Queens University Press, 2008), 67–74.

39. World Bank, "Resolution No. 93-10, Resolution No. IDA No. 93-10, September 22, 1993, The World Bank Inspection Panel," paragraph 12, in Ibrahim F. I. Shihata, *The World Bank Inspection Panel* (New York: Oxford University Press, 1994), 129.

40. Similar inspection panels, or inspection functions, were established in the other multilateral development banks, as well as in at least three public export credit and investment insurance agencies in recent years, the U.S. Overseas Private Investment Corporation (OPIC), the Canadian Export Development Corporation (EDC), and the Japan Bank for International Cooperation (JBIC).

41. See: Wade, 727–28; and see especially: Van Putten, *Policing the Banks*, 74–81.

42. Van Putten, *Policing the Banks*, 74–78, citing House Committee on Banking, Finance and Urban Affairs, *Authorizing Contributions to IDA, GEF and ADF: Hearing Before the Subcommittee on International Development, Finance, Trade, and Monetary Policy of the Committee on Banking, Finance, and Urban Affairs*, 103rd Congress, 1st sess., May 5, 1993, 1–10, 45, 51.

43. Interview with Barney Frank, in Van Putten, *Policing the Banks*, 342–45.

44. Ibid.

45. House Committee on Banking, Finance, and Urban Affairs, *World Bank Disclosure Policy and Inspection Panel: Hearing Before the Subcommittee on International Development, Finance, Trade, and Monetary Policy of the Committee on Banking, Finance, and Urban Affairs*, 103rd Congress, 2nd sess., June 21, 1994, 4–6.

46. Horta et al., 13–14.

47. Leif Christoffersen et al., *The First Decade of the GEF: The Second Overall Performance Study* (Washington, DC: Global Environment Facility, January 25, 2002), 59, http://www.thegef.org/gef/node/1914.

48. Porter et al., GEF OPS1, xv.

49. Global Environment Facility, *GEF Annual Report 2010*, 9–10.

50. Heike Mainhardt-Gibbs, "World Bank Group Energy Sector Financing Update," Bank Information Center, November 2010, bicusa.org.

51. See discussion of the World Bank/GEF Kena Tana River Primate Reserve project in Horta et al., 20–21.

52. World Bank and United Nations Development Program, *Reducing Threats to Protected Areas: Lessons from the Field* (Washington, DC, and New York: World Bank and United Nations Development Program, 2007), 66.

53. Ibid., 65–66.

54. Richard Carlos Worden and Colin Reese, *IEG Review of Twenty World Bank–Funded Projects in Tiger Landscapes*, Evaluation Brief 12 (Washington, DC: World Bank Independent Evaluation Group [IEG], 2011), 17, 16.

55. Global Environment Facility/World Bank, "Proposal for Review: India Ecodevelopment Project," 1, 4–5 (on gefonline.org, see link to pdf of "Project Document for WP").

56. Worden and Reese, *IEG Review of Twenty World Bank–Funded Projects*, 16.

57. Ibid.

58. Independent People's Tribunal on the World Bank in India, *Findings of the Jury* (New Delhi: Shivaam Sundaram, September 11, 2008), 16–17.

59. P. Devullu et al., "Indigenous and Tribal Communities, Biodiversity Conservation and the Global Environment Facility in India: General Overview and a Case Study of People's Perspectives of the India Ecodevelopment Project," May 2, 2005, 1.

60. Ibid.

61. See complaint and eligibility for inspection documents at World Bank website, worldbank.org.

62. Horta et al., 21–22.

63. Ibid.

64. World Bank, "The Inspection Panel Report and Recommendation on Request for Inspection India: Ecodevelopment Project, Rajiv Gandhi (Nagarahole) National Park," October 21, 1998, 29, paragraph 86.

65. Ibid., 13, paragraph 35.

66. For an interesting case study of the complex factors at work undermining the success

of the World Bank India Ecodevelopment Project in another one of the seven protected areas, see: Lucie Dejouhanet, "Participatory Eco-Development in Question: The Case of the Parmbikulum Wildlife Sanctuary in Southern India," *Journal of Alpine Research* 98, no. 1 (2010).

67. Ross Hughs and Fiona Flinton, *Integrating Conservation and Development Experience: A Review and Bibliography of the ICDP Literature* (London: International Institute for Environment and Development, 2001), 7.

68. Kaavya Varma, "The Asiatic Lion and the Maldharvis of Gir Forest," 158, citing T. O. McShane and S. A. Newby, "Expecting the Unattainable: The Assumptions behind ICDPs," in T. O. McShane and M. P. Wells, eds., *Getting Biodiversity Projects to Work: Towards More Effective Conservation and Development* (New York: Columbia University Press, 2004), 49–74.

69. See, for example, the Bank Management Comments, in Worden and Reese, *IEG Review of 20 World Bank–Funded Projects in Tiger Landscapes*, xiii-xvn: "Management notes that the median year of concept review of the 20 reviewed projects is 1997. Some of the design issues noted in the IEG review have been previously identified in other reviews and subsequently addressed. . . ." Nevertheless, "at the same time management recognizes that there is scope for improvement in the monitoring and reporting on environmental impacts during project implementation." And, yes, "Management appreciates the advice that the Bank should further mainstream biodiversity into sectors that can have significant impacts on biodiversity, such as infrastructure and rural development. Management agrees that mainstreaming biodiversity considerations into the design of Bank-supported projects to complement focused stand-alone biodiversity conservation efforts is key to continue advancing this agenda through proactive support to improve environmental aspects of Bank-supported projects."

70. Ibid., 5.

71. Nevertheless, the report does put forth as one of its general recommendations that better assessment of the real threats to protected areas is needed.

72. World Bank internal memo, March 26, 1993, quoted in Steve Berkman, *The World Bank and the Gods of Lending* (Sterling, VA: Kumarian Press, 2008), 28.

73. Berkman 44–45.

74. Richard Webb, "Demotion and Rededication: 1981 to the Mid-1990s," in *The World Bank: Its First Half Century*, vol. 1: *History*, ed. Devesh Kapur, John P. Lewis, and Richard Webb (Washington, DC: Brookings Institution Press, 1997), 338.

75. S. Guhan, "The World Bank's Lending to South Asia," in *The World Bank: Its First Half Century*, vol. 2, 382.

76. Wade, 733–34.

Chapter 3 Notes

1. World Bank, "Meeting of President Wolfensohn with Senior Management, March 12, 1996" (internal World Bank document), 12.

2. World Bank, "Wolfensohn Lays Out Future Direction of World Bank," News Release No. 96/S21, October 10, 1995.

3. Michael Holman, Patti Walmeir, and Robert Chote," World Bank Chief Accuses Staff of Resisting Reforms," *Financial Times*, March 29, 1996, 1.

4. Michael Holman and Patti Waldmeir, "World Bank Chief's Cry from the Heart," *Financial Times*, March 29, 1996, 4.

5. See: Garry Evans, "The World According to Wolfensohn," interview, *Euromoney*, September 1995, 45–59.

6. James D. Wolfensohn, letter to World Bank staff, June 1, 1995, as reported by Al Ka-men, "Keep It in the Family," *Washington Post,* June 9, 1995.

7. James D. Wolfensohn, *A Global Life* (New York: Public Affairs, 2010), 261–62.

8. Ibid., 269.

9. Evans, "The World According to Wolfensohn," 56.

10. Ibid.

11. Jock R. Anderson, Gershon Feder, and Sushma Ganguly, "The Rise and Fall of Train-ing and Visit Extension: An Asian Mini-drama with an African Epilogue," World Bank Policy Research Working Paper 3928, May 2006, 11–13, 22–23.

12. For example, Charles H. Antholt, a Bank senior agriculturist, concluded in a 1992 study that "without a doubt, T&V is widely considered ineffective," citing numerous examples of Bank-supported programs in Pakistan, Indonesia, India, Nepal, Thailand, Bangladesh, and Malaysia. He noted that the T&V approach "has tended to further institutionalize [agricultural] extension's top-down hierarchy and centralized manage-ment" and that its emphasis on hiring large numbers of extension staff "may have undermined [the] public sector's long-term sustainability unintentionally" through "the unacceptable strain . . . it puts on public resources." See: Charles H. Antholt, "Rel-evancy, Responsiveness and Cost-Effectiveness: Issues for Agricultural Extension in the 21st Century" (unpublished paper), July 1992.

13. World Bank, Operations Evaluation Department, Project Performance Audit Report, Kenya National Extension Project (Credit 1387-KE), draft report (Washington, DC: World Bank, January 10, 1996), 14.

14. See: Edward W. Cronin, *A Natural History of the World's Deepest Valley* (Boston: Hough-ton Mifflin Company, 1979).

15. Arun Concerned Group, Request for Inspection, World Bank Independent Inspection Panel, October 24, 1994, 8; available on World Bank website.

16. Ibid., 7; see also: Lori Udall, "Trampling on Nepal," *Multinational Monitor* 16, no. 12 (December 1994).

17. Edward W. Cronin, *A Natural History of the World's Deepest Valley.*

18. Arun Concerned Group, Request for Inspection, 2.

19. Eduardo Lachica, "Environmentalists Are Opposing Plans of World Bank to Build Dam in Nepal," *Wall Street Journal,* September 12, 1994.

20. Korinna Horta, "Monster of the Himalayas," *Washington Post,* November 11, 1994, C4.

21. Martin Karcher, interview with Environmental Defense Fund concerning the Nepal Arun III Hydroelectric Project, September 9, 1994.

22. Ibid.

23. German Federal Audit Office, "FZ-Massnahme mit Nepal; Wasserkraftwerk (WKW) Arun III," December 19, 1994, 2, 5.

24. Daniel D. Bradlow, "A Test Case for the World Bank," *American University Journal of Inter-national Law and Policy* 11, no. 2 (1996): 266.

25. World Bank, "World Bank and Nepal to Develop Energy Alternatives to Arun Proj-ect," press release, August 4, 1994. See also: Paul Lewis, "World Bank Cancels Nepal Project Loan," *New York Times,* August 16, 1995; Paul Lewis, "World Bank Ends Hey-day of the Big Project Loan," *International Herald Tribune,* August 17, 1995, 1.

26. Richard E. Bissell, "The Arun III Hydropower Project, Nepal," in *Demanding Account-ability: Civil-Society Claims and the World Bank Inspection Panel,* ed. Dana Clark, Jonathan Fox, and Kay Treakle (Lanham, MD: Rowman & Littlefield Publishers, 2003), 25–45, 31.

27. Ibid., 40. Also see discussion in Lori Udall, "The World Bank and Public Account-ability: Has Anything Changed?" in *The Struggle for Accountability: The World Bank,*

NGOs, and Grassroots Movements (Cambridge, MA, and London, UK: MIT Press, 1998), 391–436, 416–21.

28. World Bank, "Meeting of President Wolfensohn with Senior Management, March 12, 1996" (internal World Bank document), 12.

29. Daniel J. Shepard, "Donor Countries Back Wolfensohn Debt-Relief Plan, but Financing Still a Problem," *Earth Summit Times*, September 29, 1996, 1; Bread for the World Institute, "The Debt Initiative: Sham or Historic Breakthrough?" *News and Notices for World Bank Watchers*, no. 15, November 1996, 12–14.

30. World Bank Operations Evaluation Department, *OED Participation Process Review* (draft report), April 21, 1999, 12.

31. Ibid., 27–28, 24–25.

32. World Bank, Office Memorandum, "Portfolio Improvement Program: An Update," November 4, 1996.

33. "Our experiences with the Inspection Panel are teaching us that we have to be increasingly careful in setting policy that we are able to implement in practice." Myrna Alexander, OPRDR, office memorandum to various World Bank staff, March 15, 1996.

34. World Bank, "Guidance for Communicating the Compact" (internal document for managers), February 1997, World Bank Vice Presidency for External Affairs, 4.

35. Patti Waldmeir, "World Bank Defends $570 Million Restructure Plan," *Financial Times*, February 21, 1997, 6.

36. World Bank, "Meeting with Jean-Francois Rischard 10/21/96" (internal staff minutes), 2; the Bank's FY 1996 internal administrative budget was $733 million ($842 million for FY 1995). See: World Bank, *Annual Report 1996* (Washington, DC: World Bank, 1996), 170.

37. World Bank, "Questions and Answers About the Networks" (internal staff document), September 16, 1996, 2.

38. Robert Hunter Wade, "The U.S. Role in the Malaise at the World Bank: Get Up, Gulliver!" paper prepared for the G-24, 2001, also presented at the American Political Science Association Annual Meeting, San Francisco, August 28–30, 2001, 22.

39. World Bank, "Meeting with Jean-Francois Rischard 10/21/96 Summary," 9.

40. Wade, "The U.S. Role in the Malaise at the World Bank," 2.

41. World Bank Quality Assurance Group, Portfolio Improvement Program, "Portfolio Improvement Program: Reviews of Sector Portfolios and Lending Instruments: A Synthesis" (draft internal report), April 22, 1997, 15.

42. Ibid., 20.

43. World Bank, Quality Assurance Group, "Portfolio Improvement Program: Highway Sub-Sector, Review of Projects at Risk, Phase I" (internal Bank report), February 1997, 20.

44. World Bank, "Portfolio Improvement Program, Reviews of Sector Portfolios and Lending Instruments: A Synthesis," 20.

45. World Bank, Quality Assurance Group, "Review of Technical Assistance Loans in the World Bank," (internal Bank report), February 1997, 20–21.

46. World Bank, Operations Evaluation Department, *Effectiveness of Environmental Assessments and National Environmental Action Plans: A Process Study*, Report No. 15835 (Washington, DC: World Bank, June 29, 1996), 24, 25, 6–7, 38.

47. Ibid., 6.

48. Ibid., 37.

49. Ibid., 14.

50. Ibid., 8.

51. Ibid., 78.

52. James D. Wolfensohn, *A Global Life*, 295.

53. Michelle Celarier, "The Search for the Smoking Gun," *Euromoney*, September 1996, 49–52.

54. World Bank/International Monetary Fund 1996 Annual Meetings, Press Release no. 3, Address by James D. Wolfensohn to the Board of Governors of the World Bank Group, at the Joint Annual Discussion, October 1, 1996, 5; Kevin Rafferty, "Calls to Root Out Cancer of Corruption," *Emerging Markets*, October 2, 1996, 1.

55. James D. Wolfensohn, *A Global Life*, 296.

56. Thomas Kamm, "Nigeria Executions Raise Sanction Threat," *Wall Street Journal*, November 13, 1995, A10; John M. Goshko, "U.S. Censures Nigeria's Execution of Nine Activists, Installs Penalties," *Washington Post*, November 11, 1995.

57. "Papua New Guinea: Bank Signals Disquiet over Logging Tax," *Greenwire* 5, no. 242 (April 26, 1996); "Papua New Guinea: Bank Withholds Loan Over Logging Fears," *Greenwire* 6, no. 113 (October 10, 1996); "Cambodia: Inadequate Logging Policy Delays International Funding," *Greenwire*, November 15, 1996.

58. Carol Matlack, "What Happened to the Coal Miners' Dollars? At Least $100 Million from a World Bank Loan Is Lost," *Business Week*, September 8, 1997, 52, 54.

59. John Lloyd, "A Country Where the Awful Has Already Happened," *Financial Times*, October 24–25, 1998, xxvi.

60. Jeffrey A. Winters, "Down With the World Bank," *Far Eastern Economic Review*, February 13, 1997, 29; Keith Loveard, "The Dark Side of Prosperity: A World Bank Critic Alleges Waste and Graft," *Asia Week*, August 15, 1997.

61. Glenn R. Simpson, "World Bank Memo Depicts Diverted Funds, Corruption in Jakarta; Report Contrasts with '97 Denials," *Wall Street Journal*, August 19, 1998, A14.

62. Jane Loos, Regional Manager, EAPCO, "Options to Reduce Negative Impact from Corruption on Bank-Financed Activities," World Bank office memorandum to Mr. Jean-Michel Severino, Vice President, EAP, October 19, 1998. See also: Stephen Fidler, "World Bank Loans Hit by 'Corruption,'" *Financial Times*, December 8, 1998.

63. Steve Berkman, *The World Bank and the Gods of Lending* (Sterling, VA: Kumarion Press, 2008), 154.

64. World Bank Staff Association, *Proposal to Increase Effectiveness of Some Poverty Reduction Targeted Projects*, World Bank Staff Association report, undated, "Annex: Bitterness, Disillusion, and Possible Solutions," quoted in Berkman, *The World Bank and the Gods of Lending*, 145-46.

65. Kay Treakle and Elías Díaz Peña, "Accountability at the World Bank: What Does It Take? Lessons from the Yacyretá Hydroelectric Project, Argentina/Paraguay," in *Demanding Accountability: Civil-Society Claims and the World Bank Inspection Panel*, ed. Dana Clark, Jonathan Fox, and Kay Treakle (New York and London: Rowman and Littlefield, 2003), 69–90, 71.

66. Shirley Christian, "Buenos Aires Journal—Billions Flow to Dam (And Billions Down Drain?)," *New York Times*, May 4, 1990.

67. World Bank, *Accountability at the World Bank: The Inspection Panel 10 Years On* (Washington, DC: World Bank, 2003), 59.

68. Ibid., 58.

69. Ibid., 60.

70. See: Treakle and and Díaz Peña, "Accountability at the World Bank: What Does It Take?" for the most detailed account of these events; also see: World Bank, *Accountability at the World Bank: The Inspection Panel 10 Years On*, 58–68.

71. World Bank, *Accountability at the World Bank: The Inspection Panel 10 Years On*, 63–65.

72. The World Bank's Singrauli loans are discussed in greater detail in *Mortgaging the Earth*, 38–43.

73. Treakle and and Díaz Peña, "Accountability at the World Bank: What Does It Take?" 78.

74. Ibid., 77–78,

75. Ibid., 78.

76. Quoted in Treakle and and Díaz Peña, "Accountability at the World Bank: What Does It Take?" 79; see also: Mark Suzman, "Row Brews Over Bank Role in Dam Project," *Financial Times*, May 4, 1998, International Section, 4.

77. Quoted in Treakle and and Díaz Peña, "Accountability at the World Bank: What Does It Take?" 80.

78. Quoted in ibid., 80.

79. Quoted in ibid., 83.

80. World Bank Independent Inspection Panel, *Investigation Report, Paraguay—Reform Project for the Water and Telecommunications Sector (Loan No. 3842-PA); Argentina—SEGBA V Power Distribution Project (Loan No. 2854-AR)*, Report No. 27995, February 24, 2004, ix, xiii. See also: International Rivers, "World Bank Investigation Confirms Serious Problems at Yacyretá Dam," May 10, 2004.

81. World Bank Independent Evaluation Group, *Safeguards and Sustainability in a Changing World: An Independent Evaluation of World Bank Experience* (Washington, DC: The World Bank, 2010), 7.

82. See Organization for Economic Cooperation and Development (OECD), "Guidelines on Aid and Development, No. 3, Guidelines for Aid Agencies on Involuntary Displacement and Resettlement in Development Projects" (Paris: OECD, 1992).

83. Alternate U.S. executive director's statement to the World Bank/IFC board, December 1992, quoted in Susan Park, "Becoming Green: Diffusing Sustainable Development Norms throughout the World Bank Group," in *The World Bank and Governance: A Decade of Reform and Reaction*, ed. Diane Stone and Christopher Wright (London and New York: Routledge, 2007), 175.

84. Susan Park, "Becoming Green," in *The World Bank and Governance*, 174–76. On the Bío-Bío case see also: David Hunter, Cristián Opaso, and Marco Orellana, "The Bíobío's Legacy: Institutional Reforms and Unfulfilled Promises at the International Finance Corporation," in *Demanding Accountability: Civil-Society Claims and the World Bank Inspection Panel*, ed. Dana Clark, Jonathan Fox, and Kay Treakle (New York and London: Rowman and Littlefield, 2003), 115–43.

85. Jay D. Hair, et al., Pangue Hydroelectric Project (Chile): "An Independent Review of the International Finance Corporation's Compliance with Applicable World Bank Group Environmental and Social Requirements" (internal World Bank Group document), Santiago, Chile, April 4, 1997, 3, 4.

86. See: equator-principles.com.

87. See: "Members & Reporting" and "The Equator Principles: Frequently Asked Questions" at equator-principles.com.

88. Organization for Economic Cooperation and Development (OECD), Trade and Agricultural Directorate, Trade Committee, Working Party on Export Credits and Credit Guarantees, *Revised Council Recommendation on Common Approaches on the Environment and Officially Supported Export Credits*, TAD/ECG(2007)9, June 12, 2007. See also, e.g.: Bruce Rich, "Exporting Destruction," *Environmental Forum*, September-October 2000, 31–30; Bruce Rich, "A Test Case for Export Finance, *Environmental Forum*, January-February 2009, 20.

89. See, for example: Sebastian Mallaby in *The World's Banker* (New York: Penguin Press, 2004), discussed in chapter 4.

Chapter 4 Notes

1. David E. Sanger and Joseph Kahn, "World Bank Criticizes Itself Over Chinese Project Near Tibet, *New York Times*, June 27, 2000.

2. World Bank, "World Bank Approves China Western Poverty Alleviation Project," Press Release No. 99/2282/EAP, June 24, 1999.

3. World Bank Independent Inspection Panel, *The Qinghai Project, A Component of the China Western Poverty Reduction Project (Credit No. 3255 CHA and Loan No. 4501-CHA)*, April 28, 2000, xii.

4. Dana Clark and Kay Treakle, "The China Western Poverty Reduction Project," in *Demanding Accountability: Civil-Society Claims and the World Bank Inspection Panel*, ed. Dana Clark, Jonathan Fox, and Kay Treakle (Lanham, MD: Rowman & Littlefield Publishers, 2003), 211–45, 213–14.

5. Undated letter from Tibetans in Tulan Dzong to "fellow Tibetans living in independent countries," cited in Clark and Treakle, "The China Western Poverty Reduction Project," 215.

6. Ibid., 222, 232; see also: David E. Sanger, "Ideas and Trends: Karma and Helms: A Stick for China, a Carrot for Tibet's Lobby," *New York Times*, July 11, 1999.

7. "Tibetan Tinderbox," *The Economist*, June 17 1999.

8. Clark and Treakle, "The China Western Poverty Reduction Project," 221.

9. Ibid., 222.

10. Clark and Treakle, "The China Western Poverty Reduction Project," 223, 237.

11. India remained the largest cumulative borrower.

12. Clark and Treakle, "The China Western Poverty Reduction Project," 224.

13. World Bank, Press Release No. 99/2282/EAP, June 24, 1999.

14. Indira Lakshmanan, "China's Long March," *Boston Globe*, August 22, 1999, cited in Clark and Treakle, "The China Western Poverty Reduction Project," 226.

15. Clark and Treakle, "The China Western Poverty Reduction Project," 226; BBC News, World: Asia-Pacific, "China Releases Detained Tibet Activist," August 21, 1999; World Tibet Network News, "Dharamsala Urges Release of Two Detained Foreigners in Tibet (DIIR)," August 20, 1999.

16. Clark and Treakle, "The China Western Poverty Reduction Project," 227–28.

17. World Bank Independent Inspection Panel, *The Qinghai Project*, Executive Summary, paragraph 38, xxi; paragraphs 53, 60, xxiv, xxvi.

18. Ibid., paragraphs 9, 10, xiv; paragraph 14, xv.

19. Ibid., paragraph 45, xxii–xxiii.

20. "A Misguided World Bank Project, *New York Times*, July 5, 2000.

21. Jan Piercy, "Qinghai Component of Western China Poverty Reduction Project: Inspection Panel Report and Management Response," statement of U.S. executive director to the World Bank, July 6, 2000, cited in Clark and Treakle, "The China Western Poverty Reduction Project," 233.

22. Clark and Treakle, "The China Western Poverty Reduction Project," 233; Stefanie Ricarda Roos, "The World Bank Inspection Panel in Its Seventh Year: An Analysis of Its Process, Mandate, and Desirability with Special Reference to the China (Tibet) Case," in J. A. Frowein and R. Wolfrum, eds., *Max Planck Yearbook of United Nations Law*, vol. V, 2001 (Leiden, Netherlands: Martinus Nijhoff Publishers, 2001), 473–521, 479.

23. John Ackerly, International Campaign for Tibet, cited in Clark and Treakle, "The China Western Poverty Reduction Project," 238.

24. James D. Wolfensohn, *A Global Life* (New York: Public Affairs, 2010), 325.

25. Ibid., 327.

26. James D. Wolfensohn, meeting between President Wolfensohn and NGOs, including the Bank Information Center and the Center for International Environmental Law, Washington, DC, April 19, 2001, cited in Clark and Treakle, "The China Western Poverty Reduction Project," 236.

27. World Bank, Operations Evaluation Department, *OED Review of the Bank's Performance on the Environment*, July 5, 2001, 20.

28. Ibid., 23.

29. Ibid., 24–25.

30. This is the definition used by the International Commission on Large Dams (ICOLD), an industry-supported organization. See: World Commission on Dams, *Dams and Development: A New Framework for Decision Making, An Overview*, November 16, 2000, 5.

31. Sanjeev Khagram, *Dams and Development: Transnational Struggles for Water and Power* (Ithaca and London: Cornell University Press, 2004), 34.

32. Ibid., 34.

33. Ibid., 157.

34. Navroz K. Dubash, Mairi Dupar, Smitu Kothari, and Tundu Lissu, *A Watershed in Global Governance? An Independent Assessment of the World Commission on Dams* (Washington, DC: World Resources Institute, Lokayan, and Lawyer's Environmental Action Team, 2001), 27–28.

35. Dubash et al., *A Watershed in Global Governance?* 33.

36. Khagram, *Dams and Development*, 203, 205.

37. World Commission on Dams, *An Overview*, 1.

38. Dubash et al., *A Watershed for Global Governance*, 39.

39. Ibid., 53; World Commission on Dams, *An Overview*, 9.

40. Dubash et al., *A Watershed for Global Governance*, 48.

41. World Commission on Dams, *Dams and Development: A New Framework for Decision Making* (London, UK, and Sterling, VA: Earthscan, November 2000).

42. Nelson Mandela, "Address on the Occasion of the Launch of the Final Report of the World Commission on Dams," Cabot Hall, London, November 16, 2000.

43. World Commission on Dams, "Dams and Development," 13.

44. Ibid., 73, xxxi, 66–68.

45. Ibid., 75–77. The WCD could not come up with a precise figure, citing estimates of between 1 percent and 28 percent of total global greenhouse-gas emissions—the higher figure being obviously quite unlikely.

46. Ibid., 39–41.

47. Ibid., 43, 56.

48. Ibid., 207.

49. Ibid., 208.

50. Ibid., 215.

51. International Labor Organization, C169 Indigenous and Tribal Peoples' Convention 169, 16.2.

52. World Commission on Dams, *Dams and Development*, 221–43.

53. Ibid.

54. International Rivers Network, *Protecting Rivers and Rights: The World Commission on*

Dams Recommendations in Action Briefing Kit (Berkeley, CA: International Rivers Network, July 2010), 3.

55. International Rivers Network, *Citizen's Guide to the World Commission on Dams* (Berkeley, CA: International Rivers Network, 2002), 13–15.

56. Dubash et al., *A Watershed for Global Governance*, 111, 116, note 61.

57. Nirmalya Choudhury, *Sustainable Dam Development in India: Between Global Norms and Local Practices*, Discussion Paper 10, Deutsche Institut für Entwicklungspolitik ISSN 1860-0441 (Bonn: Deutsche Institut für Entwicklungspolitik, 2010), 12, 26. Choudhury notes, "In the line it follows, in the principles it formulates and in the approach it adopts to human and constitutional rights, the National Working Group's 1989 draft policy . . . is similar to the report published by the WCD in 2000." (Ibid., 26.)

58. R. R. Iyer, "Towards a Just Displacement and Rehabilitation Policy," *Economic and Political Weekly* 42, no. 30 (July 29, 2007), quoted in Choudhury, *Sustainable Dam Development in India*, 13.

59. Waltina Scheumann, German Development Institute Department of Environmental Policy and Natural Resources Management, Foreword, in Choudhury, *Sustainable Dam Development in India*.

60. World Bank, *Water Resources Sector Strategy: Strategic Directions for World Bank Engagement* (Washington, DC: World Bank, 2004), 38.

61. NGO Letter to the World Bank, Follow-up to the World Commission on Dams, March 19, 2001; see: rivernet.org.

62. World Bank, *Water Resources Sector Strategy*, 38.

63. Ibid.

64. Ibid., 46.

65. Ibid., 46–47.

66. World Bank Independent Inspection Panel, *Uganda Third Power Project, Fourth Power Project, and Proposed Bujagali Hydropower Project (2001)*, May 23, 2002, 76.

67. See Request for Inspection, Uganda National Associate of Professional Environmentalists (NAPE) and Save Bujagali Crusade, to Executive Secretary, Inspection Panel, World Bank Group, July 15, 2001.

68. World Bank, "Summary of the Discussion of the Joint Meeting of Executive Directors of the Bank and IDA and the Board of Directors of IFC," December 18, 2001, 19, quoted in Environmental Defense, Friends of the Earth, International Rivers Network, *Gambling with People's Lives: What the World Bank's New "High-Risk/High-Reward Strategy Means for the Poor and the Environment*, 2003, 31.

69. World Bank Independent Inspection Panel, *Uganda Third Power Project, Fourth Power Project, and Proposed Bujagali Hydropower Project*, 57.

70. See: International Rivers Network, "A Review of the World Bank's Inspection Panel Report on the Bujagali Hydroelectric Power Project," June 10, 2002, 7–8.

71. *Republic of Uganda, In the High Court of Uganda at Kampala, HCT-00-CV-MC-0139 of 2001 Greenwatch (U) Limited, Applicant, versus Attorney General, Respondents, Uganda Electricity Transmission Company Ltd, Before: The Honourable Mr. Justice FMS Egonda-Ntende, Ruling*, November 12, 2002.

72. Prayas Energy Group of Pune, India, "The Bujagali Power Purchase Agreement—An Independent Review: A Study of Techno-Economic Aspects of the Power Purchase Agreement of the Bujagali Hydroelectric Project in Uganda" (Berkeley, CA: International Rivers Network, November 20, 2002), 2, 3.

73. Peter Bosshard, International Rivers Network, personal communication, February 10, 2012.

74. United States Securities Exchange Commission, Form 10-Q, The AES Corporation, Quarterly Report Pursuant to Section 13 or 15(d) of the Securities Exchange Act of 1934, For the Quarterly Period ended June 30, 2003, 18.

75. Ibid., 16–18.

76. Corpwatch, "AES Backs Out of Bujagali Dam Project," August 28, 2003.

77. See, e.g.: Rich, *Mortgaging the Earth*, 26–29, 34–38.

78. World Bank Operations Evaluation Department (OED), *The World Bank Forest Strategy: Striking the Right Balance* (Washington, DC: World Bank, 2000), xx, 8.

79. Ibid., 5.

80. Ibid., 47.

81. Ibid., 27.

82. Ibid., 28.

83. Herman Daly, "The Perils of Free Trade," *Scientific American* 269, no. 5 (November 1993): 50–57.

84. Jagdish Bhagwati, "The Case for Free Trade," *Scientific American* 269, no. 5 (November 1993): 42–49; the World Bank perspective was set out in the Bank's 1992 *World Development Report: Development and the Environment* (Washington, DC: World Bank, 1992).

85. World Bank OED, *The World Bank Forest Strategy*, xxiii–xxv.

86. Ibid., 31.

87. World Bank Operational Manuel, "OP 4.36—Forests," November 2002.

88. World Bank Operations Manuel, "OP 8.60—Development Policy Lending," August 2004; see discussion in Korinna Horta, "Forests and Structural Adjustment," in *Broken Promises: How World Bank Group Policies and Practice Fail to Protect Forests and Forest Peoples' Rights* (Rainforest Foundation, 2005), 43–46, and Ricardo Carrere and Marcus Colchester, "The World Bank and Forests," in *Broken Promises*, 4–5.

89. Indigenous Pygmy Organizations and Pygmy Support Organizations in the Democratic Republic of Congo, "Request Submitted to the World Bank Inspection Panel," Kinshasa-DRC, Kinshasa-DRC, October 30, 2005, 3; see World Bank references in footnotes 3–6.

90. Ibid., 9–10; see also: Banque Mondial, Republique Democratique du Congo, Sector Forestial, Mission de Suivi Sectoriel (17–27 Avril, 2002), Aide-Memoire, 4.

91. World Bank, *Technical Annex for a Proposed Grant in the Amount of SDR 117.0 Million (US $164 Million Equivalent) and a Proposed Credit in the Amount of SDR 35.7 Million (US $50 Million Equivalent) to the Democratic Republic of the Congo for an Emergency Economic and Social Reunification Project*, (Report No. T7601-ZR), August 14, 2003, 29, 85.

92. Letter of CENADEP (Centre National d'Appui au Développement et à la Participation Populaire) and CNONGD (Conseil National des Organisations Non-Gouvernementales de Développement du Congo), to Monsieur le Représentant Résident de la Banque Mondiale à Kinshasa-Gombe, and others, Kinshasa, February 12, 2004.

93. Indigenous Pygmy Organizations, "Request," 11; see also: Simon Counsell, Rainforest Foundation, "Democratic Republic of Congo—After the War, the Fight for the Forest," in *Broken Promises*, 11–19, 15.

94. ARD, *Conflict Timber: Dimensions of the Problem in Asia and Africa*, vol. III, *African Cases*, DRCongo Case Study (Burlington, VT: USAID/ARD, May 2003), 16, 17.

95. Ibid., 41.

96. Rainforest Foundation, transcript, "VIDEO-CONFÉRENCE Concerning the Role of the World Bank in the Forest Sector of the Democratic Republic of Congo with Mr. James Wolfensohn, President of the World Bank," July 8, 2004, 4.

97. Rainforest Foundation, videoconference with James D. Wolfensohn, 13.

98. Ibid., 10.

99. Ibid., 12–13.

100. Greenpeace International, "Forest Crime File: Danzer Involved in Bribery and Illegal Logging; Greenpeace Investigation Reveals Swiss-German Company Bribing Officials in Cameroon, Democratic Republic of Congo, and Republic of Congo" (Amsterdam: Greenpeace International, June 2004).

101. Rainforest Foundation, videoconference with James D. Wolfensohn, 14.

102. Ibid., 14–15.

103. Ibid., 16.

104. Ibid., 18.

105. World Bank Inspection Panel, *Investigation Report, DEMOCRATIC REPUBLIC OF CONGO: Transitional Support for Economic Recovery Grant (TSERO) (IDA Grant No. H 1920-DRC) and Emergency Economic and Social Reunification Support Project (EESRSP) (Credit No. 3824-DRC and Grant No. H 064-DRC)* (Washington, DC: World Bank, August 31, 2007), 129–30.

106. Ibid., xiv, xxi.

107. Ibid., 91.

108. Ibid., 108.

109. World Bank News Release, "World Bank Board Discusses Inspection Panel Investigation of Forest Sector Operations in the Democratic Republic of Congo: World Bank Committed to Staying Engaged in Improving Management of Congolese Forests," News Release No. 2008/188/AFR.

110. World Bank, "Progress Report to the Board of Executive Directors on the Implementation of the Management's Action Plan in Response to the Democratic Republic of Congo Inspection Panel Investigation Report on Transitional Support for Economic Recovery Project and the Emergency Social and Economic Reunification Project," March 11, 2009; World Bank, "Second Progress Report to the Board of Executive Directors on the Implementation of Management's Action Plan in Response to the Democratic Republic of Congo Inspection Panel Investigation Report on Transitional Support for Economic Recovery Project and the Emergency Social and Economic Reunification Project," March 2011.

111. See, e.g.: Greenpeace International, "Stolen Future: Conflicts and Logging in Congo's Rainforests—the Case of Danzer" (Amsterdam: Greenpeace International, 2011).

Chapter 5 Notes

1. William H. Prescott, *History of the Conquest of Peru*, vol. 2, ed. Wilfred Harold Munro (Philadelphia and London: J. B. Lippincott Company, 1874, 1904), 130.

2. Ibid., 138–39.

3. Steven Herz, Antonio La Viña, Jonathan Sohn, eds., *Development without Conflict: The Business Case for Community Consent* (Washington, DC: World Resources Institute, May 2007), 40.

4. Ibid., 41.

5. Ibid., 42.

6. Jane Perlez and Lowell Bergman, "Tangled Strands in Fight Over Peru Gold Mine," *New York Times*, October 25, 2005.

7. Environmental Defense, Friends of the Earth, International Rivers Network, *Gambling with People's Lives: What the World Bank's New "High-Risk/High-Reward Strategy Means*

for the Poor and the Environment (Washington, DC: Environmental Defense, September 2003), 16, 18, note 47.

8. World Bank Compliance Advisor/Ombudsman (CAO), *The CAO at 10, Annual Report 2010 and Review FY 2000–10* (Washington, DC: World Bank Group Compliance Advisor/Ombudsman, 2010), 104.

9. Friends of the Earth International, *The CAO in Peru: Lessons Learned from Dialogue as a Strategy to Reduce Conflict* (Amsterdam: Friends of the Earth International, 2006), 9; Emily Caruso, Marcus Colchester, Fergus Mackay, Nick Hildyard, and Geoff Nettleton, "Synthesis Paper," in Tebtebba, Indigenous Peoples' International Center for Policy Research and Education, and Forest Peoples Programme, *Extracting Promises: Indigenous Peoples, Extractive Industries, and the World Bank* (Baguio City, Philippines: Tebtebba Foundation, 2003), 17–170, 107.

10. "Halting the Rush against Gold: Big Mining and Its Increasingly Radical Opponents," *The Economist*, February 3, 2005; Herz et al., *Development without Conflict*, 43.

11. Herz et al., *Development without Conflict*, 45.

12. "Protests in Peru, Honeymoon Over: Ollanta Humala Struggles to Contain Opposition to Mining Projects," *The Economist*, November 19, 2011; "Mining in Peru, Doing the Conga: The President Takes On the Protesters," December 10, 2011.

13. "Peru: Videomania," *The Economist*, February 8, 2001.

14. See, e.g.: Human Rights Watch, "Peru: Montesinos Asylum Claim, Panama Should Prosecute Former Peruvian Spymaster for Torture," September 27, 2000; George Washington University, National Security Archive Briefing Book No. 37, "Fujimori's Rasputin: The Declassified Files on Peru's Former Intelligence Chief, Vladimir Montesinos," November 22, 2000.

15. Perlez and Bergman, "Tangled Strands in the Fight over Peru Gold Mine."

16. Ibid.; see also: PBS Frontline, "Peru: The Curse of Inca Gold," October 2005.

17. Perlez and Bergman, "Tangled Strands in Fight Over Peru Gold Mine."

18. Ibid.

19. Ibid.

20. See, e.g.: Herz et al., *Development without Conflict.*

21. In 1998, a year of increased World Bank Group lending to stem the Asian financial crisis, financial commitments for mining, oil, and gas totaled around 5 percent of new commitments, and 15.6 percent of IFC commitments. The year 2002 marked a low point for new extractive finance, totaling around 2 percent for the entire World Bank Group, and 3 percent for the IFC. Following 2002 World Bank Group extractive industry finance would again increase, doubling by 2006.

22. World Bank Compliance Advisor/Ombudsman (CAO), *The CAO at 10*, 92–101.

23. Jeffrey D. Sachs and Andrew M. Warner, "Natural Resource Abundance and Economic Growth," Development Discussion Paper No. 517a (Cambridge, MA: Harvard Institute for International Development, October 1995), 2, 21.

24. Monica Weber-Fahr, *Treasure or Trouble? Mining in Developing Countries* (Washington, DC: World Bank and International Finance Corporation, 2002), 7.

25. Michael L. Ross, "Comments on 'Treasure or Trouble? Mining in Developing Countries,' submitted to the World Bank Extractive Industries Review," 3, cited in Scott Pegg, *Poverty Reduction or Poverty Exacerbation? World Bank Group Support for Extractive Industries in Africa* (Washington, DC: Environmental Defense, 2003), 8.

26. See, *inter alia*: Michael Ross, *Extractive Sectors and the Poor* (Boston: Oxfam America, October 2001); and Pegg, *Poverty Reduction or Poverty Exacerbation?* 8–16.

27. Paul Collier, *The Bottom Billion: Why the Poorest Countries Are Failing and What Can Be Done About It* (Oxford and New York: Oxford University Press, 2007), 17–52.

28. Andrés Liebenthal, Roland Michelitsch, and Ethel Tarazona, World Bank Operations Evaluation Department, *Extractive Industries and Sustainable Development: An Evaluation of World Bank Group Experience* (Washington, DC: World Bank, 2005), 202.

29. Bank Information Center, Bretton Woods Project, Campagna per la riforma della Banca Mondiale, "The World Bank Group's Gold Mining Operations: Tarnished Gold—Mining and the Unmet Promise of Development" (Washington, DC: Bank Information Center, September 2006), 4.

30. Desmond Tutu, quoted on cover page, Korinna Horta, Samuel Nguiffo, and Delphine Djiraibe, *The Chad-Cameroon Oil and Pipeline Project: A Call for Accountability* (Washington, DC: Environmental Defense, June 2002); also see: Paul Brown, "Chad Oil Pipeline Under Attack for Harming the Poor," *Guardian*, September 26, 2002.

31. World Bank, Project Information Document (PID), Chad-Petroleum Development and Pipeline, Project ID TDPA534, April 4, 1995; Exxon Corporation, "Exxon's Chad Doba Project" (internal World Bank document), August 15, 1996.

32. Exxon Corporation, "Exxon's Chad Doba Project" (internal Exxon document), August 15, 1996, cited in Korinna Horta, *The Chad-Cameroon Oil and Pipeline Project: Putting People and the Environment at Risk* (Washington, DC: Environmental Defense Fund, September 1999), 1.

33. Howard W. French, "Chad: Every Silver Lining Has a Cloud," *International Herald Tribune*, June 12, 1996, 2; Economist Intelligence Unit, "Country Report: Chad," 3rd Quarter Report, 1996.

34. Korinna Horta, Samuel Nguiffo, and Delphine Djiraibe, *The Chad-Cameroon Oil and Pipeline Project: A Project Non-Completion Report* (Washington, DC: Environmental Defense, April 2007), 9.

35. Korinna Horta and Scott Coverdale, "Dams and Distress for Kingdom in the Sky," *People & the Planet* 5, no. 3 (1996): 24–25.

36. Lori Pottinger, "Police Kill Striking Dam Workers in Lesotho," *World Rivers Review* 11, no. 4 (September 1996): 1, 11.

37. Brown, "Chad Oil Pipeline Under Attack," *Guardian*, September 27, 2002.

38. Claudia Frank and Lena Guesnet, *Brief 41—"We Were Promised Development and All We Got Is Misery"—The Influence of Petroleum on Conflict Dynamics in Chad* (Bonn: Bonn International Center for Conversation, December 2009), 25.

39. Exxon and Mobil merged in December 1999.

40. World Bank Independent Evaluation Group, *The World Bank Group Program of Support for the Chad-Cameroon Petroleum Development and Pipeline Construction Program Performance Assessment Report*, Chad (WB Loan 4558-CD; IDA Credits 3373-CD and 3316-CD; IFC Loan 4338), Cameroon (WB Loan 7020-CM; IDA Credit 3372-CM; IFC Loan 4338), Chad IFC Advisory Services (537745, 534603, 533974) (Washington, DC: World Bank, November 20, 2009), 5.

41. Horta et al., *The Chad-Cameroon Oil and Pipeline Project: A Project Non-Completion Report*, 7.

42. World Bank Independent Evaluation Group, *The World Bank Group Program of Support for the Chad-Cameroon Petroleum Development and Pipeline Construction Program*, 5.

43. "Africa Oil and Gas Deal of the Year 2001—Chad-Cameroon Pipeline," *Project Finance*, February 1, 2002.

44. Statement of U.S. Executive Director, World Bank, June 6, 2000, quoted in Horta et al., *The Chad-Cameroon Oil and Pipeline Project: A Call for Accountability*, 5.

45. World Bank and International Finance Corporation, *Project Appraisal Document on Proposed International Bank for Reconstruction and Development Loans in Amounts of US$39.5 Million to the Republic of Chad and US$53.4 Million to the Republic of Cameroon and on Proposed International Finance Corporation Loans in Amounts of US$ 100 Million in A-Loans and Up to US$300 Million in B-Loans to the Tchad Oil Transportation Company, S.A., and Cameroon Oil Transportation Company, S.A., for a Petroleum Development and Pipeline Project*, Report No. 19343 AFR (Washington, DC: World Bank, April 13, 2000), 12, 121.

46. U.S. Department of State, Bureau of Democracy, Human Rights, and Labor, Country Reports on Human Rights Practices, Chad, 1999; U.S. Department of State, Bureau of Democracy, Human Rights, and Labor, Country Reports on Human Rights Practices, Chad, 2000.

47. Frank and Guesnet, *Brief 41—"We Were Promised Development,"* 26–28; Horta et al., *The Chad-Cameroon Oil and Pipeline Project: A Project Non-Completion Report*, 12.

48. Horta et al., *The Chad-Cameroon Oil and Pipeline Project: A Project Non-Completion Report*, 11; see also: World Bank and IFC, *Project Appraisal Document Chad, Cameroon*, 17.

49. Horta et al., *The Chad-Cameroon Oil and Pipeline Project: A Call for Accountability*, 2; World Bank and IFC, *Project Appraisal Document Chad, Cameroon*, 141, 145.

50. World Bank and IFC, *Project Appraisal Document Chad, Cameroon*, 150.

51. Amnesty International, *Contracting Out of Human Rights: The Chad-Cameroon Pipeline Project* (London: Amnesty International UK, September 2005).

52. Netherlands Committee for IUCN Symposium, *Liability for Environmental Damage and the Chad-Cameroon Oil Pipeline Project*, the Netherlands Institute of International Relations, the Hague, February 25, 2000, cited in Maartje Van Putten, *Policing the Banks: Accountability Mechanisms for the Financial Sector* (Montreal, Kingston, London, Ithaca: McGill-Queens University Press, 2008), 225, note 50, 456.

53. Serge A. Bronkhorst, ed., *Liability for Environmental Damage and the World Bank's Chad-Cameroon Oil and Pipeline Project: Selected Papers of the NC-IUCN Symposium* (Amsterdam: Netherlands Committee for IUCN, 2000), Annex 2, 112–13, cited in Van Putten, *Policing the Banks*, 226–27.

54. Ibid.

55. Bronkhorst, *Liability for Environmental Damage*, 115, cited in Van Putten, *Policing the Banks*, 226.

56. James D. Wolfensohn, interview with Van Putten, *Policing the Banks*, 352.

57. Frank and Guesnet, *Brief 41—"We Were Promised Development,"* 51.

58. U.S. House of Representatives, Committee on International Relations, Subcommittee on Africa, *The Chad-Cameroon Pipeline: A New Model for Natural Resource Development*, hearing before the Subcommittee on Africa of the Committee on International Relations, 107th Congress, 2nd sess., April 18, 2002, Serial No. 107-75, Statement of Peter Roseblum, Director, Human Rights Program, Harvard Law School, 37, 46.

59. Ibid., 45.

60. Dino Mahtani, "World Bank Concern Over Chad's Plan for Oil Revenues," *Financial Times*, October 27, 2005.

61. J. Millard Burr and Robert O. Collins, *Darfur: The Long Road to Disaster*, 2d ed. (Princeton, NJ: Markus Wiener Publishers, 2008), 307.

62. Frank and Guesnet, *Brief 41—"We Were Promised Development,"* 53.

63. Ibid., 47, 48; see footnote 73.

64. Reuters, "Chad Decrees Avoid World Bank Controls-Analysts," February 28, 2008.

65. World Bank statement, quoted in Xan Rice, "World Bank Cancels Pipeline Deal with Chad after Revenues Misspent," *Guardian*, September 11, 2008.

66. Lydia Polgreen, "World Bank Ends Effort to Help Chad Ease Poverty," *New York Times*, September 11, 2008.

67. World Bank Independent Evaluation Group, *The World Bank Group Program of Support for the Chad-Cameroon Petroleum Development and Pipeline Construction Program Performance Assessment Report*, Report No. 50315, 38, viii, 24.

68. Ibid., xv.

69. Ibid., xi.

70. Ibid., 16.

71. Ibid., 19–20.

72. Ibid., 29.

73. Horta et al., *The Chad-Cameroon Oil & Pipeline Project: A Project Non-Completion Report*, 19–20; World Bank Independent Evaluation Group, *The World Bank Group Program of Support for the Chad-Cameroon Petroleum Development and Pipeline Construction Program Performance Assessment Report*, 30, 63.

74. Brown, "Chad Oil Pipeline Under Attack for Harming the Poor."

75. International Petroleum Industry Environmental Conservation Association (IPIECA), International Association of Oil and Gas Producers (OGP), *Industry as a Partner for Sustainable Development: Oil and Gas* (London: International Petroleum Industry Environmental Conservation Association, International Association of Oil and Gas Producers, and United Nations Environment Programme, 2002), 1, 33–34, 37–38.

76. James D. Wolfensohn, interview with Van Putten, *Policing the Banks*, 352–54.

Chapter 6 Notes

1. Kate Connoly, "World Bank and IMF Cut Short Prague Meeting," *Guardian*, September 27, 2000.

2. Tamara Straus, "The Anti-Globalization Movement Gets Global," *Alternet*, October 3, 2000.

3. Letter from James D. Wolfensohn, President, World Bank, to Dr. Emil Salim, Professor, Faculty of Economics, University of Indonesia, January 17, 2002.

4. See: World Bank, Oil, Gas, Mining Unit, "Extractive Industries Review Reports."

5. Moreover, the EIR report reinforced a number of key findings of a concurrent report of the OED on extractives, which came out in the summer of 2003. The OED report was reissued in book form in 2005; see: Andrés Liebenthal, Roland Michelitsch, Ethel Tarazona, World Bank Operations Evaluation Department, IFC Operations Evaluation Group, and MIGA Operations Evaluation Unit, *Extractive Industries and Sustainable Development: An Evaluation of World Bank Group Experience* (Washington, DC: World Bank, 2005).

6. Extractive Industries Review, *Striking a Better Balance*, vol. 1: *The World Bank Group and Extractive Industries—The Final Report of the Extractive Industries Review* (Jakarta, Indonesia, and Washington, DC: Extractive Industries Review, December 2003), 12.

7. Ibid., 14, 17.

8. Ibid., 1.

9. Ibid., 2.

10. Ibid., 3–6.

11. Ibid., 5.

12. Ibid., 6.

13. Ibid., 64–65.

14. Nicole Itano, "Proposal to Limit Oil and Coal Projects Draws Fire," *New York Times*, March 24, 2004; Demetri Sevastopulo, "Banks Contest Ban Proposed for Coal and Oil Extraction," *Financial Times*, April 5, 2004.

15. Letter from Jody Williams, Archbishop Desmond Tutu, Rigoberta Menchu Tum, Sir Joseph Rotblat, Betty Williams, and Mairead Maguire, to James Wolfensohn, President, World Bank Group, February 8, 2004; Letter from Global Legislators for a Balance Environment to James Wolfensohn, President, World Bank Group, March 16, 2004; Letter from Julie Tanner, Coordinator of Corporate Advocacy, Christian Brothers Investment Services, Lauren Compere, Chief Administrative Officer, Boston Common Asset Management, et al., to James Wolfensohn, President, World Bank Group, March 10, 2004; Letter from Monica Frassoni, Deputado al Parlamento Europeo, et al. to James Wolfensohn, President, World Bank Group, April 2, 2004; European Parliament Resolution on the World Bank-commissioned Extractive Industries Review, PE 344.189, April 1, 2004.

16. World Bank, "Striking a Better Balance—The World Bank Group and the Extractive Industries: The Final Report of the Extractive Industries Review, World Bank Group Management Response" (Washington, DC: World Bank, September 17, 2004).

17. Ibid., iv–vii.

18. Ibid., v.

19. Ibid., iv.

20. Ibid., 36, 38.

21. Bank Information Center, Bretton Woods Project, Campagna per la Riforma della Banca Mondiale, "The World Bank Group's Gold Mining Operations: Tarnished Gold," 3–4.

22. See, e.g.: BBC, "Timeline: Guatemala, A Chronology of Key Events," January 15, 2012.

23. International Finance Corporation / Multilateral Investment Guarantee Agency Compliance Advisor/Ombudsman, Assessment of a complaint submitted to CAO in relation to the Marlin Mining Project in Guatemala (Washington, DC: Office of the Compliance Advisor/Ombudsman International Finance Corporation / Multilateral Investment Guarantee Agency, September 7, 2005), 20, 27, 34–37.

24. IFC/MIGA Compliance Advisor/Ombudsman, CAO Follow-up Assessment, Guatemala, Complaint Regarding the Marlin Mining Project (Washington, DC: IFC/MIGA Compliance Advisor Ombudsman, May 2006), 3, 14.

25. Dawn Paley, "Turning Down a Gold Mine," *The Tyee*, February 7, 2007, thetyee.ca; Guatemala Solidarity Network, "Urgent Action: Flaviano Bianchini, Environmental Activist," blog posting, January 28, 2007.

26. Lyuba Zarsky and Leonardo Stanley, *Searching for Gold in the Highlands of Guatemala: Economic Benefits and Environmental Risks of the Marlin Mine* (Medford MA: Tufts University Global Development and Environmental Institute, September 2011), 12; Bretton Woods Project "Undermining Development?" *Bretton Woods Update* No. 72, September–October 2010, 2; Ahni (John Ahniwanika Schertow), "If Goldcorp Cares So Much, It Should Shut Down the Marlin Mine," *Intercontinental Cry*, June 14, 2011.

27. Goldcorp Out of Guatemala (blog), "36 European Civil Society Organizations and Networks Ask Swedish and Norwegian Pension Funds to Support Shareholder Resolution," May 13, 2011.

28. Ahni, "If Goldcorp Cares So Much."

29. Johan Van de Wauw, Roel Evens, and Lieven Machiels, "Are Groundwater Overextraction and Reduced Infiltration Contributing to Arsenic-Related Health Problems Near the Marlin Mine (Guatemala)?" University of Ghent, October 14, 2010, 1, 2–4.

30. Niladri Basu and Howard Hu, with the assistance of the International Forensic Program of Physicians for Human Rights, *Toxic Metals and Indigenous Peoples Near the*

Marlin Mine in Western Guatemala: Potential Exposures and Impacts on Health (Cambridge, MA, and Washington, DC, May 2010), 3.

31. On Common Ground Consultants, Inc., *Human Rights Assessment of Goldcorp's Marlin Mine* (Vancouver BC: May 2010), 52, 60, 180, 213.

32. Ibid., 34, 137, 149.

33. Bank Information Center, "World Bank Implicated in Controversial DR Congo Mining Contracts," November 22, 2006; Dino Mahtani, "World Bank Faces Questions Over Congo Mining Contracts," *Financial Times*, November 17, 2006; Dino Mahtani, "Transparency Fears Lead to Review of Congo Contracts," *Financial Times*, January 3, 2007.

34. John le Carré and Jason Sterns, "Getting Congo's Wealth to Its people," *Boston Globe*, December 22, 2006.

35. Bank Information Center, "IFC to Double Number of Mining Investments in Africa," March 14, 2007.

36. Bretton Woods Project," Honest Broker? The IFC, Extractive Industries, and Affected Communities," *Bretton Woods Update* No. 56, May–June 2007, 4.

37. Bank Information Center, "Newmont Prepares Mining Operations in Ghana Forest Reserve," June 21, 2008; Bank Information Center, "IFC's Support for Newmont's Ahafo Gold Mine in Ghana."

38. Bretton Woods Project, "IFC's Mining Investments: A Black Hole for Human Rights?" *Bretton Woods Update* No. 70, March–April 2010, 7.

39. Nii Ashie Kotey and Poku Adusei, "The Newmont and AngloGold Mining Projects," in Sheldon Leader and David M. Ong, *Global Project Finance, Human Rights, and Sustainable Development* (Cambridge, UK, and New York: Cambridge University Press), 467; John Hillebrand, U.S. Environmental Protection Agency Review: Newmont Ahafo South Project 28/12/05, 1, 3, cited in Kotey and Adusei, "The Newmont and Anglo-Gold Mining Projects," 478.

40. Environment News Service, "Newmont Gold Mine to Pay Ghana Millions for Cyanide Spill," January 22, 2010.

41. Ghanaweb, "15 Killed in Course of Newmont Ahafo Mine Operations," November 8, 2010.

42. Nick Magel, "Wikileaks Cables Reveal U.S. Mining Co. Negligence in Ghana Cyanide Spill," Earthworks, September 12, 2011; see: earthworksaction.org.

43. Kotey and Adusei, "The Newmont and AngloGold Mining Projects," 489.

44. Sebastian Mallaby, "NGOs: Fighting Poverty, Hurting the Poor," *Foreign Policy*, no. 144, September–October 2004, 50–52, 55.

45. Ibid., 52.

46. See, e.g.: Bretton Woods Project, "Bank, Fund Annual Meetings: The 'Mallaby Effect,'" Bretton Woods Project Update 43, November 22, 2004.

47. Sebastian Mallaby, *The World's Banker: A Story of Failed States, Financial Crises, and the Wealth and Poverty of Nations* (New York: Penguin Press, 2004).

48. See, e.g.: Jessica Einhorn, "The World Bank's Mission Creep," *Foreign Affairs* 80., no. 5 (September–October 2001): 22–35.

49. Sebastian Mallaby, "Saving the World Bank," *Foreign Affairs* 84, no. 3 (May–June 2005): 75–85, 85.

50. Mallaby, "NGOS: Fighting Poverty, Hurting the Poor," 57.

51. World Bank, *Cost of Doing Business: Fiduciary and Safeguard Policies and Compliance*, July 16, 2001, vi.

52. Author's calculations based on total and incremental cost estimates in Ibid., 9.

53. Richard Lugar, Chairman, U.S. Senate Foreign Relations Committee, "Opening

Statement Concerning Corruption in the Multilateral Development Banks," May 13, 2004; see: Senate Foreign Relations Committee, *Hearing: Combating Corruption in the Multilateral Development Banks*, 108th Congress, 2nd sess., May 13, 2004; see also: Senate Foreign Relations Committee, *Hearing: Combating Multilateral Development Bank Corruption: U.S. Treasury Role and Internal Efforts*, 108th Congress, 2nd sess., July 21, 2004.

54. Mallaby, *The World's Banker*, 357; "NGOS: Fighting Poverty, Hurting the Poor," 57–58.

55. Mallaby, "NGOS: Fighting Poverty, Hurting the Poor," 52.

56. Ibid., 52, 54.

57. Mallaby, "Saving the World Bank," 85.

58. Jim MacNeil, Former Chairman, World Bank Inspection Panel, letter to the editor, *Foreign Policy* no. 145 (November–December 2004): 6–8. See also the letters of Peter Bosshard, Policy Director, International Rivers Network, and of Bruce Rich, Senior Attorney and Director, International Program, Environmental Defense, Ibid., 6–10.

59. Mallaby, *The World's Banker*, 355–56.

60. David A. Phillips, *Reforming the World Bank: Twenty Years of Trial—and Error* (Cambridge, UK, and New York: Cambridge University Press, 2009), 212, 280.

61. Ibid., 211.

62. Ibid., 265.

63. World Bank Independent Evaluation Group, *Annual Review of Development Effectiveness 2006: Getting Results* (Washington, DC: World Bank, 2006), xxi, 27; World Bank Independent Evaluation Group, *World Bank Assistance to Agriculture in Sub-Saharan Africa* (Washington, DC: World Bank, 2007), 35.

64. International Bank for Reconstruction and Development (IBRD), *Articles of Agreement* (as amended effective February 16, 1989), Article III, sec. 4. (vii). The IDA, IFC, and MIGA Articles of Agreement all have similar provisions.

65. Kyriakos Varvaressos, "The Concept of a World Bank," *International Bank Notes* 5, no. 7 (IBRD/IDA Archives, Box No. 19), June 25, 1951, 4.

66. See: World Bank Operational Policy Manuel, "OP 8.60—Development Policy Lending," August 2004.

67. World Bank Operations Policy and Country Services, *Development Policy Lending Retrospective*, July 7, 2007, 7.

68. Atiyah Curmally, Jon Sohn, and Christopher Wright, "Multilateral Development Bank Lending Through Financial Intermediaries: Environmental and Social Challenges," World Resources Institute Issue Brief, June 2005, 2, 7–8.

69. World Bank, "Meeting of President Wolfensohn with Senior Management, March 12, 1996" (internal document), 17.

70. Ibid., 17–19.

Chapter 7 Notes

1. Bretton Woods Project, "Opposition Swells to Appointment of Wolfowitz to Head World Bank," March 17, 2005.

2. Bretton Woods Project, "Wolfowitz Era Begins: Realpolitik 1, Democracy 0," Bretton Woods Update 45, April 2005, 1.

3. "A Hawk to Ruffle the World Bank's Feathers," *The Economist*, May 21, 2005; Edward Alden, "Wolfowitz Nomination a Shock for Europe," *Financial Times*, March 16, 2005.

4. Frank Hornig and George Macolo, "Can Paul Wolfowitz Transform from Hawk to Dove?" *Der Spiegel*, June 1, 2005.

5. Bretton Woods Project, "The World Bank Weeds Out Corruption: Will It Touch the Roots?" Bretton Woods Update 50, 1, March–April 2006.

6. Steve Berkman, *The World Bank and the Gods of Lending* (Sterling, VA: Kumarian Press, 2008), 78–79.

7. See chapter 3.

8. Reuters, "U.S. Senate Panel Probes World Bank," in *Hürriet Daily News* (Turkey)," April 29, 2004; "U.S. Senator Questions World Bank," *Far Eastern Economic Review* 167, no. 17 (April 29, 2004): 8.

9. Transformation Resource Centre, "Too Many Dams, Too Little Water—Lesotho's Rivers Could Become 'Waste Water Drains,'" International Rivers Network, October 31, 2001; Metsi Consultants, "Final Draft of Instream Flow Requirements Study," Report commissioned by the LHDA, Report No. 648-F-02, Maseru, 1999, 28, quoted in Korinna Horta, "The World Bank's Decade for Africa: A New Dawn for Development Aid?" *Yale Journal of International Affairs* (Winter–Spring 2006): 16, endnote 46, 23.

10. Korinna Horta, "Corrupt Process," *World Rivers Review* 17, no. 2 (April 2002): 2.

11. Senate Foreign Relations Committee, *Hearing: Combating Multilateral Development Bank Corruption: U.S. Treasury Role and Internal Efforts*, 108th Congress, 2nd sess., July 21, 2004, Senate Hearing 108-734, Statement of Guido Penzhorn, Advocate and Senior Counsel, Durban Bar, Durban, South Africa, "Comments on the Current Lesotho Bribery Prosecutions, Presentation Before the Senate Foreign Relations Committee on 21 July, 2004," 38–43.

12. World Bank, "World Bank Sanctions Acres International Limited," Press Release No. 2005/33/S, July 23, 2004.

13. World Bank, "World Bank Sanctions Lahmeyer International for Corrupt Activities in Bank-Financed Projects," Press Release No. 129/2007/INT, November 6, 2006.

14. Gary Weiss, "Defending Wolfowitiz," *Forbes*, May 3, 2007.

15. Vikas Dhoot, "World Bank Puts on Hold a Billion Dollars for Health," *Indian Express*, April 3, 2006.

16. World Bank Group Department of Institutional Integrity, *Detailed Implementation Review, India Health Sector, 2006–2007*, vol. I, 1–2, 13, 16; Bob Davis, "World Bank Probes Health Fraud Claims," *Wall Street Journal*, March 15, 2008.

17. See, for example, Kenneth Timmerman, "World Bank Fired Wolfowitz to Hide Corruption: Former Official," *Newsmax*, August 8, 2008.

18. Quoted in Steven R. Weisman, "Wolfowitz Corruption Drive Rattles World Bank," *New York Times*, September 14, 2006.

19. World Bank Group, "Sustainable Infrastructure Plan FY 2009–2011," July 2008, iv, vii.

20. Manish Bapna, Executive Director, Bank Information Center, "Testimony before the United States Senate Committee on Foreign Relations, Infrastructure, Poverty, and the Role of the MDBS," July 12, 2006, 3.

21. World Bank Infrastructure Network, "Infrastructure: Lessons from the Last Two Decades of World Bank Engagement," Discussion Paper, January 30, 2006, 6, 11.

22. Ibid., 6, 11; see: Berkman, *The World Bank and the Gods of Lending*, 57–74, especially discussion 70–73.

23. World Bank Infrastructure Network, "Infrastructure: Lessons from the Last Two Decades of World Bank Engagement," 13.

24. Ibid., 14.

25. Ibid., 25–26.

26. Ibid., 27.

27. Ibid., x.

28. World Bank Infrastructure Network, "Scaling up Infrastructure: Building on Strengths,

Learning from Mistakes," January 30, 2006, 6.

29. Imran Ali, "Political Economy of Water Reforms in Pakistan," World Bank Country Water Resources Assistance Strategy, Background Paper No. 10, in John Briscoe and Usman Kamar, eds., *Background Papers: Pakistan's Water Economy: Running Dry* (Washington, DC, and London: World Bank and Oxford University Press, 2005), 5, 17.

30. Pervaiz Amir, "The Role of Large Dams in the Indus Valley, World Bank Country Water Resources Assistance Strategy," Background Paper No. 10, in Briscoe and Kamar, *Pakistan's Water Economy*, 25.

31. World Bank, *Pakistan Poverty Assessment—Poverty in Pakistan: Vulnerabilities, Social Gaps, and Rural Dynamics*, Report No. 24296-PAK (Washington, DC: World Bank, October 28, 2002), 88, 90.

32. Peter Bosshard and Shannon Lawrence, "Pakistan's Rot Has World Bank Roots," *Far Eastern Economic Review* 169, no. 4 (May 2006): 39–43; World Bank, *Pakistan Poverty Assessment*, 90.

33. Dan Blackmore and Faizal Husan, "Water Rights and Entitlements," Background Paper No. 6, in Briscoe and Kamar, *Pakistan's Water Economy*, 36–37.

34. Muhammad Nawaz Bhutta and Lambert K. Smedema, "Drainage and Salinity Management," Background Paper No. 15, in Briscoe and Kamar, *Pakistan's Water Economy*, 9, 13.

35. Imran Ali, "Political Economy of Water Reforms in Pakistan," 11.

36. Briscoe and Kamar, *Pakistan's Water Economy*, xviii; Peter Bosshard, "The World Bank and Pakistan's Water Sector," World Economy and Development *in Brief*, January 27, 2006.

37. Peter Bosshard and Shannon Lawrence, "The World Bank's Conflicted Corruption Fight," International Rivers Network, May 1, 2006.

38. Ibid.; Briscoe and Kamar, *Pakistan's Water Economy*, 63–69.

39. Bosshard and Lawrence, "The World Bank's Conflicted Corruption Fight."

40. Ray Fulcher, "Pakistan: Kalabagh Dam Threatens Livelihood of Millions," *Green Left Weekly* (Australia), March 15, 2006; Pakissan, "World Bank Urged Not to Release Funds for 'Bhasha' Dam," February 6, 2006.

41. Anwar Iqbal, "US and WB Renew Pledge to Finance Bhasha Dam," *Dawn* (Pakistan), April 24, 2012; "Now the World Bank," *The Nation* (Pakistan), May 12, 2012.

42. Senate Foreign Relations Committee, *Hearing: Multilateral Development Banks: Development Effectiveness of Infrastructure Projects*, 109th Congress, 2nd sess., July 12, 2006, Senate Hearing 109-912.

43. Ibid., Statement of Manish Bapna, Executive Director, Bank Information Center, Before the United States Senate Committee on Foreign Relations, 42–48.

44. Ibid., 6.

45. William Easterly, Professor of Economics, New York University, Senate Committee on Foreign Relations, *Hearing: Multilateral Development Banks: Promoting Effectiveness and Fighting Corruption*, 109th Congress, 2nd sess., March 28, 2006, Senate Hearing 109-913, 46–47.

46. Ibid., 47.

47. Thayer Scudder, Lee M. Talbot, and T. C. Whitmore, "Lao People's Democratic Republic Nam Theun 2 Hydro Project, Report of the International Environmental and Social Panel of Experts" (Vientiane, Laos PDR: Ministry of Industry and Handicraft, February 7, 1997), 11–12.

48. World Bank and MIGA (Multilateral Investment Guarantee Agency), "Project Appraisal Document on a Proposed IDA Grant (Nam Theun 2 Social and Environmental

Project) in the Amount of SDR 13.1 Million (US $20 Million Equivalent) to the Lao People's Democratic Republic, and a Proposed IDA Partial Risk Guarantee in the Amount of Up to US $50 Million for a Syndicated Commercial Loan, and Proposed MIGA Guarantees of Up to US $200 Million in Lao People's Democratic Republic and Thailand, for a Syndicated Commercial Loan to and Equity Investment in the Nam Theun 2 Power Company Limited for the Nam Theun 2 Hydroelectric Project," Report No. 31764-LA, March 31, 2005, 16.

49. Adrian Fozzard, Senior Public Sector Specialist, World Bank, "Technical Brief, Revenue and Expenditure Management, Nam Theun 2 Hydroelectric Project" (Washington, DC: World Bank, March 16, 2005), 11.

50. World Bank East Asia and Pacific Region, *Lao PDR Country Economic Memorandum: Realizing the Development Potential of Lao PDR*, Report No. 30188-LA, December 2004, 72.

51. David F. Hales, "Nam Theun: A Dam That Laos Doesn't Need," *New York Times*, April 7, 2005; David F. Hales, "Nam Theun Dam: The World Bank's Watershed Decision," *World Watch Magazine*, May–June 2005, 27–28.

52. World Bank, *Lao PDR Country Economic Memorandum*, 18.

53. Address by Pierre Lelloche, Minister of State with Responsibility for Foreign Trade, at the Nam Theun 2 Hydroelectric Dam Inauguration Ceremony, December 9, 2010.

54. Letter to Robert B. Zoellick, President the World Bank, and to Haruhiko Kuroda, President, the Asian Development Bank, Re: Unresolved issues on the Nam Theun 2 Hydropower Project and the hydropower strategy of the banks, on behalf of 34 nongovernmental organizations in 18 countries, December 6, 2010.

55. Richard Stone, "Along with Power, Questions Flow at Laos's New Dam," *Science* 38, no. 5977 (April 23, 2010): 414–15.

56. Bank Information Center, "IFC Investment in Africa Reaches $1 Billion," in *IFIs in Africa News Briefing*, No. 22, June 29, 2007.

57. "The Bujagali Hydro," *This Is Africa* (affiliated with the *Financial Times*), October 1, 2009.

58. "World Bank OKs $360 Mln in Uganda Dam Project Loans," Reuters, April 26, 2007.

59. World Bank, Inspection Panel, *Investigation Report: Uganda: Private Power Generation (Bujagali) Project (Guarantee No. B0130-UG)*, August 29, 2008, xvii.

60. Ibid., 126, 127, 130, 131.

61. Ibid., xxxvi-xxxvii.

62. Ibid., xx.

63. World Bank International Finance Corporation News, "Bujagali Hydro Earns Africa Hydro Power Deal of the Year Award," March 21, 2008.

64. See, e.g.: World Bank Independent Evaluation Group (IEG), *Annual Review of Development Effectiveness 2009: Achieving Sustainable Development* (Washington, DC: The World Bank, 2009), xvi, 53.

65. Allan Meltzer et al., *Report of the International Financial Institution Advisory Commission* (Washington, DC: U.S. Congress, 2000), 63, 67–69.

66. World Bank Independent Evaluation Group, *Development Results in Middle-Income Countries: An Evaluation of the World Bank's Support* (Washington, DC: World Bank, 2007), xiii, xiv.

67. Ibid., 20.

68. Ibid., xv.

69. Ibid.

70. Ibid., xvii, 20, 72.

71. Todd Moss and Sarah Rose, "China Exim Bank and Africa: New Lending, New Challenges," Center for Global Development Notes, November 2006; Bruce Rich, "Blank

Checks for Unsustainable Development," *Environmental Forum* 24, no. 2 (March–April 2007): 1–5; Fitch Ratings Press Release, "China Plays Crucial Role in Sub-Saharan Africa's Growth," December 7, 2001, cited in Daniel Berhane, "China EXIM Bank Tops World Bank as Africa's Lender," Danile Berhane's Blog, January 2, 2012.

72. "Brazil's Development Bank: Nest Egg or Serpent's Egg?" *The Economist*, August 5, 2010; "Brazil—Transforming the State Development Bank," *Meat Trade News Daily*, August 22, 2010.

73. "Big Spender: Brazil's International Lending Ventures," Open Society Foundation for South Africa, South African Foreign Policy Initiative, May 13, 2012.

74. Concerning BNDES and the environment, see, e.g.: NGO Reporter Brasil, "BNDES and Its Environmental Policy: A Critique from the Perspective of Organized Civil Society," February 2011; and Amazon Watch, "BNDES: Banking Amazon Destruction."

75. Françoise Crouigneau and Richard Hiault, "Wolfowitz Slams China Banks on Africa Lending," *Financial Times*, October 24, 2006; Rowan Callick, "Wolfowitz Holds Beijing to Account Over Africa," *The Australian*, October 25, 2006.

76. Francis Fukuyama, "A Battle Paul Wolfowitz Can't Win," *The American Interest*, September 16, 2006.

77. Catherine Weaver, *The Hypocrisy Trap: The World Bank and the Poverty of Reform* (Princeton, NJ, and Oxford, UK: Princeton University Press, 2008), 55; Hilary Benn, "Improving Governance, Fighting Corruption," speech to Transparency International, September 14, 2007, quoted in Weaver, *The Hypocrisy Trap*, 55.

78. Weaver, *The Hypocrisy Trap*, 134–35; "Double-Edged Sword: The World Bank's Anti-Corruption Effort Has Critics on the Inside," *The Economist*, September 14, 2006.

79. Richard Behar, "World Bank Anti-Corruption Drive Blunted as China Threatens to Halt Loans," *Fox News*, March 27, 2007; Hsieo-Yun to James W. Adams, "Re: Sanctions Reform Roll-out in EAP [East Asia and the Pacific World Bank region]—Your Feedback Needed" (World Bank internal e-mail), March 12, 2007.

80. Richard Behar, "World Bank Anti-Corruption Drive Blunted;" Richard Behar, "Paul Wolfowitz's World Bank Frustration," *Fox News*, March 26, 2007.

81. Ibid.

82. World Bank, "Strengthening World Bank Group Engagement on Governance and Anti-Corruption, Consultation Feedback, Mexico, December 18–19, 2006," Question 10: Other Key Issues.

83. Behar, "World Bank Anti-Corruption Drive Blunted."

84. *The Economist*, "Wolfowitz Agonistes," May 3, 2007.

85. See: Andrew Balls and Edward Alden, "Questions Raised about Wolfowitz Style," *Financial Times*, January 23, 2006.

86. Steve Clemons, "Paul Wolfowitz Busy Neo-Conning the World Bank: Staff Rebellion Brewing," *Huffington Post*, January 20, 2006.

87. See, e.g.: Michael Elliott, "So, What Went Wrong?" *Wired New York* (blog), September 28, 2003.

88. See, e.g.: Greg Hitt, "In World Bank Role, Wolfowitz Keeps Up Battle to Reshape Iraq," *Wall Street Journal*, October 30, 2006, A1.

89. "The Wolfowitz Affair: A Sweetheart Deal Leaves a Sour Taste in Many Mouths," *The Economist*, April 7, 2007; Bank Information Center, "All's Fair in Love and War?" Update, April 10, 2007.

90. Government Accountability Project, "Paul Wolfowitz Scandal," The Shaha Riza Scandal, whistleblower.org.

91. Bretton Woods Project, "Wolfowitz Saga Turns Ugly," Bretton Woods Project News, May 4, 2007.

92. Ibid.

93. *The Economist*, "Wolfowitz Agonistes"; "Exit Wolfowitz: Paul Wolfowitz Agrees to Quit the World Bank," *The Economist*, May 18, 2007; Steve R. Weisman, "Wolfowitz Resigns, Ending Long Fight at World Bank," *New York Times*, May 18, 2007.

94. Robert B. Holland II, "The Real World Bank Scandal: Why the Bureaucracy Wants to Oust Paul Wolfowitz," *Wall Street Journal*, April 20, 2007.

95. Kenneth R. Timmerman, "World Bank Fired Wolfowitz to Hide Corruption: Former Official," *Newsmax*, August 8, 2007.

96. Kenneth Anderson, "How the Ethics Committee Failed Wolfowitz," *Financial Times*, May 6, 2007.

97. Anonymous, Bank Information Center, "Staff Comments Posted on Internal World Bank Webpage Concerning Wolfowitz/Riza Connection" (World Bank intranet posting), April 10, 2007.

98. Steven R. Weisman, "Panel Urges World Bank to Change Antigraft Plan," *New York Times*, September 13, 2007; Bretton Woods Project, "Integrity Review Lacks Objectivity," Bretton Woods Update 55, March–April 2007, 8.

99. Krishna Guha and Eoin Callan, "Volcker Says World Bank Lax on Graft," *Financial Times*, September 13, 2007.

100. Paul A. Volcker et al., *Independent Panel Review of the World Bank Group Department of Institutional Integrity* (Washington, DC: September 13, 2007), 8, 13.

101. "A Fight Over Corruption," *Washington Post*, editorial, September 17, 2007.

Chapter 8 Notes

1. Bruce Stokes, "New Stripes at the Bank," *National Journal*, April 17, 2010, 30–36; Sebastian Mallaby, "The Quiet Revolutionary Who Saved the World Bank," *Financial Times*, February 16, 2012.

2. Stokes, "New Stripes at the Bank;" Mallaby, "The Quiet Revolutionary Who Saved the World Bank."

3. Robert B. Zoellick, Foreword, in World Bank, *World Development Report 2010, Development and Climate Change* (Washington, DC: World Bank, 2010), xiii.

4. Mallaby, "The Quiet Revolutionary Who Saved the World Bank."

5. United Nations Development Programme (UNDP), *Human Development Report 2007/2008, Fighting Climate Change: Human Solidarity in a Divided World* (New York: United Nations Development Programme, 2007), 1.

6. World Bank, *World Development Report 2010*, 5.

7. Ibid., 37.

8. Ibid., 3.

9. International Energy Agency (IEA), *World Energy Outlook 2008* (Paris: International Energy Agency, 2008), 418.

10. Ibid., 384.

11. UNDP, *Human Development Report 2007/2008*, 55.

12. IEA, *World Energy Outlook 2008*, 123–24.

13. Ibid., 75.

14. Ibid., 401; D. Archer, H. Kheshgi, and E. Maier Reimer, "Multiple Timescales for Neutralization of Fossil Fuel CO_2," *Geophysical Research Letters* 24, no. 4 (1997): 405–8; and D. Archer, "Fate of Fossil Fuel CO_2 in Geologic Time," *Geophysical Research Letters* 10 (May 2005): 1–6, cited in Worldwatch Institute, *State of the World 2009: Into a Warming World* (New York and London: W. W. Norton & Company, 2009), 23–24; and D. Archer, "Fate of Fossil Fuel CO_2 in Geologic Time," cited in Worldwatch Institute, *State of the World 2009*, 23–24.

15. James Hansen, "Letter to Michelle and Barack Obama, 29 December 2008," cited in "A Letter to Obama," *Guardian*, January 1, 2009.

16. IEA, *World Energy Outlook 2008*, 418.

17. United Nations Framework Convention on Climate Change (UNFCCC), "Investment and Financial Flows to Address Climate Change: An Update," FCCC/TP/2008/7, November 26, 2008, 54.

18. Ibid., 91.

19. Richard K. Lattanzio, "International Climate-Change Financing: The Climate Investment Funds (CIF)," Congressional Research Service, May 5, 2011, 3; "A Deal in Durban," *The Economist*, December 11, 2011.

20. World Bank Independent Evaluation Group (IEG), *Climate Change and the World Bank Group, Phase I: An Evaluation of World Bank Win-Win Energy Policy Reforms* (Washington, DC: The World Bank, 2009), xviii.

21. World Bank, *Towards a Strategic Framework on Climate Change and Development for the World Bank Group*, Concept and Issues Note, Report No. DC 2008-0002 (Washington, DC: World Bank, March 27, 2008), 12.

22. World Bank, *Development and Climate Change: A Strategic Framework for the World Bank Group*, Report to the Development Committee, October 12, 2008, 5, 8, 12.

23. The EIR recommended that "The WBG should apply carbon shadow value analysis systematically to its cost-benefit analysis and rate of return calculations in order to internalize the currently externalized costs of all energy projects, such as greenhouse gas emissions, as a follow-up to its carbon backcasting as input for its strategies to encourage investment in low- and no-carbon energy alternatives. Shadow pricing should internalize both local costs, like pollution, and global costs, such as climate change." See: Extractive Industries Review, *Striking a Better Balance*, vol. I, *The World Bank Group and Extractive Industries, The Final Report of the Extractive Industries Review* (Jakarta, Indonesia, and Washington, DC: Extractive Industries Review, December 2003), 64.

24. World Bank, *Development and Climate Change: A Strategic Framework*, 16, 32.

25. Ibid., 9, footnote 5.

26. Ibid., 9–10, footnote 6.

27. Lisa Friedman, "World Bank: South Africa Wins $3.75 Billion Coal Loan," *Climate Wire*, April 9, 2010; Ama Marston, "World Bank Energy Lending Causes Uproar," Bretton Woods Project Update 70, April 15, 2010.

28. World Bank, *Project Appraisal Document on a Proposed IBRD Loan in the Amount of $3,750 Million to Eskom Holdings Limited, Guaranteed by the Republic of South Africa for the 'Eskom Investment Support Project,'* Report No. 53425-ZA, March 19, 2010, 29–30.

29. John Vidal, "Rich Countries to Pay Energy Giants to Build New Coal-Fired Plants," *Guardian*, July 14, 2010.

30. Bretton Woods Project, "Clean Energy Targets for the World Bank: Time for a Recount," Bretton Woods Project, Briefing, May 19, 2010.

31. World Bank, *Project Document on a Proposed IBRD Loan of US $180 Million and a Grant from the Global Environment Facility Trust Fund of US $45.4 Million to India for a Coal-Fired Power Rehabilitation Project*, February 24, 2009, 6.

32. Ibid., 5.

33. Global Environment Facility, "Request for CEO Endorsement/Approval, The GEF Trust Fund, GEFSEC Project ID 100531, India Coal-Fired Generation Rehabilitation Project," March 20, 2009, 7.

34. World Bank, *Project Document on a Proposed IBRD Loan of US $180 Million,* 150, 3, footnote 7.

35. Ibid., 5.

36. UNFCCC, "Investment and Financial Flows to Address Climate Change," 53.

37. International Energy Agency (IEA), *World Energy Outlook 2010* (Paris: International Energy Agency, 2010), 417.

38. United Nations Environment Programme (UNEP), "UNEP in the GEF," unep.org /dgef.

39. Global Environment Facility, "Request for CEO Endorsement / Approval, The GEF Trust Fund, GEFSEC Project ID 100531," 35–36. The Bank's riposte was that such an attitude was unrealistic, that coal would be a big part of India's future energy portfolio in any case, and that without the projects the coal plants would be rehabilitated, but at a slower pace and with lesser energy efficiency. (Ibid.)

40. David Wheeler, "Tata Ultra Mega Mistake: The IFC Should Not Get Burned By Coal," Global Development: Views from the Center (blog of the Center for Global Development), March 12, 2008.

41. World Bank Independent Evaluation Group, *Climate Change and the World Bank Group, Phase II: The Challenge of Low-Carbon Development* (Washington, DC: World Bank, 2010), 64.

42. Wheeler, "Tata Ultra Mega Mistake."

43. Sierra Club Compass, "Sierra Club India: Coal Is Cheap? World's Largest Coal Plants Bankrupted by Skyrocketing Prices," August 15, 2011; Kartikay Mehrotra, "Tata Power Said to Seek Government Help to Curb Plant Losses as Coal Soars," Bloomberg India, August 10, 2011.

44. Natalie Obiko Pearson, "Tata Prefers Clean-Energy Projects Over Coal in Chase for Growth," Bloomberg, March 7, 2012.

45. Shakeb Afsah and Kendyl Salcito, *The World Bank's Coal Electricity Headache*, CO_2 Scorecard, May 24, 2011. "In India," the authors write, "the 4000 MW Tata Mundra coal plant will generate approximately 28–30 billion KWh of electricity per year. The Indian government has calculated that a person requires 73 KWh per person per year to meet basic energy needs—mostly lighting at night (source: WEO 2007). With envelope-back math, a fourth-grader could tell you that the scale of Tata Mundra power plant's electricity output is capable of meeting the basic needs of the 400 million Indians currently without power. Yet only 81,000 new households are promised power from this plant—a mere tenth of a percent of generated electricity is allocated for households with no access."

46. Friends of the Earth et al., *World Bank, Climate Change and Energy Financing: Something Old. Something New?* Friends of the Earth, April 2011, 35–36; Patrick Bond and Alice Thomson, "Eskom's Price Hikes Plus Climate Change Contributions Blow Citizen Fuses," *The Mercury* (South Africa), January 20, 2010.

47. Bobby Peek, Groundwork, Friends of the Earth, South Africa, "Eskom Loan Blackens the World Bank's Name," Bretton Woods Project, April 16, 2010.

48. Oil Change International, Action Aid, Vasudha (India), *Access to Energy for the Poor: The Clean Energy Option* (Washington, DC: Oil Change International, June 2011), 3, 26. The study examined and rejected several projects the Bank claimed targeted energy access for the poor, such as two natural-gas energy projects in Nigeria and Bangladesh. In both of these cases there was no increase of access by the poor to the grid, and in the Nigeria case the project document actually stated that access for the poor would have to be addressed by future projects. Ibid., 28, 29.

49. World Bank Group, Committee on Development Effectiveness (CODE), *Energizing Sustainable Development: Energy Sector Strategy of the World Bank Group*, CODE2011-0021 (draft), March 16, 2011, vii, viii.

50. Ibid., 21, 29–30.

51. Ibid., 19, 31.

52. Ibid., 21.

53. Lisa Friedman, "Developing Countries Denounce World Bank Restrictions on Coal Loans," *New York Times*, April 12, 2011; Bretton Woods Project, "World Bank Energy Strategy Stalled," June 14, 2011.

54. IEA, *World Energy Outlook 2010*, 394.

55. Ibid., 56, 247, 249, 250, 257.

56. World Bank IEG, *An Evaluation of World Bank Win-Win Energy Policy Reforms*, xv, 59.

57. IEA, *World Energy Outlook 2010*, 260; World Bank IEG, *An Evaluation of World Bank Win-Win Energy Policy Reforms*, 41–43, 45.

58. IEA, *World Energy Outlook 2010*, 3, 56.

59. World Bank IEG, *An Evaluation of World Bank Win-Win Energy Policy Reforms*, xix.

60. Ibid., 23.

61. Ibid., 24.

62. See: Bruce Rich, *Mortgaging the Earth: The World Bank, Environmental Impoverishment, and the Crisis of Development* (Boston: Beacon Press, 1994), 170–71, and endnotes 43, 44, 45, 343–42.

63. World Bank IEG, *An Evaluation of World Bank Win-Win Energy Policy Reforms*, xiv, 94.

64. Ibid., 76.

65. Ibid., 74–75.

66. Ibid., xxvi.

67. Climate Investment Funds, Meeting of the CTF Trust Fund Committee, "Trustee Report of the Financial Status of the Clean Technology Fund," May 3, 2012, 2.

68. See, e.g.: Ama Marston, "US Congress Votes against Funding World Bank Climate Fund," Bretton Woods Update 65, April 17, 2009; Joel Meister, "U.S. Congress Cuts Funds for World Bank's So-Called Clean Technology Fund," Global Development: Views from the Center (blog), February 25, 2009.

69. Clean Technology Fund, *Investment Plan for Concentrated Solar Power in the Middle East and North Africa Region*, 2, 8.

70. Bretton Woods Project, "A Faulty Model? What the Green Climate Fund Can Learn from the Climate Investment Funds," June 2011, 7.

71. Ibid., 14–15; Climate Investment Funds, Clean Technology Fund, "Non-Disclosure Agreement for Private Sector Projects," August 18, 2010.

72. Red Constantino, "Climate Sabotage: Bank Undermines Direct Access to UN Adaptation Fund," Bretton Woods Project Update No. 72, September-October 2010, 3; Richard K. Lattanzio, "International Climate Change Financing: The Climate Investment Funds," 15.

73. World Bank Independent Evaluation Group (IEG), *Trust Fund Support for Development: An Evaluation of the World Bank Group's Trust Fund Portfolio* (Washington, DC: The World Bank Group, 2011), viii.

74. Bruce Rich, Environmental Defense Fund, *Foreclosing the Future: Coal, Climate, and Public International Finance* (Washington, DC: Environmental Defense Fund, 2009), 1.

75. Tennille Tracy, "U.S Export-Import Bank Clears India Power-Plant Loan," Dow Jones Newswires, August 25, 2010.

76. Rediff Business, "Exim Bank Cowed by Lobbying on Reliance Project," July 14, 2010.

77. Banktrack, "Dodgy Deal: Sasan Ultra Mega Power Project, India," May 3, 2012.

78. Sierra Club, Pacific Environment, Ground Work, "South African Kusile 4800MW Coal-fired Power Project: Background Information and Fact Sheet."

79. Moneycontrol, "Sasan Project CERs Valued at Rs 2000cr for 10 Yrs: R-Power," February 4, 2011, moneycontrol.com; "R-Power Project Gets Nod for Carbon Credits," *Economic Times* (India), February 5, 2011.

80. World Bank, *10 Years of Experience in Carbon Finance: Insights from Working with the Kyoto Mechanism* (Washington, DC: World Bank, 2010), 2.

Chapter 9 Notes

1. The World Bank, *Annual Report 2011: Year in Review* (Washington, DC: The World Bank, 2011), 12. The *2011 Annual Report* states that the Bank is the trustee of 12 carbon funds and facilities, but in 2012 the Bank's Carbon Finance home webpage listed a total of 14.

2. United Nations Framework Convention on Climate Change (UNFCCC), Kyoto Protocol to the United Nations Framework Convention on Climate Change, 1997, Article 12, Section 2, 11–12.

3. U.S. Government Accountability Office (GAO), *International Climate Change Programs: Lessons Learned from the European Union's Emissions Trading Scheme and the Kyoto Protocol Clean Development Mechanism*, GAO-09-151, November 2008, 7; U.S. Government Accountability Office (GAO), *Climate Change Issues: Options for Addressing Challenges to Carbon Offset Quality*, GAO-11-345, February 2011, 8, 18.

4. World Bank, *10 Years of Experience in Carbon Finance: Insights from Working with the Kyoto Mechanism* (Washington, DC: World Bank, 2010), 39–42.

5. Ibid.

6. Ibid., 50–51.

7. Michael W. Wara and David G. Victor, "A Realistic Policy on International Carbon Offsets," Stanford University Program on Energy and Sustainable Development, Working Paper No. 74, April 2008, 13–15.

8. World Bank Carbon Finance Unit, Brazil: Plantar Sequestration and Biomass Use (Prototype Carbon Fund), wbcarbonfinance.org.

9. Letter of 143 Brazilian NGOs to CDM Executive Board, June 2004, cited in Tamara Gilbertson and Oscar Reyes, *Carbon Trading: How It Works and Why It Fails*, Critical Currents No. 7 (Uppsala, Sweden: Dag Hammarskjöld Foundation, 2009), 81.

10. Tamara Gilbertson and Oscar Reyes, *Carbon Trading*, 81.

11. Ibid., 83.

12. "A Gift from Scotland to Brazil: Drought and Despair," *The Scotsman*, July 7, 2007; Carbon Trade Watch, "The Carbon Connection," 2007, movie.

13. The $8–16 billion figure depends on the fluctuating price of CERs and of the similarly fluctuating dollar/euro exchange rate.

14. Blackstone, "Bujagali Energy Successfully Delivering First 50MW of Clean Energy to the Ugandan Electricity Grid," press release, March 19, 2012; Lori Pottinger, "Will Holland Fund Carbon-Credit Dam Scam?" International Rivers, December 22, 2011; Esther Nakkazi, "Bujagali Hydropower Project to Earn Carbon Credit Income," Uganda SciGirl (blog), February 1, 2012.

15. World Bank International Finance Corporation, "Allain Duhangan II, Summary of Proposed Investment, Project No. 26500" (contains summary of earlier finance and cost estimates for Allain Duhangan I), December 7, 2007; Himanshu Takkar, "The 75 Million Dollar Fraud," *Dams, Rivers & People*, May 2008, www.sandrp.in; Hydro World, "India's 192-MW Allain Duhangan Largest Hydro to Win CDM Approval," June 25, 2007, hydroworld.com,; World Bank Carbon Finance Unit, "India: Allain Duhangan Hydroelectric Project (Italian Carbon Fund)," UNFCCC Reference No. 0862;

United Nations Framework Convention on Climate Change (UNFCCC), "Project 0862 : Allain Duhangan Hydroelectric Project (ADHP)," May 17, 2007.

16. Takkar, "The 75 Million Dollar Fraud;" Nirmalya Choudhury, "Sustainable Dam Development in India: Between Global Norms and Local Practices," Discussion Paper, Deutsche Institut für Entwicklungspolitik, ISSN-0441, Bonn, October 2010, 16–19.

17. World Bank Independent Evaluation Group, *Climate Change and the World Bank Group, Phase II: The Challenge of Low-Carbon Development* (Washington, DC: World Bank, 2010), 11, 31, 78.

18. Peter Bosshard, "World Bank Hydro Project Exposes Blatant Abuse of Climate Funds," *Huffington Post*, September 20, 2011; Nick Meynen, "Belgian Cherry on Indian Pie," CDM Watch, 2009.

19. World Bank Independent Evaluation Group, *The Challenge of Low-Carbon Development*, 77; World Bank, *10 Years of Experience in Carbon Finance*, 59.

20. World Bank, *10 Years of Experience in Carbon Finance*, 61.

21. World Bank Carbon Finance Unit, China: Changshu 3F Zhonghao HFC-23 Reduction Project, UNFCCC Reference No. 0306; China: Jiangsu Meilan HFC-23 Reduction Project, UNFCCC Reference No. 0011.

22. John Heilprin, "UN Carbon Trading Scheme: $2.7 Billion Market Could Be 'Biggest Environmental Scandal in History,'" Associated Press, August 23, 2010.

23. Michael W. Wara and David G. Victor, "A Realistic Policy on International Carbon Offsets," 11–12; Michael Wara, "Is the Global Carbon Market Working?" *Nature* 445, no. 8 (February 2007): 595–96.

24. See: CDM Watch et al., "CDM Panel Calls for Investigation Over Carbon Market Scandal," July 2, 2010; Environmental Investigation Agency, "Ethically Bankrupt: World Bank Defense of the HFC 23 Scandal," August 2010.

25. Michael Szabo, "World Bank Defends Controversial HFC Carbon-Cut Plants," Reuters, August 23, 2010.

26. European Commission, "Emissions Trading: Commission Welcomes Vote to Ban Certain Industrial Gas Credits," press release, reference IP/11/56, January 21, 2011.

27. Dinakar Sethuraman and Natalie Obiko Pearson, "Carbon Credits Becoming 'Junk' Before 2013 Ban Closes Door: Energy Markets," Bloomberg, December 7, 2011.

28. Mark Shapiro, "'Perverse' Carbon Payments Send Flood of Money to China," *Yale Environment 360*, December 13, 2010.

29. Damian Carrington, "EU Plans to Clamp Down on Carbon Trading Scam," *Guardian*, October 26, 2010; PR Newswire, "World Bank Attempting to Sabotage Reform of CDM HFC-23 Projects," World Business Media, August 26, 2010; Ewa Krukowska, "World Bank Trying to 'Subvert' UN Fix for Emission Offsets, Lobby Says," Bloomberg, August 26, 2010.

30. Carrington, "EU Plans to Clamp Down"; PR Newswire, "World Bank Attempting to Sabotage Reform of CDM HFC 23 Projects"; Krukowska, "World Bank Trying to 'Subvert' UN Fix for Emission Offsets."

31. Wara, "Is the Global Carbon Market Working?"

32. Environmental Investigation Agency, "China's Greenhouse Gas Vent Threat in Bid to Extort Billions," November 8, 2011; Jonathan Watts, "Green Group Accuses China of Climate Blackmail," *Guardian*, November 9, 2011.

33. U.S. GAO, *Climate Change Issues: Options for Addressing Challenges to Carbon Offset Quality*, 14, 15.

34. Tom Young, "UN Suspends Top CDM Project Verifier Over Lax Audit Allegations," *BusinessGreen*, December 1, 2008.

35. Michael Szabo, "U.N. Panel Suspends Two More Carbon Emissions Auditors," Reuters, March 26, 2010.

36. Michael Szabo, "Emission Auditors Get Poor Grades for Second Year," Reuters, June 28, 2010; Lambert Schneider and Leonard Mohr, "2010 Rating of Designated Operational Entities (DOEs) Accredited under the Clean Development Mechanism (CDM)," Report for WWF (Berlin: Öko-Institut e.V., July 28, 2010).

37. U.S. State Department, Carbon Credits Sufficient but Not Necessary for Sustaining Clean Energy Projects of Major Indian Business Groups, Cable 08MUMBAI340, July 16, 2008; for discussions of the cable, see: Payal Prakekh, "WikiLeaks and the CDM" (blog), September 9, 2011; Quirin Schiermeir, "Clean-Energy Credits Tarnished: Wikileaks Reveals That Most Indian Claims Are Ineligible," *Nature* 477 (September 27, 2011): 517–18; Katy Yan, "WikiLeaks Cable Highlights Highlevel CDM Scam in India," International Rivers, September 20, 2011.

38. Mark Shapiro, "Conning the Climate: Inside the Carbon-Trading Shell Game," *Harpers Magazine*, February 2010, 36, cited in Christopher Barr, "Governance Risks for REDD+: How Weak Forest Carbon Accounting Can Create Opportunities for Corruption and Fraud," in Transparency International, *Global Corruption Report: Climate Change* (London and Washington, DC: Earthscan, June 2011), 338.

39. See, e.g.: Christoph Sutter and Juan Carlos Parreño, "Does the Current Clean Development Mechanism (CM) Deliver Its Sustainable Development Claim? An Analysis of Officially Registered CDM Projects," *Climate Change* 84 (July 2007): 75–90. The authors find no officially registered CDM projects likely to both deliver GHG emissions and contribute to local sustainable development, but they do, overoptimistically as later studies and examples would show, take at face value claims that most of the CDM projects would reduce GHG emissions.

40. Nathanial Gronewold, "Europe's Carbon Emissions Trading—Growing Pains or Wholesale Theft?" *New York Times*, January 31, 2011; Joshua Chaffin, "Carbon Trading: Into Thin Air," *Financial Times*, February 14, 2011.

41. Peter Younger, Interpol, quoted in Sunanda Creah, "Forest CO_2 Scheme Will Draw Organized Crime: Interpol," Reuters, May 29, 2009.

42. Transparency International, *Global Corruption Report: Climate Change,* 297–98; U.S. GAO, *Climate Change Issues: Options for Addressing Challenges to Carbon Offset Quality,* 9, 11–13, 17.

43. World Bank Operations Evaluation Department (OED), *The World Bank Forest Strategy: Striking the Right Balance* (Washington, DC: World Bank, 2000), 114.

44. World Bank Group Independent Evaluation Group, *Managing Forest Resources for Sustainable Development* (Washington, DC: World Bank Group, February 5, 2013), iii, xii, 18, 50, 100; John Vidal, "World Bank Spending on Forests Fails to Curb Poverty, Auditors Claim: Report by World Bank's Own Evaluators Say Its Investments Support Logging and Do Little to Help Rural Poor People," *Guardian*, January 29, 2013.

45. Mu Suchoa and Cecilia Wikström, "Land Grabs in Cambodia," *International Herald Tribune*, July 12, 2012; David Pred and Natalie Budalsky, "Cambodia and the Limits of World Bank Accountability," Bretton Woods Project Update 75, April 5, 2012; David Pred and Natalie Budalsky, "Accountability Squandered," Bretton Woods Project, Update 81, June 22, 2012.

46. Fran Lambrick, "Who Is Responsible for the Death of Cambodia's Foremost Forest Activist?" *Guardian*, May 1, 2012; Kanaha Sabapathy, "Cambodian Environment Journalist Found Murdered," Australian Broadcasting Company (ABC) News, September 13, 2012.

47. Richard Wainwright et al., "From Green Ideals to REDD Money—A Brief History of Schemes to Save Forests for Their Money," FERN Briefing Note 2, November 2008, 2.

48. United Nations Framework Convention on Climate Change, "Cancún Climate Change Conference," November 2010.

49. United Nations Framework Convention on Climate Change, "Outcome of the Ad-Hoc Working Group on Long-Term Cooperative Action under the Convention," Draft Decision—CP.16, paragraph 70, 10.

50. Chris Lang, "REDD: An Introduction," REDD-Monitor, February 2011; "Cancún Agreement Includes Undefined Forest Initiative," *Sustainable Business*, December 14, 2010.

51. Kemen Austin, Florence Daviet, and Fred Stolle, "The REDD+ Decision in Cancún," World Resources Institute, December 20, 2010.

52. Kate Dooley, "Forest Watch Special Report—UNFCCC Climate Talks, Cancún, December 2010," EU Forest Watch, December 2011.

53. Fiona Harvey, "If Money Grew on Trees," *Financial Times Magazine*, December 3, 2010.

54. Chris Lang, "Four Reactions to Cancún: Via Campesina, Bolivia, Friends of the Earth International, and Indigenous Environmental Network," REDD-Monitor, December 12, 2010; Meena Menon, "In Cancún, Protest Breaks Out against REDD," *The Hindu* (India), December 9, 2010, front page.

55. Lang, "Four Reactions to Cancún;" Dooley, "Forest Watch Special Report—UNFCCC Climate Talks, Cancún;" Austin et al., "The REDD+ Decision in Cancún."

56. UN Development Programme, "UN Agencies Laud Agreement on REDD+ Reached in Cancún," Newsroom, December 11, 2010; Mongabay, "Climate Agreement Reached in Cancún," December 10, 2012, mongabay.com.

57. UN Development Programme, "UN Agencies Laud Agreement on REDD+ Reached in Cancún;" UN-REDD Programme, "UN-REDD Programme Partner Countries."

58. "Forest Carbon Partnership Facility Takes Aim at Deforestation," World Bank News and Broadcast, December 11, 2011.

59. Heinrich Böll Stiftung (Foundation), North America, "Climate Funds Update, Forest Carbon Partnership Facility," June 2012; World Bank, "Forest Carbon Partnership Facility"; Kate Dooley, Tom Griffiths, Francesco Martone, and Saskia Ozinga, *Smoke and Mirrors: A Critical Assessment of the Forest Carbon Partnership Facility*, FERN and Forest People's Programme, February 2011.

60. World Bank/United Nations Development Programme, "Climate Finance Options, MDB Forest Investment Program"; Climate Investment Funds, "Forest Investment Program"; Heinrich Böll Stiftung (Foundation), North America, "Climate Funds Update, Forest Investment Program."

61. Climate Investment Funds, "Forest Investment Program."

62. John Vidal, "BP among Founding Members of World Bank Carbon Fund," *Guardian*, May 31, 2011.

63. Bretton Woods Project, "Climate Investment Funds Monitor 2, July 2010 Summary," July 27, 2010.

64. Dooley et al., *Smoke and Mirrors*, 7–8.

65. See the various iterations of the World Resources Institute's "Getting Ready with Forest Governance: A Review of the Forest Carbon Partnership Facility Readiness Preparation Proposals and the UN-REDD National Programme Documents" from 2009–12.

66. International Institute for Environment and Development (IIED), Forest Governance Group, *Just Forest Governance—for REDD, for Sanity, Progress Made by the Forest Governance Learning Group* (London: IIED, 2011), 5.

67. Transparency International, "Corruption Perceptions Index 2011."
68. Interpol and the World Bank, *Chainsaw Project: An Interpol Perspective on Law Enforcement in Illegal Logging,* October 2010, 44–45.
69. Sunanda Creagh, "Graft Could Jeopardize Indonesia's Lucrative Climate Deals," Reuters, September 17, 2010; Emy Wulandari, "Bribes Went to Forestry Ministry Officials: Trial Witness," *Jakarta Post,* October 31, 2008.
70. Interpol and the World Bank, *Chainsaw Project,* 46.
71. Ibid., 5–6.
72. "The Mask Slips: The Durban Meeting Shows That Climate Policy and Climate Science Inhabit Parallel Worlds," *Nature* 480 (December 15, 2011): 292.
73. Fiona Harvey, "Global Carbon Trading System Has 'Essentially Collapsed,'" *Guardian,* September 10, 2012.
74. World Wildlife Fund, "Stimulating Interim REDD+ Demand: The Forest Finance Facility," 2012 Brief, 2–5. WWF proposes the creation of still another "Forest Finance Facility" to keep REDD+ alive.
75. David Barton Bray, "'Toward Post-REDD+ Landscapes,' Mexico's Community Forest Enterprises Provide a Proven Pathway to Reduce Emissions from Deforestation and Forest Degradation," Center for International Forestry Research (CIFOR) info brief no. 30, November 2010, 2, 4; Gabriela Ramirez Galindo, "REDD+ Can Learn Valuable Lessons from Community-Based Forests in Latin America," Forest News, a blog by Center for International Forestry Research, December 27, 2011; Peter Cronkleton, David Barton Bray, and Gabriel Median, "Community Forest Management and the Emergence of Multi-Scale Governance Institutions: Lessons for REDD+ Development from Mexico, Brazil and Bolivia," *Forests* 2, no. 2 (April 13, 2011): 451–73.
76. Bray, "Toward Post-REDD+ Landscapes," 2.
77. Fabiana Frayssinet, "Brazil Perfects Monitoring of Amazon Carbon Emissions," Interpress Service, August 24, 2012; Adam Vaughan, "Amazon Deforestation Falls Again," *Guardian,* August 3, 2012.
78. World Bank Group Independent Evaluation Group, *Managing Forest Resources for Sustainable Development* (project ID PO80829, and PO952050), 44, 107; for a more critical, skeptical analysis of the effectiveness of these loans, see: Vincent McElhinny, "World Bank DPL to Brazil: Moving Money or Mainstreaming Environmental Sustainability?" Bank Information Center, September 9, 2009.
79. Inter-Ethnic Association for the Development of the Peruvian Amazon and Forest Peoples Programme, *The Reality of REDD+ in Peru, Between Theory and Practice,* November 2011, 6–7; see also: Chris Lang, "Interview with Andy White, Rights and Resources Initiative: 'The Global Market for Forest Carbon Is Not Going to Establish Itself Anytime Soon,'" REDD-Monitor, May 24, 2011.
80. Bretton Woods Project, "World Bank Corners Climate Funds?" Update 74, February 17, 2011; World Bank Carbon Finance, "The Partnership for Market Readiness: Shaping the Next Generation of Carbon Markets," 4.
81. Reuters Point Carbon, "'Dead' CERs to Trade Below 3 Euros Indefinitely: Barclay's," September 24, 2012.
82. Joshua Chaffin and Pilita Clark, "Carbon Collapse Raises Fears for Market's Future," *Financial Times,* January 29, 2013, 21.

Chapter 10 Notes

1. Robert B. Zoellick, "Why We Still Need the World Bank: Looking Beyond Aid," *Foreign Affairs* 19, no. 2 (March–April 2012): 66–78.

2. Ibid., 72; World Bank, News and Broadcast, "2010 Spring Meetings Endorse $86 Million Capital Increase, Voting Reforms," April 20, 2010.

3. "Report from the Executive Directors of the International Development Association to the Board of Governors, Additions to IDA Resources: Fifteenth Replenishment, February 8, 2008." "Management intends to publicly disclose the results of the independent comprehensive assessment of IDA's controls framework, scheduled for completion in early Calendar Year 2008. In addition, Management aims to implement the findings of this report [the IDA Controls Report], and provide at the IDA15 Midterm review, an update on progress made in this regard, including outlining a process for the periodic review of IDA's controls" (p. 14, paragraph 31).

4. World Bank Independent Evaluation Group (IEG), *Review of IDA Internal Controls: An Evaluation of Management's Assessment and the IAD Review*, vol. 1, *Main Text and Overall Evaluation* (Washington, DC: World Bank, 2009), xx, 14–15.

5. World Bank IEG, *Review of IDA Internal Controls: An Evaluation of Management's Assessment and the IAD Review*, vol. 2, *Completing Part II and Integrating Parts I and II* (Washington, DC: World Bank, 2009), 34.

6. Ibid., 34, 42.

7. World Bank IEG, *Review of IDA Internal Controls: An Evaluation of Management's Assessment and the IAD Review*, vol. 5, *Report on the Completion of Part IA, Process Mapping and Effectiveness of Control Design* (Washington, DC: World Bank, 2009), 18.

8. World Bank Independent Evaluation Group (IEG), *Annual Review of Development Effectiveness 2009: Achieving Sustainable Development* (Washington, DC: World Bank, 2009), 27. IEG rated only 4 percent of projects as having "high" Monitoring and Evaluation, 33 percent as "substantial," but 45 percent as "modest" and 18 percent as "negligible."

9. World Bank, Operations Policy and Country Services, "Concept Note: 2012 Development Policy Lending Retrospective: A Review Focusing on Results, Risks, and Reforms," February 2012, 6.

10. World Bank IEG, *Review of IDA Internal Controls*, vol. 2, 47.

11. See: World Bank IEG, *IDA Internal Controls: Evaluation of Management's Remediation Program, Report on Management's Implementation and IAD's Review of the Five-Point Action Plan* (Washington, DC: World Bank, 2010).

12. U.S. Government Printing Office, "The International Financial Institutions: A Call for Change, A Report to the Committee on Foreign Relations United States Senate," March 10, 2010, 111th Congress, 2nd Sess., S. Prt. 111-43, 1.

13. Ibid., 2.

14. Daniel Kaufman, "Siemens and the Illusion of CSR and Codes of Business Integrity," Kaufman Governance Post (blog), December 16, 2008.

15. United Nations Global Compact, "Overview of the UN Global Compact."

16. Siri Schubert and T. Christian Miller, "Where Bribery Was Just a Line Item," *New York Times*, December 21, 2008.

17. Ibid.

18. Richard Weiss, "Siemens Shut Out from World Bank Projects after Bribery Scandal," Bloomberg, July 2, 2009.

19. "Chronology: Twists in Siemens Corruption Scandal," Reuters, May 9, 2008.

20. Cary O'Reilly and Karin Matussek, "Siemens to Pay $1.6 Billion to Settle Bribery Cases (Correct)," Bloomberg, December 16, 2008.

21. Weiss, "Siemens Shut Out from World Bank Projects after Bribery Scandal;" World Bank, "Siemens to Pay $100M to Fight Corruption as Part of World Bank Group Settlement," World Bank Press Release No. 2009/001/EXT, July 2, 2009.

22. World Bank IEG, *Review of IDA Internal Controls*, vol. 1, xx.

23. Richard Behar, "Cyber Security Questions Persist at World Bank," *Fox News*, November 2, 2008; Beatrice Edwards, "The Satyam Fraud, Two Years Later," Government Accountability Project, The Whistleblogger, January 11, 2011.

24. Richard Behar, "Exclusive: World Bank's Web of Ties to 'India's Enron,'" *Fox News*, January 12, 2009; Heather Timmons and Bettina Wassener, "Satyam Chief Admits Huge Fraud," *New York Times*, January 8, 2009; Joe Leahy, "Satyam Chief Admits to Falsifying Books," *Financial Times*, January 7, 2009.

25. Richard Behar, "Former Top Cyber Official at Center of World Bank Scandal," *Fox News*, October 31, 2008.

26. Behar, "Cyber Security Questions Persist at World Bank."

27. Ibid.; Behar, "Exclusive: World Bank's Web of Ties to 'India's Enron.'"

28. Behar, "Cyber Security Questions Persist at World Bank;" Behar, "Exclusive: World Bank's Web of Ties to 'India's Enron;'" Richard Behar, "World Bank Under Cyber Siege in 'Unprecedented Crisis,'" *Fox News*, October 10, 2008.

29. Behar, "World Bank Under Cyber Siege in 'Unprecedented Crisis.'"

30. Behar, "Cyber Security Questions Persist at World Bank;" Behar, "Exclusive: World Bank's Web of Ties to 'India's Enron.'"

31. Richard Behar, "World Bank Admits Top Tech Vendor Debarred for 8 Years," *Fox News*, December 24, 2008.

32. Bea Edwards, "New Charges and New Arrests in the Satyam Scandal," Government Accountability Project, The Whistleblogger, November 26, 2009; Edwards, "The Satyam Fraud, Two Years Later."

33. World Bank Independent Evaluation Group (IEG), *World Bank Country-Level Engagement on Governance and Anticorruption: An Evaluation of the 2007 Strategy and Implementation Plan* (Washington, DC: World Bank, 2011), 6.

34. Ibid., 38.

35. Business Wire India, "Satyam Receives Golden Peacock Global Award for Excellence in Corporate Governance," September 23, 2008; IR Global Rankings, irglobalrankings.com.

36. World Bank Social Development Department, Sustainable Development Network, *Beyond Corporate Social Responsibility: The Scope for Corporate Investment in Community Driven Development*, Report No. 37379-GLB (Washington, DC: World Bank, December 21, 2006), 32.

37. Kaufman, "Siemens and the Illusion of CSR and Codes of Business Integrity;" Daniel Kaufman, "Satyam vs. Siemens Corruption: The Difference Is in Ponzinomics," Kaufman Governance Post (blog), January 14, 2009.

38. Behar, "Former Top Cyber Official at Center of World Bank Scandal."

39. World Bank Independent Evaluation Group (IEG), *World Bank Country-Level Engagement on Governance and Anticorruption*, 26, 28.

40. Ibid., xiv, xxxix.

41. Ibid., 28.

42. Ibid., xx, 51–52.

43. World Bank Independent Evaluation Group (IEG), *Trust Fund Support for Development: An Evaluation of the World Bank's Trust Fund Portfolio, Overview* (Washington, DC: World Bank, 2011), 8, 10, 12; see also: World Bank Group, Concessional Finance and Global Partnerships Vice-Presidency, *2011 Trust Fund Annual Report* (Washington, DC: World Bank, 2011), 5. The $67.8 billion cumulative Trust Fund contribution figure combines $57.5 billion cited by the IEG for 2002–10, with $10.3 billion for FY 2011 cited in the *2011 Trust Fund Annual Report*, 5.

44. World Bank Independent Evaluation Group (IEG), *Trust Fund Support for Development: An Evaluation of the World Bank's Trust Fund Portfolio* (Washington, DC: World Bank, 2011), 12.

45. Ibid., 69, 75, xvii.

46. Ibid., 61.

47. World Bank Independent Inspection Panel, *Accountability at the World Bank: The Inspection Panel at 15 Years* (Washington, DC: World Bank, 2009), 153.

48. World Bank, Projects and Operations, "Albania Integrated Coastal Zone Management and Clean-Up Project" (web page), Overview, Financials.

49. World Bank, "Albania Integrated Coastal Zone Management and Clean-Up Project," Financials.

50. *The Economist*, "Guilty As Charged: A Flawed Project in Albania Has Highlighted Some Broader Concerns," February 28, 2009.

51. Besar Likmeta and Gjergi Erebana, "Exclusive—World Bank Demolished Balkan Village," *Balkan Insight*, February 2, 2009; Richard Behar, "World Bank Spent More Than a Year Covering Up Destruction of Albanian Village," *Fox News*, February 9, 2009.

52. Likmeta and Erebana, "Exclusive—World Bank Demolished Balkan Village."

53. Werner Kiene, Chairperson, World Bank Independent Inspection Panel, "Memorandum to the Executive Directors and Alternates of the International Development Association, Inspection Panel Investigation Report, Albania: Integrated Coastal Zone Management and Clean-Up Project (IDA Credit No. 4083—ALB)," November 24, 2008, 3–4, 63, 64–70.

54. Ibid., 55–56.

55. Kiene, "Memorandum to the Executive Directors and Alternates of the International Development Association," 5.

56. World Bank, "World Bank Board of Executive Directors Reviews Independent Inspection Panel Report on Coastal Zone Management Project in Albania," press release, February 17, 2009.

57. Besar Likmeta, "Albanian Villagers' Hopes of Damages Recedes," *Balkan Insight*, July 11, 2011; World Bank, "Progress Report No. 4 on the Implementation of Management's Action Plan in Response to the Inspection Panel Investigation Report on the Albania Integrated Coastal Zone Management and Clean-Up Project (IDA Credit No. 4083-ALB)," Report No. 65908-AL, January 13, 2012.

58. *The Economist*, "Guilty As Charged."

59. World Bank Independent Evaluation Group (IEG), *Safeguards and Sustainability in a Changing World, An Independent Evaluation of World Bank Group Experience* (Washington DC: World Bank, 2010), 31–32.

60. World Bank, Environment Department, *Resettlement and Development: The Bankwide Review of Projects Involving Involuntary Resettlement, 1986–1993*, Environment Department Paper no. 032 (Washington, DC: World Bank, March 1996), 7, 88.

61. Dana Clark (author), André Carothers (editor), "Resettlement: The World Bank's Assault on the Poor," Center For International Environmental Law, May 2000, 6, endnote 2.

62. Personal communication, Michael Cernea, former chief World Bank sociologist, January 2012.

63. World Bank IEG, *Safeguards and Sustainability in a Changing World*, 20.

64. Personal communication, Michael Cernia.

65. World Bank IEG, *Safeguards and Sustainability in a Changing World*, 20.

66. Ibid., 79.

67. Ibid., 78.

68. Bank Information Center, "World Bank Modernization Agenda Advances, Sets Stage for Safeguard Review," June 18, 2012; Bank Information Center, "World Bank Safeguards Review," background; Kirk Herbertson, "World Bank vs. World Bank: Protecting Safeguards in a 'Modern' International Institution," World Resources Institute, May 16, 2011; World Bank, Operations Policy and Country Services, "Investment Lending Reform: Concept Note," January 26, 2009, 5, 6, 8, 9, 12.

69. Vince McElhinny, "World Bank Safeguards Policy Review: Early Issues, What to Expect?" *Biceca Boletin Mensual*, no. 26, August 2011, 3.

70. World Bank, "Investment Lending Reform: Concept Note," 4, 6; World Bank, Operations Policy and Country Services, "Moving Ahead on Investment Lending Reform: Risk Framework and Implementation Support," September 3, 2009, 16.

71. World Bank, "Investment Lending Reform: Concept Note," 12.

72. Bretton Woods Project, "World Bank Safeguards and Independent Scrutiny at Risk?" Bretton Woods Project Update 75, April 5, 2011; World Bank, Operational Manual, O.P. 9.00—Program for Results Financing, February 2012; Nancy Alexander, "The World Bank's Proposed Program for Results (P4R): Implications for Environmental, Social, and Gender Safeguards and Corrupt Practices," Heinrich Böll Foundation, April 6, 2011; Bretton Woods Project, "Programmed for Results? Concerns Raised Over New World Bank Lending Instrument," Bretton Woods Project Update 77, September 14, 2011; Vince McElhinny, "P4R Update: World Bank Approves Program for Results Policy—5% Cap over Two Year Pilot Project, but Questions Remain How P4R Expansion Will Be Conditional upon Results of Management and IEG Evaluations," February 2012.

73. World Bank/International Monetary Fund Development Committee, "New World, New World Bank Group: (II) The Internal Reform Agenda," DC2010-0004, April 20, 2010, 7.

74. World Bank IEG, *Review of IDA Internal Controls: An Evaluation of Management's Assessment and the IAD Review*, vol. I, 15.

75. John Vidal, "NGOS Criticize World Bank's New Lending Plan for Poorer Countries," *Guardian*, October 21, 2011.

76. Letter of over 200 civil-society representatives to the World Bank Executive Board, "Re: Draft Operational Policy 9.00 Program for Results Financing," October 26, 2011; Lisa Friedman, E & E, "Finance: New World Bank Funding Approach Riles Green Groups," February 2, 2012.

77. Bretton Woods Project, "Green Light for Revised P4R, but Concerns Remain," Bretton Woods Update 79, February 7, 2012; McElhinny, "P4R Update: World Bank Approves Program for Results Policy," 1–2.

78. McElhinny, "P4R Update: World Bank Approves Program for Results Policy," 5.

79. Nancy Alexander, "The World Bank Reboots: Sweeping Investment Lending Reforms in the Works," Heinrich Böll Foundation, May 10, 2010 (updated), 1, 5–6.

80. Personal communication, IFC staff member, January 2012.

81. International Finance Corporation, *2006 Annual Report* (Washington, DC: International Finance Corporation, 2006), 4; International Finance Corporation, *2011 Annual Report* (Washington, DC: International Finance Corporation, 2011), 9. These figures include finance from other institutions directly mobilized or syndicated by the IFC.

82. Peter Bakvis and Molly McCoy, "Core Labor Standards and International Organizations: What Inroads Has Labor Made?" Friedrich Ebert Stiftung Briefing Papers, no. 6/2008, 5–6.

83. International Finance Corporation, "IFC Performance Standards on Environmental and Social Sustainability, Effective January 1, 2012," 27, 28, 49–51.

84. "IFC Performance Standards," 24; International Finance Corporation, International Finance Corporation, "Policy on Environmental and Social Sustainability," January 1, 2012, paragraphs 50–52, 11–12.

85. International Finance Corporation, "Renewable Energy: IFC's Approach," September 2011, 13, 18; Viraj Desai, "World Bank's IFC Lends $300 Million for Green Energy," *Economic Times* [India], January 18, 2011; International Finance Corporation, "IFC and Minda NexGenTech to Provide Off-Grid Lighting to One Million People in Rural India," press release, June 28, 2012.

86. Bretton Woods Project, "IFC Updated Performance Standards Weak on Human Rights, Other Shortcomings," Bretton Woods Project Update no. 77, September 2011.

87. World Bank Group Independent Evaluation Group (IEG), *IEG Annual Report 2011, Results and Performance of the World Bank Group* (Washington, DC: World Bank Group, 2011), xxiv; World Bank Group Independent Evaluation Group (IEG), *IEG Annual Report 2010, Results and Performance of the World Bank Group* (Washington, DC: World Bank Group, 2010), 12.

88. International Finance Corporation, "Renewable Energy: IFC's Approach," 18.

89. See, e.g.: Bretton Woods Project, "IFC's Mining Investments: A Black Hole for Human Rights?" Bretton Woods Project Update no. 70, April 16, 2010; Bretton Woods Project, "World Bank Increases Extractives Lending Despite Human Rights Abuses," Bretton Woods Project Update no. 75, April 5, 2011; Bretton Woods Project, "The World Bank and Extractives, a Rich Seam of Controversy," Bretton Woods Project Update no. 79, February 7, 2012.

90. César Gamboa, "Camisea and the World Bank: A Lost Opportunity to Make Things Better," Bretton Woods Project Update no. 60, April 1, 2008; Oxfam, "World Bank Announces Fund Approval for Peru Pipeline Project," press release, February 6, 2008; Andrew Miller, Amazon Watch et al., "Open Letter to International Finance Corporation Regarding Financing for Camisea II," January 29, 2008.

91. Christiane Badgley, "West Africa Oil Boom Overlooks Tattered Environmental Safety Net," *iWatch News*, Center for Public Integrity, January 19, 2012; Bank Information Center, "IFC Approves Offshore Oil Projects in Ghana Despite Serious Outstanding Concerns," February 20, 2009; Pacific Environment, "Review of Environmental Material for Phase 1 of the Jubilee Oil Project Offshore Ghana," February 10, 2010; Letter of Ian Gary, Senior Policy Advisor, Oxfam America, et al., to the Board of Directors, World Bank Group, February 12, 2009.

92. World Bank Group, "The World Bank Group in Extractive Industries, 2010 Annual Review,"13.

93. Bretton Woods Project, "The World Bank and Extractives: A Rich Seam of Controversy."

94. Matthew O. Berger, "World Bank, NGOs Spar Over Indonesian Mine Project," Inter Press Service News Agency, July 14, 2010; Earthworks, "World Bank Approves Destructive Mining Project in Indonesia," July 14, 2010, yubanet.com; Scott G. Cardiff, "Supplemental Biodiversity Review of Weda Bay Nickel Project," Earthworks, July 2010, 5.

95. Berger, "World Bank, NGOs Spar Over Indonesian Mine Project."

96. World Bank Multilateral Investment Insurance Agency, "MIGA: Advancing Sustainable Investments," MIGA Brief: Environmental and Social Risks, May 2012.

97. World Bank Independent Evaluation Group, *Climate Change and the World Bank Group, Phase II: The Challenge of Low-Carbon Development* (Washington, DC: World Bank, 2010), 58–60; Bretton Woods Project, "IFC: Cowboys in the Amazon," Bretton Woods

Project Update no. 55, April 2, 2007; Bank Information Center, "World Bank Evaluation Criticizes IFC Oversight of Soy Project in Brazil," June 6, 2005.

98. "IFC Funding Linked to Soybean Purchase from Farms Using Slave Labor," May 30, 2005, amazonia.org.br.

99. Luciana Nunes Leal, "Ibama abre sindicânca sobre multo do Bertin," *Estado do São Paulo*, June 2, 2009; Greenpeace, *Slaughtering the Amazon* (Amsterdam: Greenpeace International, June 2009), 5, 71–87.

100. Frank McDonald, "IFC Withdraws Loan from Brazilian Cattle Corporation, Bertin," *Irish Times*, June 16, 2009.

101. World Bank IEG, *Climate Change and the World Bank Group, Phase II: The Challenge of Low-Carbon Development*, 58–60.

102. Ibid.

103. Ibid.

104. Ibid.

105. World Bank Group Independent Evaluation Group (IEG), *Assessing IFC's Poverty Focus and Results* (Washington, DC: World Bank Group, 2011), 39, 42, 43.

106. IFC, *2011 Annual Report*, 120.

107. World Bank Group Independent Evaluation Group (IEG), *Assessing IFC's Poverty Focus and Results*, 41, xi.

108. Ibid., xix.

109. Action Aid, Bretton Woods Project, Christian Aid, Eurodad, Campagna per la Riforma della Banca Mondiale, Third World Network, "Bottom Lines, Better Lives? Rethinking Multilateral Financing to the Private Sector in Developing Countries," March 2010, 2, 10–11.

110. Ibid.

111. Oxfam (France), Eurodad, et al., *Is the International Finance Corporation Supporting Tax-Evading Companies?* February 2010, 5.

112. DanWatch and IBIS (Uddanneise skaber udvikling), *Escaping Poverty—Or Taxes?* (Copenhagen: DanWatch, October 2011), 5.

113. World Bank Group Policy Statement on Offshore Tax Havens, 2010, cited in Nura Molina, Director, Eurodad, et al., in letter to Mr. Lars Thunell, Executive Vice President and CEO, International Finance Corporation, October 1, 2010.

114. DanWatch and IBIS, *Escaping Poverty—Or Taxes?* 4–5.

115. World Bank Group, "Policy on the Use of Offshore Financial Centers in World Bank Group Private Sector Operations, Application to IFC Operations," November 10, 2012.

116. Oxfam (France), Eurodad, et al., *Is the International Finance Corporation Supporting Tax-Evading Companies?* 11; María José Romero, "Unsafe Haven? New IFC Tax Haven Policy Questioned," Bretton Woods Project Update no. 79, February 7, 2012.

117. Nick Mead, "Developing World's Secret Offshore Wealth 'Double External Debt,'" *Guardian*, July 22, 2012.

118. Oxfam (France), Eurodad, et al., *Is the International Finance Corporation Supporting Tax-Evading Companies?* 3.

119. World Bank Group IEG, *IEG Annual Report 2011*, 50–51.

120. World Bank Group IEG, *IEG Annual Report 2011*, 75–76.

Chapter 11 Notes

1. Annie Lowrey, "Obama Candidate Sketches Vision for World Bank," *New York Times*, Global Business, April 9, 2012; on Larry Summers at the World Bank, see: Bruce Rich,

Mortgaging the Earth: The World Bank, Environmental Impoverishment, and the Crisis of Development (Boston: Beacon Press, 1994), 247–49, 263–64.

2. "Hats Off to Ngozi," *The Economist*, March 31, 2012; "The World Bank: Kim for President," blog "Feast and Famine," *The Economist*, April 16, 2012; "Obama Names Surprise World Bank Candidate Jim Yong Kim," BBC News, March 23, 2012.

3. Lowrey, "Obama Candidate Sketches Vision For World Bank," *The Economist*, "The World Bank: Kim for President"; Robin Harding, "U.S. World Bank Nominee Under Fire Over Book," *Financial Times*, March 25, 2012.

4. Joyce V. Millen, Alec Irwin, and Jim Yong Kim, "Introduction: What Is Growing? Who Is Dying?" in Jim Yong Kim, Joyce V. Millen, Alec Irwin, and John Gershman, eds., *Dying for Growth: Global Inequality and the Health of the Poor* (Monroe, ME: Common Courage Press, 2000), 7.

5. Jim Yong Kim et al., "Sickness Amidst Recovery: Public Debt and Private Suffering in Peru, in Kim et al., *Dying for Growth*, 136–37.

6. Ibid., 151.

7. "Hats Off to Ngozi," *The Economist*.

8. Lowrey, "Obama Candidate Sketches Vision For World Bank."

9. Fred Pearce, "Beyond Rio's Disappointment, Finding a Path to the Future," *Yale 360*, June 28, 2012.

10. Ibid.; Juliet Eiperin, "G20 Leaders Agree to Phase Out Fossil Fuel Subsidies," *Washington Post*, September 25, 2009; Steve Kretzman, "Report: Phasing Out Fossil Fuel Subsidies in the G20: A Progress Update," Oil Change International, June 2012.

11. Pearce, "Beyond Rio's Disappointment."

12. Bradley Brooks, "Rio+20, the Unhappy Environmental Summit," Associated Press, June 23, 2012.

13. United Nations General Assembly, Resolution 66/288, "The Future We Want," July 27, 2012, paragraph 16.

14. Jonathan Watts, "Rio+20 Summit: Walkout at 'Green Economy' Talks," *Guardian*, June 15, 2012.

15. Gwyne Dyer,"Rio+20 Culprits Set Stage for Climate Ecocide," June 24, 2012, straight.com.

16. Maria van der Hoeven, "We Can Have Safe, Sustainable Energy," *Guardian*, April 24, 2012; Fiona Harvey, "Governments Failing to Avert Catastrophic Climate Change, IEA Warns," *Guardian*, April 25, 2012.

17. Jim Leape, WWF Director General, "Rio+20 Negotiating Text Is a Colossal Failure of Leadership and Vision," press release, June 19, 2012; CARE International, "Rio+20: Nothing More than a Political Charade," press release, June 21, 2012; Barbara Stocking, Chief Executive Oxfam GB, "Oxfam Final Statement on Rio+20: Rio Will Go Down as the Hoax Summit," June 25, 2012.

18. United Nations Sustainable Development Knowledge Platform, "About Voluntary Commitments for Sustainable Development"; Anne Petermann, "Rio Earth Summit: Tragedy, Farce, and Distraction," *Z Magazine*, September 2012.

19. Mark J. Miller, "Rio+20: PepsiCo, Coca-Cola, and Other Brands Support U.N. Sustainability Goals," June 22, 2012, brandchannel.com.

20. Colin Sullivan, "Side Agreements Pitched as the Real Meat Behind Earth Summit," *Energy and Environment News*, June 22, 2010; World Bank, "Natural Capital Accounting—List of Supporters," August 8, 2012.

21. Michael Northrup, "To Understand Rio+20, Put on Your 3D Glasses," *Huffington Post*, June 27, 2012; United Nations Sustainable Energy for All, Objectives, sustainableenergyforall.org/objectives.

22. United Nations Sustainable Energy for All, High Level Group, sustainableenergyfor all.org/about-us.

23. Lisa Friedman, "Finance: Support for Mass Transit and 'Green' Accounting Moves Ahead," *Climate Wire*, June 21, 2012; Jonathan Watts, "Development Banks Pledge $175bn for Public Transport at Rio+20," *Guardian*, June 20, 2012.

24. World Bank, "Development Banks Vital to Ensuring Inclusive Green Growth Becomes Reality," press release, June 19, 2012.

25. World Bank, "Massive Show of Support for Action on Natural Capital Accounting at Rio Summit," press release, June 20, 2012.

26. World Bank, Wealth Accounting and the Valuation of Ecosystem Services, "Building Support for Natural Capital Accounting—What Can Governments and Civil Society Do?" "Frequently Asked Questions," wavespartnership.org/waves.

27. Rachel Kyte, "How a Week in Rio Leads to an Active Monday Morning," June 22, 2012, blogs.worldbank.org.

28. See, e.g.: Salah El Serafy, "Sustainability, Income Measurement, and Growth," and Jan Tinbergen and Roefie Hueting, "GNP and Market Prices: Wrong Signals for Sustainable Economic Success that Mask Environmental Destruction," in Robert Goodland, Herman Daly, and Salah El Serafy, eds., *Environmentally Sustainable Economic Development: Building on Brundtland*, World Bank Sector Policy and Research Staff, environment working paper no. 46 (Washington, DC: World Bank, July 1991), 54, 37–38; the essays in *Building on Brundtland* were subsequently published as a book, *Population, Technology, and Lifestyle: The Transition to Sustainability*, ed. Robert Goodland, Herman E. Daly, and Salah El Serafy (Washington, DC, and Covelo, CA: Island Press, 1992).

29. See, e.g., the work in the early 1990s of economist Robert Repetto at the World Resources Institute: Robert Repetto, "Balance Sheet Erosion," *International Environmental Affairs* 1, no. 2 (Spring 1989): 131–35; Robert Repetto, "Earth in the Balance Sheet: Incorporating Natural Resources in National Income Accounts," *Environment* 34, no. 7 (September 1992): 12–20, 43–45.

30. World Bank, *Inclusive Green Growth: The Pathway to Sustainable Development* (Washington, DC: World Bank, 2012), 12–13.

31. See, e.g.: Bruce Bueno de Mesquita and Alastair Smith, *The Dictator's Handbook: Why Bad Behavior Is Almost Always Good Politics* (New York: Public Affairs, 2011).

32. Bretton Woods Project, "World Bank's 'Green Growth' Approach Denounced," Update 81, July 2012.

33. Liane Schalatek and Nancy Alexander, "World Bank's 'Inclusive Green Growth' (IGG) Report—A Brief Assessment," Heinrich Böll Foundation North America, May 16, 2012, 1.

34. Banktrack, "Banktrack on the Natural Capital Declaration," Rio de Janeiro, Brazil, June 16, 2012, 1. For a sympathetic though different perspective, see: Richard Conniff, "What's Wrong with Putting a Price on Nature," *Yale Environment 360*, October 12, 2012.

35. Petermann, "Rio Earth Summit: Tragedy, Farce, and Distraction."

36. World Bank, "World Bank Group President Dr. Jim Yong Kim at Brookings Institution," Speeches and Transcripts, July 19, 2012.

37. Ibid.

38. "Former Clean Energy Czar Tries to Stop Europe's Dirtiest New Power Plant," *Environment and Energy News*, March 14, 2012.

39. Lisa Friedman, "U.S. on Both Sides of New Battle Over Assistance to 'Ugly' Coal-Fired Power Plant," *New York Times*, July 11, 2011.

40. Ibid.

41. Liza Friedman, "World Bank Studies Coal-Fired Power Plant for Kosovo," *Environment and Energy News*, January 17, 2012.

42. Letter from Daniel M. Kammen to Ms. Marisa Lago, Assistant Secretary, International Markets and Development, U.S. Department of the Treasury, March 12, 1012, www.eenews.net.

43. World Bank, "International Leader on Clean Energy Joins World Bank," press release no. 2011/084/SDN, September 9, 2010.

44. Letter from Daniel M. Kammen to Ms. Marisa Lago; Daniel M. Kammen, Maryam Mozafarir, and Daniel Prull, *Sustainable Energy Options for Kosovo: An Analysis of Resource Availability and Cost*, Energy and Resources Group, Goldman School of Public Policy, Renewable and Appropriate Energy Laboratory, University of California–Berkeley, January 15, 2012, 6; Friedman, "Former Clean Energy Czar Tries to Stop Europe's Dirtiest New Power Plant."

45. Letter from Daniel M. Kammen to Ms. Marisa Lago.

46. World Bank, "World Bank Group President Dr. Jim Yong Kim at Brookings Institution."

47. Ibid.

48. David Smith, "Desmond Tutu Expresses Outrage at Failing Politicians in South Africa," *Guardian*, September 4, 2012.

49. World Bank Group International Finance Corporation, Oil, Gas and Mining, "Lonmin Plc South Africa—Investing in Success and Sustainable Development"; World Bank Group International Finance Corporation, Oil, Gas and Mining, "IFC and Lonmin—Digging Deep for Development," www1.ifc.org.

50. Benchmarks Foundation, *The Policy Gap: A Review of the Corporate Social Responsibility Programmes of the Platinum Mining Industry in the North West Province*, 2007, 4, 9.

51. Benchmarks Foundation, *Communities in the Platinum Minefields, Policy Gap 6—A Review of Platinum Mining in the Bojanala District of the North West Province, A Participatory Action Research (PAR) Approach*, 2012, iv.

52. Ibid., 72–76.

53. Ibid., 78.

54. World Bank, Speeches and Transcripts, "Press Conference with WBG President Jim Yong Kim, S. African Finance Minister Pravin Gordhan, and WB VP for Africa Makhtar Diop," Pretoria, South Africa, September 6, 2012.

55. Bretton Woods Project, "Unearthing the IFC's Links to Mining Abuses," Bretton Woods Update 82, News, October 3, 2012.

56. "Fifth Protester Dies from Peru Clash Over Newmont Mine," Reuters, July 5, 2012; Cecelia Jasamie, "Peru Lifts State of Emergency Over Conga Mine," September 2, 2012, mining.com.

57. World Bank International Finance Corporation, *Compliance Advisor/Ombudsman (CAO) Assessment Report Regarding Community and Civil Society Concerns in Relation to IFC's Quellaveco Project ($3823)*, July 2012; International Finance Corporation, "Greystar: Summary of Proposed Investment," Overview, Sponsor/Cost/Location, Project No. 27961; Comité por la Defensa del Agua y el Páramo de Santurbán, "Complaint Submitted to the Office of the Compliance Officer/Ombudsman (CAO), June 13, 2012, 4–6, 9–11,14, 27. See also: Bretton Woods Project, "Unearthing the IFC's Links to Mining Abuses."

58. Bretton Woods Project, "Unearthing the IFC's Links to Mining Abuses;" International Finance Corporation, "Simandou III, Summary of Proposed Investment"; Barry

Fitzgerald, "World Bank Shores Up Rio's Hold Over Simandou Venture," *The Australian*, May 8, 2012.

59. Gordon Scott, "Oyu Tolgoi Copper and Gold Mine Associated Power Plant: Violations of IFC and World Bank Policies on Environmental Impacts and Criteria for Coal Projects," Sierra Club, November 2012; Kate Shepard, "The World Bank's Climate Hypocrisy," *Mother Jones*, December 14, 2012.

60. International Finance Corporation, "Oyu Tolgoi LLC, Summary of Investment Information"; Bank Information Center et al., "Complaint Filed Against Destructive Oyu Tolgoi Mine Being Considered for World Bank Support," October 12, 2012; Herder Battsengel Lkhamdoorov, quoted in Kit Gillet, "Though Not Yet Open, a Huge Mine Is Transforming Mongolia's Landscape," *New York Times*, September 13, 2012.

61. Carey L. Biron, "U.S. Abstains on Controversial World Bank Mongolia Mine Project," Inter Press Service, March 7, 2013; U.S. Department of Treasury, United States Position, Mongolia Oyu Tolgoi Mining Project, February 28, 2013.

62. Punan Chuhan-Pole et al., *Africa's Pulse: An Analysis of Issues Shaping Africa's Economic Future* 6 (October 2012): 20.

63. Ibid.

64. Shantayanan Devarajan, World Bank Chief Economist for Africa, quoted in Mark Tran, "Africa's Mineral Wealth Hardly Denting Poverty Levels, Says World Bank," *Guardian*, October 5, 2012.

65. World Bank, "Massive Show of Support for Natural Capital Accounting at Rio Summit."

66. Chuhan-Pole et al., *Africa's Pulse*, 21.

67. Bretton Woods Project, "CSO Townhall with Jim Yong Kim and Christine Lagarde," minutes of meeting, October 11, 2012.

68. Ibid.

69. Ibid.

70. Ibid.

71. Ibid.

72. World Bank Group Independent Evaluation Group (IEG), *Assessing IFC's Poverty Focus and Results* (Washington, DC: World Bank Group, 2011), 39, 42, 43, 51.

73. World Bank, "Remarks as Prepared for Delivery: World Bank Group President Jim Yong Kim at the Annual Meeting Plenary Session," Tokyo, Japan, October 11, 2012.

74. Ibid.

75. Bretton Woods Project, "World Bank-IMF Annual Meetings 2012," Conclusions and Wrap-Up, News, October 16, 2012.

76. World Bank, "Remarks as Prepared for Delivery: World Bank Group President Jim Yong Kim at the Annual Meeting Plenary Session."

Chapter 12 Notes

1. World Bank and Potsdam Institute for Climate Impact Research and Climate Analytics, *Turn Down the Heat: Why a 4 °C Warmer World Must Be Avoided* (Washington, DC: World Bank, November 2012), 11–12.

2. Ibid.; see also: Reuters, "World Bank Climate Change Report Says 'Turn Down the Heat' on Warming Planet," November 18, 2012.

3. See chapter 7, 130–32; see also: World Bank Independent Evaluation Group, *Development Results in Middle-Income Countries: An Evaluation of the World Bank's Support* (Washington, DC: World Bank, 2007), xii, 20, 72.

4. World Bank Independent Evaluation Group, *Development Results in Middle-Income Countries*, xii, 20, 72; concerning "sequencing," see chapter 6, 97–98, chapter 4, 94.

5. China Exim Bank, *2011 Annual Report*, 9.

6. World Bank Independent Evaluation Group, *Climate Change and the World Bank Group, Phase II: The Challenge of Low-Carbon Development* (Washington, DC: World Bank, 2010), 43–44.

7. World Bank Independent Evaluation Group (IEG), *Climate Change and the World Bank Group, Phase I: An Evaluation of World Bank Win-Win Energy Policy Reforms* (Washington, DC: The World Bank, 2009), xxxiv, xxxvi.

8. Paul A. Volcker et al., *Independent Panel Review of the World Bank Group Department of Institutional Integrity* (Washington, DC: September 13, 2007), 8, 13.

9. See: Raymond W. Baker, *Capitalism's Achilles Heel: Dirty Money and How to Renew the Free-Market System* (Hoboken, NJ: John Wiley & Sons, 2005).

10. Global Financial Integrity, "Tip Sheet: Illicit Financial Flows from Developing Countries Over the Decade Ending 2009," December 15, 2011; see also: Dev Kar and Sarah Freitas, *Illicit Financial Flows from Developing Countries Over the Decade Ending 2009*, Global Financial Integrity, December 2011.

11. See: Global Financial Integrity, "Tip Sheet: Illicit Financial Flows from Developing Countries Over the Decade Ending 2009."

12. Raymond Baker, "Letter from the Director," in Dev Kar, *The Drivers and Dynamics of Illicit Financial Flows from India: 1948–2008*, Global Financial Integrity, November 2010, iii.

13. Astrophysicists think that more than 70 percent of the cosmos consists of invisible dark energy and matter. See: NASA Science Astrophysics, "Dark Energy, Dark Matter," science.nasa.gov.

14. For official development-assistance flows, see: Organization for Economic Cooperation and Development (OECD), "Development: Aid to Developing Countries Falls Because of Global Recession," Chart 2: Components of DAC Donors Net ODA, April 4, 2012.

15. Baker, *Capitalism's Achilles Heel*, 237.

16. See, e.g.: Global Financial Integrity, Task Force on Financial Integrity and Economic Development, "Trade Mispricing," and "Beneficial Ownership."

17. Baker, *Capitalism's Achilles Heel*, 257.

18. World Bank Operational Procedure 10.04, "Economic Evaluation of Investment Operations," September 1994, paragraph 4, in World Bank Group Independent Evaluation Group, *Cost-Benefit Analysis in World Bank Projects* (Washington, DC: World Bank, 2010), 55.

19. Ibid., paragraph 7.

20. World Bank Group Independent Evaluation Group, *Cost-Benefit Analysis in World Bank Projects*, 4.

21. Ibid., 5.

22. Ibid., 46.

23. Ibid.

24. Chairperson's Summary: Committee on Development Effectiveness (CODE), in World Bank Group Independent Evaluation Group, *Cost-Benefit Analysis in World Bank Projects*, 10, 11.

25. John A. Gould and Matthew S. Winters, "Petroleum Blues: The Political Economy of Resources and Conflict in Chad," in Päivi Lujala and Siri Aas Rustad, *High-Value Natural Resources and Post-Conflict Peacebuilding* (New York: Earthscan, 2012), 333.

26. See chapter 3, 44–45; see also: World Bank Quality Assurance Group, Portfolio Improvement Program, "Portfolio Improvement Program: Reviews of Sector Portfolios and Lending Instruments: A Synthesis" (draft internal report), April 22, 1997, 15.

27. David A. Phillips, *Reforming the World Bank: Twenty Years of Trial—and Error* (Cambridge, UK, and New York: Cambridge University Press, 2009), 81–82.

28. Abhihit Banerjee (MIT), Angus Deaton (Princeton), Nora Lustig (UNDP), Ken Rogoff (Harvard), *An Evaluation of World Bank Research 1998–2005*, September 24, 2006, 5, 6, 20–21, 126–27; see also: Eon Callan, "World Bank 'Uses Doubtful Evidence to Push Policies,'" *Financial Times*, December 22, 2012.

29. Kate Bayliss, Ben Fine, and Elisa van Waeyenberge, *The Political Economy of Development: The World Bank, Neoliberalism, and Development Research* (London: Pluto Press, 2011); Bretton Woods Project, "Evaluations Suggest IMF, World Bank Research Ideologically Driven," Update 77, September 14, 2011.

30. Jessica Lecroy, "An Evaluation of World Bank Research: 1998–2005," *Foreign Affairs*, January 2007.

31. Robert B. Zoellick, "Why We Still Need the World Bank: Looking Beyond Aid," *Foreign Affairs* 19, no. 2 (March-April 2012): 75.

32. Publish What You Fund, "The World Bank Demands Open Data in Google Mapping Project," April 11, 2011.

33. Nancy Birdsall, "From Zoellick to Kim: Three Seedlings to Nourish," Global Development: Views from the Center, Center for Global Development, May 17, 2012.

34. Zoellick, "Why We Still Need the World Bank," 76.

35. Evgeny Morozov, *The Net Delusion: The Dark Side of Internet Freedom* (New York: Public Affairs, 2011), 15.

36. Ibid., 46, 58, 86–87.

37. Ibid., 305.

38. Ibid., 257–58; see also: *Wildlife Extra*, "Rare Iranian Salamander in Danger of Extinction Due to Internet Pet Trade," March 2010, wildlifeextra.com.

39. World Bank Group Independent Evaluation Group, *Global Program Review: Multi-Donor Trust Fund for the Extractive Industries Transparency Review* (Washington, DC: World Bank Group IEG, February 18, 2011), vii, xvi.

40. Morozov, *The Net Delusion*, 306.

41. Nancy Birdsall, "The World Bank and Climate Change: Forever a Big Fish in a Small Pond?" Center for Global Development Policy Paper 007, July 2012.

42. Ibid., 26.

43. See chapter 10, 192–93; see also: World Bank, "Investment Lending Reform: Concept Note," 4, 6; World Bank, Operations Policy and Country Services, "Moving Ahead on Investment Lending Reform: Risk Framework and Implementation Support," September 3, 2009, 16.

44. See chapter 6, 110; see also: Kyriakos Varvaressos, "The Concept of a World Bank," *International Bank Notes* 5, no. 7, June 25, 1951 (IBRD/IDA Archives, Box No. 19), 4.

45. See: Export Development Corporation Canada, "Compliance Officer," edc.ca; World Bank Group CAO, "About the CAO: Partners, Independent Accountability Mechanisms."

46. World Bank Independent Evaluation Group (IEG), *Safeguards and Sustainability Policies in a Changing World: An Independent Evaluation of World Bank Group Experience* (Washington, DC: World Bank, 2010), 37–38.

47. See chapter 6, 104–05; see also: Nii Ashie Kotey and Poku Adusei, "The Newmont and AngloGold Mining Projects," in Sheldon Leader and David M. Ong, *Global Project Finance, Human Rights, and Sustainable Development* (Cambridge, UK, and New York: Cambridge University Press, 2011), 489; Nirmalya Choudhury, *Sustainable Dam Development in India: Between Global Norms and Local Practices*, Discussion Paper 10, Deutsche

Institut für Entwicklungspolitik ISSN 1860-0441 (Bonn: Deutsche Institut für Entwicklungspolitik, 2010), 27–28.

48. Bruce Bueno de Mesquita and Alastair Smith, *The Dictator's Handbook: Why Bad Behavior Is Almost Always Good Politics* (New York: Public Affairs, 2011), vii, 181.

49. Between 1945 and 2011 India had borrowed $88.7 billion from the Bank, far ahead of China ($49.6 billion), Brazil ($50.0 billion), and Indonesia ($43.3 billion); see: World Bank, *Annual Report 2011*, "IBRD and IDA Cumulative Lending by Country/Fiscal 1945–2011."

50. Paul Rogers, "India's 21st Century War," *Sustainable Security*, November 2009, citing Prakash Nanda, "India's Deadliest War Within," UPI India Online, November 4, 2009; Jim Yardley, "Maoist Rebels Widen Deadly Reach Across India," *New York Times*, November 1, 2009; Sunil Raman, "Leak Reveals India Maoist Threat," BBC News, Delhi, September 21, 2009; Arundhati Roy, "The Heart of India Is Under Attack," *Guardian*, October 30, 2009.

51. Roy, "The Heart of India Is Under Attack;" Rogers, "India's 21st Century War."

52. Rogers, "India's 21st Century War."

53. Aristotle, *The Politics*, trans. T. A. Sinclair (London: Penguin Books, 1962), book 1, chap. ix, 84–85.

54. Kenneth Rogoff, "Rethinking the Growth Imperative," Project Syndicate, January 2, 2012.

55. George Soros, *The Age of Fallibility: Consequences of the War on Terror* (New York: Public Affairs, 2006), 102; Hans Küng, *A Global Ethic for Global Politics and Economics* (New York: Oxford University Press, 1998), 204.

56. Adam Smith, *The Theory of Moral Sentiments*, vol. 1 (1817; repr., Washington, DC: Regnery, 1997), 63–64..

Index

Mexico, 174, 223

Meyer, Eugene, 114

Millennium Development Goals, 23

Mineral extraction. *See* Extractive industries

Mission creep, 106

Mongolia, Oyu Tolgoi gold and copper mine, 216

Monitoring and evaluation (M&E), 27, 62, 120, 235

Montesinos, Vladimiro, 81

Montreal Protocol, 165

Morozov, Evgeny, 231

Morse, Bradford, 23–24

Morse Commission, 24, 25, 26, 207

Mortgaging the Earth (Rich), viii

Movement for the Survival of the Ogoni People (Nigeria), 47

Movement of Dam-Affected People (Brazil), 62

Muhsin, Mohamed Vazir, 181–182, 184

Multilateral Investment Guarantee Agency (MIGA), 3, 53, 54, 69, 82, 84, 85, 103, 196–197, 211, 216, 232

Murdy, Wayne, 82

Musharraf, Pervez, 123

Nagarhole conflict, India Ecodevelopment Project, 30

Nakai Plateau (Laos), 126–128

Nam Theun 2 Dam (Laos), 125–128, 203

Narmada Sardar Sarovar dam project (India), 23–25, 26, 38, 62–63, 67

National Association of Professional Environmentalists (NAPE) (Uganda), 129

National Bank for Economic and Social Development (BNDES) (Brazil), 132

National Environmental Action Plans (NEAPs), 18, 45–46, 179

National Agricultural Extension Project (Kenya), 37

National Policy on Developmental Resettlement of Project-Affected People (India), 66

National Rehabilitation and Resettlement Policy (India), 67

National Thermal Power Corporation (NTPC) Project (India), 50

National Wildlife Federation, 55

Natural capital accounting, 208–209

Natural Habitats Policy (World Bank), 97

Nepal, 37–40, 65

Networks (World Bank), 43, 61, 109. *See also* Matrix management

Newmont mining corporation, 80, 81–82, 104

Newmont Ghana Ahafo mine, 104

"Next Steps" plan, 24–25

Nguiffo, Samuel, 94

Nigeria, 47, 116, 223

Ninth IDA Replenishment, 18

Nippon Export Insurance (NEXI), 156

"No-go" zones, 97, 99

Non-project lending, 73, 103, 110–111, 178–179, 189, 193, 195–196. *See also* Development policy loans; Governments, loans for support of; Poverty Reduction Strategy Credits; Structural adjustment loans

Norway, 70, 166, 207

Ocampo, José Antonia, 202

Odima, Bongo, 217

Oeko Institute (Germany), 166

Offshore tax havens, 199–200

Ogoni tribe (Nigeria), 47

Oil Industry. *See* Petroleum industry

Okonjo-Iweala, Ngozi, 202, 204

Open Data Initiative (World Bank), 230

Operation Green Hunt (India), 237

Operational Directives (World Bank), 42

Operational Procedure 10.04, Economic Evaluation of Investment Operations, 226

Operations Evaluation Department (OED), 7, 41, 45, 46, 61, 71, 72, 107, 236. *See also* Independent Evaluation Group

Organization for Economic Cooperation and Development (OECD), 53, 56, 108

Organized crime, 172–173

Oxfam, 196, 206

Oyu Tolgoi mine (Mongolia), 216

Ozone depletion, 19, 165

Pakistan, 121–123

Pakter, Medha, 63

Pandav, Bivash, 5

Pangue Dam (Chile), 54–55

Panthera, 5

Papua New Guinea, 47, 54, 73, 169, 173

Paradox of plenty. *See* Resource curse

Paraguay, Yacyretá Dam and, 49–52

About Island Press

Since 1984, the nonprofit Island Press has been stimulating, shaping, and communicating the ideas that are essential for solving environmental problems worldwide. With more than 800 titles in print and some 40 new releases each year, we are the nation's leading publisher on environmental issues. We identify innovative thinkers and emerging trends in the environmental field. We work with world-renowned experts and authors to develop cross-disciplinary solutions to environmental challenges.

Island Press designs and implements coordinated book publication campaigns in order to communicate our critical messages in print, in person, and online using the latest technologies, programs, and the media. Our goal: to reach targeted audiences—scientists, policymakers, environmental advocates, the media, and concerned citizens—who can and will take action to protect the plants and animals that enrich our world, the ecosystems we need to survive, the water we drink, and the air we breathe.

Island Press gratefully acknowledges the support of its work by the Agua Fund, Inc., The Margaret A. Cargill Foundation, Betsy and Jesse Fink Foundation, The William and Flora Hewlett Foundation, The Kresge Foundation, The Forrest and Frances Lattner Foundation, The Andrew W. Mellon Foundation, The Curtis and Edith Munson Foundation, The Overbrook Foundation, The David and Lucile Packard Foundation, The Summit Foundation, Trust for Architectural Easements, The Winslow Foundation, and other generous donors.

The opinions expressed in this book are those of the author(s) and do not necessarily reflect the views of our donors.